D0414628

CAXTON

THE HISTORY OF REYNARD THE FOX

EARLY ENGLISH TEXT SOCIETY
No. 263
1970

that ſawe thiſe Jewellis / J ſente thyſe to my lady the
quene/for J haue founden her good & gracious to me, this
Combe myght not be to moche preyſed / Hit was made
of the bone of a clene noble beeſt named Panthera,
Whiche fedeth hym bytwene the grete Inde and erthly
paradyſe, he is ſo luſty fayr & of colour/ that ther is no colour vnder the heuen, but ſomme lyknes is in hym, therto
he ſmelleth ſo ſwete that the ſauour of hym boteth alle
ſykneſſis & for his beaute and ſwete ſmellyng all other
beeſtis folowe hym/for by his ſwete ſauour they ben heled
of alle ſykneſſis / this panthera hath a fair bon brode &
thynne, whan ſo is that this beeſte is ſlayn al the ſwete
odour reſtid in the bone whiche can not be broken ne ſhal neū

h 2

The History of Reynard the Fox, 1481, f. h2r

Reproduced by kind permission of the Governors of the John Rylands Library, Manchester

hated hym to fore/yf he had the ring vpon hym/they shold
forgete theyr angre as sone as they sawe hym / Also
though he were al naked in a felde agayn an hondred
armed men, he shold be wel herted & escape fro them with
worship/but he muste be a noble gentle man/and haue no
chorles condicions/ffor thenne the stone hath no myght
& by cause this stone was so precious & good/I thought
in my self that I was not a ble ne worthy to bere it/and
there fore i sente it to my dere lord the kyng/for i knowe
hym for the most noble that now lyueth,& also alle our
welfare & worship lyeth on hym/and for he shold be kepte
fro alle drede nede and vnghelucke.

I Fonde this rynge in my faders tresour/and in the
same place I toke a glasse or a mirrour & a combe
Whiche my wyf wold algates haue [illegible]

THE HISTORY OF REYNARD THE FOX

TRANSLATED FROM THE DUTCH ORIGINAL

BY

WILLIAM CAXTON

EDITED BY

N. F. BLAKE

Published for

THE EARLY ENGLISH TEXT SOCIETY

by the

OXFORD UNIVERSITY PRESS

LONDON NEW YORK TORONTO

1970

PRINTED IN GREAT BRITAIN

PREFACE

FOR almost five centuries *The History of Reynard the Fox* has remained the most popular of Caxton's translations. Yet till now, no modern edition to meet the needs of the scholar has been produced. I hope it may be thought appropriate that such an edition should appear at this time. Firstly, as we get ready to celebrate the quincentenary of the first book printed in English, it is fitting that our first printer's best-loved work should be made more generally available. Secondly, scholarly work on various aspects of the Reynard story has recently grown quite spectacularly. The new edition by M. Roques of *Le Roman de Renart* is now complete, and the first volume of the new edition of the Dutch texts by W. Gs. Hellinga has been available for some years. J. Flinn's far-reaching investigation into the spread of the Reynard story and K. Varty's work on its iconography illustrate different aspects of this renewed interest in Reynard. But Caxton's own contribution has been unjustly neglected. It is to be hoped that this new edition may serve to encourage both a juster assessment of Caxton's text in the growth of the Reynard story and a greater interest in Caxton's translations.

I should like to thank the Librarians of the British Museum, the John Rylands Library, the Pierpont Morgan Library, and Eton College for allowing me to consult the incunabula in their care. I am particularly grateful to the Governors of the John Rylands Library for their permission to reproduce a leaf of their copy of Caxton's edition as my frontispiece.

The bulk of the edition was completed at Liverpool, and I am indebted to the staff of the Harold Cohen Library for their unfailing courtesy and helpfulness. I should also like to thank the Council of the University for several small research grants awarded to me during the preparation of this edition. I also worked on the edition during a year I spent as a visitor at the University of Toronto. I should like to thank the Librarian of Massey College, Toronto, for his help in acquiring many books that I needed while I was there.

When I embarked on my edition some years ago, the Hon. Secretary of the Early English Text Society put me in touch with

Mrs. M. Y. Offord, who was engaged on an edition of the *Knight of the Tower* for the Society. She has advised and helped me at all stages in the preparation of this edition. I should like to thank her for her constant assistance, so generously given, throughout all these years. Professor Simeon Potter read through my typescript and made many suggestions. I am also indebted to the Hon. Director and the previous Hon. Secretary of the Early English Text Society for their patience and helpful comments. Finally, I should like to thank my wife and Miss Margaret Burton for their help in the preparation of my typescript.

Additional Note Since this edition went to press, the Mercers' Company has acquired a late fifteenth-century manuscript of privileges granted to the Merchant Adventurers in the Low Countries. These privileges are in Latin, French and Dutch, with English translations. The translations of the privileges in Dutch are of particular interest as they contain some of the words listed in the Introduction, § 2. But as the translations were probably made after RF was printed, my conclusions in introduction, §2, will not be affected. I hope to publish a note on the vocabulary of the translations from Dutch shortly in *Notes and Queries*; and a full account of the manuscript by Miss Jean Imray will be published in due course in the *Journal of the Society of Archivists*.

CONTENTS

The History of Reynard the Fox, 1481, f. h2^r *Frontispiece*

Abbreviations ix

Introduction

1. The Development of the Medieval Beast-Epic xi
2. Dutch Loan-words in *The History of Reynard the Fox* xxi
3. The Translation xlvii
4. Editions of *The History of Reynard the Fox* lix
5. The Present Edition lxiii

Select Bibliography lxvii

Sigla of Copies of *The History of Reynard the Fox*, 1481 lxxii

The History of Reynard the Fox 1

Notes 113

Glossary 141

Index of Names 169

ABBREVIATIONS

For abbreviations of parts of speech used in the Glossary and Introduction, § 2, see the preface to the Glossary. Editions of *Reynard the Fox* printed after 1550 are referred to by the date of their issue and are not listed here. For fuller bibliographical details of the works listed below, consult the Select Bibliography.

AN.	Anglo-Norman.
Arber	E. Arber, *The History of Reynard the Fox*, 1878.
Blake	N. F. Blake, *Bulletin of the John Rylands Library*, xlvi (1963–4), 298–325.
C	William Caxton's *The History of Reynard the Fox*, 1st ed., 1481 (for abbreviations of individual copies see Sigla of Copies of *The History of Reynard the Fox*, 1481).
de Reul	P. de Reul, *The Language of Caxton's Reynard the Fox*, 1901.
English Versions	N. F. Blake, *Studies in Philology*, lxii (1965), 63–77.
Flinn	J. Flinn, *Le Roman de Renart*, 1963.
JEGP.	*Journal of English and Germanic Philology.*
Jente	R. Jente, *Proverbia Communia*, 1947.
LDE.	J. F. Bense, *A Dictionary of the Low-Dutch Element in the English Vocabulary*, 1926–39.
Lenaghan	R. T. Lenaghan, *Caxton's Aesop*, 1967.
McCulloch	F. McCulloch, *Mediaeval Latin and French Bestiaries*, rev. ed., 1962.
MD.	Middle Dutch.
ME.	Middle English.
MED.	*Middle English Dictionary*, 1952—
MLG.	Middle Low German.
MNW.	E. Verwijs, J. Verdam, and F. A. Stoett, *Middelnederlandsch Woordenboek*, 1885–1941.
Morley–Thoms	W. J. Thoms, *Early English Prose Romances*, rev. ed., 1907.
Muller I	J. W. Muller, *Van den Vos Reinaerde*, vol. i, 1939.
Muller II	J. W. Muller, *Van den Vos Reinaerde*, vol. ii, 1942.
Muller–Logeman	J. W. Muller and H. Logeman, *Die Hystorie van Reynaert die Vos, naar den Druk van 1479*, 1892.
NPT.	*The Nun's Priest's Tale* (references to F. N. Robinson, *The Works of Geoffrey Chaucer*, 2nd ed., 1957).
NQ.	*Notes and Queries.*
ODEP.	*The Oxford Dictionary of English Proverbs*, 2nd ed., 1948.
OE.	Old English.

ABBREVIATIONS

OED.	*The Oxford English Dictionary*, 1933.
OF.	Old French.
P	*Die Hystorie van Reynaert die Vos*, printed by Gerard Leeu, 1479.
PL	William Caxton's *The History of Reynard the Fox*, 2nd ed., 1489.
RI	*Reinaert I*, earlier poetic version (thirteenth century) [A = Comburg MS.].
RII	*Reinaert II*, later poetic version (fourteenth century) [B = Brussels MS.; C = The Hague MS.].
RP	*The History of Reynard the Fox*, printed by Richard Pynson, *c.* 1494.
RR.	*Le Roman de Renart* (references to individual branches are to E. Martin's edition, 1882–7).
Sands	D. B. Sands, *The History of Reynard the Fox*, 1960.
Stallybrass	W. S. Stallybrass, *The Epic of the Beast*, 1924.
S.T.C.	*A Short-Title Catalogue of Books Printed in England, Scotland, & Ireland 1475–1640*, 1926.
Teirlinck	Is. Teirlinck, *De Toponymie van den Reinaert*, 1910–12.
TG	*The History of Reynard the Fox*, printed by Thomas Gaultier, 1550.
Thoms	W. J. Thoms, *The History of Reynard the Fox*, 1844.
Tinbergen–Dis	D. C. Tinbergen and L. M. van Dis, *Van den Vos Reinaerde*, 14th ed., 1956.
WW	*The History of Reynard the Fox*, printed by Wynkyn de Worde, *c.* 1515.

INTRODUCTION

1. THE DEVELOPMENT OF THE MEDIEVAL BEAST-EPIC

THE characteristic feature of medieval stories about Reynard the fox is that whereas the protagonists have human names and ranks, they nevertheless retain their animal individuality and behave in accordance with their animal nature. Although Reynard is a courtier, owns a castle, and is willing to undergo a pilgrimage, he is still a fox who steals fowls and preys on smaller animals. The animals never become mere personifications of human vices and virtues, for they continue to live in a non-human world. Yet Reynard is never an individual fox, he is the type of all foxes: his exploits stem from the fox's nature. The animals in the beast-epic do not become wholly human or wholly animal, and the charm of the Reynard stories consists to a large part in this blend of the human with the animal. They are more profound than fable and not as dry as allegory. It has been suggested that the medieval beast-epic came into being when the animals of the earlier fables were given human names.[1] These names in the Reynard stories fall into two broad categories. The first consists of simple human names which can generally be traced back to a Germanic origin, such as Reynard and Isegrim. The second and later group is of French origin and the names in it imply the character or a particular characteristic of the animal in question: Noble (the lion), Chanteclere (the cock). Yet although the older group of names is Germanic, the stories about Reynard and his companions originated in medieval France and spread from there to other West European countries. Nevertheless behind the French *Le Roman de Renart* (RR.) there lies a long history of animal literature, which we must now briefly consider.

Collections of animal stories are found in the literature of almost all peoples and among the more famous of the older ones are the Indian Pantchatantra and Aesop's fables. It is from the latter that

[1] G. Paris, *Mélanges de Littérature française du Moyen Age*, 1912, pp. 357 f. [Bibliographical details of works mentioned in the footnotes will be found in the Select Bibliography.]

RR. is ultimately descended. Aesop's fable of the sick lion appears to have been the central one in the medieval precursors of RR.; it is the seed from which later accounts grew. In Aesop when the lion falls sick, the wolf accuses the fox, who is not present, of disrespect for not attending on the lion. The fox appears and claims he has been looking for a cure for the lion. In order to be healed the lion must wrap himself in the wolf's warm hide. This he does and is cured. In this story, as is typical both in classical fable and in folktale, the animals are not named. Quite apart from the more direct influence of Aesop's fables on RR. by the transmission of fables through the Middle Ages until they were included in RR., there is an indirect influence exerted by Aesop's fables upon the later beast-epic. The fables had a wide currency in antiquity and were adopted by the early Christian church as exempla to illustrate Christian morals and beliefs. The most influential collection of Christian animal fables was the *Physiologus*, which may have been written as early as the second century A.D. In it a brief description of each animal is followed by a Christian interpretation. The *Physiologus* was drawn upon by Ambrose and other Christian writers; and in its Latin prose version, the *Bestiarius*, it became very popular. The picturesque details of the fables, the simple morals, and the adaptability of the subjects for pictorial reproduction made the Bestiary one of the commonest books in the Middle Ages and it was translated into most of the vernacular languages of Western Europe.[1] It is hardly surprising that some of the themes in the Bestiary should have found their way into the Reynard cycle.[2]

The Middle Ages did not know Aesop's fables in Greek, but Latin collections of fables based on Aesop were common. Two of the earlier Latin adaptations were those of Phaedrus in verse written in the first century A.D. and of Avianus in prose written some three centuries later. These collections may well have been used in the schools and many of the fables were widely disseminated. The early Latin collections gave birth to various imitations and copies, the most important of which is known as the Romulus. Written in prose, it appears nevertheless to be a reworking of the fables of Phaedrus completed in the tenth century or earlier. It is

[1] See particularly F. Lauchert, *Geschichte des Physiologus*, 1889, and McCulloch.

[2] As, for example, the story of the fox feigning death in order to entice the crows near enough for him to be able to catch one; see pp. 52–3.

extant today in various guises in a large number of manuscripts: clearly it had soon ousted the Phaedrus in popularity. In its turn the Romulus served as a pattern and source for later collections of fables, notably the poetic version of the fables attributed by Hervieux to Walther of England, a chaplain to Henry II.[1] It was probably composed shortly before 1177. This poetic version was in Latin, but there was also an English translation of the Romulus, which some scholars attribute to Henry I.[2] Marie de France in the epilogue to her collection of fables written shortly after 1189[3] informs us that she had translated them from English. There are, however, in Marie's collection fables which have been influenced by or perhaps even borrowed from RR.

Stories about animals were popular in medieval Europe and the first author of RR. merely followed a trend. But although RR. can be shown to have used many motifs and episodes from the Romulus and associated collections, the fable of the sick lion which is one of the central episodes of RR. is not found in the Romulus. The absence of the fable in this work may well be fortuitous, for it was known in the Middle Ages, as a late eighth-century version of the tale ascribed to Paulus Diaconus testifies.[4] This version is of great interest because, although it resembles the fable in Aesop, it has certain additions and differences. The prime difference is that it is the bear and not the wolf who loses his skin; and the fable by Paulus Diaconus thus sets itself aside from not only the earlier but also the later accounts. Nevertheless it does contain the main framework of the fable as found in Aesop, and it also contains newer features which are found again in later medieval versions. Such an innovation is the production by the fox of the shoes which he has worn out in his search for a cure. It is not clear how Paulus Diaconus got his information, but it may well be that he heard the story from oral sources.

After Paulus Diaconus we next meet the fable of the sick lion in a Latin poem called *Ecbasis cuiusdam captivi per tropologiam*.[5] It

[1] L. Hervieux, *Les Fabulistes latins*, 1884, i. 447.

[2] Ibid., p. 584.

[3] A. Ewert and R. C. Johnston, *Marie de France, Fables*, 1942, p. x.

[4] Edited by E. Duemmler, *Poetae Latini Aevi Carolini*, 1881, i. 62–4. An English translation is available in E. H. Zeydel, *Ecbasis Cuiusdam Captivi*, 1964.

[5] E. Voigt, *Ecbasis Captivi*, 1874. This edition contains a full introduction where problems of authorship, date, etc., are discussed. It has also been edited by K. Strecker, *Ecbasis Cuiusdam Captivi*, 1935. A new edition with a brief survey of the relevant scholarship is now available in E. H. Zeydel, op. cit.

was written between 1043 and 1046 by a Cistercian monk of Germanic stock who spent some of his life near Toul. The author had read fairly widely in both classical and Christian literature, though he borrows most often from Horace and Prudentius. The poem is noticeably different from the fables not only in its length, but also because various beast stories are linked together for the first time and presented as a continuous story. The fables and the bestiaries are collections of unconnected animal stories which are brought together merely because they all happen to deal with animals of one sort or another. But in the *Ecbasis captivi* an attempt is made to link certain beast fables together into a coherent poem in which one episode is made dependent upon another. The author has not been altogether successful in this, for his poem consists of two halves, usually known as the outer and inner fable. The main outline of the story is as follows. A young calf who had been left alone in the stall without his mother gets restless and longs for freedom. So he breaks free and enjoys himself in the meadow till evening. Then being tired he seeks the shelter of a wood where he falls in with a wolf who takes him to his cave (? castle). While having dinner that evening the wolf decides to eat the calf on the following day; and although the wolf suffers from a bad dream that evening, which forebodes his death, he will not release the calf. In the morning the calf's absence is noted, and led by the dog, the whole herd goes in search of him. The wolf is surprised in his castle, but is not dismayed as he cannot see the fox among his attackers and trusts in the strength of his castle. The story of the castle is then told in the inner fable. The lion had once fallen ill and he had called an assembly of the beasts. The wolf calumniated the fox who had failed to attend and said he showed no respect for the king. The king in his anger at this condemned the fox to death; the wolf prepared a gallows. The panther, who is in league with the fox, brings him to court; the fox then relates how he has been wandering throughout the world looking for a cure. The king demands to know the cure. It is that the fox should rub a special herb on the king and also that the lion should wrap himself in the wolf's hide. The treatment, which naturally involves the wolf's death, is carried out and amid great festivities the lion is cured. The fox is raised to a position of great honour and he receives among other things the castle as a fief. But the wolf's son had revenged his father by managing to rob the fox of the castle. So the wolf of the outer fable is anxious that the fox should not be among his attackers for he knows the layout of the castle and is eager to have his revenge on the wolf. The outer fable continues with the wolf discovering that the fox has in fact joined his attackers. The fox, however, is able by flattery to persuade the wolf to leave his castle, whereupon he is seized by the bull and tossed into a tree. In the meantime the calf has escaped and returned home. The fox regains possession of his castle; the wolf is left dead on the field of battle. The *Ecbasis captivi* is an allegory of the monk who leaves his cloister and of the dangers he meets. He is saved only by his fellow monks, and he returns to his true vocation in the monastery. For us its interest lies in the attempt by a poet to write a beast-epic, the first of its kind that is extant today. It is noticeable, too, that part of the action springs from the antagonism of the fox and the wolf, for this opposition is later to become one of the central starting-points of RR. Furthermore it is in the *Ecbasis captivi* that the wolf and the fox are first said to be uncle and nephew. Other points of interest that should be noticed because they occur here for the first time are: the wolf erects a gallows for the fox; the fox is warned of the impending danger by his friend, the panther; and the animal kingdom is compared with the feudal hierarchy. These features all appear in the later stories about Reynard.

The beast-epic which is inaugurated by the *Ecbasis captivi* develops a stage further with another Latin poem called *Ysengrimus*.[1] This poem of 6,574 lines was completed in 1149 by a Master Nivardus, who was a monk in Flanders. From various references in the poem it would appear that Master Nivardus was a learned cleric who was well acquainted with the Low Countries and France. *Ysengrimus* contains many episodes, most of them taken from earlier fables or beast stories, which are all fashioned into a unified whole by subordinating them to the general theme of the enmity of the fox and the wolf. One of the fables, that of the fox and the hen, does not fall within this general pattern, but as it is linked together with the preceding fable the unity of the poem is not disrupted. The wolf generally comes out on the losing side, and

[1] The poem was entitled *Reinardus Vulpes* in F. J. Mone's edition (1832). It is edited with full commentary by E. Voigt, *Ysengrimus*, 1884. See also L. Willems, *Étude sur l'Ysengrinus*, 1895. A German translation is available in A. Schönfelder, *Isengrimus*, 1955. Scholars have called the poem either *Ysengrimus* (Voigt) or *Ysengrinus* (Willems).

thus the poem becomes really the tale of Isegrim's discomfiture. It is not possible to give a summary of the poem here, but the majority of the episodes reappear in RR. and ultimately, though often in an altered form, in C. Among these are the following episodes: Reynard teaches Isegrim to fish; Isegrim becomes a monk; the rape of the wolf's wife; the wolf and the mare; and the division of the cow by the wolf. *Ysengrimus* also contains one or two individual scenes, such as the death of the wolf, which do not reappear in later versions. It is not only because it manages to unite a great many episodes in a unified poem that it is important; it is also in *Ysengrimus* that the animals are given names for the first time. They begin to develop their own characters and to act in accordance with them. In the *Ecbasis captivi* the animals were unnamed and were mere allegorical figures; but in *Ysengrimus* they live in their own right. Admittedly the intention of the poem is satirical; but like *Gulliver's Travels* the story can be read for its own sake, as the author's use of dialogue and description has made *Ysengrimus* one of the more notable medieval Latin poems. It is the ancestor of all the later Reynard stories in that here for the first time we meet the use of satire, the use of dialogue, the names of the animals, the epic descriptions of the court, the use of proverbial expressions, and the general framework of the enmity of the fox and the wolf.

That *Ysengrimus* and RR. are closely related no one would now deny, though not all scholars have accepted Foulet's theory that *Ysengrimus* was RR.'s major source.[1] Others prefer to think that *Ysengrimus* and RR. arose independently.[2] Since the results of Foulet's investigations were published, however, most scholars have been less ready to accept that RR. arose from oral tradition and folklore, as had been strongly urged by Grimm and Sudre.[3] The former, paying due attention to the Germanic roots of many of the animal names, suggested that an oral beast-epic existed among the primitive Germanic peoples and that this had been borrowed and expanded by later French writers. The latter, on the other hand, compared the episodes in RR. with fables from places as far apart as Scandinavia and India, and he was able to point to

[1] L. Foulet, *Le Roman de Renard*, 1914.

[2] See K. Voretzsch, *Introduction to the Study of Old French Literature*, 1931, pp. 360–8 and references there.

[3] J. Grimm, *Reinhart Fuchs*, 1834, and L. Sudre, *Les Sources du Roman de Renart*, 1893.

many parallels. Although the actions are frequently attributed to different animals, the general theme and working out of the fables in folklore are often very similar to the corresponding episodes in RR. Among those episodes which have close parallels from the East may be noted the tale of the sick wolf, the story of the fox, the crow and the cheese, and the account of the division of the cow (or whatever animal it might happen to be) by the wolf. It is possible that, apart from the written accounts which are found in Latin medieval works of one sort and another, there were also oral accounts in existence which traced their descent back ultimately to the East. We have already seen in discussing the fable of the sick lion by Paulus Diaconus that he might have learned of it through an oral tradition. Foulet was perhaps too quick to dismiss oral tradition altogether. The authors of RR. may have found some of their inspiration and themes from stories handed down orally, but they also drew extensively upon written collections of fables and other beast stories.[1] Just how much RR. owes to the one and to the other has not yet been decided.

RR. as it exists today is an agglomeration of stories in verse in which the ever-changing relationship between the fox and the wolf is the constant feature. It was made up of various branches[2] which were assembled in the thirteenth century. It is now clear that these branches were composed at different times by different poets, the later ones often being imitations or adaptations of the earlier ones. The thirteenth-century compilers have not preserved the branches in their chronological order of composition and in discussing the poem one has to take almost each single branch as a separate entity. The earliest part of RR. was probably composed about 1175, for before that date there are no references to Reynard and Isegrim in contemporary literature, whereas after that time references to them occur fairly frequently. The last part may well have been written as late as 1250, though continuations, which really form separate poems, were still being

[1] The matter is discussed further in H. R. Jauss, *Untersuchungen zur mittelalterlichen Tierdichtung*, 1959.

[2] The various sections of RR. are called branches by modern scholars, for this is the name given to them in RR. itself. Martin's numbering of the branches is used throughout this book; see E. Martin, *Le Roman de Renart*, 1882–7. For a short introduction to RR. see R. Bossuat, *Le Roman de Renard*, 1957. The most recent study of the poem is J. Flinn's *Le Roman de Renart*, 1963. (Some scholars prefer to use the modern form *Renard*; others retain the OF. spelling *Renart*.)

written after that. However, sixteen branches were composed between 1175 and 1205 and they appear in almost all the manuscripts and may be said to form the poem RR.[1] But it is also possible to trace a more primitive version composed of only six branches written between 1175 and 1190,[2] for this version was used as the basis for the German *Reinhart Fuchs*, which was written about 1180 or a little later.

The earliest part of RR., which consists of branches II and Va, was written by a certain Peter of St. Cloud about whom we know nothing. It contains the adventures of Reynard against the wolf and against certain other animals. Although he manages to get the better of Isegrim, he is himself worsted by the animals weaker than himself such as the crow and the cat whom he tried to dupe. He prospers only when faced by brute force in the person of Isegrim. The poem was both a *conte à rire* and a satire, in which much of the humour springs from the parody of medieval feudal society and courtly romances.[3] It apparently achieved immediate popularity. The success of Peter's poem led to the writing of continuations and adaptations which it is impossible to enumerate here. But mention must be made of branch I, which is always placed at the beginning of each manuscript of RR. This branch tells of Noble's court, how the animals raised charges against Reynard and how he answered them. Consequently it has become known as the *branche du Plaid*. Although not the oldest branch, it was the one upon which the Middle Dutch adaptation was based and has thus come to be the prototype of all modern stories about Reynard. Before the Middle Dutch versions are discussed, however, a few words should be said about the German version of the Reynard story, *Reinhart Fuchs*, written about 1180 by a certain Heinrich der Glichezaere.[4] It contains three sections: the worsting of Reynard by some weaker animals such as the cock; the repeated victory of Reynard over Isegrim; and the tale of the sick lion. These three sections echo the stories found in the earliest branches of RR.

[1] The oldest branches in their suggested order of composition are II, Va, III, V, XV, IV, XIV, I, X, VI, XII, VIII, Ia, VII, XI, IX, XVI, XVII.

[2] See particularly L. Foulet, p. 100 ff.

[3] 'Mais dans les meilleures branches la satire reste liée, sinon subordonée, au désir d'amuser, tout en raillant, plutôt que de créer des ouvrages d'une âpre critique. Quand l'intention satirique prédomine sur le comique, on est arrivé aux branches postérieures du *Roman de Renart*' (Flinn, p. 9). See further Flinn, p. 35 ff.

[4] Edited by G. Baesecke, *Heinrich des Glichezaeres Reinhart Fuchs*, 1925.

During the last century it was commonly held that *Reinhart Fuchs* was not descended from RR. as it exists today, but from much earlier French poems no longer extant. Now the earlier branches of RR. are considered to have been written before the composition of *Reinhart Fuchs* and to have been the source of the German poem. This poem is accepted as a free adaptation of the six oldest branches in RR. and, the first of several medieval adaptations, it testifies to the immediate popularity of RR.[1] The importance of *Reinhart Fuchs* is that it shows how a poet could use RR. and yet produce an organized and unified work.

The most important and influential adaptation of RR. was the one written in Middle Dutch. There are two extant poetic versions of the Reynard story in Middle Dutch, *Reinaert I* (RI) and *Reinaert II* (RII).[2] RI, the older version, survives complete in two manuscripts, the Comburg MS. and the Dyck MS., both of which were copied in the first half of the fourteenth century. The poem itself was almost certainly written in the thirteenth century, though some scholars put the date of its composition in the late twelfth century.[3] We do know, at least, that it must have been written before 1274, for a Baldwin the Younger dedicated a Latin translation of RI to Jan van Dampierre, Dean of Bruges. Jan held this office from 1269 to 1274. RI is a poem of about 3,500 lines, the model for which was the first branch (*branche du Plaid*) of RR. Because it is built round the court scene and the plot is based on the summons and trial of Reynard, it has far more unity than its source. The poem is satirical, but it never becomes dogmatic: the actions are allowed to speak for themselves. The poem, which is notable for its use of proverbs and legal terms, does not lag and the action keeps going at a quick pace. A continuation to RI was made by a second author in the latter part of the fourteenth century. This version, RII, survives complete in only one manuscript, the Brussels MS., and an extensive fragment is to be found in a manuscript now at The Hague. The continuation contains a great deal of material which is not properly related to Reynard, such as the parable of the serpent and the man (cf. pp. 70–3). Also some of the episodes found in the earlier part are used again by the poet

[1] See Flinn, pp. 549–97; cf. H. R. Jauss, pp. 142–64.

[2] All the Middle Dutch versions and Baldwin's Latin translation are edited in W. Gs. Hellinga's *Van den Vos Reynaerde: I Teksten*, 1952.

[3] For a discussion of the problems involved in the composition of RI see particularly M. Delbouille, *Revue Belge de Philologie et d'Histoire*, viii (1929), 19–52.

of RII so that the continuation is very repetitive. Thus in C, chapter 23 (p. 51) we learn that the king is holding another feast and complaints are again raised against Reynard. Once more the king is angry with Reynard, and Grimberd has to warn him and bring him to court. On his way to the court Reynard makes a second confession to Grimberd. And so it goes on with the second part following the general pattern of the first. The second part is more openly satirical and didactic. The poet is not content to let the incidents speak for themselves, but he must add his own views and interpretations. The speech by the fox in which he criticizes the habits of contemporary clerics (cf. C, p. 60) is typical of the didactic approach of the poet of RII. This distinction between the styles of RI and RII can be traced in Caxton's translation, where the first part is light and fast-moving whereas the second, which begins at chapter 23, is heavier and long-winded.

Gerard Leeu printed a prose version of the Reynard story in 1479 at Gouda. This is a prose re-telling of RII which follows the poetic version very closely, often making use of the same words. The translator altered the story little and its only importance for us is that it was the Gouda edition which Caxton used as a basis for his translation, which he printed in 1481. Some scholars have suggested that there was a prose version of RII made in the early fifteenth century which is no longer extant and that it was this version and not the Gouda edition which was used by Caxton for his translation. But this theory is open to serious objections.[1] It is best to accept that Caxton used the Gouda edition. The changes that Caxton made from the Gouda text will be discussed in section 3 of the Introduction, though it may be said here that in general C reflects the Dutch version faithfully. This is why it is possible to trace the differences between RI and RII in C.

Caxton's edition became very popular in England, as many subsequent versions show. Yet even before 1481 animal stories in general, and stories about Reynard and his companions in particular, were known and enjoyed in England. There was, as we have already seen, an English translation of the Romulus fables, and the bestiaries had a great vogue in England. One of the episodes found in RR. had appeared as a separate poem in England about 1260. *The Fox and the Wolf* relates how the fox who had fallen into a well managed to escape by enticing the wolf to jump into the other

[1] See further below, Introduction, §3.

bucket. The wolf does so thinking thereby to enter into paradise, but his only reward is a beating from the friars. The names of the animals must have been known in England in the thirteenth century, for in the poem, *The Fox and the Wolf*, we find both *Sigrim* and *Reneuard* named. And in the fourteenth century the fox in *Sir Gawain and the Green Knight* is called *Renaud* (l. 1898), *Renaude* (l. 1916), and *Reynarde* (l. 1920). Chaucer contributed to the popularity of animal stories by his tale of the fox and the cock in the Nun's Priest's Tale, which need hardly be discussed further here. Although in this tale Chaucer calls the fox *daun Russell* (l. 3334), he knew the name *Renard* for he employed it in *The Legend of Good Women* (l. 2448.) These are merely a few of the indications of the popularity of Reynard and his companions in England.[1] Furthermore, it should also not be forgotten that the fox and the other animals appear in innumerable pictures and carvings in English manuscripts and churches.[2] The ground was well prepared for the reception of Caxton's translation.

2. DUTCH LOAN-WORDS IN REYNARD THE FOX

Caxton made his translation of Reynard from the Dutch prose version *Die Hystorie van Reynaert die Vos* printed by Gerard Leeu at Gouda in 1479 (P).[3] Because he translated so quickly, as we shall see in the next section, he often took over a word from his Dutch original and included it in the English text. Yet not only are Dutch and English closely related languages whose vocabularies are similar, but also throughout the later Middle Ages there was a rising volume of commerce between England and Holland which had led to the introduction of many Dutch loan-words into English.[4] Consequently it is not always possible to tell whether a word in C represents a Dutch loan-word occurring in English for the first time, an anglicized version of an earlier Dutch loan, or even an otherwise unrecorded English word. For example, P uses *ruymen*, 'to vacate, abandon', frequently. Normally Caxton translates this as *rome*, *romed*, but once he uses *ruymed* (57/32), in which form Dutch influence is apparent. OED. *Room*, *v.*[1] 3b records that this verb was

[1] See particularlv F. Mossé, *Les Langues modernes*, xlv (1951), 70–84.

[2] See K. Varty, *Reynard the Fox*, 1967.

[3] See Blake, pp. 298–311.

[4] See particularly J. F. Bense, *Anglo-Dutch Relations from the Earliest Times to the Death of William the Third*, 1925.

known in English only from 1393 to 1566 in this meaning. This sense is a normal semantic development from the other meanings that the word had in ME., though it is possible that this semantic tendency was strengthened by the meaning of the cognate word in MD. As the word appears with a Dutch spelling in C, and as this sense is recorded only once in English before 1481, it is probable that Caxton borrowed the word straight from P. Furthermore this meaning was not to survive long in English; indeed it may never have entered the spoken language, for Wynkyn de Worde in his reprint (WW) altered *rome* to *voyd*. So words like this one in C are probably loans from MD., although in some cases Caxton used the ME. word suggested by the MD. cognate form. Nevertheless I have decided in the following list of Dutch loans in C to include only those words which are not recorded earlier than 1481 in OED.[1], or which are recorded so much earlier that it may be accepted without hesitation that Caxton reintroduced the word. Naturally words which are found in MED. but which are not recorded fully in OED. are likewise excluded. Thus *clere*, as an adverb 'completely, entirely' is first recorded in OED. in 1513, but there are many examples of it under MED. *cler*, *adv*. 3 (a). It is possible that other words in the list would have been excluded if all volumes of MED. had been issued. I have also excluded from the list the animal names, such as *Bruin*, and the various Dutch senses given to the prepositions and conjunctions in C.[2] Nevertheless I have thought it of some interest to follow the history of the loan-words through the many reprints of C. The most important of these are those by Caxton himself in 1489 (PL), by Pynson in 1494 (RP), by de Worde in 1515 (WW), and by Gaultier in 1550 (TG).[3] It should be borne in mind in the discussion that follows that PL and RP are both independent reprints of C. But WW is a reprint of PL and TG a reprint of WW. It will often be noted that RP has a different reading from the other versions because it stands outside the general line of descent of the Reynard reprints. The versions

[1] Thus I have excluded such a word as *wysehede* (65/2) which is recorded in the *Ayenbite of Inwit* (1340), even though it may never have entered the spoken language. It was certainly used in C because it appeared in P.

[2] The various exceptional uses of these parts of speech are listed in the Glossary.

[3] For details of these texts see *S.T.C.*, no. 20920–2 and E. G. Duff, *Fifteenth Century English Books*, 1917. For a discussion of the relationship of these editions see *English Versions*.

made after TG are more like retellings of the story than reprints, so that a word for word comparison is often impossible. But where it is both possible and necessary to compare a word in the versions printed after 1550 with a Dutch loan-word in C, I have included a selection of the occurrences of the word from these later texts. Texts printed after 1550 are referred to by the date of their printing.[1] In general it may be said that apart from RP each version is a reprint based on the last printed version; so that as soon as a Dutch loan-word has been eliminated from one text, it has not been thought necessary to continue the search in later versions.

A list of Dutch loan-words in English was given by T. de Vries in his *Holland's Influence on English Language and Literature*, 1916, pp. 98–142. The list, which is a translation of that found in W. de Hoog, *Studiën over de Nederlandsche en Englesche Taal en Letterkunde en haar wederzijdschen Invloed*, 1902–3, is very slight. It contains only a very few of the words listed below, and even then gives no more than a translation and the Dutch form. A more comprehensive list is that given by J. F. Bense in his *A Dictionary of the Low-Dutch Element in the English Vocabulary*, 1926–39, (LDE.). Bense, however, appears to have relied on OED. for the Dutch loan-words in C. Thus wherever in the following list a word is said not to be listed in OED., it is to be understood that it is not listed in LDE. either. However, LDE. often contains fuller discussions of individual words than those found in OED. and in these cases the reference to LDE. has been given.

In the following list I have included the context from C in which the word occurs when this helps to explain the meaning of the loan-word. This is particularly so in the case of doublets, though it should be remembered that Caxton's doublets are not always made up of synonyms, e.g. *locked ne take* (see *Lock*, below). I have also included other translations in C of the same Dutch word, as these also help to illuminate the meaning of the loan. Where necessary to explain the relevant meaning of the MD. word, I have referred to the *Middelnederlandsch Woordenboek* compiled by E. Verwijs and J. Verdam, 1885–1941, (MNW.), which still remains the most comprehensive collection of MD. vocabulary. I have not normally considered it necessary to investigate to what dialect within the Low-Dutch complex individual MD. words

[1] See *S.T.C.*, no. 20923 ff. and C. C. Mish, *The Huntington Library Quarterly*, xvii (1953–4), 327–44.

belonged. P was printed in Holland, but is based on an original written in the Flemish dialect. In most cases Caxton has borrowed the word straight from the printed text, though in individual instances he was influenced by his knowledge of the spoken language. Although he travelled extensively in the Low Countries, he was most often at Bruges where he no doubt would have spoken the Flemish dialect. But in the following list, by Dutch or MD. is meant the whole Low-Dutch complex without reference to a particular dialect unless such a dialect is mentioned.[1] The words are arranged alphabetically, the alphabetical arrangement being the same as the one found in the glossary. References to C are to page and line of the present edition; references to the other English printed versions are to the foliation of the text in question; references to the Dutch text are to line references to P in Hellinga's edition, unless otherwise stated.

ABODE AFTER *phr.* (*pt. s.*) 'remained unaccomplished, came to nothing': *thus abode the treson of bruyn by my subtylte after* (38/24–5) translating *bleef . . . after* (1834–5). The verbal phrase is thus a calque on MD. *achterbliven*, see MNW. *Achterbliven*, 2) c); it is not recorded in OED. Cf. *abode . . . after* PL c5^{v}, RP b6^{v}; *abode . . . behinde* TG f8; *defeated* 1640 g3^{v}.

AFTERDELE *n.* 'disadvantage': *he was at an afterdele* (100/16–17). The word translates *quaet* (5566), but *afterdeel*, *achterdeel* is a common MD. word, see MNW. *Achterdeel.* OED. *Afterdeal* records the word from 1481 to 1634, but does not suggest that it is a Dutch loan. LDE. *After-deal* suggests that it might have been an English word although it is not recorded before Caxton. Cf. *afterdele* TG r4^{v}; *found nothing but despaire in the conflict* 1629 s2^{v}.

AFTERFEET *n. pl.* 'hindlegs': *on his afterfeet* (45/34) translating *op sijn afterste voet* (2246–7), but cf. *aftersten voeten* (532) which Caxton renders *hynder feet* (15/35). It is not recorded in OED. Cf. *afterfeet* PL d2; *after fet* RP c4; *hynder fete* TG h1^{v}.

AFTERWARD *adv.* 'back, away from': *drawe al afterward from hym* (74/2–3) translating *dat si hem afterwaerts setten* (3875–6), where the

[1] Our knowledge of MD. dialects still remains imperfect, but for a general introduction to the problems involved see C. B. van Haeringen, *Netherlandic Language Research*, 2nd ed., 1960.

meaning is probably just 'they forget him', see MNW. *Achterwaert*, *a*) 2). OED. does not record the word in this sense. Cf. *afterward* PL f4[v]; RP e4[v]; *backewarde* TG m8[v].

BALK *v. intrans.* 'be angry': *Ysegrym balked and sayde* (31/18) translating *ballech* (1419). The meaning of the word is disputed, see note to 31/18; but the meaning given above seems most probable, see Muller–Logeman, p. l and MNW. *Belgen.* OED. *Balk*, *v.*[1] 3 records this example as the first in the sense 'to stop short'; it is not recorded in LDE. Cf. *balked* PL c1, RP b3[v], TG e6[v]; *halfe angry* 1629 f2[v].

BANNE *n.* 'excommunication, ecclesiastical interdict': *in the popes banne and sentence* (41/29) translating *in des paeus banne* (2012–13). Elsewhere Caxton translates *banne* as *curse* (42/1: P 2028; etc.). OED. *Ban*, *sb.* 4 gives this as the first quotation of the noun in this sense, but the verb *banne* 'to curse' is known in England from *c.* 1275. The word is not recorded in LDE. Cf. *banne* PL c7[v], RP c2; it is omitted in later versions.

BELYKE *v.* 'be like, resemble': *He belyketh me so wel* (25/3) translating *hi ghelijcket mi seer wel* (1050). See MNW. *Geliken*, *Intr.* 1). There does not appear to be a MD. verb *beliken*, but Caxton often alters the prefixes of his Dutch loans. This is the only quotation under OED. *Belike*, *v.*[1] 2; it is not in LDE. Cf. *belyketh* PL b4[v], RP b1; *he lyketh me so well* TG d5[v].

BERYSPE *v.* 'censure, reprove': *he shal*, *beryspe me* (92/3) translating *berispen* (5035); see MNW. *Berispen*, 3). This is the only quotation under OED. *Berisp*, *v.* Cf. *beryspe* PL g8[v]; *take me in my wordes* TG q1[v].

BETEL *n.* 'wedge'; at 15/15, 15/29 translating *beytels* (501) and *beitele* (521). OED. *Beetle*, *sb.*[1] 1 quotes forms from *c.* 897 to the present day in the sense of 'a hammer, a hammer-like instrument'. It does not give the sense of 'wedge'. In MD. the word originally meant 'an instrument with a sharp edge used for cleaving' (cf. MD. *biten* in the sense 'to cleave'), hence 'a wedge', see MNW. *Beitel.* The meaning 'wedge' is the only appropriate one in P and C. It is not in LDE. In BM[1] *weg(g)e* is added in handwriting above the two words, see Introduction, §4. Cf. *betels* PL, RP; *wedges* TG b8, b8[v].

BYDRYUE, BEDRYUE *v.* (i) 'have sexual intercourse with': *I haue bydryuen wyth dame erswynde* (27/26) translating *bedreuen* (1202); (ii) 'perpetrate, accomplish, do', (74/8, 107/10) translating *bedreue*, *bedriuen* (3883, 5986). The sense of MD. *bedriven* is 'to do, commit an action', see MNW. *Bedriven*, 1), and (i) is a specialized sense. OED. *Bedrive, v.* gives a quotation from Laȝamon (*c.* 1205) and these three examples only. Cf. (i) *bydryuen* PL b6ᵛ; *bedreuen* RP b2; *mysdone* TG e1; (ii) *bedryue* is retained in PL and RP, but is superseded in TG by *do* (n1, s5).

BYDWYNGE *v.* 'subdue, render submissive': *I shal bydwynge and subdue the* (81/2–3) translating *Ic en sal di nv dwinghen* (4372). The form with the prefix occurs also in P (see next entry). Cf. Caxton's translation of *diese bedwonghe* (1705–6) as *that myght rewle them* (36/21). OED. *Bedwynge, v.* records two quotations from Caxton only, the other being from his version of Ovid's *Metamorphoses* (1480). Cf. *bydwynge* PL g1; *rule* TG o2ᵛ.

BYDWONGEN *pp. adj.* (i) 'subjugated, enslaved': *were not bydwongen* (36/19) translating *onbedwonghen* (1702); (ii) 'forced, made under duress': *bydwongen oth· or oth sworn by force* (48/1) translating *bedwonghen eede* (2372). See also *Bydwynge* above. Cf. (i) *bydwongen* PL c4; *bonden* RP b6; *kepte vnder* TG f5; (ii) *bydwongen* PL d3ᵛ, RP c5; it is omitted in later versions.

BYSLABBED *pp. adj.* 'beplastered': *They were byslabbed and byclagged . . . in her owen donge* (93/3–4) translating *Si waren beslabbet ende becladdet* (5101). This is the only quotation given under OED. *Be-, prefix* 1. LDE. *Beslabbed, ppl. adj.* suggests that 'cœno conspersus' would be a more accurate meaning for the word. Cf. *byslabbed* PL h1; *beslabbed* TG q2ᵛ; *dawb'd* 1629 r1.

BYTE *v.* 'kill by biting, bite to death': *whom Reynart the foxe hath byten* (12/19–20) translating *die reynaer die vos . . . verbeten heeft* (337–8). It also occurs at 51/5 (*verbiten* 2546) and 89/36 (*ghebeten* 4914). At 65/23–4 we find *byten and slayn her* translating *hebse doot ghebeten* (3384). Caxton has not retained the Dutch prefixes *ver-* or *ghe-*, but the sense intended in all these passages in C must clearly be 'bitten to death', cf. MNW. *Verbiten*, 2) and *Gebiten*. This sense is not recorded under OED. *Bite, v.* In another instance Caxton translates *verbeet ic* (1545–6) as *I slowe* (33/30). Cf. *bytyn* PL a4ᵛ; *biten* RP a3ᵛ; *bytten* TG b4; *slaine* 1640 b4ᵛ.

BONSSYNG *n.* 'polecat'; at 74/34 translating *bonssinc* (3968). OED., following Arber, and LDE. record under *Boussyng;* but all forms in MD. have an internal *n*, see MNW. *Bonsinc*. See further note to 74/34. This appears to be the sole occurrence of the word in English; it survives in PL, RP, and TG, but is omitted in all later versions.

BROKE *n.* 'crime': *brokes* (42/30) translating *brueken* (2068), *gylty in ony feat or broke* (64/8) translating *in enighen daden brokich* (3301–2); cf. Caxton's translation of *broeken* (2547) as *ony forfayte* (51/5). No other examples are listed under OED. *Broke*, *sb.* 4. It is not listed in LDE. Cf. *brokes* PL c8, RP c2ᵛ; *felony* TG g5ᵛ.

BUFF NE BAFF 'not a single word'; at 99/34 translating *boe noch bau* (5531); see MNW. *Ba.* OED. *Buff*, *sb.*[5] and *int.* records this as the earliest known example. It is not listed in LDE. The English phrase is probably an anglicized version of the Dutch idiom. It is retained in PL and TG, but is dropped from later versions.

BULE *n.* 'swelling'; at 81/26 translating *bulen* (4411). This is the only quotation given under OED. *Boil*, *sb.*[1] 1b. Cf. *bules* PL g1ᵛ; *byles* TG o3; the passage is rewritten in later versions.

CAM BY (SOMEONE/SOMETHING) TO *phr.* (*pt. s.*) 'arose, was brought about (through the agency of a person or thing)': *that cam by me to* (8/5) translating *ouermits mi* (86), *the moste parte of alle cam to by the vertue of the wode* (80/16–17) translating *dit quam al meestendeel toe by des edelen houtes crachte* (4329–30). The presence of *to* suggests that this is a loan from Dutch, for MD. *toe* while preserving an adverbial function is often linked to verbs and modifies their meaning, see MNW. *Toe*, *bijw.*, and cf. *Go to*, *See to* (below). The phrase is not recorded in OED. It is retained in PL, but the *to* is dropped in RP and TG.

CAM OF *phr.* (*pt. s.*) 'escaped from (an enemy)': *cam I of his clawes* (52/11) translating *ic ontquam . . . wt sinen fellen poeten* (2613–14). It seems likely that *cam of* is a calque on (*ont*)*quam wt*; see MNW. *Comen*, A. (1c). The nearest equivalent in OED. is that listed under *Come*, *v.* 61 f 'to leave the field of combat; to extricate oneself from any engagement', which is first quoted from 1596. It is not listed in LDE. Cf. *cam I of* PL d6, RP d1; *lepte fro* TG i2ᵛ.

CAMPYNG *n.* 'battle, single combat'; at 95/36 translating *campspel* (5291). But a MD. *campinge* exists with the sense 'single combat', see MNW. *Campinge*. This is the only example quoted under OED. *Camping*, *vbl. sb.*[1] 1 which suggests a derivation from Flemish *kampen*. It is not in LDE. It survives in PL and TG, but falls in later versions.

CYBORE *n.* 'vermilion colour of cinnabar'; at 78/28 translating *cyber* (4225). This is hardly a genuine loan-word since P's *cyber* is probably a mistake for *cynober* (cf. RII *synoper* B 5498). It occurs somewhat later in P as *cynober* (4339), which Caxton translates as *cynope* (80/20).

Elsewhere Caxton uses *cybory* as 'the ark of the Jewish tabernacle', see OED. *Cybory*. Despite its origin it survives as *cybore* in PL, RP, and TG, and is still *cybor* in 1640 o3^{v}.

CLERLY *adv.* 'without entanglement': *it may not clerly be done* (60/17) translating *is waerliken so claer niet te doen* (3083). In C ME. *clerly* has adopted the sense of MD. *claer*, see MNW. *Clare*, 7), a sense which OED. *Clearly, adv.* 10 records only from 1607–12 onwards. MED. *clerli, adv.* 1 (c) records the very similar sense 'with purity, blamelessly, guiltlessly' from the fifteenth century. It is not in LDE. The word survives in PL, RP, and TG, but the passage is rewritten in later versions.

CLOPE *n.* 'blow, strike'; at 101/8 translating *clop* (5625). This is the only quotation given under OED. *Clope, sb.* Cf. *clappe* TG r5^{v}; the passage is omitted in later versions.

CLUSE *n.* 'eremitical cell'; at 10/11 translating *cluse* (212). This is the only quotation under OED. *Cluse*. Cf. *cluse* PL a3, RP a2^{v}; *heremitage* TG b1.

COMPLAYN OUER *v. phr.* 'raise a charge (against someone)': *there is moche thynge complayned ouer you* (24/8–9) translating *ouer v gheclaghet* (1003). The Dutch construction is usually translated by Caxton as *complayn on*, e.g. 24/18, but in this instance he has taken over the *ouer* from the Dutch. OED. and LDE. do not list the phrase. Cf. *complayned ouer* PL b4, RP a8^{v}; *complayned on* TG d4^{v}.

COSTE *n.* 'food, sustenance'; at 9/29 translating *cost* (181), which has the meaning 'food, provisions' in MD., see MNW. *Cost*, 3). The word is not listed in OED. in this sense. *Coste* survives in PL a2^{v} and RP a2^{v}, but is replaced in TG a8^{v} by *vitailes*.

CRYTE *v. intrans.* 'cry, howl': *tho whyned he and cryted* (92/11–12) translating *Doe begont hi te criten* (5050–1). OED. does not give this word, as Arber emended to *cryed*; but *criten* is a common MD. verb, see MNW. *Criten*, and there is no need to emend C's form. Cf. *cryted* PL g8^{v}; *cryed* TG q1^{v}.

DAY *v.* 'summon someone to appear on an appointed day': *that he shold be sente fore and dayed* (19/19–20, cf. 19/30, 23/27) translating *datmen hem te houe dagen soude* (742–3). This is the only quotation under OED. *Day*, $v.^{2}$ 1; it is not recorded in LDE. Cf. *dayed* PL, RP, TG; *summoned* 1629.

DASSE *n.* 'badger'; it occurs frequently in C translating P's *das.* OED. *Das,* 1 records this word from C only. In PL *dasse* is replaced by *brocke* or *gray,* though it is retained in RP. In isolated instances it is retained in PL as well, e.g. *the cattes and the dassen* (C 38/16), where the inflexional *-n* helped to disguise the word. *Dassen* remains in this context in RP and TG; it appears as *dassens* in editions of 1629, 1640, 1681, and 1701; and the passage is rewritten in the 1756 edition.

DOOLE *v. intrans.* This word occurs three times in C as a translation of two MD. words: (i) *they studye so moche . . . that they therin doole* (60/2–3) translating *verdwalen* (3062); *Ther is no man so wyse/ but he dooleth otherwhyle* (62/6–7) translating *dwaelt* (3188); and (ii) *but I wente dolynge on the heeth/ and wist not what to doo for sorowe* (64/17–18) translating *dolen* (3317). Both *dwalen* and *dolen* mean 'to go astray, lose one's way' in MD., see MNW. *Dolen, Dwalen,* and this must be the meaning of Caxton's *doole* (i). Neither OED. nor LDE. records *doole* in the sense of 'to go astray', but under OED. *Dole, v.*[2] 1 the example in (ii) is recorded in the sense 'to mourn, grieve'. Possibly the compilers were influenced by the parallel phrase *and wist not what to doo for sorowe,* which has no equivalent in the Dutch text. But MD. *dolen* does not have this sense and Caxton's doublets are not always an accurate guide to the meanings of the words of which they are composed. Translate *dolynge* as 'behaving like a madman', for MD. *dolen* can mean 'out of one's senses' as well. The word is not listed in LDE. All examples are unchanged in PL and RP, but in TG the two examples from (i) appear as *dull(eth),* and that from (ii) as *wandrynge.*

DOW *v.* (i) 'press, squeeze, wring': *the foxe dowed and wronge his genytours* (104/16) translating *dat hem reynaer alsoe zere duwede* (5831). OED. *Dow, v.*[4] records this and the following example as the only two occurrences of the word. *Dowed* does not survive in the later versions in this passage. (ii) 'hit, nip': *I dowed the cony bytwene his eeris* (58/22–3) translating *duwede* (2967). OED. does not distinguish between meanings (i) and (ii), taking both in the sense of (i); but MD. *duwen* has a wide range of meanings, including 'to hit', see MNW. *Duwen, Trans.* Cf. *dowed* PL e2^{v}, RP d3^{v}; *nypped* TG k3^{v}.

DUBBE *v.* 'hit, nip': *dubbed me in the necke bytwene myn Eeris* (52/8–9) translating *dubbede* (2610). The word is used in the same context as *dow* (ii). OED. *Dub, v.*[2] 1 records *dub* only in the sense 'to thrust' and that only from 1513 onwards; although it compares the word with E. Frisian *dubben,* 'to butt, strike, beat'. For the sense 'to hit' see MNW. *Dubben,* 3. Cf. *dubbed* PL, RP, TG; *gaue me such a blow* 1629 k1.

ENDE *conj.* 'and'; at 17/6 Caxton has mechanically taken over P's *ende* (599). It is naturally not recorded in OED. or LDE. It survives in PL a7^{v}, but appears as *and* in RP a5^{v} and TG c2^{v}.

ENDWYTE *v.* 'reproach': *may noman endwyte me* (108/3) translating *verwyten* (6033–4). It is not clear how Caxton formed this word or whether it should be classified as a loan. Perhaps C's *end-* corresponds to the MD. prefix *ont-*, though no MD. *ontwiten* in this sense is recorded. MD. *verwyten* would normally give *forwyte* in C (cf. *Forwyttyng* below). The word could have been formed from an English base for the word *wite* exists in ME. in this sense, see OED. *Wite, v.*[1]; and possibly its form was influenced by *edwite*, which died out in the fifteenth century. *Endwyte* is not recorded in OED. It survives in PL i3; it appears as *endyte* in TG s6 and as *accuse* in 1629 t2^{v}.

FALACYE *n.* 'guile, trickery': *how wel can ye your falacye and salutacion* (63/18) translating *fallacie ende salutacie* (3259–60). OED. *Fallacy*, 1 gives this quotation as the first occurrence of the word (the next is from 1607), and suggests that it replaces *fallace*. In this context the form of the word is taken over from Dutch, see MNW. *Fallacie*, though it is not listed in LDE. It is retained in all later editions.

FALDORE, VALDORE *n.* 'trap-door', (i) *faldore* (27/8) and (ii) *valdore* (27/19) both translating *valdoer* (1170, 1191). This is the only example under OED. *Fall-door*; it is not in LDE. Cf. (i) *faldore* PL b6, RP b2, TG d8^{v}; *falldore* 1629 e4; *false door* 1681 e4; (ii) *valdore* PL b6, RP b2; *fall dore* TG e1; *trap dore* 1629 e4.

FEDE *v. refl.* 'live, exist': *whiche fedeth hym* (78/10–11) translating *voedet* (4190). In MD. the verb is intrans. and not refl., see MNW. *Voeden*, II. *Intr.* This sense is not recorded in OED. Cf. *fedeth* PL f7^{v}, RP e6, TG n6^{v}; *liveth* 1640 o3.

FOOTSPORE *u.* 'track 'foot-print'; at 37/21, 60/29 translating *voetsporen* (1767–8, 3102–3). OED. *Foot, sb.* 35 has only a quotation from the Leechdoms (*c.* 1000) and the first of these two examples from C; and LDE. *Footspore, sb.* accepts its use in C as a Dutch loan. There was a form *spor* in OE., but it appears not to have survived into ME. Cf. *footspore* PL c4^{v}, RP b6^{v}; *fotespur* TG f6^{v}; *print of his foot* 1629 g3.

FOR SLYNGER *v.* 'beat, belabour': *they wappred and al for slyngred hym* (17/2) translating *wapperen ende slingeren* (594). This is the only quotation under OED. *Forslinger, v.* LDE. *Forslinger, vb.* remarks that there is no recorded MD. *verslingeren*, only *slingeren* being found. It suggests that Caxton might have used *for-* in the sense of the English prefix 'all over', see OED. *For-*, *pref.*[1] 7, in order to translate *om sijn lijf* in P. But the prefix *ver-* is common in MD, and in its anglicized form *for-* it is found in many Dutch loan-words. It seems possible therefore that the verb *verslingeren* was found in MD., but is not recorded today; or (more probably) that Caxton added the prefix *for-* on the analogy of such pairs as *sling/forsling*, see *Forslongen*. Caxton does not seem to have been very careful in his use of prefixes. Cf. *for slyngred* PL a7, RP a5^{v}; *to bette* TG c2^{v}.

FORSLONGEN *pp.* 'swallowed, devoured': *hath this theef forslongen them* (11/36–12/1) translating *verslonden* (306). This is the only example under OED. *Forsling*, *v*. *Forslongen* is closely associated with *slange* (see below). In both cases Caxton replaces MD. (*ver*)*slinden* by a form (*for*)-*sling* with a *g*. The verb *verslingen* is not found in MD. Muller–Logeman, p. lii, suggest that Caxton took the word from P, even though it represents a dialect different from the one he spoke. LDE. *Forsling*, *vb.* records a form *vorslingen* in MLG. But as LDE. points out it is not likely that Caxton borrowed this word from MLG.; and therefore LDE. further suggests that the printer made a typographical error by inserting a *g* for a *d*. Although this is a possibility, it seems somewhat improbable in view of the two forms *forslongen* and *slange*; and notice the change of *stont* to *slonk* (see below). It would seem that Caxton had some definite verb in mind; but its origin remains uncertain. *Forslongen* is replaced in TG b3^{v} by *fordone*.

FORWYNTERD *pp. adj.* 'reduced to straits by the winter'; at 7/29 translating *verwintert* (73). This is the only example under OED. *For-*, *pref.*[1] 5c; it is not in LDE. Cf. *forwynterd* PL a1^{v}, RP a1^{v}; *forwyntred* TG a6; *halfe starved* 1629 a4^{v}.

FORWYTTYNG *n.* 'reproach'; at 86/6 translating *verwijt* (4682). OED. *Forwitting*, *sb.* has only this example and thinks the noun is formed from the MD. verb *verwijten*. But LDE. *Forwitting*, *sb.* rejects this and suggests it is a borrowing of the MD. or Flemish noun *verwitinge* (*verwitinghe*), which is a somewhat older variant of the form *verwijt* found in P; see also MNW. *Verwitinge*. The word is retained in PL and RP, but it is omitted in later editions.

FORWROUGHT *pp.* 'destroyed, sinned against': *I haue forwrought and angred my frendes* (50/16–17) translating *ic mijn vriende verwrocht hebbe* (2513–14). OED. *Forwork*, *v.* 2 lists only a quotation from Laȝamon (*c.* 1205) in the sense 'To do wrong to, injure'. It records the example from C under sense 1 'To forfeit (a possession, privilege, etc.), ruin (oneself) by one's own conduct'. But the sense of *forwrought* in C is much closer to OED.'s sense 2 for it is clearly an anglicized form of *verwrocht*, which has this meaning, see MNW. *Verwerken*, I. *Trans.* B. 2). Cf. *forwrought* PL d5, RP c6, TG h8; *wrong and abuse* 1629 i3.

FRIESE *adj.* 'Frisian'; at 41/6 translating *vriese* (1977). OED. *Friese, a.* and *sb.* has quotations from C and a work of 1675 only. Cf. *frise* PL c7; *friese* RP c2; *Frise* TG g3; *Fryer* 1640 g4ᵛ.

GALP *v. intrans.* 'cry aloud, yell': *he mawede and galped so lowde* (22/11) translating *hi mauwede ende galpte soe luyde* (895–6); and *she galped and cryde so lowde* (89/28) translating *si galpede soe lude* (4898). Only these two examples are listed under OED. *Galp, v.* 3, 'To yelp'. But LDE. *Galp, vb.* suggests that earlier English examples from *Kyng Alisaunder*, *Piers Plowman*, and *Political Poems* (1401), listed under OED. *Galp, v.* 1 'To gape, yawn', might also mean 'to cry, yell', even though in the latter two cases the verb is used of persons. OED. suggests the alternative translation 'to bell' for the example in *Kyng Alisaunder*, l. 462, and this is the meaning accepted by G. V. Smithers in his edition (*Kyng Alisaunder*, vol. ii, 1957, p. 178), who takes it from MD. *galpen*. MED. *galpen, v.* (c) quotes the example from *Kyng Alisaunder* as the only one in the sense '? to bellow'. The forms remain in PL, RP, and TG, but they are omitted in all later editions.

GLAT *adj.* 'smooth': *also glat and slyper* (97/2) translating *alsoe glat* (5339). It is the only example recorded under OED. *Glat, a.* It survives in PL, but is omitted in later editions.

GLYMME *v. intrans.* 'shine, gleam': *glymmed* (92/30) translating *glimmeden* (5081–2). This is the only example listed under OED. *Glim, v.* 1. Cf. *glymmed* PL h1, TG q2ᵛ; *glimmering and sparkling* 1629 q4ᵛ.

GO TO *v. phr.* 'shut (of a trap)': *the grynne wente to* (22/2) translating *die stricke ghinck toe* (881–2). Only this example is recorded under OED. *Go, v.* 91d; it is not in LDE. Cf. *wente to* PL b2ᵛ, RP a7ᵛ; *went togyder* TG d1ᵛ; *running close together* 1629 d4.

GRATE *n.* 'bone, backbone (of a fish)': *the grate or bones* (9/6) translating *die grate* (145–6). This is the only example under OED. *Grate, sb.*³ LDE. *Grate, sb.* questions OED.'s interpretation 'backbone' because of Caxton's doublet *bones*. Not only does MD. *grate* appear to mean both 'backbone' and 'bone', see MNW. *Graet*, but also one cannot be certain that Caxton's doublets are made up of synonyms. Cf. *grate or bones* PL a2ᵛ, RP a2; *the greate bones* TG a7ᵛ.

GREPE *pt. s.* 'gripped': at 104/12 translating *greep* (5825). OED. *Grip, v.*[1] records only weak forms of the preterite of this verb in English; but MD. *gripen* is a strong verb. Cf. PL *grepe* h8v; *toke* TG s1v.

GROWLE *v. impers.* 'feel terror for': *hym myght growle* (74/5) translating *hem gruwelen mocht* (3879–80), and *me growleth of thyse . . .* (94/22) translating *mi gruwelt soe sere van desen . . .* (5206–7); see MNW. *Gruwelen*, 1). The first example is the only occurrence of the word given under OED. *Growl, v.*[1] The word also occurs in the seventeenth-century epilogue to PL. Cf. *growle* PL f4v, RP e4v; *wepe and bewayle* TG n1; *I am sore afearde* TG q4v.

HAMME *n.* 'buttock, back of thigh': *he satte vpon his hammes* (18/38) translating *hammen* (713); see MNW. *Hamme*, 1) b). The first quotation in this sense under OED. *Ham, sb.*[1] 1b is from 1552. Cf. *buttockes* PL a8v; *hammes* RP a6v.

HEED OFFYCER *n.* 'principal officer'; at 42/12 it translates *huusgenote* (2043), which has the meaning 'trusted friend, servant', see MNW. *Huusgenoot*, 1). Compounds with the first element *hovet* are common in MD., e.g. *hovethere*, *hovetman*, and it is probable that Caxton made up his *heed offycer* from these MD. parallels. But *head* is also used as the first element of compounds in English, if not very frequently at this date; see OED. *Head, sb.* 63, which does not however record this word. Cf. *heed offycers* PL c8, RP c2v, TG g5; *chiefe and supreme Officers* 1640 h1.

HOLDE OF *v. phr.* 'fear'; at 53/11–12 it translates *houde van* (2674), but at 53/36 it translates a different construction. It would seem that *hold of* is a calque on MD. *houden van*, for the meaning of which see MNW. *Houden*, I. *Trans.* 7) b), although MD. *houden af* is also found. This sense is not recorded in OED. The forms are retained in PL, RP, and TG, but the passages are rewritten in later editions.

HUMAYNLY *adj.* 'in the manner of human beings'; at 69/20 translating *menschelic* (3612), 'of or pertaining to a man', see MNW. *Mensce-like*. OED. *Humanly, adv.* 1 records the adverb 'After the manner of man, etc.' from 1613 onwards. But in C the word is probably an adjective and almost certainly a calque on *menschelic*. Cf. *humaynly* PL, RP, and TG; *humane and manly* 1640 n1v.

LAADEN *v.* 'load, load up': *he hath do laaden torches* (56/6–7) translating *toertsen laten laden* (2827). OED. *Load, v.* has its earliest quotation for this verb from 1495 and suggests that the verb is formed from the noun. But the *aa* in C's *laaden*, which is not recorded in any other example in OED., shows that C's form is taken direct from the Dutch. The verb *laden* is common in MD., see MNW. *Laden.* It is not recorded in LDE. Cf. *laaden* PL d8v; *laden* RP d2v; *lade* TG i8; the passage is rewritten in subsequent versions.

LASTE *n.* 'distress, sorrow': *in this grete laste and harme* (60/3–4) translating *in desen groten last* (3063–4). For the meaning of MD. *last* see MNW. *Last*, 1). OED. *Last*, *sb.*[3] records the word only in the sense 'a fault, vice, sin, blame' and not in the sense given above. Caxton's word is certainly a loan from MD. It is not in LDE. Cf. *laste* PL e3v, RP d4; *losse* TG k5v.

LYE ON *v. phr.* (i) 'come in question': *ther lyeth not on* (20/2) translating *daer en ligt niet an* (764–5); (ii) 'be dependent on': *alle our welfare and worship lyeth on hym* (78/2–3) translating *al onse salicheyt ende onse ere an hem leit* (4175). For the meaning of the MD. *an liggen* see MNW. *Liggen*, B. 7). The phrase is not recorded in OED. It would appear to have been taken straight over from the Dutch by Caxton. Cf. (i) *lyeth not on* PL b1, RP a7; *lyeth it not* TG c6v; (ii) it is retained till TG, but then the passage is rewritten.

LYF SCATHE *n.* 'mortal injury': *lyf. scathe and hurte* (61/36–7) translating *lijfscade* (3175). Caxton's word has often been misinterpreted as two words by earlier commentators; but the juxtaposition of 'life' and 'scathe' makes nonsense of the sentence. The Dutch word *lijfscade* shows that C's *lyf scathe* is one word; RII has *lijfs scade* (B 4250). It is not recorded in OED. Cf. *lyf. scathe* PL e4v; *lyf schate* RP d5; *lyfe, scathe* TG k8; *misery* 1640 l4.

LOCK *v.* 'entice': *to be locked ne take by chaf* (103/28–9) translating *diemen mit kaue locken mach* (5794–5). This is the first quotation under OED. *Lock*, *v.*[2] See further LDE. *Lock*, *vb.* The word is retained in PL and RP, but the passage is rewritten in later editions.

LOOS *adj.* 'free from moral restraint': *thyse loos prelates* (60/29) translating *dese lose prelaten* (3103). OED. *Loose*, A. *adj.* 7 records an example from Henryson (*c.* 1470) and then the next from Lindesay (*c.* 1578), both of whom are Scottish authors. No doubt in Caxton the word was a loan from MD.; see MNW. *Loos*, *bnw.* 1). It is not in LDE. Cf. *loos* PL e4; RP d4v; in TG the passage is somewhat rewritten but *loos* is superseded by *crafty* (k6v).

LOSSE, LOSSEM *n.* 'lynx'; in C the losse and the leopard are the marshals of the lists. It occurs (i) *losse* (98/19) translating *los* (5437); and (ii) *lossem* (104/32) translating *loessem* (5849; cf. *los* RII C 7360). Caxton omits another example of *lossen* (P 3985) at 75/4, which might indicate some uncertainty on his part about this form. OED. *Loss, sb.*[2] records the word first from C and then from 1598; but it can find no explanation for the variant *lossem*. LDE. *Loss, sb.* accepts that C's *lossem* comes from a corrupt form *loessem* in P, and Muller–Logeman, p. 201, suggest that P's *loessem* might have arisen from a reading like *die loesse in dat crijt* . . ., though this seems improbable. The form *losse* survives till the seventeenth century; but *lossem* which survives till TG becomes *Lesson* in 1640 s4v.

MAW *v. intrans.* 'mew (like a cat)': *he mawede and galped* (22/11) translating *hi mauwede ende galpte* (895–6). This is the only example under OED. *Maw, v.* It is not recorded in LDE. Cf. *mawede* PL b2v, RP a8; *mawed* TG d1v; *mewed* 1629 d4.

MERCATTE *n.* 'monkey'; at 92/33 translating *meercat* (5086). OED *Meerkat*, 1 records the word from C and then from 1559. The word survives in seventeenth-century editions.

MERMOYSE *n.* 'monkey'; at 92/32–3 translating *marmoeyse* (5085–6). OED. *Mermoyse* records only this quotation and refers to *Marmoset*, 1 'A grotesque figure'. But the reference should have been to *Marmoset*, 2 'A monkey'. See further Muller–Logeman, pp. 194–5, and MNW. *Marmoset*, 2). Cf. *mermoyse* PL h1, TG q2v, *Marmozin* 1640 q4v.

MYSDELE *v. intrans.* 'distribute unfairly': *how ye mysdeled on the plays* (9/3–4) translating *misdeylde* (141). This is the only example under OED. *Misdeal, v.* 1. It is not listed in LDE. Cf. *mysdeled* PL a2v, RP a2; *misdelte* TG a7v; *cheated* 1629 b2.

MYSSAKE *v.* 'deny, renounce'; at 109/2 translating *missaken* (6079–80). This is the only quotation under OED. *Missake, v.* Cf. *myssake* PL i3v; *forsake* TG s7v.

MUSEHONT *n.* 'weasel'; at 74/32 translating *muushont* (3965); later at P 5886 the word *muyshont* occurs again, but with *muys* on f. 106r and *hont* on f. 106v, so that Caxton translated as *mowse* (105/17). OED. *Mouse-hunt*,[1] glosses as 'A weasel' with the first quotation from C. LDE. *Mouse-hunt, sb.* suggests that in P the word means 'cat' rather than 'weasel' and compares MNW. *Muushont*. The arguments are hardly convincing particularly as MNW. accepts the translation 'weasel' in RII. For its occurrence in Modern English dialects see *The English Dialect Dictionary*, s.v. *Mouse*, II (8). Cf. *musehont* PL f5; *musehount* RP e4^{v}; *moushound* TG n1^{v}; it is omitted in later editions.

NYCKER *n.* 'demon, devil'; at 94/22 translating *nickers* (5207). The English word meaning 'a water-demon' is known from Anglo-Saxon times to 1568, but the meaning 'demon, devil' is confined to this example in English, see OED. *Nicker, sb.*[1] 2; cf. MNW. *Nicker*. Cf. *nyckers* PL h2; *gobelyns* TG q4^{v}.

OCH, ACH *interj.* 'Oh, Ah'; at 31/35, 91/8, and 102/33 translating *och* or *aey* (1444, 4987, 5727). They are not recorded so early in OED. They are kept in PL and RP, but superseded by *O* and *A* in TG.

OFFRYNG CANDEL *n.* 'candle used in act of worship'; at 22/18 translating *offer kaerse* (907), see MNW. *Offerkerse*. It is not recorded in OED. It survives through all reprints of Reynard.

OSTROLE *n.* This word is of uncertain meaning, but at 74/34 it translates *ostrole* (3968, cf. *oostraelle* RII B 5186). The meaning and etymology of MD. *ostrole* are not clear, see MNW. *Ostrale*. The word is not recorded in OED. Cf. *astrole* PL f5, RP e4^{v}, TG n2; it is omitted in later editions.

OUEREST *adj. superl.* 'highest in quality': *taste of the ouerest wysehede* (65/1–2) translating *die ouerste wijsheyt smaket* (3349). OED. *Overest*, A. *adj.* 2 gives this as its first example in this figurative sense. The word was used in its literal sense in England from the fourteenth century and the figurative sense could have developed within English. Nevertheless the figurative sense was common in MD., see MNW. *Overste*, I. 2), and Caxton probably took the word straight from P. It is not recorded in LDE. PL and RP keep *ouerest*; but in TG l4 it is changed to *vtmoste*.

OUER REDYNG *n.* '(superficial) reading (of a document)': *not wyth ones ouer redyng* (6/16) translating *met een ouerlesen* (23). OED. records a verb *Over-read* from *c.* 1000 onwards, but it has no examples of the verbal noun; it is not recorded in LDE. The word is probably a calque on the MD. *overlesen*, possibly also influenced by MD. *overlesinge*. *Ouer redyng* survives in PL, RP, and TG, but the preface is omitted in later editions.

PALSTER *n.* 'pilgrim's staff'; at 45/7 and 45/23 translating *palsterkijn* (2202) and *palster* (2229), the former of which is a diminutive. Just before Caxton translated *palster* (2163) as *staff* (44/21). OED. *Palster* records the word only from Caxton's works, though *palstr* 'a spike, etc.' existed in Old English. PL and RP retain *palster*, but TG replaces it with *palmers staffe* (g8^{v}) and *staffe* (h1^{v}).

PERSONABLY *adv.* 'with such an appearance as to create a favourable impression'; at 45/22 translating *persoenliken* (2227), for which see MNW. *Persoonlike*, 3). No doubt *personably* is an anglicized form of *persoenliken*; its form was no doubt influenced by the adjective *personable*, recorded from the early fifteenth century. It is the only quotation under OED. *Personably*, *adv.* 1; see also Muller–Logeman, p. 174, who gloss 'like an important person'. It is not recorded in LDE. W. Matthews, *Later Medieval English Prose*, 1963, p. 284, wrongly modernizes this word as 'parson-ably'. *Personably* is unchanged in PL, RP, and TG, but becomes *personable Reynard was* in 1640 h4.

PLAGHE *v.* 'afflict, torment': *god sholde plaghe me* (66/7) translating *god die soude mi plaghen* (3415–16). The verb *plague* is first recorded here in English, see OED. *Plague*, *v.* 1, but the noun which was a loan from French was known in England from the fourteenth century. Caxton's example is certainly a borrowing from MD. as the spelling shows, but later examples of the verb may well have been formed from the noun; see LDE. *Plaghe*, *vb.* Cf. *plaghe* PL e7^{v}; *plage* RP e1; *smyte* TG 16.

PLAT BLYNDE *adj. phr.* 'completely blind'; at 99/11 translating *plat blint* (5485). OED. *Plat*, B. *adv.* 3 records examples of *plat* in the sense 'entirely, absolutely' in the fourteenth and fifteenth centuries including this example from C. But in the other examples *plat* is used by itself, whereas here *plat blynde* appears to be a complete word, cf. OED. *Stark blind*, *a.* Muller–Logeman, p. liv, class it as a doubtful loan; it is not recorded in LDE. Cf. *plat blynde* PL h5; *starke blynde* WW.

PLOMPE *adj.* 'foolish, ignorant': *so plompe and folisshe* (61/22) translating *soe plomp* (3150); and cf. *rude and plompe beestis* (94/15) translating *ruydi ongheuallighen beesten* (5194–5). Under OED. *Plump*, *a.*[1] 1 the word is recorded in C and not again till *c.* 1620; see further LDE. *Plump*, *adj.* Cf. *plompe* PL e4^{v}, RP d5; *blunte* TG k7^{v}, q4^{v}.

RASYNG *n.* The sense is somewhat uncertain, but is best taken as 'a fit of madness (preceding death)'. Caxton's *it was a rasyng ayenst his deth* (85/3–4) translates *dat was een ruer teghen sijnre doot dat hij alsoe rasede* (4618–20), where *rasede* has the sense of 'raged, acted madly'. A MD. *rasinge*, 'folly, madness', does exist upon which Caxton's *rasyng* may have been formed, see MNW. *Rasinge* (cf. *Ouer redyng* above). Otherwise he may have formed it directly from MD. *rasen.* This example is not found in OED.; but compare the verb *rase* listed under OED. *Rase*, *v.*[3] 'To be furious, to rage'. Cf. *rasyng* PL g4; *rassyng* RP f3; *fransy* TG o8.

RATTE *n.* 'wheel (used for torture)'. At 13/18 C's *sette yow on the ratte* corresponds to P's *raedebraken* ('break you on the wheel' 386). One must assume that Caxton's *ratte* is based on MD. *rat*, 'a wheel', as suggested by LDE. *Rat*, *sb.*[1] It is the first quotation listed under OED. *Rat*, *sb.*[3] But elsewhere Caxton translates *raden* (1009) as *racke* (24/12), and it is not impossible that he meant this at 13/18 as well. Cf. *ratte* PL a5; *rette* RP a4; *racke* TG b5ᵛ.

REKEN *v.* 'reckon out, allege'; at 33/32 and 33/33 translating *rekende* (1548) *rekenen* (1549). Under OED. *Reckon*, *v.* 1e this sense is first recorded from Douglas (1513), but it is quite possible that the sense was already in existence in England. Caxton might have taken over the sense from Dutch, however, see MNW. *Rekenen*, I. *Trans.* 6). The words survive till TG and are replaced by *unfolded* in 1640 f4.

RICHE *adj.* 'almighty': *The riche god* (20/17) translating *Die rijke god* (786). MD. *rijke* has the sense 'almighty' when describing the Divinity, see MNW. *Rike*, *bnw.* A. 1), but this sense is not recorded for ME. *riche*. Yet OED. *Rich*, I. *adj.* 1 records the sense 'powerful, mighty' for *riche* in the fifteenth century. Nevertheless it would seem that the sense 'almighty' for C's *riche* was taken over from MD. It is not in LDE. The word survives till TG, but the passage is rewritten in later editions.

RORE *v.* (i) 'move': *rore ne meue ony Ioynte* (43/9–10) translating *hande noch voete rueren en mochten* (2090); and (ii) 'affect with some feeling': *I am . . . rored and prycked in my conscience* (60/18–19), where P has *ghewecket* (3086). OED. *Rore*, *v.* records as sense 1 'To turn over, to stir about or up, to trouble' from *c.* 1440 to 1565, but this does not quite fit the meaning of our *rore* (i). Here the simple translation 'move' is best, this being the commonest meaning of MD. *roren*, see MNW. *Roeren*, I. *Trans.* 1). Nevertheless *rore* in sense (i) must remain a doubtful loan. Under sense 3 of the same verb, OED. has the quotation in (ii) as its sole example. This sense is certainly from MD., see MNW. *Roeren*, I. *Trans.* 2). Cf. (i) *styre* PL c8ᵛ; *rore* RP c3; (ii) *rored* PL e3ᵛ, RP d4ᵛ; *touched* TG k6.

ROUYNGE *n.* 'robbery, theft': *your steelyng and rouynge* (25/18) translating *stelens ende rouens* (1071); but cf. *thefte* (28/9) translating *rouen* (1234). Caxton may have been influenced by MD. *rovinge* which has the same meaning as *roven*. The word is not recorded under OED. *Roving*, *vbl. sb.*[2] until *c.* 1513. It is not listed in LDE. Cf. *rouynge* PL b5, RP b1; *robbynge* TG d6.

ROWME *adj.* 'far, advanced': *herde that it stode so rowme* (101/36) translating *dattet alsoe rume stont* (5667–8). OED. *Room, a.* 1c glosses it as 'Open to choice' and the only quotation is this one from C. Sands, p. 216, regards the OED. listing as 'questionable' and glosses the word as 'far'. As Caxton borrowed the word directly from MD. *rume*, for which see MNW. *Rume*, 1), it may be assumed that the general sense is 'far, advanced to such a stage (that only one of two choices is now possible)'. It is not in LDE. Cf. *rowme* PL h7, TG r6; the passage is rewritten in later editions.

RUTSELE *v. intrans.* 'slide': *rutsele ouer his tayl* (18/38) translating *rutselen ouer sinen stert* (714). This is the only example given under OED. *Rutsel, v.* Cf. *rutsele* PL a8[v], RP a6[v]; *rustle* TG c5.

SCATTE *n.* 'treasure': *so grette scatte and good* (34/9–10) translating *so groten scat* (1570). Elsewhere Caxton translates *scat* by *good and richesse* (34/12) or simply *rychesse* (34/13, 14). It is the only quotation under OED. *Scat, sb.*[2] Cf. *scatte* PL c2[v], RP b5; *a multitude of gold* TG f2.

SCATTE *v.* 'oppress by exactions': *scatte and pylle the peple* (107/7–8) translating *scatten si dezen* (5982). For the meaning in MD. see MNW. *Schatten*, 1). It is the first quotation under OED. *Scat, v.*[1], the next being from 1543. Cf. *scatte* PL i2; *poll* TG s5.

SEE TO *v. phr.* 'take care': *see wel to* (26/34) translating *siet ymmer toe* (1152); the phrase occurs frequently in C. OED. *See, v.* 25 records *see to* in the sense 'To be solicitous about' only from 1389. It is not recorded in LDE., but is clearly a loan from MD., see MNW. *Sien*, II. *Intr.* 2). The phrase is kept in PL and RP, but is generally superseded in WW and TG by *take* (*good*) *hede*.

SHORN *pp. adj.* 'deprived of privileges, possessions'; at 107/12 and 107/21 translating *onbescoren* (5988) and *beschoren* (6008) respectively. For the meaning of the MD. words see MNW. *Scheren*, 1). This meaning of *shear* is recorded in OED. *Shear, v.* 4 from 1740 onwards; it is not recorded in LDE. Cf. *shorn* PL i2[v]; *scorned* TG s5, s5[v].

SIDE HOLE *n.* 'smaller hole leading off a larger one': *by or side holes* (47/29) translating *sidel gaten* (2362). It is perhaps not a proper compound in C, but compare such words as *sidepath*, *sidedoor*, etc. and there are compounds in MD. with a first element composed of *side(l)*. *Side hole* can be accepted as a calque on MD. *sidel gate* or *sidegat*, for which see MNW. *Sidegat*. The word is not recorded in OED. It is retained until TG, but the passage is rewritten in later editions.

SIEDE *v.*, SYEDYNG *pr. p.* 'boil(ing)'; at 30/7 and 107/3 translating *sieden* (1350) and *siedende* (5975). Forms with an internal *d* are not recorded in ME., the ME. equivalent being *seethe*. The sense is the same for ME. *seethe* and MD. *siede*, but the spelling in C would seem to indicate a borrowing from MD. See OED. *Siede*, *v.* TG replaces the Dutch forms by *sethe* (e4^{v}) and *sethyng* (s5).

SYKERNES *n.* 'promise, faith': *Thus helde . . . tibaert his sykernes* (82/32–3) translating *zekerheit* (4482), for which see MNW. *Sekerheit*, 5). This meaning of *sickerness* is not known otherwise in English and is not recorded in OED. But the context assures us that Caxton had the MD. sense in mind here. The word is retained until TG, after which the passage is rewritten.

SYTE *v.* 'summon to court'; at 66/11 translating *citeren* (3421). OED. *Cite*, *v.* 1 records its earliest quotation from Caxton's Cato (1483) and its second from 1583. It derives the word from OF. *cite-r*, but in C and Cato it must have come via MD. It is not recorded in LDE. Cf. *sytte* PL e7^{v}, RP e1; *syt* TG 16; it is rewritten in later editions.

SYTTE OF *v. phr.* 'dismount': *now sytte of I wil reste me* (80/39) translating *Nv sit of ick wil mij rusten* (4366). The phrase is taken direct from MD. It is not recorded in OED. Cf. *sytte of* PL g1; *syt of* TG o2; *alight* 1640 p1.

SKYLLE (QUYTE) *v. phr.* 'make free or quit of': *hath skylled hym quyte of* (42/29) translating *heeft hem alle sine brueken quijt gelaten* (2067–8). Although there is no parallel to *skylled* in P, the word must have been formed from MD. *schillen*, see MNW. *Schelden*, 2); (V) *Schellen*. OED. *Skill*, *v.*[1] 1c records only this example; it is not recorded in LDE. Cf. *skylled* PL c8, RP c2^{v}; *quit* (*v.*) TG g5^{v}.

SKRABBE *v.* 'scrape, scratch': *skrabbing and casting wyth his feet the duste* (99/14) translating *scrabben in dat stof* (5490); cf. MNW. *Schrabben*, I. *Intr.* OED. *Scrab*, *v.* records only this example before 1808. LDE. *Scrab*, *vb.* thinks it might have been reintroduced after Caxton by Flemish and Dutch settlers in the Eastern counties and Ireland, because the word occurs locally in those areas. Cf. *scrapynge* WW, TG r3.

SLANGE *pt. s.* 'swallowed, devoured': *he slange them in* (53/3) translating *slant hi* (2661). The change of the MD. *t* to *g* is difficult to account for, cf. *Forslongen* above. The word is not recorded in OED. Cf. *slange* PL d6v, RP d1; *deuoured* TG i3v.

SLEPE *v.* 'drag': *They slepid hym and drewe hym* (27/1) translating *Si sleepten hem* (1159–60); for which cf. MNW. *Slepen*, I. *Trans.* B. 1). This is the only example quoted under OED. *Slepe*, *v.* Cf. *slepyd* PL b6; *sleped* RP b2; *toke* TG d8.

SLEPTE *pp.* 'digested by means of sleep': *haue ye slepte your dyner* (59/25–26) translating *Hebdi v eten verslapen* (3037–8). One must assume that Caxton's *slepe* is a bold adaptation of MD. *(ver)slapen*, for the meaning of which see MNW. *Verslapen*, I. *Trans.* 2). It is the only quotation under OED. *Sleep*, *v.* 8; it is not listed in LDE. *Slept* is retained in PL, RP, and TG, but replaced by *outslept* in 1640 l3.

SLONK *v.* 'devour, swallow greedily': *the false keytyf ete and slonked her in* (53/1–2) translating *dese valsche keytijf stont ende at* (2658), where *stont* means 'stood'. OED. *Slonk*, *v.* and Muller–Logeman, p. 176, suggest that Caxton might have misread *stont* as *slont* (and LDE. *Slonk*, *vb.* erroneously thinks that P's reading is in fact *slont*). It is possible that Caxton connected the word with *slange*, see *Forslongen* above, although *slonk* is a weak verb in C, whereas *slange* is the preterite of a strong verb. LDE. suggests that *slonk* might have been formed by Caxton through confusion of MD. *slinden*, 'to swallow', with its synonym MD. *slocken* and thus 'Caxton formed what we may perhaps call an early "portmanteau" loan-word'. The explanation of the word remains uncertain. Cf. *slonged* PL d6v; *slonked* RP d1; *slonged* TG i3v; *deuoure vp* 1629 k1v.

SMOLDRE *v. intrans.* 'smother, suffocate': *hit stanke that I was almost smoldred therof* (93/4–5) translating *ick nae ghesmoert hadde* (5103–4). Caxton's *smoldre* does not correspond to P's *smoeren*, but it may be based on MD. *smolen*, see MNW. *Smolen*. This example is the first occurrence of the verb in this sense recorded under OED. *Smoulder*, *v.* 1, though the noun occurs earlier. It is possible that the verb was formed in English from the noun. It is not listed in LDE. Cf. *smoldred* PL h1; *smodred* TG q2v; *poysoned* 1629 r1.

SONDRELY *adv.* 'especially, particularly': *my wyf his sondrely wyse* (66/27) translating *sonderlinghe* (3451). Under OED. *Sunderly*, *adv.* 2 there is a quotation from the OE. Bede (*c.* 900), and the only other example is this one from C. It is not recorded in LDE. Cf. *sondrely* PL e7v, RP e1; *marueilous* TG l6v.

SOROWE FOR *v. phr.* 'provide for': *the vytayller and he that sorowed for malperduys* (25/8–9) translating the noun *die besorgher* (1059). Caxton's *sorowe for* is probably based on MD. *versorgen*, see MNW. *Versorgen*, I. *Trans.* 1), which also has the sense 'to provide for'. OED. *Sorrow*, *v.* 1c records only this example and one from 1545; it is not recorded in LDE. The phrase is kept in PL, RP, and TG, but it is omitted in later versions through a revision of the passage.

SOULDYE *n.* 'salary, wages': *their souldye or wagis* (38/2) translating *den solt* (1823). The MD. word appears in several forms: *soudie*, *souldie*, *zoudie*, etc., see MNW. *Soudie, Soldie.* OED. *Souldie* records examples from Caxton's *The Game and Play of the Chess* (1474) and from 1555, apart from this one. It is retained in PL, RP, and TG, but is omitted in later editions. See also note to 38/2.

SPYNDE *n.* 'larder, pantry'; at 26/11, 12 translating *spijnde* (1112, 1115). The first is the only example recorded under OED. *Spinde.* It remains in PL and TG, but is omitted through revision in later editions.

SPYTY *adj.* 'scornful': *spyty worde* (95/24) translating *spytich* (5272). This is the only quotation under OED. *Spity*, *a.* Cf. *spyty* PL h3; *spitefull* TG q6.

SPRYNKLIS *n. pl.* 'spots, speckles': *somme sprynklis therin lyke purpure* (77/26) translating *somme dropele yn recht als purpur* (4144–5). But C's *sprynklis* must be based on MD. *sprenkel*, *sprinkel*, 'spot, speckle', see MNW. *Sprenkel*, 2). OED. *Sprinkle*, *sb.*[1] 2 records this example from C and one from 1577 only; it is not recorded in LDE. Cf. *sprynklis* PL f7, RP e6; *spryncles* TG n5[v]; *spots* 1640 o3.

STARE *v. intrans.* 'gaze lifelessly, be glazed (as in death)': *lyke a dede keytyf / hys eyen stared* (52/28) translating *Sijn oghen staerden hem* (2639–40). The English verb *to stare* has a similar sense in 'to gaze fixedly', see OED. *Stare*, *v.* 1, but the specialized sense in C is not recorded elsewhere in English; it is not found in OED. For the sense of the MD. verb, see MNW. *Staren*, 2). Cf. *stared* which remains in PL, RP, and TG, and which becomes *staring* in later editions.

STOKKE *n.* 'stick, stave': *wyth stokkes and staues* (26/35) translating *mit stocken ende mit stauen* (1153–4). OED. *Stock*, *sb.*[1] 1 records the sense of 'tree-stump', but not that of 'stick, cudgel', which Caxton must have taken over from MD., see MNW. *Stoc*, 8). Cf. *stokkes* PL b6; *stockes* RP b2; *clubbes*, *styckes* TG d8.

STOPPELMAKER *n.* 'reaper of stubble'; at 17/13 translating *stoppelmader* (613). OED. *Stopple, sb.*[1] 1 shows that *stopple* in the sense 'cork, plug' was known in England before 1481 and it relates *stoppelmaker* to this sense of *stopple*, even though this is the only occurrence of the word in English. LDE. *Stoppelmaker, sb.* rejects OED.'s translation and suggests the one given above. In P *stoppelmader* is used in a derogatory sense which implies that the man was a fool, i.e. he was someone who mowed the stubble after the corn had been harvested, see MNW. *Stoppelmader*. I think one must assume with LDE. that this is the sense meant for *stoppelmaker* in C as well. Cf. *stoppelmaker* PL a7ᵛ, RP a5ᵛ; *stoppell maker* TG c3; *Steeplemaker* 1629 d1.

STRYKE *n.* 'trap, snare': *and his croppe dyde hym woo of the stryke* (32/12) translating *strick* (1464), though elsewhere *strick* is translated as *gryn*, as at 21/25, 37. The word is not recorded in OED. Cf. *strike* PL c1ᵛ; *strycke* RP b4; *and the strokes greued him sore* TG e7ᵛ.

STROPE *n.* 'noose': *make a rydynge knotte or a strope* (32/34) translating *maket een strop* (1500). Elsewhere MD. *strop* is translated by Caxton as *halter* (31/19) or *corde* (32/11), which are the senses it has in MD., see MNW. *Strop*. OED. *Strop, sb.* 1 records an example from *c.* 1050 before this one; the word is not recorded in LDE. It is retained until TG, but the passage is rewritten in later editions.

STUFS *n.* 'dust': *ful of stufs* (100/15–16) translating *vol stofs* (5564); in the rest of the fight between Reynard and Isegrim Caxton translates *stof* as *dust*. This is the only quotation before the nineteenth century under OED. *Stuff, sb.*[2] Cf. *stuf* PL h6; *duste* TG r4ᵛ.

TATELYNG *n.* 'stammering, faltering'; at 61/27 translating *tatelen* (3159). OED. *Tattling, vbl. sb.* 1 records this example and one from 1749 only; it is not recorded in LDE. Muller–Logeman, p. liv, reject this as a loan-word because they say that examples are found in *Promptorium Parvulorum*, though no forms or references are quoted. OED. *Tattle, v.* 1 accepts the form in C as a genuine loan from MD. *tatelen*, a parallel form of the more usual *tateren*. It is the loan based on *tateren* which is found in *Promptorium Parvulorum*, see OED. *Tatter, v.*[2]. Cf. *tatelyng* PL e4ᵛ, RP d5; *tatling* TG k7ᵛ; *ratling* 1629 l3ᵛ.

THURGH SODEN *pp. adj.* 'very sodden'; at 106/27 and 107/2 translating *doer versoden* (5958–9) and *doerzoden* (5973–4). The use of *dore-* as a prefix is common in MD.; see MNW. *Dore*, II. 3). *Thurgh soden* is not recorded in OED. It is kept in PL and TG, but is omitted in later editions through revision of the contents.

VYSEUASE *n.* 'trifle'; at 9/24 translating *vyseuase* (174); see MNW. *Visevase*, 1). Only this example is recorded under OED. *Visevase*; see further LDE. *Visevase, sb.* Cf. *vyseuase* PL a2[v]; *tryfle* TG a8.

VNBERISPED *pp. adj.* 'without censure or blame': *to saye vnberisped* (35/9) translating *omberispet wtspreken* (1631); see *Beryspe* above. OED. *Unberisped, ppl. a.* records only this example. Cf. *vnberysped* PL c3, RP b5[v]; *openly* TG f3[v].

VNGHELUCK *n.* 'misfortune'; at 78/4 translating *onghelucke* (4177). The word is not recorded in OED., but there can be no doubt that it is a MD. loan. Cf. *vngheluck* PL f7; *vngeluck* RP e6; *vnlucke* TG n6.

VNROUSED *pp. adj.* The sense of this word is obscure; it is not recorded in OED. Perhaps the best translation of *Vnroused be it* (86/4) would be 'let it not be bruited about, i.e. I don't want to make a great deal out of this'. The positive *roused* is recorded under OED. *Roused, ppl. a.*[1] as meaning 'aroused, awakened' from the sixteenth century; the verb *rouse* was not common before then. The passage in P which 86/4 translates has no corresponding word, though *vnroused* may have been meant as a translation of *onuerweten* (4678–9), which means 'secretly, unknown to you'. It is not certain that this word is a MD. loan-word, though there is a MD. verb *rusen*, 'to make a fuss, noise', upon which it could be based; see MNW. *Rusen*. The meaning of this MD. word is applicable, but it is very rare in MD. and so any derivation from it must remain tentative. Sands, p. 215, says it is an 'expression of doubtful meaning, perhaps equivalent to "unnoticed as it was",' though C's *be it* would hardly support this suggestion. Stallybrass does not translate or comment on the word. It is not listed in LDE. The word is retained until TG, after which the passage is rewritten.

VNSHOED *pp. adj.* 'with shoes removed': *whan Isegrym was vnshoed* (44/1) translating *ontscoeyt* (2131). C's form is definitely modelled on the Dutch. OED. *Unshoe, v.* records this example and the next one from 1530; see further LDE. *Unshoe, vb.* The word is retained until TG, after which the passage is rewritten.

WAPPER *n.* and *v.* 'a strap with a leaden ball attached, to hit someone with such a weapon': *and that other a grete leden wapper/ ther wyth they wappred and al for slyngred hym* (17/1–2) translating *wappere . . . wapperen* (593–4). This is the only example under OED. *Wapper, sb., v.*[1]; see further LDE. *Wapper, sb., vb.* Cf. *wapper . . . wappred* PL a7, RP a5[v]; *whip . . . to scourged* TG c2[v].

WARANDE *n.* 'hunting land, abode of animals': *vpon a warande in the wyldernesse* (41/4–5) translating *op die warande in die woestine* (1973–4). For MD. *warande* see MNW. *Warande.* OED. *Warren, sb.* records forms without a medial *d* from *c.* 1377 onwards, but the word in the form *warren* is a loan from OF. The example from C is the first occurrence of the form with a medial *d* and in this instance the word is almost certainly a loan from MD.; see further LDE. *Warande, sb.* The word remains unchanged until TG, but it is omitted in later editions.

WENTLE *v. intrans.* 'roll, tumble about': *he wentled and tombled* (19/1) translating *so wentelde hi* (715); see also 19/4, 23/12. OED. *Wentle, v.* records forms from C and *The Four Sons of Aymon* (1489) only. The word survives in PL and RP, but is superseded by *tumbling* in TG.

WYDE *adv.* The sense of this word is doubtful, though perhaps it means 'with a wide open expression', for MD. *wide zien* means 'to look with wide open eyes', see MNW. *Wide, bijw.* 1). C's *they gapeden wyde on me* (92/35–6) translates P's *doe gaepten si mi wyde toe* (5091), which has no parallel in RII. This sense is not recorded in OED. The word is retained in later editions till late in the seventeenth century.

WYDER *adv. comp.* 'with longer steps': *The wulf strode wyder than reynard dyde* (99/7–8) translating *die wolf die screet wyder dan reynaer dede* (5480). As with *wyde* (above) the meaning is not altogether clear, though the context provides a general sense. One can assume that this specialized sense was developed in P from the original meaning 'further', see MNW. *Wide, bijw.* 1). This meaning was then taken over directly from P. OED. *Wide, adv.* 2 records the special sense 'with long steps' for this quotation; it is not recorded in LDE. *Wyder* survives in PL, RP, and TG, but is replaced by *taking larger strides* in 1640 s2.

WYGHTIS *n. pl.* 'children'; at 95/7 translating *wichteren* (5247). This sense is not recorded in OED.; for the meaning of the Dutch form see MNW. *Wicht,* 3). Cf. *wyghtes* PL h2^{v}; *beastes* TG q5^{v}.

WYKE *v. intrans.* 'withdraw, give way': *haue wyked and goon theyr way* (63/33) translating *ontweecken* (3284), and *we wyke and departe* (67/25) translating *wi wijcken* (3510). OED. *Wyke, v.*[2] records only these two examples. LDE. *Wyke, vb.*[2] suggests that the meaning of *wyked* in the first example is 'avoided, kept out of the way (of a person)' rather than 'gave way' as suggested in OED. But in view of the parallel *goon theyr way* and the meaning of MD. *wiken* (upon which Caxton's word was no doubt formed, rather than on *ontweecken*, the corresponding word in P), OED.'s translation is quite satisfactory; see MNW. *Wiken,* 1). The word survives unchanged in PL and RP, but is changed to *walked* (l2ᵛ) and *go* (18) in TG.

WORME *n.* 'monster'; at 94/25 translating *wormen* (5211), for the sense of which see MNW. *Worm*, 3). OED. *Worm, sb.* 2b records this example under the sense 'Applied (like *vermin*) to four-footed animals considered as noxious or objectionable', though the meaning in C would seem to be a little stronger and more definite than that. It is not recorded in LDE. It is retained in PL and RP, after which the passage is rewritten.

WRAWEN *v. intrans.* 'cry aloud, screech': *began he to wrawen* (22/2) translating *moest hi wrauwen* (882). OED. *Wraw, v.* lists this quotation and one from 1662, but the meaning it gives, 'to mew like a cat', is too specialized. LDE. *Wraw, vb.* suggests that *wrawen* means 'to mourn, feel grief', from MD. *wrauwen* (for the meaning of which see MNW. *Wrauwen*) and that Caxton misunderstood P, which was slightly corrupt and which ought to read 'Then Tibert began to grieve because he had betrayed himself'. This seems the most sensible solution, but it is not to be understood that Caxton meant *wrawen* to have that meaning in this context. The word is retained till TG, but is omitted after then.

WRYUE *v.* 'rub': *they rubbed and wryued hym* (109/14) translating *si wreuen hem* (6100). This is the only quotation under OED. *Wrive, v.* Cf. *wryued* PL i3ᵛ; *chafed* TG s8.

YAMER *v. intrans.* 'grieve, have pity': *as he hadde yamerde in his herte* (45/10) translating *iammerde* (2206); otherwise MD. *iammeren* is translated as *ermed* (46/1) or *haue pyte* (59/31–2, etc.). OED. *Yammer, v.* records an earlier fifteenth-century example from the North, but the word is otherwise extremely rare; see further LDE. *Yammer, vb.* Cf. *yamerde* PL d1ᵛ, RP c3ᵛ; *sorowed* TG h1.

YESTER MOROW *n.* 'yesterday morning'; at 52/3 translating *Ghisteren morgen* (2598). OED. records a *yestermorn* from 1702 and a *yestermorning* from 1654–5, but it has no example of *yester morow*; so we may accept that Caxton's form is a Dutch loan. It is not recorded in LDE. Cf. *yester morow* PL d6; *yester morowe* RP c6ᵛ; *yesterday in the mornyng* TG i2.

YONNE *v.* 'wish': *whiche yonned hym but lytyl good* (62/23) translating *gonden* (3215), the preterite of *gonnen*, for which see MNW. *Gonnen.* This is the only example under OED. *Yon, v.* which is glossed as 'To wish'. LDE. *Yon, vb.* suggests from the MD. parallels that Caxton's verb means more correctly 'To be willing or disposed to allow (a person) to have, receive, earn, or gain (something)'. Cf. *yonned* PL e5, RP d5ᵛ; *wysshed* TG l1.

YONSTE *n.* 'favour, good will': *the very yonste and good wyl* (15/4–5) translating *met gunsten* (480); see MNW. *Gonste.* This is the only example under OED. *Yonste.* The word survives in PL and RP, but is omitted in later versions.

Now that the loans have been listed, a few general features about them may be noted. Many of the verbs are common English ones which have taken on new meanings through the addition of adverbial prepositions: *go to*, *cam to* (*by*), *see to*, *abode after*, and *complayn ouer*. Some of these, like *see to*, may actually have entered Caxton's speech, for *see to* occurs commonly in C and is also found in Caxton's translations from French. Caxton frequently anglicizes many of the Dutch loans by changing the endings. The verbal noun suffix *-ing* is often used to replace MD. *-en* or some other ending or occasionally no ending at all: *tatelyng* (tatelen), *rouynge* (rouens), *bonssyng* (bonssinc), *campyng* (campspel), and *forwyttyng* (verwijt). He also changes *persoenliken* to *personably*. Caxton varies from his source considerably in the use of verbal prefixes. Although some MD. prefixes are kept, others are omitted or altered, and occasionally Caxton adds a prefix where there was none in MD.: *byte* (verbiten, ghebiten), *doole* (verdwalen), *slepte* (verslapen), *wyke* (ontweecken), *endwyte* (verwyten), *belyke* (ghelijcket), and *forslynger* (slingeren). The list contains a number of calques on MD. words: *humaynly* (menschelic), *offryng candel* (offer kaerse), *ouer redyng* (ouerlesen), and *side hole* (sidel gaten). In general, though, the majority of the words in the list appear to have been taken straight over from P. Caxton probably did not bother to think what the English word was or whether the Dutch word itself made sense. How else can we account for *ende*, *cybore*, and *ostrole*? The words are not part of an attempt to enrich the English vocabulary and most of them were quickly forgotten. Only a few lived on, but their survival is generally attributable to causes other than their appearance in C.

3. THE TRANSLATION

Before a discussion of how Caxton translated the Dutch *Die Hystorie van Reynaert die Vos* can be attempted, it is necessary to try to find answers to two important problems: firstly, which Dutch version of the story Caxton used; and secondly, how accurately the printed version represents Caxton's translation. The first is perhaps the easier to solve, though different solutions have been suggested at various times. Of all the Dutch versions it is P, printed by Gerard Leeu at Gouda in 1479, which C most closely resembles.[1] It had been generally accepted that Caxton used a copy of P for his translation until Muller–Logeman suggested that Caxton had used an earlier prose version no longer extant which was also used by Leeu as the basis for his printing of P.[2] Their main arguments were that in some places C seems to be more like RII than P; there are mistakes in C which suggest that Caxton made his translation as a young man before he became fluent in Dutch and therefore before P was printed; and it would be easier for Caxton to get a copy of a Dutch (or possibly Flemish) manuscript prose version than it would be for him to get hold of a copy of P in London shortly after it had been printed. I have suggested elsewhere that these arguments are inconclusive.[3] As we shall see shortly there are many differences between C and P. In general these are small changes made by Caxton to make the work more intelligible to his English audience. The few examples where C does not reproduce P fairly closely which Muller–Logeman adduced, which are not in any case very similar to the corresponding passages in RII, are part of this general improvement of the story. Secondly, the mistakes which occur in C result not from a lack of knowledge of Dutch on Caxton's part, but from the speed at which the translation was made. This type of mistake is found in all his other translations. Finally, we now know that there was a flourishing book trade between England and the Low Countries in the latter part of the fifteenth century and that Caxton was himself engaged in it. Books made their way over the Channel very quickly. There is, therefore, no proof that Caxton did not use P as the source for his translation, and unless further evidence is brought forward it may be accepted that C is a translation of P.

It has long been recognized that the compositor of an early printed book was allowed a certain amount of freedom in setting

[1] For a brief discussion of the Dutch versions and their inter-relationship see Introduction, § 1.

[2] Muller–Logeman, pp. xi ff. and xli ff., and Muller I, p. 49.

[3] Blake, pp. 298–311. A recent article by W. Krogmann, *Jahrbuch des Vereins für niederdeutsche Sprachforschung*, lxxxvii (1964), 29–55, repeats Muller–Logeman's arguments in support of the view that C is a translation of a version earlier than P. As no new arguments are presented, the objections advanced in Blake, pp. 298–311, may be held to apply to Krogmann's work as well.

up his copy. This freedom embraced not only spelling, but also word order and even omissions and additions.[1] The problem arises therefore how accurately the printed version C represents Caxton's own translation, for until we can answer this we cannot always be sure whether in the places where C differs from P the change was made by Caxton or by his compositor. Some alterations were clearly made by Caxton, as when a lengthy passage in P is omitted in C. But changes of this scope are infrequent. Normally the differences between P and C are of a minor nature: two or three words are added or omitted here and there, and the word order is altered occasionally. For example, in C direct speech is introduced far more frequently by 'said the fox', 'said the wolf', etc., than it is in P, where it is sometimes difficult to grasp who is speaking.[2] Perhaps these introductions were added by Caxton as part of his attempt to make the text more intelligible to his English readers. On the other hand, these phrases are introduced quite haphazardly and they are often not found in places where one would expect them.[3] Furthermore in each subsequent reprint of *Reynard the Fox* there are more examples of 'said the fox', 'said the wolf', etc., than there are in the version from which it was reprinted. It is improbable that every master-printer, or whoever was responsible for preparing the copy for the compositor, would introduce a few more of these introductory phrases; it is much more reasonable to assume that the compositors themselves occasionally added phrases of this sort. Moreover it not infrequently happens in manuscripts that *he quath* is added by a scribe where it ought not to be;[4] and the compositors probably did the same. Unfortunately there is no hard and fast rule for determining the respective contributions of editor and compositor in incunabula.[5] Nevertheless in the following discussion I have tried as far as possible to use examples of changes which can be attributed to the editor rather than to the compositor, though certainty is seldom demonstrable.

Before Caxton's translation is discussed in detail, it might be as

[1] See particularly *English Versions*, pp. 63–77.

[2] In 21/15–18 *quod he* (i.e. the cat) is added twice and *quod the catte* (C *foxe*) is added once.

[3] In the same passage, the fox's speech, 21/15, is not introduced by a *quod he* or *quod the foxe*.

[4] See K. Sisam, *Fourteenth Century Verse and Prose*, revised ed., 1950, pp. 25 (*Sir Orfeo*, l. 382) and 210. Cf. also *The Finnsburh Fragment*, l. 24.

[5] I have suggested some tentative conclusions in *English Versions*, pp. 74–7.

well to consider how Caxton viewed the work as a whole and why he translated it. Even if it is accepted that Caxton's purpose was to make money, the book would have belonged in his opinion to a money-making class of books. What class was this? Admittedly an answer to this question can be only speculative, but there are certain facts to be taken into consideration. In most lists of Caxton's translations *Reynard the Fox* is entered under the heading of satire and is the only book found in that class.[1] But I am somewhat doubtful whether Caxton regarded this work as predominantly either a satire or a parody and whether he printed it because he thought satirical works were popular. I am rather inclined to the view that Caxton regarded it as a moral fable not unlike Aesop's fables.[2] Two major reasons lead me to this conclusion: the general development of the Reynard story and Caxton's treatment of the Dutch prose version. When the poet of RI composed his poem there is no doubt that he intended it as a parody of the heroic epic and the courtly romance.[3] Noble and his beasts sit in court in a circle like Arthur with his knights at the Round Table, and Noble sends out his animals on quests. But instead of returning with fame and honour they come back in shame and humiliation, for here cunning is more potent than good. At the same time there is a great deal of implied social criticism and satire: Reynard manages to escape punishment because he plays on the avarice of the king. The satire and parody are not laboured in RI. In RII, however, the delicacy of the satire has been lost and the attitude of the poet is more openly didactic. The conclusion of the prologue sets the tone:

> Mer ic bid v so wat ic toge
> Hoort die woorden ende merct den syn
> Onthout dair leit veel wijsheit in. (B 42–44)

The parody is no longer so keenly felt for the poet introduces long moral attacks on the various social sins of his day. The characters become less lifelike because the poet introduces stereotyped

[1] For example, H. B. Lathrop, 'The First English Printers and their Patrons', *The Library*, 4th ser., vol. iii (1922–3), 69–96, particularly p. 78.

[2] N. S. Aurner, *Caxton: Mirrour of Fifteenth-Century Letters*, 1926, discusses them together in her chapter entitled 'Beast Tales' (p. 156 ff.) and so she presumably thought of them as forming a common class.

[3] Muller I, p. 30 ff.; cf. P. H. van Moerkerken, *De Satire in de Nederlandsche Kunst der Middeleeuwen*, 1904, pp. 38–53.

allegorical figures like Sir Rapiamus and Bishop Prendelor, whose qualities are proclaimed by their names, and because he introduces animal fables with didactic morals. Reynard and his companions are reduced to the level of exempla for a moral, to the level of the frogs and the stork, the horse and the deer, and the dog with a bone. Their courtliness and human qualities become jarring as they become more like animals in a moral allegory. The process inaugurated by the poet of RII is carried on in P. A prologue is included in P which underlines the way in which the reader is to understand the text.[1] Although the book deals with wicked animals, the reader will learn from this how to avoid wickedness and the book has been written 'for nede and prouffyte of alle god folke'. This attitude is reinforced in P's epilogue. There are many amusing episodes in the book, but the reader will understand that they are exempla which are employed to encourage the reader to improve himself. 'Late euery man take his owne part as it belongeth and behoueth/ and he that fyndeth hym gylty in ony dele or part therof/ late hym bettre and amende hym' (112/10–12). The purpose of the book is the improvement of the reader. Caxton translated these moral exhortations and no doubt read the book in the light of the prologue and epilogue. His translation was popular and it was constantly reprinted with the moral nature of the work becoming continually more explicit. In the early seventeenth century the morals for each chapter were printed in the margin so that no one could be in any doubt as to the interpretation of individual passages. Finally these morals were incorporated into the text.[2] Thus although the story of Reynard was originally a humorous parody with satirical overtones, it quickly developed into a moral fable in which the satire is mordant and heavily didactic: the parody becomes allegory.[3] Caxton's translation comes at a time after this trend was well established, and so I find it difficult to accept that Caxton himself regarded the work primarily as a satire or a parody. This does not mean that Caxton did not find the stories amusing and colourful, for this aspect of the story undoubtedly contributed greatly to the book's popularity. Yet many of the medieval versions of Aesop's fables are

[1] Cf. C's translation, 6/2–19.

[2] The later versions of *Reynard the Fox* are investigated by C. C. Mish, *The Huntington Library Quarterly*, xvii (1953–4), 327–44.

[3] A similar change can be noted in the development of RR. and its continuations, see Flinn, pp. 35–157.

no different in this, and Caxton regarded them principally as moral exempla.[1]

In Caxton's treatment of P we find that he often omits some of the features which had helped to create the parody in earlier versions. The poet of RI had parodied the courtly Arthurian romances by substituting animals for knights. One of the characteristics of the Arthurian court was that the knights sat in a circle to signify all were of equal rank. This feature is also found at Noble's court in the Dutch versions and it helps to build up the suggested similarity between Noble's and Arthur's court. Caxton probably did not realize this, for generally the 'ring' in which the animals sit is not included in his translation. Note the following translations: *inden rinc* (78): *in emonge them* (7/34); *midden inden rinck* (1296): *in the mydel of the place* (29/10–11); and *daer mede inden rinck* (4627): *ther by* (85/6–7); but it is retained once: *te ringe* (2038): *in a rynge* (42/8), when Noble tells the animals to be seated in a ring. It would seem as though Caxton was not aware of the significance of this feature. The details become blurred and the parody is lost, for instead of being mock-Arthurian, Noble's court merely becomes just another court. This tendency can also be traced in the Dutch prose version: RII's *inden rijnck* (B 343) becomes P's *inden gedinghe* (243; C omits, 10/32). By the time the story reached Caxton many of the satirical features were becoming obscured, and Caxton did not appreciate many of those that were left. The most likely conclusion is that he neglected features of this type because he did not think they were important. He saw *Reynard the Fox* as primarily a moral fable, not as a parody or a gentle satire.

Scholars are divided on the question of how well Caxton knew Dutch. Blades thought Caxton an excellent linguist and claimed that he was almost as fluent in Dutch as in English.[2] Muller–Logeman, however, on the basis of his translation of *Die Hystorie van Reynaert die Vos* thought that his knowledge of Dutch was slight when he attempted the translation.[3] Our sole evidence for Caxton's knowledge comes from this translation,[4] though as he

[1] The high regard for moral fable and allegory in the later Middle Ages is stressed by J. W. H. Atkins, *English Literary Criticism: The Medieval Phase*, 1943, p. 163 ff.

[2] W. Blades, *The Biography and Typography of William Caxton*, 2nd ed., 1882, p. 88.

[3] Muller–Logeman, p. xlix: 'Men ziet het, met de weinige kennis die Caxton van 't Nederlandsch had, was zijn onderneming een gewaagde zaak.'

[4] It is possible that the *Dialogues in French and English* may have been trans-

lived in the Low Countries for thirty years there is much to be said for the assumption that he must have had at least a fairly competent working knowledge of the language. Nevertheless the accuracy of the translation leaves much to be desired. There are many examples of an imperfect command of Dutch on Caxton's part. The sentence *Doe ghinct mit reynert vten spul* (P 1388) is translated by Caxton as *tho lyste not he to pleye* (30/33). But the MD. idiom *uten spele gaen met* means 'things begin to look bad for (someone)' and this makes much more sense in the passage. Caxton, however, understood *spul* in its sense of 'play' and made up his translation accordingly. On another occasion Caxton translates *heeruaert gheboden* (P 2824) as *commanded . . . for to be here* (56/4). But *heeruaert* is here a noun meaning 'levy, armed expedition', and the Dutch means that the king 'summoned out the levy'. Caxton understood *heeruaert* to be *heerwaert*, 'hither, to here'.[1] It does not follow that these mistakes prove that Caxton's knowledge of Dutch was very limited, for another explanation is possible. These mistakes may have been caused by the speed at which Caxton completed his translation. He often misread his text in a way that does not reflect on his knowledge of Dutch, but which strongly suggests that he was not concentrating as much on his translation as he ought to have been. For example, his translation of *Alsoe dat hij alle den hoep begaf* (P 5492–3) as *in suche wyse that he muste leue the rennyng after hym* (99/15–16) can only be explained on the assumption that Caxton misread *hoep* as *loep*, which he then translated as *rennyng*. When Caxton mistranslates *Segt ons bellijn* (P 2468, 'Tell us, Bellin') as *saye on bellyn* (49/27), it is not credible that he did not know the meaning of *ons*, 'us', for he translates it accurately in many other places. In his haste he presumably misread *ons* as *on*.[2] Caxton often varies his translation of Dutch words and phrases, sometimes taking the Dutch over into English and sometimes finding the correct English equivalent. This is particularly true with respect to prepositions, which in any language are often among the most troublesome words to translate. Thus the phrase *onder sine oeghen*, 'in his eyes', is translated as 'and gaf the wulf a stroke wyth his tail ful of pysse *in his eyen*' (100/11–12)

lated from Flemish or Dutch, see H. Bradley, *Dialogues in French and English by William Caxton*, EETS., o.s. 79, 1900, p. vi. But see N. F. Blake, *English Language Notes*, iii (1965–6), 7–15.

[1] For further examples see Muller–Logeman, pp. xlvii–xlix.

[2] For further examples see Blake, pp. 306–7.

and 'he swange his tayl wyth pysse ofte *vnder his eyen*' (100/27–8). A glance at the glossary will reveal that many of the other prepositions are also influenced by the meaning of the Dutch prepositions from time to time. Similarly in translating other parts of speech Caxton sometimes created an anglicized version of the Dutch word and sometimes used the correct English equivalent. At 34/10 Caxton translates MD. *scat* (P 1570) as *scatte*, but a few lines later it is translated as *good and richesse* (34/12) or simply *rychesse* (34/13, 14). At 100/16 Caxton translates *stofs* (P 5564) as *stufs*; but whenever *stof* occurs again in the battle scene it is translated as *dust* (e.g. 100/36).[1] Were it not for the cases where the word is replaced by its English equivalent, it would be easy to think that Caxton did not understand the Dutch word and so merely carried it over into English. These examples show that he knew what the Dutch words meant; it was merely that in his haste he did not bother to find the correct English word.

A further small point which intimates that Caxton's translation was made in a hurry is that there are a number of cases of influence of the Dutch text on his orthography. It is true that even in the texts translated from French there are instances of Dutch spellings. But in C they are of a somewhat different nature, they occur more frequently and they also occur haphazardly. Sometimes, for example, *rook* appears in C as *roke* (52/21), but more frequently it appears as *roek* (52/24) or *roeck* (63/22), both of which spellings must have been taken over from the Dutch text. Similarly we find both *romed* (30/37) and *ruymed* (57/32) in C, where the latter form is influenced by the Dutch. Indeed it is not uncommon to find examples of Dutch diphthongal spellings in C. Yet these never became part of Caxton's regular orthographic practice. He was merely influenced now and again by the spellings in his original. In the spellings of the consonants also Dutch influence can often be noted in such pairs as *vlycche*: *flycche* and *valdore*: *faldore*. Caxton knew how such words were normally spelt in English, but in his haste he took over the Dutch spellings without thinking—and his compositors did not correct them.

The orthographic evidence is perhaps not so telling as that from the loan-words.[2] In either case it is the variation between a Dutch

[1] Other examples may be found in Introduction, § 2.

[2] A similar variation between Dutch and English can be noted in C's syntax, see Blake, pp. 323–5.

form and an English form which is important. For this variation shows that Caxton knew the meaning of the Dutch and appreciated the difference in spelling between Dutch and English. It shows that it was not an ignorance of Dutch which is responsible for many of the mistakes in Caxton's translation. Some of them may admittedly have been caused by such ignorance, but generally it would seem that Caxton altered what he failed to understand.[1] The mistakes in the text are often the result of his misreading the Dutch, and the misreadings seem to have sprung from a hasty superficial 'ones ouer redyng'. I find it difficult to believe that Caxton would not have corrected most of the mistakes if he had made a thorough revision of his translation before printing.[2]

Although many features of Caxton's translation have already been mentioned incidentally, the translation as a whole may now be considered in greater detail. An interesting feature of C is that the quality of the translation improved as it went along: the earlier part is more mechanical, whereas the later part is somewhat freer.[3] Consequently in order to get an impression of Caxton in his full powers of translation a passage towards the end of the book is more appropriate. A suitable passage would be his translation of the story of Paris and the golden apple (78/29–79/22). This story had already been translated by Caxton once before in his *Recuyell of the Historyes of Troye*.[4] The passage in C corresponds to P 4226–81, which is too long an extract to be quoted here. Before the passage is discussed in detail, though, it should be noted that Caxton includes this section even though it has no proper connection with the story of the fox; it is a digression pure and simple. Indeed Caxton only once omits a lengthy section of the book, though he does make many shorter omissions.[5] In general he includes all episodes in P and he keeps them in the same order in which they occur. Although he was prepared to make changes within each episode, as we shall see, the progression and framework of the story are the same in C as they were in P. Caxton was

[1] This feature is discussed below, p. lviii.

[2] It is interesting to note that in Caxton's second edition of 1489, which was not collated with the Dutch text, some of the Dutch loan-words, such as *dasse* and *hamme*, were replaced by English words. See further Introduction, § 2, and *English Versions*, pp. 72–3.

[3] Blake, p. 311 ff.

[4] H. Oskar Sommer, *The Recuyell of the Historyes of Troye*, 1894, ii. 520–2.

[5] For examples see Blake, pp. 317–19.

not prepared to reorganize or in any way substantially reshape the story.

Although Caxton did not omit the full story of Paris, he did modify it to a considerable extent by omitting, adding, or altering certain passages. This can be clearly seen by comparing the opening sentences in each account.

Ende is die histori hoe dat venus juno ende pallas enen appel van finen goude hadden onder hem drien ghemene Ende een yeghelijc die wouden allene hebben daer si langhe omme twisten Ende quame des ten lesten ouer een Dat si parijs den gulden appel doen souden Ende wie die schoenste vanden drien waer dyen soude hi den appel weder geuen openbaerlijke

(P 4226–35)

And ther in is thistorye how venus Iuno and pallas strof for thapple of gold/ whiche eche of them wold haue had/ whiche contrauersye was sette vpon parys/ that he shold gyue it to the fayrest of them thre.

(C 78/29–32)

Caxton omits that the apple belonged to all three of them, that they had contended over it for a long time and that they finally agreed that they should give the apple to Paris. Nevertheless he is able to give a coherent account with all the essential information contained in it. Throughout the episode information of this sort is omitted in C: we are not told that Paris is a handsome young man or that Hecuba is his mother. Even some of the adjectives in P are omitted in C: thus *die meesten scat den edelsten ende den besten* (P 4252–3) becomes *the richest tresour* (79/7). This is quite a notable omission, for Caxton is often accused of creating too many doublets. Yet here he forgoes the opportunity to create one. Throughout C, and particularly in the second half, there are omissions of what was in the Dutch text. Most of these were not caused by Caxton's ignorance of the Dutch language,[1] but appear to have been an expression of his policy to cut down irrelevant material.

We saw in the last paragraph that Caxton omitted that the goddesses decided to give Paris the apple. Yet a few lines later he does include the words *whan he had resceyuid thapple* (78/34).

[1] This was the reason given in Muller–Logeman for the many omissions in C; see Muller–Logeman, pp. xliv–xlv.

Perhaps he excluded the earlier account because he knew he was going to include this clause here. Or else he might have done this as a correction or improvement to the story, for in the *Recuyell* the apple is given to him by Mercury and not by the goddesses as implied in P.[1] Moreover it provides a suitable transition between Paris guarding the sheep and the offers of the goddesses. In P this change is abrupt, as can be readily appreciated if the added sentence is omitted. Other changes were made by Caxton. He added the name *menelaus* at 79/16 and was therefore able to exclude a sentence about Menelaus later (cf. P 4275–6). Instead of the rather indeterminate *dit lant veer ende nae* (P 4249–50) Caxton has *asye* (79/5). It was, of course, well known that Troy was in Asia and this would have been known to Caxton anyway from his own translation of the *Recuyell*.[2] Other details were added by Caxton which he might also have learnt from his translation of the *Recuyell*. After Paris had brought Helen to Troy C adds *and wedded her* (79/20). In the *Recuyell* the marriage and the joy it occasioned are stressed.[3] Similarly when Pallas offers her gift to Paris, C adds *she wold gyue hym wysedom and strengthe* (79/1). Whereas *strengthe* might be considered an amplification of *and make hym so grete a lorde that he shold ouercome alle his enemyes*, the translation of what is found in the Dutch, *wysedom* is somewhat different. Also when Venus disparages the offers of the other two goddesses she says only *what nedest thou richesse or strengthe* (79/3–4); nothing is said of wisdom. Yet it is wisdom which is traditionally associated with Pallas and which she is said to offer Paris in the *Recuyell*.[4] These additions are pieces of information which Caxton introduced from his own reading or general knowledge. Other additions of this type are found occasionally in C. Caxton added one or two details from *The Canterbury Tales* such as the name Pertelot, Chanteclere's wife.[5] Similarly he also adds after *the holy thre kynges* the words *of coleyne* (36/10). Caxton had visited Cologne where he had learned the art of printing, and no doubt during his visit to *the holy cyte of Colen*[6] he would have visited the famous relics of the three holy kings.

The additions made from Caxton's reading or general knowledge are not the only ones found in C. Another type is the introduction

[1] Sommer, ii. 521. [2] Ibid. i. 37. [3] Ibid. ii. 536–7. [4] Ibid. ii. 522.

[5] See Muller–Logeman, p. xlvi (note), and Blake, pp. 309–10.

[6] Sommer, i. 3.

of a word or phrase to form a doublet: P's *sijns vaders scapen* (4237–8) becomes *his faders beestis and sheep* (78/33–34). Unless one should count *wysedom and strengthe* (79/1) as a doublet, this is one of the two new doublets formed by Caxton[1] and it is typical that it is found at the beginning of the paragraph. For I have shown elsewhere that new doublets are normally created in passages which demand the high style or at the beginning or end of a paragraph.[2] In passages of narration there are fewer doublets, and it is noteworthy, as was pointed out above, that Caxton omits one doublet in the Dutch. Other additions made by Caxton are designed to make the story more intelligible to an English audience[3] or to help the flow of the story. It was noted earlier how effective was the inclusion of *whan he had resceyuid thapple*. A little later when Venus tells Paris of the most beautiful woman, Paris 'prayd her to name this fayr lady/ that was so fair and *where she was*' (79/14–15), in which the italicized phrase is an addition in C. Many of the inclusions throughout C are designed to fill gaps in P as, for example, the phrase *on whiche sware the wulf* (98/19–20) which is not found in P.[4] Without this addition the passage would hardly be intelligible. Otherwise when Caxton could not understand the Dutch in his original, often because it was corrupt, he inserted something which he thought would make sense. Thus Caxton clearly made no sense of P's corrupt reading at 1452–3: *Ic ben des op deser vren al ghetroest*, so he inserted instead *I wote wherto I shal* (32/5). Nevertheless not all the additions which Caxton made are executed with polish. Particularly some of those in the earlier part of the translation are included without due regard for style. The first addition of all, chapter heading 3 in the table of contents, is one of these. To *The complaynt of curtoys the hound* (cf. P, p. 1) Caxton added *and of the catte Tybert* (3/6–7). It might seem from this that Tibert also made a complaint against Reynard in this chapter. On the contrary Tibert defends Reynard in the chapter and the *of* must mean 'concerning, about'. Similarly Caxton added *hede ne foote* (15/32) in the following sentence: 'in suche wyse as he coude not gete out wyth myght ne wyth crafte/ *hede ne foote*' (cf. P 526–7). Here the

[1] There is a second doublet in a sentence which Caxton added: 'and brynge a man in very *Ioye and blysse*' (79/13), though this is not of course a doublet formed from a word already in the text.

[2] Blake, pp. 319–22; but cf. Lenaghan, p. 21.

[3] See particularly Muller–Logeman, pp. xlv–xlvii, and Blake, pp. 307–8.

[4] See further Blake, pp. 303–4.

addition has been made rather mechanically by merely joining it on to the end of the sentence which reads quite well enough without it. At the beginning of his translation Caxton was less willing to rearrange his sentences than he was at the end.

It will be appreciated from this investigation of the Paris episode that Caxton's translation was by no means unintelligent. Small details within the story were added, omitted, or changed either to bring the story into line with the account already known to Caxton or else to make the story flow more naturally. The story was not omitted altogether nor was it basically altered. In the *Recuyell*, for instance, Paris is not a herdsman. He goes on a hunting expedition and having become separated from his men he rests and falls asleep. In his sleep he has a vision in which Mercury leads the three goddesses to him and explains why they are quarrelling among themselves. None of these details are included by Caxton and it is unlikely that he consulted the *Recuyell* when making his translation of *Reynard the Fox*. The details he includes are those which he could remember: he made no attempt to harmonize the two versions.[1] The changes could therefore be said to be largely superficial: the basic framework of *Reynard the Fox* remains unaltered. Caxton was not prepared to create his own version of the tale, since he did not want to spend time on such a project. He was content to take over the Dutch story and to adapt small details here and there in order to make it more acceptable to his English audience.

4. EDITIONS OF *THE HISTORY OF REYNARD THE FOX*

Caxton concluded his translation of C on 6 June 1481 and it is assumed that the book was printed sometime later in the same year. This first edition of 1481 is known to survive in at least six copies.[2] The following is a general description of the edition; individual variations are noted under the separate copies.[3]

[1] The same conclusion would be reached from a comparison of the other fables in C with the accounts in Aesop's fables, which were translated and printed by Caxton in 1484. The references to the corresponding passages in Aesop's fables are given in the Notes.

[2] S. de Ricci suggested that a seventh copy might exist, but see N. F. Blake, 'A Possible Seventh Copy of Caxton's "Reynard the Fox" (1481)?', *NQ*. ccviii (1963), 287–8.

[3] The fullest descriptions of the edition are to be found in: W. Blades, *The Life and Typography of William Caxton*, ii, 1863, No. 32, pp. 87–8; S. de Ricci,

The book is a folio with no title-page. The collation of its 84½ folios is a–h^8, π, i^8, k–l^6. a1 and l6 are blanks which are not found in all copies; π is a half-page without a signature inserted between h8 and i1, probably because a page of type was omitted by the compositor. The book begins on a2^r with the words ¶ *This is the table of the historye of reynart the foxe*, and the story itself opens on a3^v with the words ¶ *Hyer begynneth thystorye of reynard the foxe*. It ends halfway down l5^v with the words ¶ *Here endeth the historye of Reynard the foxe etc*. There are no catchwords in this edition. It is printed throughout in black letter with Caxton's type No. 2*, and a full page of type, as a8^r, measures 120 mm. across and 195 mm. from top to bottom. Spaces two lines deep were left for the initial capitals, which, like the paragraph marks, were to be filled in later by hand. Guide letters or directors were printed for the capitals to help the decorator, these being all in small letters except for the second guide letter on a4^r which is a capital I. There are twenty-nine lines of print on a full page; π^r has fifteen and π^v has fourteen lines. All copies consulted had horizontal chain lines and vertical wire lines with the 'shears' type of watermark, except that PM e7 has the hand or glove with the fleur-de-lis.

The following description of the six extant copies is meant as a supplement to the description of the edition found in S. de Ricci's *A Census of Caxtons*, No. 87. Those who wish for information on early owners, binding, etc., should consult de Ricci's book.

1. John Rylands Library, 15392 [JR]. JR is perfect except that it lacks the initial and final blanks. All paragraph marks and initial capitals have been inserted by hand in blue or red. The copy has had lines ruled in under each line of type so that it has the general appearance of a manuscript. Apart from the printed ones, the guide letters on b3^r (a), c1^r (r) and i2^v (r) have also been written in by hand. JR differs from the other copies particularly in the half-page π; it is probable that this half-page is a facsimile.[1] This copy

A Census of Caxtons, 1909, No. 87, pp. 88–9; E. Gordon Duff, *Fifteenth Century English Books*, 1917, No. 358, p. 99. See also J. Ames, *Typographical Antiquities*, 1749, pp. 21–3; J. Ames and W. Herbert, *Typographical Antiquities*, i, 1785, pp. 27–30; J. Ames, W. Herbert, and T. F. Dibdin, *Typographical Antiquities*, i, 1810, pp. 114–19, 364–6; L. Hain, *Repertorium Bibliographicum*, i, 1826, No. 861, p. 93; W. A. Copinger, Supplement to Hain's *Repertorium Bibliographicum*, i, 1895, No. 861, p. 21.

[1] I suggest that the half-page π in JR is a facsimile for the following reasons. (1) Variant readings: π^r l. 5 *skynn* (JR), *skynne* (C); l. 7 *shame And as*

is first mentioned in a bibliographical work by Ames–Dibdin, p. 366.[1]

2. British Museum, C. 11. c. 3 [BM[1]]. This copy belonged to Joseph Ames and is first mentioned in his *Typographical Antiquities* of 1749 (pp. 21–3). BM[1] is perfect except that it also lacks the initial and final blanks. The paragraph marks and initials have not been added. In BM[1] the half-page π was torn into five pieces at some time. The pieces have been stuck together, but one small piece in the middle of the page has been stuck in the wrong way round. Another piece of paper was fastened to the bottom of the half-page, thus making it full size. A few things have been written in BM[1] in what seems to be an almost contemporary hand. Thus *weg(g)e* is added on b2^r and b2^v above *betels* and a *w* before *alke* on b6^v. A part of the text is copied in the margin of d6^r and there are scribbles on several pages.[2]

3. British Museum, G. 10545 [BM[2]]. BM[2] is perfect except that a4 and a5 have been transposed and the blanks are missing. The initial capitals and paragraph marks have been inserted in red, though this has not been carried out so completely as in JR. It is first mentioned by W. Blades, *The Life and Typography of William Caxton*, 1863, No. 32.

4. Eton College, Cg.2.3.12 [EC]. This was bequeathed in 1799 by A. M. Storer to Eton College. It is bound in blue morocco, possibly by Henry Walther for Storer. It is imperfect as it lacks folios a2, a7, and a8. These have been replaced by manuscript facsimiles of a fairly poor quality. Possibly Storer had the facsimiles

(JR), *shame/ Alas* (C); l. 5 *departyng.* (JR), no full-stop in other texts; π^v l. 7 *trespaced/* (JR), no stroke in other texts. (2) Variant letter forms: π^r l. 2 *haue*, in JR the *a* of the digraph *ha* is written far above the line, in the other texts it is on the line; l. 5 *skynn(e)*, the second upright of the second *n* reaches below the line in JR but not in the other texts; π^v l. 11 *Reynart*, the back curl of the capital *R* hardly reaches the line in JR, in the other texts it continues below the line and turns forwards and upwards again; ll. 12 and 14 the bottom loop of the swash form of capital *I* stretches back and then upwards in JR, whereas in the other texts after stretching back it curls down and right round to cross itself. (3) The chain lines of π in JR measure 3·3 cm. The chain lines of all other pages in JR and of all pages in the other texts measure 3·8 cm.

[1] See also *English Incunabula in The John Rylands Library*, 1930, pp. 68–9.

[2] See also R. Proctor, *An Index to the Early Printed Books in The British Museum*, 1898–1903, No. 9639. This copy was used for the *S.T.C.* microfilm series (Ann Arbor), reel 12.

made before the book was bound. The original blanks are also missing. The initials and paragraph marks have been painted in as far as b1^{r} in gold, red, and blue, so that the first pages of this copy are rather ornate. These ornamental initials and paragraph marks also appear on the facsimile folios. The paragraph marks have been placed in the margin; but none are to be found in the table of contents. The borders on each page have been drawn in with red ink. A copy of Bagford's spurious picture of Caxton has been pasted in at the front. EC does not seem to be mentioned before the time of Storer, and it is first fully described in W. Blades, *The Life and Typography of William Caxton*, 1863, No. 32.

5. Pierpont Morgan Library, 20893 [PM]. This is the copy which was formerly in the Christie–Miller Collection at Britwell. It was sold at Sotheby's on 16 December 1919 and was bought by Quaritch for the Pierpont Morgan Library. It is perfect and includes the two blanks. It does not contain any initial capitals or paragraph marks. Some of the letters have apparently been touched up on k2^{r}, though this has not been professionally executed. On h3^{r} a stroke has been added above the *e* of *me* in ink. There are scribbles on several pages of this copy. On the verso of the final blank there is written *Constat Ricd Gough*, who was presumably the early owner of the book. PM contains worm holes, many of which have been patched up. PM was known to exist by Blades, but it was not fully described until S. de Ricci, *A Census of Caxtons*, 1909, No. 87.[1]

6. Bibliotheca Bodmeriana, Geneva. This copy, which formerly belonged to the Duke of Newcastle, was sold at Sotheby's on 21 June 1937 where it was bought by Maggs for Martin Bodmer. I was refused permission to see this copy. It is said to be perfect except for the final blank which is missing. The initial capitals are supplied in red.[2] It was first described by W. Blades, *The Life and Typography of William Caxton*, 1863, No. 32.

The story of Reynard the Fox proved to be as popular in England as it was on the Continent. Caxton himself printed a second

[1] See also *Book-Prices Current Oct. 1919–Aug. 1920*, p. 560; F. R. Goff, *Incunabula in American Libraries. A Third Census*, 1964, No. R137, p. 524; *The Britwell Handlist*, 1933, ii. p. 821; A. Thurston and C. F. Bühler, *Check List of Fifteenth-Century Printing in the Pierpont Morgan Library*, 1939, No. 1771, p. 167.

[2] See *Book-Prices Current Oct. 1936–Aug. 1937*, pp. 685–6.

edition in 1489, and his translation was reprinted with some modifications by Richard Pynson, Wynkyn de Worde, and Thomas Gaultier. Many versions were also printed in the seventeenth and eighteenth centuries. Although all the later versions printed before Goethe's rendering of the Reynard story became known in England can be traced back ultimately to Caxton's translation, the seventeenth- and eighteenth-century editions differ considerably from it because each version appears to be a reworking of the previous one. Thus there was a continuous process of modernization, adaptation, and interpolation at work. But a return to Caxton's original was made in 1844 when W. J. Thoms produced his edition of *Reynard the Fox* based on Caxton's text of 1481.[1] Thoms's text retained the original spelling, but had modernized punctuation. In general the text is reliable, although the editor has made several emendations and improvements silently and has sometimes modernized the spelling. Another edition of Caxton's text was prepared by Edward Arber for the English Scholar's Library. This edition, which appeared in 1878 and again in 1895, attempts to reproduce the original spelling and punctuation, though it is by no means free from textual errors. It is hardly surprising that a story which was so popular and which had been translated by Caxton should also have been printed privately in the late nineteenth century when private presses were numerous. Two private printings of C were made at this time: one for the Bibliotheca Curiosa in 1884 and the other by the Kelmscott Press in 1892. The former appears to have been based on Arber's edition and contains many of the mistakes found in that edition; the text of the latter is unreliable and the punctuation in it has been modernized. Quite apart from these four editions which set out to reproduce Caxton's original text of 1481, the last hundred years has seen the appearance of a host of modernized versions, metrical adaptations, renderings for children, etc. Yet despite this continued interest in the Reynard story there is no text that meets the demands of modern scholarship.

5. THE PRESENT EDITION

The purpose of this edition is to present as reliable a text of Caxton's original as possible. But in order to make it acceptable to

[1] For details of this and the other modern editions see the Select Bibliography.

modern readers and to prevent excessively high printing costs, a certain amount of standardization has been essential. The following editorial principles have been observed.

C was printed with Caxton's type 2*, a complete fount of which amounted to 254 sorts. The variety which resulted from this large number of sorts has not been retained here. The ligatures are printed as two letters, such as *we*, *wo*, etc. Individual letters have only one form in the upper and the lower case. For example, long and short *s* appear as *s*; no attempt is made to discriminate between forms of *d* or *g* with or without a tail, or of *l* with or without a stroke; and the ordinary and the swash form of capital *i* both appear as *I*. But the variation between *v*, used initially, and *u*, used medially and finally, has been retained. In the glossary words beginning with a *v*, whether this represents a modern *v* or *u*, are grouped under one head, as are words beginning with *i* or *j*. The only punctuation marks used in C are the stroke and the full-stop. In this edition the varying forms and uses of these marks are standardized into two forms in each case. The stroke appears in a long and short form, the former of which corresponds to Caxton's full-length stroke, the latter to any other size of stroke. This latter form can appear in a high, mid, or low position in Caxton, but here it always appears in the low position corresponding to the modern comma. Likewise in this edition the full-stop appears in its normal modern position or in a position a little higher than this, which can be characterized as a mid-position. This latter full-stop is used for all examples of the full-stop in the original which are not situated in the normal modern position. Capitalization and paragraphs represent the original faithfully, except that initial *ff* appears as *F*. Spaces for the paragraph marks were left by the printer to be filled in by hand later, and there is a divergence among the copies as to how many have been included. In this edition JR has been used as a guide for the paragraph marks.

Not many abbreviations are used in C. *Capitulo* appears frequently in a suspended form in the chapter headings and these abbreviated forms have been retained. All other abbreviations are expanded silently in the text, though doubtful cases are mentioned in the footnotes. The commonest abbreviation is the ampersand, which occurs about as commonly as the expanded form. The superior stroke is used for an abbreviated *n* (102 examples), *m* (24) or *i* (3). Arber expands the stroke as *n* in this last case as well, thus giving *reputaconn* for *reputacōn*. But that the stroke here stands for *i* is proved by Caxton's second edition, medieval Latin manuscripts, and fifteenth- and sixteenth-century English letters. The other abbreviations which occur are *qd* for *quod* (4), 9 for *com-* (1), ' for *-er* (1), and *willm* for *william* (1). There are no examples of such abbreviated forms as w^t^ or þ^t^.

A characteristic of English incunabula is the frequent occurrence of turned letters, especially *n*, *u*, and *m*. C is no exception and there are 71 examples of turned *u*, 16 of turned *n*, and 5 of turned *m*. There is also one example of a turned *r* and one of a turned ligature *ra*. These mistakes are corrected silently. All other mistakes which have been emended are recorded in the footnotes. Generally only those mistakes which are purely typographical errors are corrected. Many of the spelling variations, however, such as *behoefful* (81/34) have been introduced from the Dutch through a too hasty translation on Caxton's part. In this case there is no corresponding word in P, but the *oe* spelling may well have arisen in C from MD. *behoevelijc*. On the other hand, it is not impossible that C's reading ought to be emended to *behouefful*. An editor must use his discretion. I have preferred to adopt a fairly conservative approach to the text and not to remove the variants, unless I can be reasonably sure that the variant arose from some typographical error. Where Caxton or the compositor has made a more important mistake such as substituting *catte* for *foxe*, this has been corrected and recorded.

It is difficult to be certain where Caxton divided some of his words, and in doubtful cases I have used my discretion. But where Caxton joined two words together, I have separated them and recorded the form in the footnotes, except in the case of words beginning with *no-* such as *noman*, which can be regarded as a single word. Where a word has been divided into two, I have joined the two parts together only when the division does not coincide with the syllabic division. Thus *ta ughte* appears as *taughte*, but *by cause* and *to fore* remain unchanged.

Some of the details mentioned above may be noted on f. h2^r^, which is reproduced as the frontispiece to this edition. There are examples of the long and short stroke in the top line, but notice the different position of the short stroke in other lines. The ampersand appears frequently (l. 4, etc.) and *ff* appears in *ffor* (l. 6), which is reproduced as *For* in this edition. Capital *F* also occurs, as in

Fonde (l. 13). There is a turned *u* in *mirrour* (l. 14) and *colour* (ll. 21–22). This last form also exhibits the hyphen, which is naturally not reproduced in the edition. Occasionally, however, the hyphen is found within the line and these cases are noted in the apparatus criticus. The turned ligature *ra* occurs in *gracious* (l. 17), although this example is not entirely unambiguous. Words joined together can be seen in *acombe* (l. 14). The problem of word division in C is shown by the word *able* (l. 8), which I have read as one word, but which could be read as two. The following contractions are found on this page: *brokē* (for *broken*) and *neů* (for *neuer*), both of which are on the last line.

The folio number is given in square brackets at the beginning of each folio. The signatures, which are printed in lower-case letters and arabic numerals (see frontispiece), appear on the recto pages of the first four folios of a quaternion and of the first three folios of a ternion. In the edition this numbering has been extended to all folios, recto and verso.

I have collated five of the extant copies of C for this edition. All variants, which are largely of a minor character, have been recorded in the apparatus criticus.

SELECT BIBLIOGRAPHY

Bibliographical

N. F. Blake, 'A Possible Seventh Copy of Caxton's "Reynard the Fox" (1481)?', *NQ*. ccviii (1963), 287–8.

S. de Ricci, *A Census of Caxtons* (Illustrated Monographs issued by the Bibliographical Society, XV). London, 1909.

Dictionaries and Language

J. F. Bense, *A Dictionary of the Low-Dutch Element in the English Vocabulary*. London, 1926–39.

N. F. Blake, 'Caxton's Language', *Neuphilologische Mitteilungen*, lxvii (1966), 122–32.

G. N. Clark, *The Dutch Influence on the English Vocabulary* (Society for Pure English Tract No. XLIV). Oxford, 1935.

W. de Hoog, *Studiën over de Nederlandsche en Engelsche Taal en Letterkunde en haar wederzijdschen Invloed*. 2 vols. Doordrecht, 1902–3.

E. C. Llewellyn, *The Influence of Low Dutch on the English Vocabulary* (Publications of the Philological Society). London, 1936.

P. de Reul, *The Language of Caxton's Reynard the Fox. A Study in Historical English Syntax* (Université de Gand: Recueil de Travaux publiés par la Faculté de Philosophie et Lettres, fasc. 26e). Ghent and London, 1901.

H. Römstedt, *Die englische Schriftsprache bei Caxton*. Göttingen, 1891.

F. A. Stoett, *Middelnederlandsche Spraakkunst: Syntaxis*. 2nd edition. The Hague, 1909.

J.-M. Toll, *Niederländisches Lehngut im Mittelenglischen*. Halle, 1926.

E. Verwijs, J. Verdam, and F. A. Stoett, *Middelnederlandsch Woordenboek*. 11 vols. The Hague, 1885–1941.

T. de Vries, *Holland's Influence on English Language and Literature*. Chicago, 1916.

H. Wiencke, *Die Sprache Caxtons* (Kölner anglistische Arbeiten, XI). Leipzig, 1930.

Editions and Translations of The History of Reynard the Fox, 1481

E. Arber, *The History of Reynard the Fox Translated and Printed by William Caxton June 1481* (English Scholar's Library, I). London, 1878.

F. S. Ellis, *The History of Reynard the Fox*. London, 1894. [A verse translation; reissued 1897].

E. Goldsmid, *The History of Reynard the Fox. Translated and Printed by William Caxton, 1481* (privately printed: Bibliotheca Curiosa, X and XI). Edinburgh, 1884.

H. Morley, *The History of Reynard the Fox*, in *Early Prose Romances*, pp. 41–166 (The Carisbrooke Library, IV). London, 1889.

H. Morley, *The History of Reynard the Fox* (printed in W. J. Thoms, *Early English Prose Romances*, pp. 41–166). London, 1907. [A reprint of the above.]

D. B. Sands, *The History of Reynard the Fox Translated and Printed by William Caxton in 1481*. Cambridge, Mass., and London, 1960.

H. H. Sparling, *The History of Reynard the Foxe by William Caxton*. Privately printed: Kelmscott Press, Hammersmith, 1892.

W. S. Stallybrass, *The Epic of the Beast, Consisting of English Translations of The History of Reynard the Fox and Physiologus*, with an Introduction by William Rose (Broadway Translations). London and New York, 1924.

W. J. Thoms, *The History of Reynard the Fox, from the Edition printed by Caxton in 1481* (Percy Society, XII). London, 1844.

Editions and Translations of Earlier Continental Versions of the Reynard Story

E. Colledge and A. J. Barnouw, *Reynard the Fox and other Mediaeval Netherlands Secular Literature* (Bibliotheca Neerlandica, I). London, New York and Leyden, 1967.

W. Gs. Hellinga, *Van den Vos Reynaerde: I Teksten, diplomatisch uitgegeven naar de bronnen vóór het jaar 1500*. Zwolle, 1952.

P. de Keyser, *Reinaerts Historie. Hs. Koninklijke Bibliotheek 14601* (Rijksuniversiteit te Gent: Werken uitgegeven door de Faculteit van de Wijsbegeerte en Letteren, Extra Serie: Facsimiles I). Antwerp, 1938.

E. Martin, *Reinaert. Willems Gedicht van den Vos Reinaerde und die Umarbeitung und Fortsetzung Reinaerts Historie*. Paderborn, 1874.

J. W. Muller and H. Logeman, *Die Hystorie van Reynaert die Vos, naar den Druk van 1479, vergeleken met William Caxton's Engelsche Vertaling*. Zwolle, 1892.

J. W. Muller, *Van den Vos Reinaerde, naar de thans bekende Handschriften en Bewerkingen critisch uitgegeven met eene Inleiding* (Koninklijke Vlaamsche Academie voor Taal- en Letterkunde, Publicaties reeks 3, No. 22). Ghent and Utrecht, 1914.

J. W. Muller, *Van den Vos Reinaerde* (Leidsche Drukken en Herdrukken, groote reeks No. 1 and 2). 2nd edition, 2 vols. Leiden, 1939–42.

D. C. Tinbergen, *Van den Vos Reinaerde*. 14th edition revised by L. M. van Dis. Groningen, 1956.

E. Martin, *Le Roman de Renart*. 3 vols. and supplement. Strassburg, 1882–7.

A. P. Paris, *Les Aventures de Maître Renart et d'Ysengrin son Compère, mises en nouveau Langage, racontées dans un nouvel Ordre et suivies de nouvelles Recherches sur le Roman de Renart*. Paris, 1861. [The translation alone was republished in a private edition by the Club des Libraires de France, 1963.]

M. Roques, *Le Roman de Renart, édité d'après le manuscript de Cangé* (Les Classiques français du Moyen Age, 78, 79, 81, 85, 88, 90). Paris, 1951–63.

G. Baesecke, *Heinrich des Glichezaeres Reinhart Fuchs* (Altdeutsche Bibliothek, VIII). Halle, 1925.

J. Grimm, *Reinhart Fuchs*. Berlin, 1834.

J. Grimm, *Sendschreiben an Karl Lachmann. Über Reinhart Fuchs*. Leipzig, 1840.

A. Michel, *Die Ecbasis Cuiusdam Captivi per Tropologiam, ein Werk Humberts, des späteren Kardinals von Silva Candida* (Sitzungsberichte der Bayerischen Akademie der Wissenschaften, Phil.-Hist. Klasse, I). Munich, 1957.

K. Strecker, *Ecbasis Cuiusdam Captivi per Tropologiam* (Scriptores rerum germanicarum in usum scholarum). Hanover, 1935.

E. Voigt, *Ecbasis Captivi, das älteste Thierepos des Mittelalters* (Quellen und Forschungen zur Sprach- und Culturgeschichte der germanischen Völker, VIII). Strassburg, 1874.

E. H. Zeydel, *Ecbasis Cuiusdam Captivi: Escape of a Certain Captive* (University of North Carolina Studies in the Germanic Languages and Literatures, 46). Chapel Hill, 1964.

A. Schönfelder, *Isengrimus. Das flämische Tierepos aus dem Lateinischen verdeutscht* (Niederdeutsche Studien, 3). Münster and Cologne, 1955.

E. Voigt, *Ysengrimus*. Halle, 1884.

Studies on the Reynard Story and Allied Topics

N. F. Blake, 'William Caxton's *Reynard the Fox* and his Dutch Original', *Bulletin of the John Rylands Library*, xlvi (1963–4), 298–325.

N. F. Blake, 'English Versions of *Reynard the Fox* in the Fifteenth and Sixteenth Centuries', *Studies in Philology*, lxii (1965), 63–77.

R. Bossuat, *Le Roman de Renard* (Connaissance des Lettres, 49). Paris, 1957.

M. Delbouille, 'La Composition du *Reinaert I*, Arnout, Willem et le *Roman de Renart* français', *Revue Belge de Philologie et d'Histoire*, viii (1929), 19–52.

J. Flinn, *Le Roman de Renart dans la Littérature française et dans les Littératures étrangères au Moyen Age* (University of Toronto Romance Series, 4). Toronto and Paris, 1963.

W. Foerste, 'Von Reinaerts Historie zum Reinke de Vos', *Münstersche Beiträge zur niederdeutschen Philologie*, vi (1960), 105–46.

L. Foulet, *Le Roman de Renard* (Bibliothèque de l'École des Hautes Études, Sciences Historiques et Philologiques, fasc. 211e). Paris, 1914.

J. Graven, *Le Procès criminel du Roman de Renart*. Geneva, 1950.

W. Gs. Hellinga, *Naamgevingsproblemen in de Reynaert* (Bijdragen en Mededelingen der Naamkunde-Commissie van de Koninklijke Nederlandse Akademie van Wetenschappen te Amsterdam, III). Amsterdam, 1952.

H. R. Jauss, *Untersuchungen zur mittelalterlichen Tierdichtung* (Beihefte zur Zeitschrift für romanische Philologie, 100). Tübingen, 1959.

M. W. J. A. Jonckbloet, *Étude sur Le Roman de Renart*. Groningen, 1863.

P. Jonin, 'Les Animaux et leur Vie psychologique dans *Le Roman de Renart* (branche I)', *Annales de la Faculté des Lettres d'Aix*, xxv (1951), 63–82.

W. Krogmann, 'Die Vorlage des "Reynke de Vos" ', *Jahrbuch des Vereins für niederdeutsche Sprachforschung*, lxxxvii (1964), 29–55.

C. C. Mish, '*Reynard the Fox* in the Seventeenth Century', *The Huntington Library Quarterly*, xvii (1953–4), 327–44.

F. Mossé, 'Le *Roman de Renart* dans l'Angleterre du Moyen Age', *Les Langues modernes*, xlv (1951), 70–84.

J. W. Muller, 'Reinaert-Studiën: II Navolging en Parodie van Heldenepos en Ridderroman', *Tijdschrift voor Nederlandsche Taal- en Letterkunde*, lii (1933), 217–63.

J. W. Muller, *Critische Commentaar op Van den Vos Reinaerde naar de thans bekende Handschriften en Bewerkingen*. Utrecht, 1917.

G. Paris, *Le Roman de Renard* (Extrait du *Journal des Savants*: Septembre, Octobre, et Décembre 1894, Février 1895). Paris, 1895. [Reprinted in *Mélanges de Littérature française du Moyen Age*, edited by M. Roques, Paris, 1912, pp. 337–423.]

D. B. Sands, 'William Blades' Comment on Caxton's "Reynard the Fox": the Genealogy of an Error', *NQ*. cxcix (1954), 50–1.

L. Sudre, *Les Sources du Roman de Renart*. Paris, 1893.

Is. Teirlinck, *De Toponymie van den Reinaert* (Koninklijke Vlaamsche Academie voor Taal- en Letterkunde, Reeks IIIe. No. 19). Ghent, 1910–12.

I. W. Trillitzsch, 'Die *Ecbasis Captivi* im Lichte der Forschung', *Forschungen und Fortschritte*, xxxv (1961), 146–52.

C. Voretzsch, 'Jacob Grimms Deutsche Thiersage und die moderne Forschung', *Preussische Jahrbücher*, lxxx (1895), 416–84.

L. Willems, *Étude sur l'Ysengrinus*. (Université de Gand: Recueil de Travaux publiés par la Faculté de Philosophie et Lettres, fasc. 13e.) Ghent, 1895.

Miscellaneous

N. S. Aurner, *Caxton: Mirrour of Fifteenth-Century Letters. A Study of the Literature of the first English Press*. London and Boston, 1926.

N. F. Blake, *Caxton and his World*. London, 1969.

A. B. Ferguson, *The Indian Summer of English Chivalry*. Durham, North Carolina, 1960.

R. Jente, *Proverbia Communia. A Fifteenth Century Collection of Dutch Proverbs together with the Low German Version* (Indiana University Publications: Folklore Series, 4). Bloomington, Indiana, 1947.

W. W. Lawrence, *Medieval Story*. Revised edition. New York, 1926.

R. T. Lenaghan, *Caxton's Aesop*. Cambridge, Mass., 1967.

F. McCulloch, *Mediaeval Latin and French Bestiaries* (University of

North Carolina Studies in the Romance Languages and Literatures, 33). Revised edition. Chapel Hill, 1962.

A. L. Meissner, 'Die bildlichen Darstellungen des Reineke Fuchs im Mittelalter', *Archiv für das Studium der neueren Sprachen und Literaturen*, lvi (1876) 265–80; lviii (1877), 241–60; lxv (1881), 199–232.

P. H. van Moerkerken, *De Satire in de Nederlandsche Kunst der Middeleeuwen*. Amsterdam, 1904.

M. Schlauch, *Antecedents of the English Novel 1400–1600 (from Chaucer to Deloney)*. Warsaw and London, 1963.

W. G. Smith, J. E. Heseltine and P. Harvey, *The Oxford Dictionary of English Proverbs*. 2nd edition. Oxford, 1948.

F. A. Stoett, *Nederlandsche Spreekwoorden, Spreekwijzen, Uitdrukkingen en Gezegden*. 2nd edition, 2 vols. Zutphen, 1915–16.

K. Varty, *Reynard the Fox*. Leicester, 1967.

Sigla of Copies of *The History of Reynard the Fox*, 1481

BM[1]	British Museum, C. 11. c. 3
BM[2]	British Museum, G. 10545
EC	Eton College, Cg.2.3.12
JR	John Rylands Library, 15392
PM	Pierpont Morgan Library, 20893

NOTE. The copy in the Bibliotheca Bodmeriana, Geneva, was not available for collation and thus does not appear in the apparatus criticus. Further details of individual copies may be found in Introduction, § 4.

THE HISTORY OF REYNARD THE FOX

[a2] ℭ This is the table of the historye of reynart the foxe

In the first how[1] the kynge of alle bestes the lyon helde his court capitulo ℭ .primo.

How Isegrym the wolf complayned first on the foxe ca .ij.

The complaynt of curtoys the hound and of the catte Tybert capitulo ℭ .iij.

How grymbert the dasse the foxes susters sone answerd for the foxe to the kynge capitulo ℭ .iiij.

How chantecler the cok complayned on the foxe ca. .v:

How the kynge sayde touchyng the complaynt ca ℭ .vj.

How bruyn the bere spedde wyth the foxe capitulo ℭ .vij:

How the bere ete the hony capitulo ℭ .viij.

The complaynt of the bere vpon the/ foxe capitulo ℭ .ix.

How the kynge sente Tybert the catte for the foxe ca .x.

How grymbert brought the foxe to the lawe ca ℭ .xj.

How the foxe was shryuen to grymbert capitulo/ ℭ .xij.

How the foxe cam to the court and excused hym ca ℭ .xiij·

How the foxe was arestid and Iuged to deth ca ℭ .xiiij.

How the foxe was ledde to the galwes capitulo ℭ .xv.

How the foxe made open confession to fore the kynge and to fore alle them that wold here it capitulo ℭ .xvj

How the foxe brought them in danger that wold haue brought hym to deth And how he gate the grace of the kyng capitulo ℭ .xvij.

[1] hoow C

How the wulf and the bere were arestyd by the labour of the foxe capitulo ℂ .xviij.

How the wulf and his wyf suffred her shoys to be pluckyd[1] of And how the foxe dyde them on his feet For to [a2v] go to rome capitulo ℂ .xix.

How kywart the hare was slayn by the foxe capitulo .xx.

How the foxe sente the hares heed to the kynge by bellyn the Ramme capitulo. ℂ .xxj.

How bellyn the ramme and alle his lynage were Iugged to be gyuen to the wulf and to the bere capitulo ℂ .xxij:

How the kynge helde his feste/ and lapreel the cony complayned to hym of the foxe capitulo. ℂ .xxiij.

How corbant the roek complayned on the foxe for the deth of his wyf capitulo. ℂ .xxiiij.

How the kynge was angry of these complayntes. ca ·xxv.

How grymbert warned the foxe that the kynge was wroth and wold slee hym capitulo ℂ .xxvj.

How the foxe cam agayn to the court and of his shrifte capitulo ℂ .xxvij·

How the foxe excused hym byfore the kynge. ca .xxviij.

How dame Rukenawe the she ape answerd For the foxe capitulo ℂ ·xxix·

A parable of a man whiche delyuerd a serpent fro deth capitulo ℂ .xxx.

Of them that were frendis and/ kyn to the foxe. ca .xxxj·

How the foxe subtylly excused hym of the deth of the hare and of other maters and/ how he gate his pees ca ·xxxij.

How the wulf complayned on the foxe capitulo .xxxiij.

A parable[2] of the foxe and the wulf capitulo ℂ .xxxiiij·

[1] pulckyd C [2] Aparable C

How the wulf caste his gloue to fight with the foxe capitulo ℂ ·xxxv.

How the foxe toke vp the gloue/ And the kynge sette them day And felde for to fighte ca. ℂ .xxxvj. [a3]

How dame rukenawe the she ape counseylled the foxe How he shold doo in the feld[1] ayenst the wulf. ca .xxxvij.

How the foxe cam in to the feld capitulo ℂ xxxviij

How the foxe and the wulf foughten to gydre. ca .xxxix.

How the foxe beyng vnder the wulf with glosyng and flateryng wordes cam to his aboue capitulo ℂ xl

How ysegrym the wulf was ouercomen and the batayl fynysshyd and how the foxe had the worship capitulo ℂ xlj

An example that the foxe told to the kyng whan he had wonne the felde capitulo ℂ ·xlij·

How the foxe with his frendes departed nobly fro the kynge and wente to his castel maleperduys/ capitulo ℂ xliij [a3v]

[1] fold C

¶ Hyer begynneth thystorye of reynard the foxe

In this historye ben wreton the parables/ goode lerynge/ and dyuerse poyntes to be merkyd/ by whiche poyntes men maye lerne to come to the subtyl knoweleche of suche thynges as dayly ben vsed and had in the counseyllys of lordes and prelates gostly and worldly/ and/ also emonge marchantes and other comone peple/ And this booke is maad for nede and prouffyte of alle god folke/ As fer as they in redynge or heeryng of it shal mowe vnderstande and fele the forsayd subtyl deceytes that dayly ben vsed in the worlde/ not to thentente that men shold vse them but that euery man shold eschewe and kepe hym from the subtyl false shrewis that they be not deceyuyd/ Thenne who that wyll haue the very vnderstandyng of this mater/ he muste ofte and many tymes rede in thys boke and ernestly and diligently marke wel that he redeth/ For it is sette subtylly/ lyke as ye shal see in redyng of it/ and not ones to rede it For a man shal not wyth ones ouer redyng fynde the ryght vnderstandyng ne comprise it wel/ but oftymes to rede it shal cause it wel to be vnderstande/ And for them that vnderstandeth it/ it shall be ryght Ioyous playsant and prouffitable

¶ How the lyon kynge of alle bestis sent out his mandementis that alle beestis sholde come to his feest and court capitulo primo

[a4]

IT was aboute the tyme of penthecoste or whytsontyde/ that the wodes comynly be lusty and gladsom/ And the trees clad with leuys and blossoms and the ground with herbes and flowris swete smellyng and also the fowles and byrdes[1] syngen melodyously in theyr armonye/ That the lyon the noble kynge of all beestis wolde in the holy dayes of thys feest holde on open Court at stade/ whyche he dyde to knowe ouer alle in his lande/ And commanded by strayte commyssyons[2] and maundements that euery beest shold come thyder/ in suche wyse that alle the beestis grete and smale cam to the courte sauf reynard the fox/ for he knewe hym self fawty and gylty in many thynges ayenst many beestis that thyder sholde comen that he durste not auenture to goo thyder/

[1] andbyrdes C [2] conmyssyons C

whan the kynge of alle beestis had assemblid alle his court/ ther was none of them alle/ but that he had complayned sore on Reynart the foxe·

¶ The first complaynt made Isegrym the wulf on Reynart capitulo ·ij·

ISegrym the wulf wyth his lynage and frendes cam and stode to fore the kynge/ And sayde hye and myghty prynce my lord the kynge I beseche yow that thurgh your grete myght/ ryght/ and mercy that ye wyl haue pyte on the grete trespas and the vnresonable mysdedes that reynart the foxe hath don to me and to my wyf that is to wete he is comen in to my hows ayenst the wylle of my wyf/ And there he hath be pyssed my chyldren where as they laye in suche wyse as [a4v] they therof ben woxen blynde/ wherupon was a day sette/ and was Iuged that reygnart shold come and haue excused hym hierof/ and haue sworen on the holy sayntes[1] that he was not gylty therof/ And whan the book wyth the sayntes was brought forth/ tho had reygnart bythought[2] hym other wyse/ And wente his waye agayn in to his hole/ as he had nought sette therby/ And dere kynge this knowen wel many of the bestes that now be comen hyther to your court/ And yet hath he trespaced to me in many other thinges/ he is not lyuyng that coude telle alle that I now leue vntolde/ But the shame and vyllonye that he hath don to my wyf/ that shal I neuer hyde ne suffre it vnauengyd but that he shal make to me large amendes/

¶ The complaynt of Courtoys the hounde capitulo iij

Whan thyse wordes were spoken so stode there a lytyl hounde and was named courtoys/ and complayned to the kynge/ how that in the colde wynter in the harde froste he had ben sore forwynterd/ in suche wyse as he had kepte nomore mete than a puddyng/ wyche puddyng reygnard the foxe had taken away from hym

¶ Tho spak tybert[3] the catte

Wyth this so cam Tybert the catte wyth an Irous moed/ and sprang in emonge them and sayde My lord the kyng/ I here hier that reygnart is sore complayned on/ and hier is none but that

[1] sayn/ |tes C [2] bythouht C [3] thybert C

he hath ynowh to doo to clere hym self/ that courtoys hier complayneth of [a5] that is passyd many yeres goon/ how be it that I complayne not/ that pudyng was myne/ For I hadde wonne it by nyghte in a mylle/ The myllar laye and slepe/ yf courtoys had ony parte hieron/ that cam by me to/ Thenne spak panther/ Thynke ye Tybert that it were good that reynard sholde not be complayned on/ he is a very murderer/ a rouer/ and a theef/ he loueth noman so wel/ not our lord the kyng here that he wel wold that he shuld lese good and worshyp/ so that he myght wynne as moche as a legge of a fat henne/ I shal telle yow what I sawe hym do yesterday to Cuwaert the hare that hier standeth in the kynges pees and saufgarde/ he promysed to Cuwart and sayde he wold teche hym his credo/ and make hym a good chapelayn/ he made hym goo sytte bytwene his legges and sange and cryde lowde Credo. Credo. my waye laye ther by there that I herde this songe/ Tho wente I ner and fonde maister reynard that had lefte that he fyrst redde and songe/ and bygan to playe his olde playe/ For he had caught kywaert by the throte/ and had I not that tyme comen he sholde haue taken his lyf from hym like as ye hiere may see on kywaert the hare the fresshe[1] wounde yet/ For sothe my lord the kynge yf ye suffre this vnpunysshyd and lete hym go quyte that hath thus broken your peas/ And wyl do no right after the sentence and Iugement of your men/ your Chyldren many yeris herafter shal be myspreysed and blamed therfore/ Sykerly panther sayd Isegrym ye saye trouthe/ hit were good that right and Iustyse were don/ for them that wolde fayn lyue in peas/

❡ How grymbart the dasse the foxes susters sone spack [a5v] For reynart and answerd to fore the kynge. capitulo .iiij.

Tho spack Grymbart the dasse/ and was Reynarts suster sone wyth an angry moed/ Sir Isegrym that is euyl sayd it is a comyn prouerbe An Enemyes mouth/ sayth seeld wel/ what leye ye/ and wyte ye myn Eme Reynart/ I wold that ye wolde a venture that who of yow tweyne had moste trespaced to other sholde hange by the necke as a theef on a tree/ But and yf he were as wel in this court and as wel wyth the kynge as ye be/ it shold not be thought in hym/ that it were ynowh/ that ye shold come and aske hym

[1] fresse C

forgyuenes ye haue byten and nypte myn vncle wyth your felle and sharp teeth many mo tymes than I can telle/ yet wil I telle some poyntes that I wel knowe/ knowe not ye how ye mysdeled on the plays/ whiche he threwe doun fro the carre/ whan ye folowed after fro ferre/ And ye ete the good plays allone/ and gaf hym nomore than the grate or bones/ whyche ye myght not ete your self/ In lyke wyse dyde ye to hym also of the fatte vlycche of bacon/ whiche sauourd so wel/ that ye allone ete in your bely/ and whan myn Eme askyd his parte/ tho answerd ye hym agayn in scorne/ Reynart fayr yonglyng I shal gladly gyue you your part/ but myn eme gate ne had nought/ ne was not the better/ Notwithstandyng he had wonnen the flycche of bacon[1] wyth grete drede/ For the man cam and threw hym in a sacke/ that he scarsely cam out wyth his lyf/ Suche maner thynges hath reynart many tymes suffred thurgh ysegrym. [a6]

O ye lordes thynke ye that this is good/ yet is ther more/ he complayneth how that reynart myn eme hath moche trespaced to hym by cause of his wyf/ Myn Eme hath leyn by her but that is wel seuen yer to fore/ er he wedded her/ and yf reynart for loue and curtosye dyde with. her his wille/ what was that/ She was sone heled therof/ hierof by ryght shold be no complaynt were Isegrym wyse. he shold haue lefte that he doth to hym self no worshyp thus to sklaundre his wyf/ She playneth not/ now maketh kywaert the hare a complaynt[2] also/ that thynketh me a vyseuase/ yf he rede ne lerned a right his lesson/ sholde not reynard his maister bete hym therfore/ yf the scolers were not beten ne smyten and reprised of their truantrye/ they shold neuer lerne/

Now complayneth Courtoys that he with payne had goten a puddyng[3] in the wynter/ at suche tyme as the coste is euyl to fynde Therof hym had be better to haue holde his pees/ for he had stolen it/ Male quesisti et male perdidisti hit is ryght that it be euil loste/ that is euil wonne who shal blame Reynart/ yf he haue taken fro a theef stolen good hit is reson who that vnderstandeth the lawe and can discerne the right/ and that he be of hye burthe as myn Eme reynart is whiche knoweth wel how he shal resseyue stolen good/ ye al had he courtoys hanged whan he fonde hym with the menowr/ he had not moche mysdon ne trespaced/ Sauf

[1] bacion C [2] acomplaynt C [3] apuddyng C

ayenst the crowne/ that he had don Iustyse wythoute leue wherfore for the honour of the kynge he dyde it not/ all hath he but lytyl thanke/ what skatheth[1] it hym that he is thus complayned on/ Myn Eme is[2] [a6v] a gentil and a trewe man he may suffre no falshede/ he doth nothyng but by his prestes counseyl And I saye yow syth that my lorde the kynge hath do proclamed his pees he neuer thoughte to hurte ony man/ For he eteth no more than ones a day/ he lyueth as a recluse/ he chastiseth his body and wereth a sherte of heer/ hit is more than a yere that he hath eten no flesshe/ as I yesterday herd saye of them that cam fro hym he hath lefte and geuen ouer his Castel maleperduys/ And hath bylded a cluse/ theryn dwelleth he/ and hunteth nomore/ ne desyreth no wynnynge but he lyueth by almesse and taketh nothyng but suche as men gyue hym for charyte and doth grete penance for his synnes/ and he is woxen moche pale and lene of prayeng and wakyng For he wolde be fayn wyth god/ Thus as grymbert his eme stode and preched thise wordes/ so sawe they comen doun the hylle to hem chauntecler the cock and brought on a biere[3] a deed henne of whom reynart had byten the heed of/ and that muste be shewed to the kynge for to haue knowleche therof.

How the Cocke complayned on reynart capitulo ¶ .v°.

CHauntecler cam forth and smote pyteously his handes and his fetheris and on eche side of the byer wenten tweyne sorouful hennes that one was called cantart and that other goode henne Crayant they were two the fayrest hennes that were bytwene holland and arderne/ Thise hennes bare eche of them a brennyng[4] tapre whiche was longe and strayte/ Thise two hennes were coppens susters And they cryed so pitously/ Alas and weleaway [a7] for the deth of her dere suster coppen/ Two yonge hennes bare the byere whiche kakled so heuyly and wepte so lowde for the deth of coppen their moder that it was ferre herde/ thus cam they to gydre to fore the kynge/ And chantecleer tho seyde/ Mercyful lord/ my lord the kynge plese it yow to here our complaynte/ And abhorren the grete scathe that reynart hath don to me and my children that hiere stonden/ it was so that in the begynnyng of appryl whan the weder is fayr/ as that I was[5] hardy and prowde/

[1] skathed C [2] is JR, BM1, PM; is BM2, EC
[3] abiere C [4] brennyg C [5] as C

bycause of the grete lynage that I am comen of and also hadde/ For I had viij fayr sones and seuen fayr doughters whiche my wyf had hatched. and they were alle stronge and fatte and wente in a yerde[1] whiche was walled round a boute/ In whiche was a shadde where in were six grete dogges whiche had to tore and plucked many a beestis skyn in suche wyse as my chyldren were not aferd/ On whom Reynart the theef had grete enuye by cause they were so sure that he cowde[2] none gete of them/ how wel oftymes hath this fel theef goon rounde aboute this[3] wal/ and hath leyde for vs in suche wyse that the dogges haue be sette on hym and haue hunted hym away/ And ones they leep on hym vpon the banke/ And that cost hym somwhat for his thefte/ I saw that his skyn smoked neuertheles he wente his waye/ god amende it/

Thus were we quyte of reynart a longe whyle/ atte laste cam he in lyknes of an heremyte/ and brought to me a lettre for to rede sealed wyth the kynges seal/ in whiche stode wreton that the kynge had made pees oueral in his royame/ and that alle maner beestis and [a7v] fowlles shold doo none harme ner scathe to ony other/ yet sayd he to me more/ that he was a cloysterer or a closyd recluse be comen/ And that he wolde receyue grete penance for his synnes/ he shewd me his slauyne and pylche and an heren sherte ther vnder/ and thenne sayd he/ syr Chaunteclere after thys tyme be no more aferd of me ne take no hede/ For I now wil ete nomore flesshe/ I am forthon so olde/ That I wolde fayn remembre my sowle I wil now go forth/ for I haue yete to saye my sexte/ none/ and myn euensonge to god I bytake yow/ Tho wente reynart thens sayeng his Credo/ and leyde hym vnder an hawthorn/ Thenne/ was I glad and mery/ and also toke none hede/ And wente to my chyldren and clucked hem to gydre And wente wythout the wal for to walke[4] wherof is moche harme comen to vs/ for reynart laye vnder a busshe and cam krepyng bitwene vs and the yate/ so that he caught[5] one of my chyldren and leyd hym in his male/ wherof whe haue had grete harme/ for syth he hath tasted of hym/ ther myght neuer hunter ne hounde[6] saue ne kepe hym from vs/ he hath wayted by nyghte and daye in suche wyse that he hath stolen so many of my chyldren that of ·xv. I haue but foure/ in suche wyse hath this theef

[1] ayerde C [2] hecowde C [3] aboutethis C
[4] waske C [5] caght C [6] hoūnde C

forslongen them/ And yet yesterday was coppen my doughter that hier lyeth vpon the byer with the houndes rescowed This complayne I to yow gracious kynge/ haue pyte on myn grete and vnresonable damage and losse of my fayre chyldren/

¶ How the kyng spack touchyng this complaynt ca .vj:

Thenne spack the kynge/ Syre dasse here ye this wel of the recluse your Eme he hath fasted and prayde [a8] that yf I lyue a yere he shal abye it/ Nowe herke chauntecler/ your playnt is ynough your doughter that lyeth here dede/ we wyl gyue to her the dethes right we may kepe her no lenger/ we wil betake her to god/ we wylle syngen here vygylie/ and brynge her worshipfully on erthe/ and thenne we wille speke wyth thise lordes and take counseyl how we may do ryght and Iustyse of thys grete murdre/ and brynge this fals theef to the lawe/ Tho begonne they placebo domino/ with the verses[1] that to longen whiche yf I shold saye/ were me to longe/ whan this vigilye was don and the commendacion/ she was leyde in the pytte/ and ther vpon was leyde a marble stone polyshed as clere as ony glas and theron was hewen in grete lettres in this wyse coppe chanteklers doughter/ whom Reynart the foxe hath byten lyeth hier vnder buryed/ complayne ye her For/ she is shamefully comen to her deth/ after this the/ kynge sente For his lordes and wysest of his counseyl for to take aduys/ how this grete murdre and trespaas shold be punysshyd on reynart the foxe/ Ther was concluded and apoynted for the beste/ that reynart shold be sent Fore and that he lefte not for ony cause/ But he cam in to the kynges court For to here wat shold be sayd to hym/ And that bruyn the bere shold do the message. the kynge thought[2] that alle this was good and saide to brune the bere syr brune I wyl that ye doo this message/ but see wel to for your self/ For reynart is a shrewe/ and felle and knoweth so many wyles that he shal lye and flatre/ and shal thynke how he may begyle deceyue and brynge yow to some mockerye/ tho sayd brune what good lord late it [a8v] allone/ deceyueth me the foxe/ so haue I ylle lerned my casus/ I trowe he shal come to late to mocque me/ Thus departed brune meryly fro thens/ but it is to drede that he cam not so meryly agayn/

[1] with the/ verses BM[1] [2] thou-| ught C

¶ how brune[1] the beere was sped of Reynart the foxe/ capitulo ¶ .vij°.

NOw is brune goon on his waye toward the foxe wyth a stowte[2] moede/ whiche supposed wel that the foxe sholde not haue begyled hym/ as he cam in a derke wode in a forest were as reynard had a bypath whan he was hunted/ ther bysyde was an hie montayne and lande/ and there muste brune in the myddel goon ouer for to goo to maleperduys/ for reynart had many a dwellyng place/ but the castel of maleperduys was the beste and the fastest burgh that he had/ Ther laye he Inne whan he had nede and was in ony drede or fere/ Now whan bruyn was comen to maleperduys he fonde the yate fast shette/ tho wente he to fore the yate and satte vpon his taylle and called Reynart be ye at home I am brownyng/ the kynge hath sente me for yow that ye sholde come to court/ for to plete your caas/ he hath sworn there by his god/ come ye not/ or brynge I yow not with me for tabyde suche right and sentence as shal be there gyuen/ it shal coste you your lyf he wyl hange yow/ or sette yow on the ratte/ reynart doo by my counseyl and come to the court/ Reynart laye within the gate as he ofte was wonte to doo for the warmth of the sonne/ whan reynart herd bruyn tho wente he Inneward in to his hole/ for maleperduys was ful of hooles/ hier one hool and there an other and yonder an other/ narowe. [b1] croked and longe wyth/ many weyes to goo out/ whiche he opend and shette after that he had nede/ whan he had ony proye brought home/ or that he wiste that ony sought hym for hys mysdedes and trespaces/ thenne he ran and hydde hym fro his enemyes in to hys secrete chambres/ that they coude not fynde hym/ by whiche he deceyuyd many a beest that sought hym/ and tho thought reynart in hym self how he myght best brynge the beere in charge and nede/ and that he abode in worship/

IN this thoughte reynart cam out and sayde bruyn eme ye be welcome/ I herde you wel to fore/ but I was in myn euesong therfore haue I the lenger taryed a lytyl/ dere eme he hath don to you no good seruyse and I can hym no thank that hath sente you ouer this longe hylle/ for I see that ye be also wery that the swete renneth doun by your chekys/ it was no nede/ I had neuertheles comen to court to morowe but I sorowe now the lasse/ for your

[1] brūne C   [2] astowte C

wyse counseyl shal wel helpe me in the court/ and coude the kyng fynde none lasse messager but yow For to sende hyther/ that is grete/ wonder/ For next the kynge ye be the mooste gentyl and richest of leeuys and/ of lande/ I wolde wel that we were now at the court but I fere me that I shal not conne wel goo thyder/ for I haue eten so moche new mete/ that me thynketh my bely wylle breke or cleue asonder and by cause the mete was nyewe/ I ete the more/ tho spack the bere lyef neue what mete haue ye eten that maked yow so ful/ dere eme that [b1v] I ete what myght it helpe yow that yf I tolde yow/ I ete but symple mete a poure[1] man is no lord that may ye knowe eme by me/ we poure folke muste ete oftymes suche as we gladly wolde not ete yf we had better/ they were grete hony combes which I muste nedes ete for hunger/ they haue made my bely so grete/ that I can nowher endure/ Bruyn tho spack anone/ alas reynart what saye ye/ sette ye so lytyl by hony/ me ought to preyse and loue it aboue alle mete/ lief reynart helpe me that I myght gete a deel of this hony/ and as longe as I lyue I shal be to you a tryew friende and abyde by yow as ferre as ye helpe me that I may haue a parte of thys hony/

ℂ how bruyn ete the hony capitulo. ℂ .viij:

BRuyn eme I had supposed that ye had iaped therwyth/ so help me god reynart nay/ I shold not gladly iape with yow/ thenne spacke the rede reynart is it thenne ernest that ye loue so wel the hony/ I shal do late you haue so moche that ten of yow shold not ete it at one mele/ myght I gete therwith your friendship/ not we ten reyner neue sayd the bere how shold that be had I alle the hony that is bytwene this and portyngale I shold wel ete it allone· reynard sayde· what saye ye Eme/ hier by dwelleth an husbondman named lantfert whiche hath so moche hony that ye shold not ete it in ·vij. yere whiche ye shal haue in your holde. yf ye wille be to me friendly and helpyng ayenst myn enemyes in the kynges court/ thenne promysed bruyn the bere to hym. that yf he[2] myght haue his bely full· he wold [b2] truly be to hym to fore alle other a faythful frende/ herof laughed reynart the shrewe and sayde/ yf ye wolde haue vij hamber barelis ful I shal wel gete them and helpe you to haue them/ These wordes plesyd the bere so wel and made hym so moche to/ lawhe/ that he coude not wel stande Tho thought

[1] apoure C [2] be C

reynart/ this is good luck I shal lede hym thyder that he shal lawhe by mesure/

Reynart sayd thenne/ this mater may not be longe taryed/ I muste payne my self for you/ ye shal wel vnderstande the very yonste and good wyl that I bere to you ward I knowe none in al my lygnage that I nou wolde laboure fore thus sore/ that thanked hym the bere and thought he taryed longe/ Now eme late vs goo a good paas and folowe ye me/ I shal make you to haue as moche hony as ye may bere/ the foxe mente of good strokes but the caytyf markyd not what the foxe mente/ and they wente so longe to gydre that they cam vnto lantferts yerde tho was sir bruyn mery/ now herke of lantfert is it true that men saye/ so was lantfert a stronge carpenter of grete tymbre/ and had/ brought that other day to fore in to his yerde a/ grete oke whiche he had begonne to cleue And as men be woned he had smeten two betels therin one after that other in suche wyse the oke was wyde open wherof reynart was glad/ for he had founde it right as he wisshed/ And sayde to the bere all lawhyng/ see nou wel sharply/ to/ in this tree is so moche hony that it is without mesure/ asaye yf ye can[1] come therin and ete but lytil for though the hony combes be. swete and good yet beware [b2v] that ye ete not to many. but take of them by mesure. that ye cacche no harme in your body· for swete eme I shold be blasmed yf they dyde you ony harme. what reynart cosyn sorowe ye not for me. wene ye[2] that I were[3] a fole· mesure is good in alle mete· reynart sayde· ye saye trouthe. wherfore shold I sorowe· goo to thende and Crepe theryn bruyn the bere hasted sore toward the hony. and trad in wyth his two formest feet: and put his heed ouer his eeris in to the clyft of the tree. And reynart sprang lyghtly and brak out the betle of the tree. Tho helped the bere nether flateryng ne chydyng. he was fast shette in the tree thus hath the neueu wyth deceyte brought his eme in pryson in the tree in suche wyse as he coude not gete out wyth myght ne wyth crafte/ hede ne foote/

What prouffyteth bruyn the bere that he stronge and hardy is/ that may not helpe hym/ he sawe wel that he begyled was he began to howle and to braye/ and cratched[4] wyth the hynder feet and made suche a noyse and rumour that lantfert cam out hastely/

[1] cam C [2] yt C [3] woere C [4] crutched C

and knewe nothyng what this myght be/ and brought in his hand a sharp hoke/ bruyn the[1] bere laye in the clyfte of the tree in grete fere and drede/ and helde fast his heed and nyped both his fore feet/ he wrange he wrastled/ and cryed/ and all was for nought/ he wiste not how he myght gete out/ reynar the foxe sawe fro ferre how that lantfert the carpenter cam and tho spack reynart to the bere/ is that hony good how is it now/ ete not to moche it shold do you harme/ ye shold not thenne wel conne goo to the court whan lantfert cometh [b3] yf ye haue wel eten he shal yeue you better to drynke and thenne it shal not styke in your throte/

AFter thise wordes tho torned hym reynart toward his castel and lantfert cam and fonde the bere fast taken in the tree/ thenne ranne he faste to his neyghbours and sayde/ come alle in to my yerde/ ther is a beere taken/ the worde anone sprange oueral in the thorpe/ ther ne bleef nether man ne wyf/ but alle ranne theder as fast as they coude/ eueryche wyth his wepen/ some wyth a staf/ some with a rake/ some with a brome/ some with a stake of the hegghe and some wyth a flayel/ and the preest of the chirche had the staf of the crosse/ and the clerk brought a vane The prestis wyf Iulok cam with her dystaf/ she sat tho and spanne/ Ther cam olde wymen that for age had not one toeth in her heed/ now was bruyn the bere nygh moche sorowe/ that he allone muste stande ayenst them alle whan he herde alle this grete noyse and crye/ he wrastled and plucked so harde and so sore/ that he gate out his heed/ but he lefte behynde alle the skyne and bothe his eeris/ In suche wyse that neuer man sawe fowller ne lothlyer beest/ for the blode ran ouer his eyen/ and or he coude gete/[2] out his/ feet/ he muste lete there his clawes or nayles and his[3] roughe hande/ This market cam to hym euyl. For he supposed neuer to haue goon/ his[4] feet were so sore/ and he myght not see for the blode whiche ran so ouer his eyen/ lantfert cam to hym wyth the preest and forth with alle the parysshe/ and began to smyte and stryke sore vpon his heed and visage he receyuyd there many a sore [b3ᵛ] stroke/ euery man beware hierby. who hath harme and scathe/ euery man wil be ther at and put more to/ That was wel seen on the bere/ for they were alle fiers and wroth on the bere grete and smal/ ye hughelyn wyth the croked lege· and ludolf with the brode longe noose/ they were

[1] de C [2] gete- C [3] this C [4] is C

booth wroth That one had an leden malle· and that other a grete leden wapper/ ther wyth they wappred and al for slyngred hym/ syr bertolt with the longe fyngers lantfert. and ottram the longe. thyse dyde to the bere more harme than al the other that one had a sharp hoke/ and that other a croked staf wel leded on thende for to playe at the balle/ Baetkyn/ ende aue abelquak my dame baue. and the preest with his staf/ and dame Iulok his wyf thise wroughten to the bere so moche harme/ that they wold fayn haue brought hym fro his lyf to deth/ they smote and stacke hym al that they cowde/ bruyn the beere satte and syghed and groned/ and muste take suche as was gyuen to hym/ but lantfert was the worthiest of byrthe of them alle/ and made moste noyse/ for dame pogge of chafporte was his moder/ and his fader was Macob the stoppelmaker/ a moche stowte man there as he was allone/ bruyn receyued of hem many a caste of stones/ Tofore hem alle sprang forst lanteferts brother with a staf/ and smote the bere on the heed that he ne herde ne sawe/ and there with the bere sprange vp bytwene the bushe and the ryuer emonge an heep of wyuis that he threwe a deel of hem in the ryuer whiche was wyde and depe/ ther was the persons wyf one of them wherfor he was ful of sorow whan he sawe his wyf lye in the water/ hym lusted [b4] no lenger to smyte the bere/ but called dame Iuloke in the water now euery man see to/ Alle they that may helpe her/ be they men or/ wymen/ I gyue to hem alle pardon of her penance and relece alle theyr synnes/ alle they thenne lefte bruyn the bere lye/ And dyde that the preest badde

Whan bruyn the bere sawe that they ranne alle fro hym and ranne to saue the wymen/ tho sprange he in to the water and swame alle that he coude/ Thenne made the preest a grete showte and noyse and ran after the bere wyth grete anger and said come and torne agayn thow false theef/ The bere swame after the beste of the streme/ and lete them calle and crye/ for he was glad that he was so escaped from them/ he cursed and banned the hony tree/ and the foxe also that had so betrayed hym/ that he had cropen therin so depe that he loste boothe his hood and his eeris/ And so forth he droof in the streem wel a ij or iij myle/ Tho waxe he so wery that he wente to lande for to sitte and reste hym/ For he was heuy/ he groned and syghed/ and the blode lepe ouer his eyen/ he drough his breth lyke as one sholde haue deyde/

NOw herke how the foxe dyde/ er he cam fro lantferts hows he had stolen a fatte henne and had leyde her in his male And ranne hastely away by a by path were he wende that noman shold haue comen/ he ranne toward the Ryuer that he swette/ he was so glad that he wist not what to[1] do for Ioye/ For he hoped [b4v] that the bere had be dede/ he sayde/ I haue now wel spedde for he that sholde moste haue hyndred me in the court is now dede/ and none shal wyte me therof/ may I not thenne by right/ be wel glad/ with thise wordes the foxe loked to the ryuer ward and espyed where bruyn the bere laye and rested hym/ Tho was the foxe sorier and heuyer than he to fore was mery/ and was as angry and sayde In chydyng to lantfert/ alas lanfert lewde fool god gyue hym a shames deth that hath loste suche good venyson whiche is good and fatte/ and hath late hym goo whiche was taken to his hande many a man[2] wolde gladly haue eten of hym. he hath loste a riche[3] and fatte bere/ Thus al chydyng he cam to the ryuer/ where he fonde the beere sore wounded/ bebled/ and right seke/ whiche he myght thanke none better therof than Reynart whiche spack to the bere in skorne/ Chiere priestre/ dieu vous garde wylle ye see the rede theef sayde the bere to hym self/ the rybaud and the felle diere here I se hym comen/ Thenne sayd the foxe/ haue ye ought forgoten at lantferts. haue ye also payd hym for the hony combes that ye stale fro hym/ yf ye haue not. it were a grete[4] shame and not honeste/ I wyl rather be the messager my self for to goo and paye hym/ was the hony not/ good/ I knowe yet more of the same prys. dere Eme telle me er I goo hens/ In to what ordre wille ye goo. that were this newe hode/ were be[5] ye a monke[6] or an abbot· he that shoef your crowne/ hath nyped of your eeris/ ye haue lost your toppe And don of your gloues/ I trowe veryly that ye wyl go synge complyn· alle this herde bruyn the bere/ and wexe alle angry and sory for he myght not [b5] a venge hym/ he lete the foxe saye his wylle And wyth grete payne suffred it. and sterte agayn in the ryuer/ and swam doun wyth the streem to that other syde/ now muste he sorowe how that he sholde come to the court/ for he had loste his eeris/ and the skynne wyth the clawes of his forefeet/ for though a man sholde haue slayn hym he coude not go/ And yet he muste. nedes forth/ but he wist not how Now here how he dyde. he satte vpon his hammes/ and began to rutsele ouer his tayl/ and

[1] whatto C [2] aman C [3] ariche C
[4] agrete C [5] be *omitted in* C [6] amonke C

whan he was so wery/ he wentled and tombled nyghe half a myle/ this dyde he with grete payne so longe tyl atte laste he cam to the courte/ And whan he was seen so comyng fro ferre/ Some doubted what it myght be that cam so wentelyng The kynge atte laste knewe hym/ and was not wel payd and sayde This is bruyn the bere my frende/ lord god who hath wounded hym thus he is passyng reed on his heed. me thynketh he is hurte vnto the deth where may he haue ben therwyth is the bere come to fore the kynge and sayde/

¶ The complaynt of the bere vpon the foxe· cap^{o} ·ix^{o}

I complayne to yow mercyful lorde syre kynge/ so as ye may see how that I am handled prayeng you tauenge it vpon reynart the felle beest· For I haue goten this in your seruyse. I haue loste bothe my formest feet/ my chekes and myn eeris by his false deceyte and treson The kynge sayde how durst this fals theef Reynart[1] doo this/ I saye to yow bruyn and swere by my crowne/ I shal so auenge you on hym/ that ye shal conne me thanke/ he [b5^{v}] sente for alle the wyse beestis/ and desired counseyl how that he myght auenge this ouer grete wronge/ that the foxe had don/ Thenne the counseyl concluded olde and yong/ that he shold be sente fore and dayed ernestly agayn for tabyde suche Iugement as shold there be gyuen on hym of alle his trespaces And they thought that the catte tybert myght best do this message yf he wolde/ for he is right wyse/ The kynge thought this counceyl good/

How the kynge sente another tyme tybert the catte for the foxe/ and how tybert spedde with reynart the foxe/ ca^{o} x^{o}·

Thenne the kynge saide sir tybert/ ye shal now goo to reynart and saye to hym this seconde tyme that he come to court vnto the plee for to answere/ for though he be felle to other beestis· he trusteth you wel/ and shal doo by your counseyl. and telle yf he come not/ he shal haue the thirde warnyng and be dayed and yf he thenne come not/ we shal procede by ryght ayenste hym and alle hys lygnage wythout mercy/ Tybert spack/ My lord the kynge/ they that this counseylde you were not my frendes what shal I doo there/ he wil not for me neyther come ne abyde/ I beseche you dere kynge sende some other to hym/ I am lytyl and feble/ bruyn the bere whiche was so grete and stronge/ coude/[2] not brynge hym/ how shold I thenne take it on honde/ nay said the

[1] Reynat C [2] coude- C

kynge sir tybert ye ben wyse and wel lerned/ Though ye be not grete/ ther lyeth not on/ many do more wyth crafte and connyng/ than with myght and strengthe/ thenne said the catte/ syth it [b6] muste nedes be don/ I muste thenne take it vpon me/ god yeue grace that I may wel achieue it/ for my herte is heuy/ and euil willed therto/ Tybert made hym/ sone redy toward maleperduys/ and he saw fro ferre come fleyng one of seynt martyns byrdes/ tho cryde he lowde and saide al hayl/ gentyl byrde/ torne thy wynges hetherward and flee on my right side/ the byrde flewh forth vpon a tree whiche stoode on the lift side of the catte/ tho was tybert woo/ For he thought hit was a shrewd token and a sygne of harme/ for yf the birde had flowen on his right side/ he had ben mery and glad/ but now he sorowed that his Iourney shold torne to vnhappe/ neuertheles he dyde as many doo/ and gaf to hym self better hope than his herte sayde/ he wente and ronne to maleperduys ward/ and there he fonde the foxe allone standyng to fore his hous/ tybert saide/ The riche god yeue you good euen reynart/ the kyng hath menaced yow/ for to take your lyf from yow/ yf ye come not now wyth me to the court/ The foxe tho spack and saide/ Tibert my dere cosyn ye be right welcome/ I wolde wel truly that ye had moche good lucke/ whad hurted the foxe to speke fayre/ though he sayd wel his herte thoughte it not and that shal be seen/ er they departe/ reynart sayde wylle we this nyght be to gydre/ I wyl make you good chyere and to morow erly in the dawnyng we wyl to gydre goo to the court/ good neue late vs so doo/ I haue none of my kyn/ that I truste so moche to as to yow/ hier was bruyn the bere the traytour he loked so shrewdly on me/ and me thoughte he was so stronge/ that I wolde not for a thousand marke haue [b6v] goon[1] with hym/ but cosyn I wil to morow erly goo with yow/ Tybert saide/ it is beste that we now goo/ for the mone shyneth also light as it were daye/ I neuer sawe fayrer weder/ nay dere cosyn/ suche myght mete vs by daye tyme/ that wold make vs good chiere/ and by nyghte[2] parauenture myght doo vs harme/ it is suspecyous to walke[3] by nyghte. Therfore a byde this nyght here by me Tybert sayde/ wat sholde we ete/ yf we abode here/ reynart sayde/ here is but lytel to ete ye maye wel haue an hony combe good and swete/ what saye ye/ Tybert wyl ye ony therof/ tybert answerd I sette nought therby haue ye nothyng ellis yf ye gaf me a good[4] fatte mows/ I shold be better plesyd/ a fatte mows said reynard/

[1] goon/ PM [2] nyghtte C [3] alke C [4] agood C

dere cosyn what saye ye/ here by dwelleth a preest and hath a barne by his hows ther in ben so many myse/ that a man shold not lede them a way vpon a wayne/ I haue herd the preest many tymes complayne that they dyde hym moche harme O dere reyner lede me thyder for alle that I may doo for yow/ ye tybert saye ye me trouthe/ loue ye wel myes/ yf I loue hem wel said the catte/ I loue myes better than ony thyng that men gyue me· knowe ye not that myes sauoure better than veneson/ ye than flawnes or pasteyes wil ye wel doo. so lede me theder where the myes ben· and thenne shal ye wynne my loue. ye al had ye slayn my fader moder and alle my kyn.

Reynart sayd ye moke and Iape therwyth· the catte saide so helpe me god I doo not. Tybert said the foxe wiste I that veryly I wolde yet this nyght make that ye shuld be ful of myes. reynart[1] quod he· ful that were many. tyberte [b7] ye Iape/ reynart quod he in trouth I doo not/ yf I hadde a fatte/ mows/ I wold not gyue it for a golden noble/ late vs goo thenne/ tybert quod the foxe I wyl brynge yow to the place/ er I goo fro you/ reyner quod the catte[2]/ vpon your saufconduyt/ I wolde wel goo wyth you to monpelier/ late vs thenne goo said the foxe we tarye al to[3] longe/ Thus wente they forth withoute lettyng to the place/ where as they wold be to the prestes barne whiche was faste wallid aboute with a mude wal and the nyght to fore the foxe had broken in/ and had stolen fro the preest a good fatte henne/ and the preest alle angry had sette a gryn to fore the hool to auenge hym/ for he wold fayn haue take the foxe/ this knewe wel the felle theef the foxe And said sir tybert cosyn[4] crepe in to this hool/ and ye shal not longe tarye but that ye shal catche myes by grete heepis/ herke how they pype. whan ye be ful/ come agayn/ I wil tarye here after you be fore this hole/ we wil to morowe goo to gyder to the court/ Tybert why tarye ye thus longe come of/ and so maye we retorne sone to my wyf. whiche wayteth after vs/ and shal make vs good chiere Tybert saide/ reynart cosyn is it thenne your counseyl that I goo in to this hole. Thise prestes ben so wyly and shrewyssh/ I drede to take harme/ O ho tybert said the fox I sawe you neuer so sore aferde/ what eyleth yow/ the catte was ashamed and sprange in to the hoole/ And anon he was caught in the gryn by the necke er he wyste/ thus deceyuyd reynart his ghest and cosyn/

[1] rrynart C [2] foxe C [3] alto C [4] rosyn C

AS tybert was waer of the grynne/ he was a ferde and sprange forth/ the grynne wente to/ thenne [b7v] began he to wrawen/ for he was almost y stranglyd/ he called he cryed and made a shrewd noyse/ reynart stode to fore the hool and herde al/ and was wel a payed and sayde/ tybert loue ye wel myes/ be they fatte and good/ knewe the preeste herof or mertynet/ they be so gentyl that they wolde brynge yow sawce/ Tybert ye synge and eten/ is that the guyse of the court/ lord god yf ysegrym ware there by yow in suche reste as ye now be thenne shold I be glad/ for ofte he hath don me scathe and harme/ tybert coude not goo awaye/ but he mawede and galped so lowde/ that martynet sprang vp/ and/ cryde lowde/ god be thanked my gryn hath taken the theef that hath stolen our hennes/ aryse vp we wil rewarde hym/

Wyth these wordes aroose the preest in an euyl tyme and waked alle them that were in the hows/ and cryde wyth a lowede vois/ the foxe is/ take there leep and ranne alle that there was the preest hym self ranne al moder naked/ mertynet was the first that cam to tybert the preest toke to locken his wyf an offryng candel and bad her lyght it atte fyer/ and he smote tybert with a grete staf/ Ther receyuid tybert many a grete stroke ouer alle his body/ mertynet was so angry that he smote the catte an eye out/ the naked preest[1] lyfte vp and shold haue gyuen a grete stroke to tybert/ but tybert that sawe that he muste deye sprange bytwene the prestes legges wyth his clawes and with his teeth that he raught out his ryght colyon or balock stone/ that leep becam yl to the preest and to his grete shame. [b8]

This thynge fyl doun vpon the floer/ whan dame Iulocke knewe that/ she sware by her faders sowle/ that she wolde it had coste her alle thoffryng of a hole yere/ that the preest had not had that harme hurte and shame/ and that it had not happed and said/ in the deueles name was the grynne there sette/ see mertynet lyef sone/ this is of thy faders harneys/ This is a grete shame and to me a grete hurte/ for though he be heled herof yet he is but a loste man to me and also shal neuer conne doo that swete playe and game/ The foxe stode wythoute to fore the hole and herde alle thyse wordes/ and lawhed so sore that he vnnethe coude stonde/ he spack

[1] prerst C

thus al softly/ dame Iulock be al stylle/ and lete your grete sorowe synke/ Al hath the preest loste one of his stones it shal not hyndre hym he shal doo wyth[1] you wel ynowh ther is in the world many a chapel/ in whiche is rongen but one belle/ thus scorned and mocked the foxe/ the prestes wyf dame iulock that was ful of sorowe/ The preest fyl doun a swoune/ they toke hym vp and brought hym agayn to bedde. tho wente the foxe agayn in to his borugh ward/ and lefte tybert the catte in grete drede and Ieopardye/ for the foxe wiste none other[2] but that the catte was nygh deed/ but whan tybert the catte sawe them al besy aboute the preest tho began he to byte and gnawe the grenne in the myddel a sondre/ and sprange out of the hool and wente rollyng and wentlyng towards the kyngs court or he cam theder it was fayr day and the sonne began to ryse/ And he cam to the court as a poure wyght/ he had caught harme atte prestes hows by the helpe and counseyl of the foxe/ his [b8v] body was al to beten/ and blynde on the one eye/ whan the kynge wyste this/ that tybert was thus arayed/ he was sore angry and menaced reynart/ the theef sore/ and anone gadred his counseyl to wyte what they wold auyse hym/ how he myght brynge the foxe to the lawe and how he sholde be fette

Tho spack sir grymbart whiche was the foxes suster sone and saide ye lordes/ thowgh myn eme were twyes so bad and shrewessh/ yet is ther remedye ynough/ late hym be don to/ as to a free man whan he shal be Iuged/ he muste be warned the thirde tyme for al and yf he come not thanne/ he is thenne gylty in alle the trespaces that ben leyd ayenst hym and his or complayned on/ grymbert who wolde ye that sholde goo and daye hym to come/ who wil auenture for hym his eeris/ hys eye or his lyf whiche is so fel a beest/ I trowe ther is none here so moche a fool/ grymbart spack/ so helpe me god I am so moche a fool/ that I wil do this message my self to reynart/ yf ye wille commande me/

¶ How grymbert the dasse brought the foxe to the lawe to fore the kynge/ capitulo ¶ .xjº.

NOw go forth grymbart and see wel to fore yow reynart is so felle and fals and so subtyl/ that ye nede wel to loke aboute yow/ and to beware of hym/ Grimbert said he shold see wel to[3]/

[1] w th C (*tail of* y *visible*)   [2] ocher C   [3] welto C

thus wente grymbart to maleperduys ward/ and whan he cam theder/ he fonde reynart the foxe at home/ and dame ermelyn his wyf [ci] laye by her whelpis in a derke corner/ Tho spack grymberd and salewed his eme and his aunte/ and saide to reynart eme beware that your absence hurte yow not in suche maters as be leyde and complayned on yow but yf ye thynke it good/ it is hye tyme that/ ye come wyth me to the court/ The wythholdyng you fro it can doo yow no good there is moche thynge complayned ouer you/ and this is the thirde warnyng/ and I telle you for trouth yf ye abyde to morow al day/ ther may no mercy helpe you ye shal see that wyth in thre dayes that your hows shal be byseged al aboute/ and ther shal be made to fore it galowes and racke/ I saie you truly ye shal not thenne escape neyther with wyf ne wyth chylde/ The kynge shal take alle your liuys fro yow/ therfore it is beste that ye goo wyth me to the court/ your subtyl[1] wyse counseyl shal parauenture auaylle you/ ther ben gretter auentures falle er this for it may happe ye shal goo quyte of all the complayntes that ben complayned on you/ and alle your enemyes shal abyde in the shame/ ye haue oftymes don more and gretter thingis than this.

REynart the foxe answerd/ ye saye soth/ I trowe it is beste that I goo wyth/ you for ther lacketh my counseyl parauenture the kynge shal be mercyful to me yf I maye come to speke wyth hym/ and see hym vnder his eyen/ though I had don moche more harme/ the court may not stonde without me/ that shal the kynge wel vnderstande· Though some be so felle to me ward/ yet it goth not to the herte/ alle the counseyl shal conclude [ci^{v}] moche by me/ where grete courtes ben gadred of kynges or of grete lordes/ where as nedeth subtyl counseyl/ ther muste reynart fynde/ the subtyl meanes/ they maye wel speke and saye theyr aduys but the myne is beste/ and that goth to fore alle other/ in the courte ben many that haue sworen to doo me the werst they can/ and that causeth me a parte to be heuy in my herte/ For many maye doo more than one allone/ that shal hurte me/ neuertheles neuew it is better that I goo wyth yow to the court and answere for my self/ than to sette me/ my wyf/ and my chyldren in a venture for to be loste/ aryse vp late vs goo hens/ he is ouer myghty for me/ I muste doo as he wylle/ I can not bettre[2] it I shal take it paciently and suffre it.

[1] sultyl C [2] bectre C

REynert saide to his wyf dame ermelyn I betake yow my chyldren that ye see wel to hem/ and specyally to reynkyn my yongest sone/ He belyketh me so wel I hope he shal folowe my stappes And ther is rosel a passyng[1] fayr theef/ I loue hem as wel as ony may loue his chyldren/ Yf god gyue me grace/ that I may escape I shal whan I come agayn thanke yow wyth fair wordes Thus toke Reynart leue of his wyf/ A gods/ how sorouful a bode ermelyn wyth her smale whelpis/ For the vytayller and he that sorowed for malperduys was goon his way/ And the hows not pourueyed ne vitaylled.

¶ How reynard shroef hym[2] capitulo. ¶ xij. [c2]

WHan reynart and grymbert had goon a whyle to gydre/ tho saide reynart/ dere cosyn now am I in grete fere/ for I goo in drede and ieopardye of my lyf/ I haue so moche repentaunce for my synnes that I wil shryue me dere cosyn to yow/ here is none other preest to gete yf I were shryuen of my synnes/ my soule shold be the clerer/ grymbert ansuerde/ Eem wil ye shryue you/ thenne muste ye promyse first to leue your steelyng and rouynge reynart saide that wiste he wel/ now herke dere cosyn what I shal saye/ Confiteor tibi pater of alle the mysdedes that I haue don/ And gladly wil receyue penance for them/ Grymbert sayde what saye ye/ wylle ye shryue yow/ thenne saye it in englissh that I may vnderstande. yow reynart sayde/ I haue trespaced ayenst alle the beestis that lyue in especyal ayenst bruyn the bere myne Eem whom I made his crowne al blody/ ¶ And taughte[3] tybert the catte to[4] catche myes for I made her leepe in a grenne wher she was al to beten/ also I haue trespaced gretly ayenst chanteclere with his children/ for I haue made hym quyte of a grete dele of hem

The kynge is not goon al quyte/ I haue sklandred hym and the quene many tymes/ that they shal neuer be cleer therof yet haue I begyled ysegrym the wulf ofter than I can telle wel I called hym eme/ but that was to deceyue hym/ he is nothyng of

[1] apassyng C [2] hym̄ BM[1], BM[2], PM, EC; hym JR
[3] ta ughte JR, BM[1], BM[2], EC; taughte PM [4] catteto C

my kyn/ I made hym a monke/ at[1] Eelmare/ where I my self also becam one/ And that was to his hurte and no prouffyte/ I made bynde his [c2v] feet to the belle rope/ the ryngyng of the belle thought hym so good that he wolde lerne to rynge wherof he had shame/ For he range so sore that alle the folke in the strete were aferd therof and meruaylled what myght be on the belle/ And ranne thyder to fore he had comen to axe the religyon/ wherfore he was beten almost to the deth/ after this I taught hym to catche fyssh where he receyuid many a stroke/ also I ledde hym to the richest prestes hows that was in vermedos/ This preest had a spynde[2] wherin henge many a good flitche of bacon/ wherin many a tyme I was wonte to fyl my bely/ in this spynde I had made an hole/ in whiche I made ysegrym to crepe/ There fonde he tubbes wyth beef and many goed flytches of bacon wherof he ete so moche withoute mesure/ that he myght not come out at the hole where he wente in/ his bely was so grete and ful of the mete/ and whan he entred his bely was smal/ I wente in to the village and made there a grete showte/ and noyse/ yett herke what I dyde thenne I ranne to the preest where he satte at the table and ete/ And hadde to fore hym as fatte capone as a man myght fynde/ that capone caught I and ranne my weye therwith al that I myghte/ the preest cryed out and said/ take and slee the foxe/ I trowe that neuer man sawe more wonder/ the foxe cometh in my hows and taketh my capoone fro my table/ where sawe euer man an hardyer theef/ and as me thought he toke his table knyf and casted it at me/ but he touched me not I ranne away/ he shoof the table from hym/ and folewed me cryeng kylle and slee hym/ I to goo and they after and many moo cam after [c3] whiche alle thought to hurte me/

I Ranne so longe that I cam where as isegrym was/ and there I lete falle the capone/ for it was to heuy for me/ and ayenst my wille I lefte it there/ and thenne I sprange thurgh an hole where as I wolde be/ and as the preest toke vp the capone. he espyed isegrym and cryde smyte doun here frendes here is the theef the wulf/ see wel to that he escape vs not· they ranne alle to gydre wyth stokkes and staues and made a grete noyse that alle the neyghbours camen oute. and gauen· hym many a shrewde stroke/ and threwe at hym grete stones/ in suche wyse that he fyl doun as he had

[1] at *omitted in* C [2] aspynde C

ben deed/ They slepid hym and drewe hym ouer stones and ouer blockes wythout the village and threwe hym in to a dyche and there he laye al the nyght/ I wote neuer how he cam thens syth I haue goten of hym/ for as moche as I made hym to fylle his bely/ that he sware that he wolde be myn helpe an hole yere/

Tho ledde I hym to a place where I tolde hym ther were vij· hennes and a cocke whiche satte on a perche and were moche fatte/ And ther stode a faldore by/ and we clymmed ther vp/ I sayde to hym yf he wolde bileue me/ and that he wolde crepe in to the dore/ he sholde fynde many fatte hennes/ Isegrym wente al lawhyng to/ the dore ward and crope a lityl in/ and tasted here and there/ and at laste he sayde to me reynarde ye borde and iape with me/ for what I seche I fynde not thenne said I/ eme yf ye wyl fynde crepe forther in/ he that wil wynne/ he muste laboure and auenture/ [c3v] They that were wonte to sytte there/ I haue them a waye thus I made hym to seche ferther in/ and shooue hym forth so ferre/ that he fylle doun vpon the floer for the perche was narow/ and he fill so grete a falle/ that they sprange vp alle that slepte/ and they that laye nexte the fyre cryden that the valdore was open and/ somthyng was falle and they wiste not wat it myght be/

They roose vp and lyghte a candel/ and whan they sawe hym they smeton beten[1] and wounded hym to the deth/ I haue brought hym thus in many a iepardye/ moo than I can[2] now rekene/ I sholde fynde many moo/ yf I me wel bythoughte/ whiche I shal telle you here after/ Also I haue bydryuen wyth dame erswynde his wyf/ I wolde I had not don it/ I am sory for it/ hit is to her grete shame/ and that me repenteth/ grymbert saide/ Eme I vnderstande you not/ he sayde I haue trespaced with his wyf/ ye shryue you/ as though ye helde somwhat behynde/ I wote not what ye mene ne where ye haue lerned this langage/ Ach dere eme it were grete shame yf I shold saye it oppenly as it happed/ I haue leyen by myn aunte/ I am your eme I shold angre you yf I spak vylanye of wymmen/ neueu now haue I tolde yow alle that I can thynke on/ sette me penaunce/ and assoylle me/ For I haue grete repentaunce/ Grymbert was subtyl and wyse/ he brake a rodde of a tree and saide/ eme now shal ye smyte your self thryes with this rodde on your body/ And thenne leye it doun vpon the

[1] betēn C [2] gan C

grounde/ and sprynge thre tymes ther ouer without bowyng [c4] of your legges and wythout stomblyng/ and thenne shul ye take it vp and kysse it frendly in token of mekenes and obedience of your penance that I gaf yow/ herwith be ye quyte of alle synnes that ye haue don to this day for I forgeue it yow al/ the foxe was glad/ tho sayd grymbert to his eme/ Eme see now forthon/ that ye doo good werkis/ rede your psalmes/ goo to chirche faste and kepe your halydayes/ and gyue your allmesse/ and leue your synful and yl lyf/ your thefte and your treson and so maye ye come to mercy/ the foxe promysed that he wold so doo/ and thenne wente they bothe to gydre to the court ward/

A Lytel besyde the waye as they wente stode a cloyster of black[1] nonnes. where many ghees/ hennes and capones wente withoute the walles/ and as they wente talkynge the foxe brought grymberte out of the right waye thyder and wythout the walles by the barne wente the polayle/ The foxe espyed them and saw a fatte yong capone whiche wente allone fro his felaws/ and leep and caught hym that the fethers flewh aboute his eeris but the capone escaped/ grymbert sayde what eme cursyd man what wil ye doo/ wille ye for one of thise poletes falle agayn in alle your synnes of whiche ye haue shryuen yow/ ye ought sore repente you/ reynart answerd/ truly cosyn I had al forgoten/ praye god that he forgeue it me for I wil neuer do so more/ thenne torned they agayn ouer a lityl[2] brydge/ yet the foxe alway loked after the polaylle/ he coude not refrayne hym self/ that whiche cleuid by the bone/ [c4v] myght not out of the flesshe/ though he shold be hanged/ he coude not lete the lokyng after the polayll as fer as he myght see them/ ℭ Grymbert sawe his maner and sayde/ Fowle false deceyuour/ how goo your eyen so after the poleyl/ The foxe sayde/ cosyn ye/ mysdoo to saye to me ony suche wordes/ ye brynge me out of my deuocion and prayers/ late me saye a pater[3] noster For alle the sowles of polaylle and ghes that I haue betrayed/ and ofte wyth falsheed stolen from thyse holly nonnes/ Grymbert was not wel a payd but the foxe had euer his eyen toward the polayl/ til atte laste they cam in the waye agayn/ And thenne torned they to the court warde/ how sore quaked tho reynard whan they aproched the court/ For he wiste wel that he had for to answere to many a fowle[4] feet and theft that he had doon/

[1] back C [2] alityl C [3] apater C [4] afowle C

¶ How the foxe cam to the court/ and how he excused hym to fore the kynge/ capitulo ¶ .xiij°

AT the first whan it was knowen/ in the court that reynart the foxe and grymbaert his cosyn were comen to the court/ Ther was none so poure nor so feble of kynne and frendes/ but that he made hym redy for to complayne on reynart the foxe/ reynart loked as he had not ben aferd/ and helde hym better/ than he was for he wente forth proudly with his neueu thurgh the hyest strete of the courte/ right as he had ben the kynges sone and as he had not trespaced to ony man the value of an heer/ and wente [c5] in the mydel of the place stondyng to fore noble the kynge and sayde/ God gyue yow grete honour and worship/ Ther was neuer kyng/ that euer had a trewer seruant/ than I haue ben to your good grace and yet am· Neuertheles dere lorde I knowe wel that ther ben many in this courte that wolde destroye me yf ye wold[1] byleue them/ but nay god thanke yow/ hit is not syttyng to youre crowne to byleue thise false deceyuars and lyars lyghtly/ To god mote it be complayned/ how that thise false lyars and flaterers now adayes in the lordes courtes ben moste herde and byleuyd/ the shrewes and false deceyuers ben borne vp for to doo to good men alle the harme and scath they maye/ Our lorde god shal ones rewarde them their hyre/ the kynge sayde/ pees reynard false theef and traytour/ how wel can ye brynge forth fayr talis/ And alle shalle not helpe yow a strawe/ wene ye wyth suche flateryng wordes to be my frende/ ye haue so ofte seruyd me soo as ye now shal wel knowe/ The pees that I haue comanded and sworn/ that haue ye wel holden/ haue ye/ chauntecler coude no lenger be stylle but cryde/ alas what haue/ I by this pees loste/ be stylle chaunteclere[2] holde your mouth late me answere this fowle theef/

THow shrewd felle theef saide the kynge/ thou saist that thow louest me wel· that hast thou shewd wel on my messagers these poure felaws/ Tibert the cat and bruyn the bere/[3] whiche yet ben al blody whiche chyde not ne saye not moche/ but that shal this day coste the thy lyf/ In nomine pater· criste. filij. sayd the foxe dere lord and myghty kyng· yf bruyns crowne be blody/ what is that [c5v] to me/ whan he ete hony at lantferts hows in the vyllage and dyde hym hurte and scathe/ there was he beten therfore

[1] yewold C [2] chaũtetlere C [3] bere- C

yf he had willyd he is so stronge of lymmes/ he myght wel haue be auengid er he sprang in to the water/ Tho cam tybert the catte whom I receyued frendly/ yf he wente out without my counseyl for to stele myes to a prestes hows/ and the preest dyde hym harme sholde I abye that thenne myght[1] I saye I were not happy not so my liege lorde/ ye may doo what ye wille/ thowh my mater be cleer and good. ye maye siede me/ or roste/ hange. or make me blynde. I may not escape yow. we stonde alle vnder your correccion. ye be myghty and stronge. I am feble/ and my helpe is but smal/ yf ye put me to the deth. hit were a smal vengeance whiles they thus spack. sprange vp bellyn the rame and his ewe dame olewey and saide my lord the kynge here oure complaynt/ bruyn the bere stode vp wyth al his lygnage and his felaws. Tibert the catte Isegrym the wulf. kywart the hare/ and panther the boore· the camel and brunel the ghoos the kyde and ghoot. boudewyn the asse. borre the bulle/ hamel the oxe· and the wesel. Chantecler the cock· pertelot wyth alle theyr children· alle thise made grete rumour and noyse. And cam forth openly to fore their lorde the kynge. ℂ And made that the foxe was taken and arested/

ℂ How the foxe was arestid and Iuged to deth capitulo ℂ ·xiiij°· [c6]

HEre vpon was a parlament/ and they desired that reynart sholde ben deed and what somme euer they sayden ayenst the foxe/ he answerde to eche to them/ neuer herde man of suche beestis/ suche playntis of wyse counseyl/ and subtyl Inuencions and on that other syde/ the foxe made his excuse so wel and formably theron that they that herde it wondred therof/ they that herde and sawe it/ may telle hit forth for trouthe/ I shal shorte the mater and telle yow forth of the foxe/ The kynge and the[2] counseyl herde the witnessis of the complayntes of reynarts mysdedes/ hit wente with hem as it ofte doth the feblest hath the worst/ They gafe sentence and Iuged that the foxe sholde be dede and hanged by the necke tho lyste not he to pleye alle his flateryng wordes and deceytes coude not helpe hym/ The Iugement was gyuen and that muste be don/ grymbert his neueu/ and many of his lignage myght not fynde in their hertes to see hym dye but token leue soroufully/ and romed the court/

[1] mygyht C   [2] eth JR, BM[2], PM; the BM[1], EC

The kynge bithoughte hym and marked how many a yonglyng departed from thens al wepyng/ whiche were nyghe of his kynne/ and sayde to hym self/ hier behoueth other counseyl herto/ Though reynart be a shrewe/ ther be many good of his lignage/ tybert[1] the catte sayde/ sir bruyn and sir Isegrym/ how be ye thus slowe. it is almost euen/ hier ben many busshes and hedges. yf he escaped from vs. and were delyuerd out of this paryl he is so subtyl and so wyly and can so many deceytes that he shold neuer [c6v] be taken agayn/ shal we hange hym how stonde ye al thus er the galewis can be made redy it shal be nyght/ Isegrym bethought hym tho and seyde/ hier by is a gybet or galewis/ And wyth that worde he sighed/ and the catte espyed that and sayde/ Isegrym ye be aferd/ ys it ayenst your wylle/ thynke ye not that he hym self wente and laboured that bothe your brethern were hanged/ were ye good and wyse ye sholde thanke hym/ and ye sholde not therwith so longe tarye/

ℭ How the foxe was ledde to the galewis/ cap° ·xv°·

Ysegrym balked and sayde/ ye make moche a doo sir tybert hadde we an halter whiche were mete for his necke and stronge ynough/ we shold sone make an ende/ reynert the foxe whiche longe had not spoken/ saide to Isegrym shorte my payne/ Tyberte hath a stronge corde whiche caught hym in the prestes hous/ whan he bote of the prestes genytoirs/ he can clyme wel and is swyft late hym bere vp/ the lyne/ Isegrym and bruyn thys becometh yow wel that ye thus doo to your neuew/ I am sory that I lyue thus longe/ haste you ye be sette therto/ it is euyl doo that ye tarye thus longe/ goo to fore bruyn ande lede me Isegrym folowe fast. and see[2] wel to and beware that reynart go not away· tho sayd bruyn it is the best counseil that I euer yet herde/ that reynart there seith Isegrym commanded anon and badde his kyn and frendes. that they sholde see to reynart that he escaped not. For he is so wyly and fals. They helden hym by the feet. by the berde. and so kepte [c7] hym that he escaped not from hem/ The foxe herde alle thyse wordes/ whiche touchid hym/ nygh/ yet spak he and sayde/ Och dere eme/ me thynkyth ye payne your self sore/ for to doo to[3] me hurte and scathe/ yf I durste I wolde pray you of mercy/ thaugh my hurte and sorow is playsant to you/ I wote wel

[1] thybert C [2] andsee C [3] do C

yf myn aunte your wyf bethought her wel of olde ferners· she wolde not suffre that/ I shold haue ony harme/ but now I am he/ that now ye wille doo on me what it shal plese yow/ ye bruyn and/ tibert[1]/ god gyue you shames deth but ye doo to me your werst/ I wote wherto I shal/ I may deye but ones I wolde that I were dede al redy I sawe my fader deye he had sone donne/ Isegrym sayde late vs goo/ For ye curse vs bi cause we lengthe the tyme/ euyl mote he fare yf we abyde ony lenger/ he wente forth wyth grete enuye on that one side and bruyn stoode on the other syde/ and so lede they hym forth to the galowes warde/ Tybert ranne with a good wil to fore/ and bare the corde and his throte was yet sore of the grynne/ and his croppe dyde hym woo of the stryke that he was take in that happed by the/[2] counseil of the foxe/ and that thought he now to quyte/

Tybert ysegrym and bruyn wente hastely wyth reinert to the place/ there as the felons ben wonte to be put to deth/ Nobel the kynge and the quene/ and alle that were in the court folowed after for to see the ende of reynart/ the foxe was in grete drede yf hym myshapped/ and bethought hym ofte/ how he[3] myghte saue hym fro the deth/ And tho thre that so sore desireden [c7v] hys deth how he myght deceyue them/ and brynge them to shame/ and how he myght brynge the kynge wyth lesyngis For to holde wyth hym ayenst hem/ This was alle that he studyed/ how he myght putte away his sorowe wyth wylys/ And thought/ thus though the kynge and many one be vpon me angry/ it is no wonder for[4] I haue wel deseruid it/ neuertheles I hope for to be yet hir best frende/ And yet shal I neuer do them good/ how strong that the kynge be/ and how wyse that his counseil[5] be/ yf I may brouke my wordes/ I knowe so many an inuencion/ I shal come to myn aboue/ as fer as they wolde comen to the galewes/

Tho saide ysegrym/ sir bruyn[6] thynke now on your rede crowne whiche by reynarts mene ye caughte we haue now the tyme that we may wel rewarde hym/ Tybert clyme vp hastyly and bynde the corde faste to the lynde/ and make a rydynge knotte or a strope/ ye be the lyghtyst/ ye shal this day see your wylle of hym· Bruyn

[1] thibert C [2] the- C [3] be C
[4] for-| C [5] tounseil C [6] brūyn C

see wel to that he escape not. and holde faste. I wil helpe that the ladder be sette vp/ that he may goo vpwart theron. bruyn saide. do. I shal kepe[1] hym wel The foxe sayde now may my herte be wel heuy for grete drede· For I see the deth to fore myn eyen. and I may not escape· my lorde the kynge and dere quene and forth alle ye that here stande. er I departe fro this worlde I pray you of a bone. that I may to fore you alle make my confession openly and telle my defaultes also clerly that my sowle be not a/ combred/ and also that noman [c8] here after/ bere no blame for my thefte ne for my treson my deth shal be to me the esyer/ and praye ye alle to god that he haue mercy on my sowle.

¶ How the foxe made openly his confession to fore the kynge and to fore al them that wold here it cap° xvj°

Alle they that stoden there had pyte whan reynart saide tho wordis and said it was/ but a lytyl requeste yf the kynge wolde graunte it hym/ and they prayde the kynge to graunte it hym/ The kyng gaf hym leue/ reynart was wel glad and hoped that it myght falle better/ And said thus/ now helpe spiritus domini/ for I see hier noman but I haue trespaced vnto/ Neuertheles yet was I vnto the tyme that I was wened fro the tete/ one the best chylde that/ coude ouwher be founden/ I wente tho and pleyde wyth the lambes by cause I herde hem gladly blete/ I was so longe wyth hem that at the laste I bote one/ there lerned I fyrst to lapen of the bloode hit sauourd wel/ me thought it right good/ And after I began to taste of the flessh/ therof I was lycourous/ so that after that I wente to the gheet in to the wode. there herde I the kyddes blete and I slewe of them tweyne/ I began to wexe hardy after I slew hennes/ polayl and ghees/ where euer I fonde hem/ Thus worden my teeth al blody after this I wexe so felle and so wroth/ That what somme euer I founde that I myght ouer/ I slowe alle/ Therafter cam[2] I by Isegrym now in the wynter/ where he hydde hym vnder a tree. And rekened to [c8v] me that/ he was myn eme whenne I herde hym thenne rekene allyance we becomen felaws whiche I may wel repente/ we promysed eche to other to be trewe and to vse good felawship/ and began to wandre to gyder/ he stal the grete thynges and I the smalle and all was comyn bytwene vs/ yet he made it so

[1] helpe C [2] Ther aftercam C

that he had the beste dele I gate not half my parte/ whan that ysegrym gate a calf/ a ramme or a weder thenne grimmed he/ and was angry on me and droof me fro hym/ and helde my part and his to/ so good is he.

YEt this was of the leste/ but whan it so lucked that we toke an oxe or a cowe/ thenne cam therto his wyf wyth .vij. children so/ that vnto me myght vnnethe come one of the smallest rybbes/ and yet had they eten alle the flessh therof/ ther with all muste I be content not for that I had so grete nede. For I haue so grette scatte and good of syluer and of gold that seuen waynes shold not conne carye it away/ whan the kynge herde hym speke of this grete good and richesse he brenned in the desyre and couetyse therof and sayde reynart where is the rychesse becomen/ telle me that· the foxe saide my lord I shal telle yow/ the rychesse was stolen/ and had it not be stolen[1]/ it shold haue coste yow/ your lyf and shold haue ben murdred whiche god forbede and shold haue ben the gretest hurte of the worlde/ whan the quene herde that she was sore aferde and cryde lowde/ alas and weleaway reynart what saye ye/ I coniure yow by the longe waye that youre soule shal goo/ that ye telle [dɪ] vs openly the trouthe herof as moche as ye knowe of this grete murdre that sholde haue be doon on my lorde/ that we alle may here it now herkene how the foxe shal flatre the kynge and quene/ and shal wynne bothe their good willes and loue/ And shal hyndre them that laboure for his deth/ he shal vnbynde his packe and lye and by flaterye and fayr wordes shal brynge forth so his maters/ that it shal be supposed for trouthe/

IN a sorouful contenance spack the foxe to the quene I am in suche caas now that I muste nedes deye/ and hadde ye me not so sore coniured/ I wil not Ieoparde my sowle/ and yf I so dyde I shold goo therfore in to the payne of helle/ I wil saye nothyng but that I wil make it good/ for pytously he shold haue ben murthred of his owen folke. neuertheles they that were most pryncypal in this feat. were of my next kynne· whom gladly I wold not bewraye. yf the sorow were not of the helle. The kynge was heuy of herte and saide/ reynart saiste thou to me the trouthe. ye said the foxe.

[1] bestolen C

see ye not how it standeth with me. wene ye that I wil dampne my sowle. what shold it auaylle me yf I now saide other wise than trouthe. my deth is so nyghe· ther may nether prayer ne good helpe me Tho trembled the foxe by dyssymylyng[1] as he had ben a ferde The quene had pyte on hym. And prayde the kyng to haue mercy on hym in eschewyng of more harme/ and that he sholde doo the peple holde their peas and gyue the foxe Audience. and here what he shold saye/ Tho commanded the kynge openly that eche of [d1v] them shold be stylle/ and suffre the foxe to saye vnberisped what that he wolde. thenne saide/ the foxe/ be ye now alle stylle. syth it is the kynges wille. and I shal telle you openly this treson. And therin I wil spare noman that I knowe gylty.

¶ How the foxe brought them in daunger/ that wolde haue brought hym to deth. and how he gate the grace of the kyng.

capitulo ¶ .xvij°:

NOw herkene how the foxe began. in the begynnyng he appeled grymbert his dere cosyn. whiche euer had holpen hym in his nede/ he dyde so bycause his wordes sholde be the better byleued. and that he forthon myght the better lye on his enemyes thus began he firste and saide. my lorde my fader had founden kyng ermeryks tresour doluen in a pytte. and whan he had thys grete good. he was so prowde and orguillous that he had alle other beestis in despyte whiche to fore had ben his felaws he made tybert the catte to goo in to that wylde lande of ardenne to bruyn the bere for to do to hym homage. and bad hym saye yf he wolde be kynge that he shold come in to flaundres/ bruyn the bere was glad hierof/ For he had longe desired it/ And wente forth in to flaundres where my fader receyued hym right frendly/ anone he sente for the wyse grymbert myn neuewe/ And for ysegrym the wulfe/ and for tybert the catte/ Tho these fyue camen bytwene gaunt and the thorpe callyd yfte/ there they helden their counseyl an hole derke nyght longe/ what wyth the deuels helpe and craft and for my faders richesse they concluded/ and swore there the kyngys deth/ [d2][2] now herkene and here this wonder the foure sworen vpon ysegryms crowne/ that they sholde make bruyn a kynge and a lorde/ And brynge hym in the stole at akon and sette

[1] dyssymlyyng C [2] 2 *upside down* C

the crowne on his heed/ and yf there were ony of the kynges frendes or lignage/ that wolde be contrarye or ayenst this/ hym sholde my fader wyth his good and tresour fordryue and take from hym his myght and power/

IT happed so that on a morowtyde erly that grymbert my neuew was of wyne almost dronke/ that he tolde it to dame sloepcade his wif in counseyl/ and badde her kepe it secrete/ but she anone forgate it/ and saide it forth in confession to my wyf/ vpon an[1] heth where they bothe wenten a pylgremage/ but she must firste swere by her trouthe and by the holy thre kynges of coleyne that for loue ne for hate she sholde neuer telle it forth but kepe it secrete but she helde it not/ and kepte it no lenger secrete but tyl she cam to me/ and she thenne tolde to me alle that she herde/ but I muste kepe it in secrete/ and she tolde me so many tokenys/ that I felte wel it was trouthe and for drede and fere myn heer stode right vp/ and my herte becam as heuy as leed/ and as colde as Ise/ I thought by this a lyknesse whiche hier a fore tyme byfylle to the frosshis/ whiche were free/ and complayned that they had none lorde/ ne were not bydwongen/ for a comynte without a gouuernour was not good[2]/ and they cryden to god with a lowde voys/ that he wolde ordeyne one that myght rewle them/ this was al that they desired/ god herde theyr requeste/ for it was resonable and sente to them a storke/ whiche ete and swolowed [d2v] them in as many as he coude fynde/ he was alway to hem vnmercyful/ tho complayned they theyr hurte/ but thenne it was to late/ they that were to fore free and were a ferde of no body/ ben now bonde and muste obeye to strengthe theyr kynge/ hyer fore ye riche and poure I sorowed that it myght happen vs in lyke wyse/

THus my lord the kyng I haue had sorowe for you wherof ye can me but lytyl thanke/ I knowe bruyn the bere for suche a shrewe and rauener/ wherfor I thoughte yf he were kynge we shold be alle destroyed and loste/ I knowe our souerain lord the kyng of so hye byrthe/ so myghty so benyngne and mercyful/ that I thought truly it had ben an euyl chaunge for to haue a foule stynkynge theef and to refuse a noble myghty stately lyon/ For the

[1] and C [2] god C

bere hath more madde folye in his vnthrifty heed and al his auncestris/ than ony other hath/ thus had I in myn herte many a sorowe/ and thought alway how I myght breke and fordoo my faders fals counseyl whiche of a chorle and a traytour and worse than a theef wolde make a lorde and a kynge/ alway I prayd god that he wolde kepe our kyng in worship and good helthe and graunte hym long lyf/ but I thought wel yf my fader helde his tresour/ he shold with his fals felaws wel fynde the waye[1] that the kyng shold be deposed and sette a syde/ I was sore bethought how I myght beste wyte where my faders good laye/ I a wayted at al tymes as nygh as I coude/ in wodes in bushes in feeldis/ where my fader leyde his eyen/ were it by nyght or by daye/ colde or weet I was alway by hym to espye and knowe where [d3] his tresour was leyde/

ON a tyme I laye doun al plat on the grounde/ and sawe my fader come rennyng out of an hole/ Nowe herke what I sawe hym doo/ whan he cam out of the hole/ he loked fast a boute yf ony body had seen hym/ And whan he coude nowher none see/ he stopped the hole with sande and made hit euen and playn lyke to the other grounde by/ he knewe not that I sawe it/ and where his footspore stood/ there stryked he with his tayl and made it smothe with his mouth that noman shold espye it/ that lerned I there of my fals fadre and many subtylitees that I to fore knewe nothyng of/ thenne departed he thens and ran to the village warde for to doo his thyngis/ and I forgate not but sprange and lepe to the hole ward/ and how wel that he had supposed that he had made al faste I was not so moche a fool but that I fonde the hole wel/ and cratched and scraped with my feet the sande out of the hole/ and crepte therin/ there fonde I the moste plente of siluer and of golde that euer I sawe/ hier is none so olde that euer so moche sawe on one heep in alle his lyf/ Tho toke I ermelyne my wyf to helpe/ and we ne rested nyght ne day to bere and carye a waye with grete labour and payne this riche tresour in to another place that laye for vs better vnder an hawe in a depe hole/ in the/ mene whyle that myn husewyf and I thus labouryd my fader was with them that wolde betraye the kynge/ now may ye here what they dede/ bruyn the bere and ysegrym the wulf sente alle the londe a boute/ yf ony man

[1] wa ye C

wolde take wages/ that they [d3v] shold come to bruyn[1]/ and he wolde paye them their souldye or wagis to fore. my fader ranne ouer alle the londe and bare the lettres. he wist lytil that he was robbed of his tresour. ye though he myght haue wonnen al the world. he had not conne fynde a peny therof.

Whan my fader hadde ben oueral in the lande bytwene the elue and the somme. And hadde goten many a souldyour that shold the next somer haue comen to helpe bruyn. tho cam he agayn to the bere and his felowis. and tolde them in how grete a venture he had be to fore the borughes in the londe of saxone/ and how the hunters dayly ryden and hunted with houndes after hym in suche wise that he vnnethis escaped with his lyf/ whan he had tolde this to thise foure false traytours/ thenne shewde he them lettres that plesyd moche to bruyn there in were wreton xij ·C· of ysegryms lignage by name withoute the beres/ the foxes/ the cattes and the dassen/ alle thise had sworn that wyth the first messager that shold come for them they shold be redy and come for to helpe the bere/ yf they had their wages a moneth to fore/ This aspyed I/ I thanke god/ after thise wordes my fader wente to the hole where his tresour had leyn and wolde loke vpon it/ tho began he a grete sorowe/ that he soughte he fonde nothyng/ he fonde his hole broken and his tresour born away/ there dede he that I may wel sorowe and bewaylle/ for grete anger and sorowe he wente and hynge hym self/ thus abode the treson of bruyn by my subtylte after/ Now see myn Infortune/ thise traytours ysegrym and bruyn/ ben now most preuy of counseyl [d4] aboute the kynge/ and sytte by hym on the hye benche[2]/ And I poure reynart haue no thanke ne reward/ I haue buryed myn owen fader by cause the kynge sholde haue his lyf/ my lorde saide the foxe/ where ben they that so wolde doo/ that is to destroye them self for to kepe yow/

The kynge and the quene hoped to wynne the tresour and wyth oute counceyl toke to them reynart and prayde hym that he wold do so wel as to telle them were this tresour was/ reynart saide how shold I telle the kynge or them that wolde hange me/ for loue of the traytours and murderars whiche by her flaterye wolde fayne brynge me to deth/ shold I telle to them where my good is/ thenne were I out of my wytte/ The quene tho spak nay reynart the kyng

[1] bruyñ C [2] bouche C

shal lete you haue your lyf/ and shal al to gydre forgyue you/ and ye shal be fro hensforth[1] wyse and true to my lorde. the foxe answerd to the quene. dere lady yf the kynge wil beleue me and that he wil pardone and forgyue me alle my olde trespaces ther was neuer kynge so riche as I shal make hym for the tresour that I shal doo hym haue/ is right costely and may not be nombred/ The kynge saide ach dame. wille ye beleue the foxe. sauf your reuerence he is borne to robbe/ stele and to lye/ this cleuid to his bones and can not be had out of the flessh/ the quene saide/ nay my lorde ye may now well byleue hym/ though he were here to fore felle/ he is now chaunged otherwise than he was ye haue wel herde that he hath appechid his fader and the dasse his neuew/ whiche he myght wel haue leyde on other bestes/ yf he wold [d4v] haue ben false/ felle/ and a lyar/ The kynge saide dame wille ye thenne haue it soo/ and thynke ye it best to be don/ though I supposed it sholde hurte me/ I wille take alle thise trespaces of reynart vpon me/ and bileue his wordes/ But I swere by my crowne/ yf he euer here after mysdoo and trespace/ that shal he dere abye and alle his lignage vnto the .ix· degree/ The foxe loked on the kyng stoundmele and was glad in his herte/ and saide my lorde/ I were not wyse/ yf I sholde saye thynge that were not trewe/ The kynge toke vp a straw fro the ground/ And pardoned and forgaf the foxe alle the mysdedes and trespaces of his fader and of hym also/ yf the foxe was tho mery and glad it was no wonder/ For he was quyte of his deth and was alle free and franke of alle his enemyes/

THe foxe saide my lord the kynge and noble lady the quene god rewarde yow/ thys grete worship that ye do to me/ I shal thynke and also thanke you for hit/ in suche wise that ye shal be the richest kynge of the world/ For ther is none lyuyng vnther the sonne/ that I vouchesauf better my tresour on/ than on yow bothe/ Thenne toke the foxe vp a straw and profred it to the kyng and saide my moste dere lord plese it yow to receyue hiere the ryche tresour whiche kynge ermeryk hadde/ for I gyue it vnto you wyth a fre wylle/ and knowleche it openly/ The kynge receyuid the straw and threwe it meryly fro hym with a Ioyous visage/ And thanked moche the foxe/ The foxe laughed in hym [d5] self/ The kynge thenne herkened after the counseyl of the foxe/ And alle that ther were/ were at his wylle/ My lorde sade he/ herkene and marke wel

[1] frohens forth C

my wordes/ in the west side of flaundres ther standeth a woode and is named hulsterlo/ And a water that is called krekenpyt lyeth therby/ This is so grete a wyldernesse/ that ofte in an hole yere man ner wyf cometh therin/ sauf they that wil/ and they that wille not eschewe it/ There lyeth this tresour hydde/ vnderstande wel that the place is called krekenpit/ for I aduyse you for the leste hurte/ that ye and my lady goo bothe thyder/ For I knowe none so trewe that I durste on your behalue truste wherfore goo your self/ And whan ye come to krekenpyt ye shal fynde there two birchen trees standyng alther next the pytte/ my lorde to tho byrchen trees shal ye goo/ there lyeth the tresour vnther doluen/ There muste ye scrape and dygge a way a lytyl the mosse on the one side/ Ther shalle ye fynde many a Iewel of golde and syluer. and there shal ye fynde the crowne whiche kynge Ermeryk ware in his dayes that sholde bruyn the bere haue worn yf his wyl had gon forth ye shal see many a costly Iewel with riche stones sette in golde werk whiche coste many a thousand marke/ My lord the kynge whan ye now haue alle this good/ how ofte shal ye saye in your herte and thynke/ O how true art thou reynart the foxe. that with thy subtyl wytte daluyst and hyddest here/[1] this grete tresour/ god gyue the good happe and welfare where euer thou bee/ [d5v]

THe kynge sayde/ sir reynart ye muste come and helpe vs to dygge vp this tresour/ I knowe/ not the way/ I sholde neuer conne fynde it/ I haue herde ofte named/ parys/ london akon and coleyn/ As me thynketh this tresour lyeth/[2] right as ye mocked and Iaped/ for ye name kryekenpyt/ that is a fayned[3] name/ these wordes were not good to the foxe/ and he sayd wyth an angry mode/[4] and dissymyled and saide/ ye my lord the kynge/ ye be also nyghe that as fro rome to maye/ wene ye that I wille lede yow to flomme iordayn·/ Nay I shal brynge you out of wenyng and shewe it you by good[5] wytnes/ he called lowde kywart the hare/ come here to fore the kynge The bestes sawe alle thyder ward and wondred what the kynge wold/ the foxe sayde to the hare/ kywart ar ye a colde/ how tremble ye and quake so/ be not a ferd/ and telle my lorde the kynge here the trouthe/ And that I charge you by the fayth and/ trouthe that ye owe hym and to my lady the quene of suche thyng. as I shal demaunde of you/ Kywaert saide I shal saye the trouthe though I shold lose my necke therfore/ I shal not lye

[1] here- C [2] lyeth- C [3] afayned C [4] mode- C [5] gdod C

ye haue charged me so sore/ yf I knowe it/ Thenne saye/ knowe ye not where krieken pyt standeth/ is that in your mynde/ the hare saide/ I knewe that wel .xij. yer a goon/ wher that stondeth/ why aske ye that. It stondeth in a woode[1] named hulsterlo vpon a warande in the wyldernesse/ I haue suffred there moche sorowe for hunger and for colde/ ye more than I can telle/ Pater symonet the friese was woned to make there false money/ wherwyth he bare hym self out and al his felawship/ but that was to fore er I had [d6] felawship wyth ryn the hounde/ whiche made me escape many a daunger/ as he coude wel telle yf he were here/ and that I neuer In my dayes trespaced ayenst the kynge other wyse than I ought to doo with right/ reynart sayd to hym go agayn to yonder felawship here ye kyward/ my lorde the kynge desyreth nomore to knowe of yow/ the hare retorned and wente agayn to the place he cam fro/ The foxe sayde my lord the kynge is it trewe that I saide/ ye reynart said the kynge/ For gyue it me/ I dyde euyl that I beleuid you not/ Now reynart frende fynde the waye that ye goo wyth vs to the place and pytte/ where the tresour lyeth/ the foxe saide it is a wonder thyng wene ye that I wolde not fayne goo with yow/ yf it were so wyth me that I myght goo wyth yow/ in suche wise that it no shame were vnto your lordshyp/ I wold goo but nay it may not bee/ herkene what I shal saye and muste nedes thaugh it be to me vylonye and shame/ whan Isegrym the wulf in the deuels name wente in to religion and become a monke shorn in the ordre/ tho the prouende of sixe monkes was not suffycient to hym/ and had not ynough to ete he thenne playned and waylled so sore/ that I had pyte on hym/ for he becam slowe and seke/ and by cause he was of my kynne I gaf hym counceyl to renne away and so he dyde/ wherfore I stonde a cursed and am in the popes banne and sentence I wil to morow bytymes as the sonne riseth take my waye to rome for to be assoyled and take pardon and fro rome I wil ouer the see in to the/ holy/ lande and wil neuer retorne agayn til I haue doon so moche good that I may [d6v] with worship goo wyth yow/ hyt were greet repref to you my lord the kyng/ in what londe that I accompanyed you that men shold saye ye reysed and accompanyed your self with a cursyd and a persone agrauate/ The kynge sayde sith that ye stande a cursyd in the censures of the chirche yf I wente wyth you/ men sholde arette vilonye vnto my crowne/ I shal thenne take kywaert or somme other to goo with me to kryekenpytte/ and I

[1] awoode C

counseylle you reynart that ye put you your self out of this curse/ my lord quod the foxe/ therfore wylle I goo to rome as hastely as I may/ I shal not reste by nyght ner day til I bee assoylled/ reynart said the kynge/ me thynketh ye ben torned in to a good waye/ god gyue you grace taccomplyssh wel your desyre/

As sone[1] as this spekyng was don/ noble the kyng wente and stode vpon an hygh stage of stone/ And commanded[2] sylence to alle the bestes/ and that they shulde sytte doun in a rynge rounde vpon the grasse eueriche in his place after his estate and byrthe/ reynart the foxe stode by the quene/ whom he ought wel to loue/ Thenne said the kynge/ here ye alle that be poure and riche yong and olde that stondeth here/ reynart one of the heed offycers of my hows had don so euyl whiche this daye shold haue ben hanged/ hath now in this courte don so moche/ that I and my wyf the quene haue promysed to hym our grace and frendshyp/ The quene hath prayde moche/ for hym/ in so moche that I haue made pees wyth hym/ And I gyue to hym his lyf and membre/[3] [d7] frely. agayn/ and I comande you vpon your lyf/ that ye doo worship to/ reynart his wyf and to his chyldren/ where someuer ye mete hem by day or by nyght/ and I wil also here nomoo complayntes of reynard/ yf he hath hier to fore mysdon and trespaced/ he wil nomore mysdo ne trespace/ but now bettre hym/ he wylle to morowe/ erly goo to the pope for pardone and foryeuenes of alle hys synnes and forth ouer the see to the holy lande/ and he wil not come agayn til he brynge pardon of alle his synnes/ This tale herde tyselyn the rauen/ and leep to ysegrym/ to bruyn/ and to tybert there as they were/ and saide ye caytyfs/ how goth it now/ ye vnhappy folke what do ye here/ reynard the foxe is now a squyer[4] and a courtyer and right grete and myghty in the court/ The kynge hath skylled hym quyte of alle his brokes and forgyuen hym alle his trespaces and mysdedes/ And ye be alle betrayed and apechyd/ ysegrym saide how may this be/ I trowe tyselyn that ye lye I do not certaynly saide the rauen/ Tho wente the wulf and the bere to the kynge Tybert the catte was in grete sorowe he was so sore a ferde/ that for to haue the foxes frendship/ he wold wel forgyue reyner the losse of his one eye that he loste in the prestes hows/ he was so woo/ he wist not what to doo/ he wolde wel that he neuer had seen the foxe/

1 Assone C
2 conmanded C
3 membre/ BM[1], BM[2], EC, PM; membre JR
4 asquyer C

¶ How the wulf and the bere were arestyd by the labour of reynart the foxe capitulo ¶ .xviij°.

YSegrym cam proudly ouer the felde to fore the kynge/ and he thanked the quene/ and spack [d7v] wyth a felle[1] moed ylle wordes on the foxe/ in suche wise that the kynge herde it/ and was wroth and made the wulf and the bere anon to be arestyd/ ye sawe neuer wood dogges do/ more harme/ than was don to them they were bothe fast bounden so sore that alle that nyght/ they myght not stere hande ne foot/ They myght scarsely rore ne meue ony Ioynte/ Now here how the foxe forth dyde/ he hated hem/ he laboured so to the quene that he gate leue for to haue as moche of the beres skyn vpon his ridge as a foote longe and a foot brode for to make hym therof a scryppe/ thenne was the foxe redy yf he had foure stronge shoon/ now here how he dyde for to gete these shoon/ he said to the quene/ madame I am youre pylgrym/ here is myn eme sir Isegrym that hath .iiij. strong shoon whiche were good for me/ yf he wolde late me haue two of them I wolde on the waye besyly thynke on your sowle/ For it is right that a/ pylgrym shold alway thynke and praye for them/ that doo him good/ Thus maye ye doo your sowle good yf ye will/ And also yf ye myght gete of myn aunte dame eerswyn also two of her shoon to gyue me/ she may wel doo it/ For she gooth but lytil out/ but abydeth alway at home/ thenne sayde the quene/[2] reynard yow behoueth wel suche shoes/ ye may not be wythout them/ they shal be good for you to kepe your feet hool for to passe with them many a sharpe montayn and stony roches/ ye can fynde no better shoes for you/ than suche as Isegrym and his wyf haue and were/ they be good and stronge/ though it sholde touche their lyf eche of them shal gyue you two shoes for to [d8] accomplissh wyth your hye pilgremage/

¶ How ysegrym and his wyf ereswyn muste suffre her shois to be plucked of/ And how reynard dyde on the shoys for to goo to rome wyth/ capitulo ¶ ·xix°.

THus hath this false pylgrym goten fro Isegrym ij shooes fro his feet/ whiche were haled of the clawes to the senewis ye sawe neuer foule that men rosted laye so stylle/ as Isegrym dyde/ whan his shoes were haled of/ he styred not/ and yet his feet bledde/

[1] afelle C [2] quene- C

thenne whan Isegrym was vnshoed/ Tho muste dame eerswyn his wyf lye doun in the grasse wyth an heuy chere/ And she loste ther her hynder shoes/ Tho was the foxe glad and saide to his aunte in scorne/ My dere aunte how moche sorow haue ye suffred for my sake/ whiche me sore repenteth/ sauf this/ herof I am glad For ye be the lyeuest of alle my kyn/ Therefore I wyl gladly were your shoen/ ye shal[1] be partener of my pylgremage/ and dele of the pardon that I shal with your shoen fecche ouer the see/ dame erswyne was so woo that she vnnethe myght speke/ Neuertheles this she sayde/ A reynart that ye now al thus haue your wyl/ I pray god to wreke it/ ysegrym and his felaw the bere helden their pees and wheren al stylle/ they were euyl at[2] ease/ For they were/ bounden and sore wounded had tybert the catte haue ben there/ he shold also somwhat haue suffred/ in suche wyse/ as he sholde not haue[3] escaped thens wythout hurte and shame· [d8v]

THe next day whan the sonne aroos reynard thenne dyde grece his shoes whiche he had of ysegrym and erswyn his wyf/ and dyde hem on and bonde hem to his feet/ and wente to the kynge and to the quene and said to hem with a glad chere/ Noble lord and lady god gyue you good morow and I desire of your grace that I may haue male and staff blessyd as belongeth to a pilgrym Thenne the kynge anone/ sent for bellyn the ramme/ and whan he cam he saide/ sir bellyn ye shal do masse to fore reynart/ for he shal goo on pylgremage/ and gyue to hym male and staf/ the ram answerd agayn and said/ my lord I dare not do that/ For he hath said that he is in the popes curse/ The kynge said/ what therof/ mayster gelys hath said to vs/ yf a man had doo as many synnes as al the world/ and he wold tho synnes forsake/ shryue hem and resseyue penance/ and do by the prestes counseyl/ god wil forgyue them and be mercyful vnto hym now wil reynard goo ouer the see in to the holy lande and make hym clere of al his synnes/ Thenne ansuerd bellyn to the kynge I wil not doo litil ne moche herin/ but yf ye saue me harmles in the spirituel court byfore the bysshop prendelor and to fore his archedeken loosuynde/ and to for sir rapiamus his offycyal/ the kynge began to wexe wroth and saide/ I shal not bydde you so moche in half a yere/ I had leuer hange yow than I shold so moche praye you for it/ whan the rame sawe that the kynge was angry/ he

[1] slal C [2] al C [3] haue *omitted in* C

was so sore aferd that he quoke for fere/ and wente to the awter and sange in his bookes and radde suche as hym thought good ouer reynart/ whiche lytyl sette ther by/ [e1] sauf that he wold haue the worship therof

Whan bellyn the ramme had alle sayd his seruyse deuoutly/ thenne he hynge on the foxes necke/ a male couerd wyth the skynne/ of bruyn the bere/ and a lytil palster therby. tho was reynart redy toward his Iourney. tho loked he toward the kynge as he had ben sorowful to departe and fayned as he had wepte. right as he hadde yamerde in his herte· but yf he had ony sorow/ it was by cause al the other that were there were not in the same plyght as the wulf and bere were brought in by hym. neuertheles he stood and prayd them alle to praye for hym. lyke as he wold praye for them the foxe thought that he taryed longe and wold fayn haue departed for he knewe hym self gylty/ the kynge saide reynart I am sory ye be so hasty/ and wil no lenger tarye/ nay my lord/ it is tyme/ for me ought not spare to doo wel/ I pray you to gyue me leue to departe I muste doo my pylgremage/ the kynge sayd/ god be wyth yow[1] now/ and commanded alle them of the court to go and conueyne reynart on his way sauf the wulf and the bere/ whyche fast laye bounden/ ther was none that durst be sory therfore/ and yf ye had seen reynart how personably he wente wyth hys male and palster on his sholder and the shoes on his feet/ ye shold haue laughed/ he wente and shewde hym outeward wysely/ But he laughed in his herte that alle they brought hym forth/ whiche had a lytyl to fore been/ with. hym so wrooth/ And also the kynge whiche so moche hated hym/ he had made hym suche a fool that he[2] brought hym to his owne entente [e1v] he was a pylgrym of deux aas.

MY lord the kyng sayd the foxe I pray you to retorne agayn I wil not that ye goo ony ferther with me. ye myght haue harme therby. ye haue there two morderars arestyd/ yf they escaped you. ye myght be hurt by them y pray god kepe you fro mysauenture· wyth these wordes he stode vp. on his afterfeet. And prayde alle the beestys grete and smal that wolde be parteners of his pardon that they shold praye for hym/ They sayde that they alle wolde remembre[3] hym/ Thenne departed he fro the kynge so

[1] yow *omitted in* C [2] be C [3] remenbre C

heuyly that many of them ermed/ Thenne saide he to kyward the hare/ and to bellyn the[1] ramme meryly/ dere frendes shal we now departe/ Ye wil and god will accompanye me ferther/ ye two made me neuer angry/ ye be good for to walke wyth/ courtoys/ frendly and not complayned on of ony beeste ye be of good condicions/ and goostly of your lyuyng/ ye lyue bothe as I dyde/ whan I was a recluse/ yf ye haue leeuis and gras ye be plesyd/ ye retche not of brede/ of flesshe/ ne suche maner mete/ with suche flateryng wordes hath reynard thise two flatred/ That they wente wyth hym tyl they camen to fore his hows/ maleperduys/

❡ How kywart the hare was slayn by the foxe/ cap° .xx°

WHan the foxe was come to fore the yate of his hows he sayde to bellyn the ramme/ cosyn ye shal abide here withoute/ I and kywart wille [e2] goo in/ For I wille praye kywart to helpe me to take my leue of ermelyn my wyf/ and to conforte her and my chyldren/ bellyn sayde I praye hym to comforte them wel/ wyth suche flateryng wordes brought he the hare in to his hole in an euyl hour/ There fonde they dame ermelyn lyeng on the grounde with her yonglyngis/ whiche had sorowed moche For drede of reynarts deth/ but whan she sawe hym come she was glad/ but whan she sawe his male and palster/ and espyed his shoes/ she meruailled and sayd dere reyner/ how haue ye spedd/ he sayd I was arestid in the court/ But the kynge lete me gon/ I muste goo a pilgremage/ Bruyn the bere and ysegrym the wulf they be plegge for me/ I thanke the kynge/ he hath gyuen to vs kywart hier/ For to doo with hym what we wyl/ The kynge saide hym self that kywart was the first that on vs complayned/ And by the fayth that I owe yow I am right wroth on kywart/ whan kywart herde thise wordes he was sore aferde/ He wold haue fledde/ but he myght not/ For the foxe stode bytwene hym[2] and the yate/ And he caught hym by the necke/ Tho cryed the hare helpe bellyn helpe/ Where be ye This pilgryme sleeth me/ but that crye was sone doon/ for the foxe had anon byten his throte a two/ Tho sayd he late vs go ete this good fatte hare/ the yonge whelpes cam also/ Thus helde they a grete feste/ For kywart had a good fatte body/ ermelyn ete the flessh and dranke the blood/ she thanked ofte the kynge that he had made

[1] th C [2] hym JR, BM[2]; hym (*but with* y *very faint*) PM, EC, BM[1]

them so mery/ The foxe saide ete as moche as ye maye/ he wil paye for it/ yf we will/ feche it. [e2v]

SHe sayd reynart I trowe ye mocke/ telle me the trouthe how ye be departed thens/ dame I haue so flaterid the kynge and the quene/ that I suppose the frendship bytwene vs shal be right thynne whan he shal knowe of this/ he shal be angry/ and hastely seke me for to hange me by myne necke/ Therfore late vs departe and stele secretly a way in somme other foreste/ Where we may lyue wythoute fere and drede/ and there that we may lyue vij yere and more and fynde vs not/ there is plente of good mete of partrychs/ wodekokkis[1] and moche other wilde fowle/ dame and yf ye wil come with me thyder/ ther ben swete welles and fayr and clere rennyng brokes/ lord god how swete eyer is there/ There may we be in pees and ease and lyue in grete welthe/ For the kynge hath lete me gon by cause I tolde hym that ther was grete tresour in krekenpyt/ but there shal he fynde nothyng though he sought euer/ This shal sore angre hym whan he knoweth that he is thus deceyuid what trowe ye how many a grete lesynge muste I lye/ er I coude escape from hym/ It was harde that I escaped out of pryson/ I was neuer in gretter paryl ne nerrer my deth/ but how it euer goo/ I shal by my wille neuer more come in the kynges daunger/ I haue now goten my thombe out of his mouth/ that thanke I my subtylyte.

DAme ermelyne saide reynart I counseyle that we goo not in to another foreste/ where we sholde be strange and elenge we haue here al that we desyre/ And ye be here lorde of our neyghbours/ wherfore shalle we leue this place/ And auenture vs in [e3] a worse/ we may abyde her sure ynough/ yf the kynge wold doo vs ony harme or besiege vs/ here ben so many by or side holes/ in suche wyse as we shal escape fro hym/ in abydyng here/ we may not doo amys/ we knowe alle bypathes ouer alle/ and er he take vs with myght/ he muste haue moche helpe therto but that ye haue sworen that ye shal goo ouersee and abide there/ that is the thyng that toucheth me moste/ nay dame care not therfore/ how more for sworn/ how more forlorn/ I wente ones with a good man/ that said

[1] wododekkis C

to me/ that a bydwongen oth· or oth sworn by force. was none oth. Though I wente on this pilgremage it shold not auaylle me a cattes tayl. I wil abyde here and folowe your counseyl/ yf the kyng hunte after me. I shal kepe me as wel as I maye. yf he be me to myghty. yet I hope wyth subtylte to begyle hym. I shal vnbynde my sack. yf he wil seche harm he shal fynde harme.

NOw was bellyn the ramme angry that kywart his felawe was so longe in the hole. and called lowde. come out kywarte in the deuels name. how longe shal reynart kepe you there. haste you and come late vs goo/ whan reynard herde this· he wente out and saide softly to bellyn the ramme. lief bellyn wherfore be ye angry kywart speketh wyth his dere aunte. me thynketh ye ought not to be dysplesid therfore. he bad me saye to yow ye myght wel go to fore· And he shal come after· he is lighter of fote than ye. he muste tarye a whyle wyth his aunte and her chyldren. they wepe and crye by cause I shal goo fro them. bellyn sayde· what dyde kyward. me [e3v] thoughte he cryed after helpe/ the foxe answerd/ what saye ye bellyne wene ye that he shold haue ony harme/ now herke what he thenne dyde/ whan we were comen in to myn hows/ and ermelyn my wyf vnderstode that I shold goo ouer see she fyl doun in a swoun and whan kywart sawe that/ he cryed loude bellyn come helpe myn aunte to brynge her out of her swoun thenne sayde the ramme In fayth I vnderstode that kywart had ben in grete daunger/ the foxe sayde/ nay truly/ or kyward shold haue ony harme in my hows/ I had leuer that my wyf and chyldren shold suffre moche hurte/

¶ How the foxe sente the heed of kywart the hare to the kynge by bellyn the ramme· capitulo ¶ xxj°.

THe foxe saide/ bellyn remembre ye not that yesterday the kynge and his counseyl commanded me that er I shold departe out of this lande/ I shold sende to hym two lettres. dere cosyn I pray you to bere them. they be redy wreton. the ramme sayde I wote neuer yf I wiste that your endyttyng and wrytyng were good/ ye myght pareuenture so mocche praye me that I wold bere them/ yf I had ony thyng to bere them in/ reynard saide ye shal not fayle to haue somwhat to bere them in/ rather than they shold be vnborn I shal rather gyue yow my male that I bere. and put the kynges lettres therin. and hange them aboute your necke ye shal haue of the kynge grete thanke therfore and be right welcomen to hym. hier vpon bellyn promysed hym to bere thise lettres· tho retorned reynart in to his hows and toke the male and put therin kywarts heed and brought it [e4] to bellyn for to brynge hym in daunger/ And henge it on his necke/ and chargyd hym not for to loke in the male/ yf he wolde haue the kyngis frendship and yf ye wil that the kynge take you in to his grace and loue you/ saye that ye your self haue made the lettre and endited it/ and haue gyuen the counseyl[1] that it is so wel made and wreton/ ye shal haue grete thank therfore/ bellyn the ramme was glad herof and thought he shold haue grete thank and saide reynard I wote wel that ye now doo for me/ I shal be in the court gretly preysed whan it is knowen that I can so wel endyte and make a lettre[2]/ thaugh I can not make it/ ofte tymes it happeth that god suffreth somme to haue worship and thanke of the labouris and connyng of other men/ and so it shal bifalle me now/ Now what counseyle ye reyner/ shal kywaert the[3] hare come wyth me to the court/ nay sayd the foxe/ he shal anone folowe yow/ he may not yet come/ for he muste speke wyth his aunte/

NOw goo ye forth to fore/ I shal shewe to kywart secrete thyngis whiche ben not yet knowen/ bellyn sayd fare wel reynart/ and wente hym forth to the court/ and he ran and hasted so faste that he cam to fore mydday to the court/ and fonde the kynge in his palays wyth his barons/ the kynge meruaylled whan he saw hym brynge the male agayn whiche was made of the beres skyn/ the kyng saide saye on bellyn fro whens come ye/ where is the foxe/ how is it that he hath not the male with hym/ bellyn sayd my lord I shal saye yow al that I knowe/ I accompanyed[4] reynard vnto his hows/ And whan he was redy he asked me yf that I[5] wold For your saacke bere two. lettres [e4v] to yow/ I saide for to do you playsir and worship/ I wold gladly bere to yow vij. tho brought he to me this male where in the lettres be/ whiche ben endyted by my connyng and I gaf counseyl of the makyng of them/ I trowe ye sawe neuer lettres better ne craftelyer made ne endyted/ the kynge commanded anon bokart his secretarye to rede the lettres/ For he vnderstode al maner langages/ tybert the catte and he toke the male

[1] coũnseyl C [2] alettre C [3] he C
[4] accompayned C [5] I that C

of bellyns necke/ and bellyn hath so ferre sayd and confessyd/ that he therfore was dampned.

THe clerke bokart vndyde the male/ and drewe out kywarts heed and said alas what lettres ben these/ certaynly my lord this is kywarts heed/ alas sayde the kynge that euer I beleuid so the foxe/ There myght men see grete heuynesse of the kynge and of the quene/ the kyng was so angry that he helde longe doun his heed And atte laste after many thoughtes/ he made a grete crye/ that alle the bestys were aferde of the noyse/ Tho spack sir firapeel the lupaerd whiche was sybbe somwhat to the kynge/ and saide/ sire kyng how make ye suche a noyse ye make sorow ynough thaugh the quene were deed/ late this sorowe goo/ and make good chere/ it is grete shame/ be ye not a lorde and kynge of this londe/ Is it not alle vnder yow. that here is/ the kynge sayde sir firapeel how sholde I suffre this/ one false shrewe and deceyuar hath betrayed me and brought me so ferre/ that I haue forwrought and angred my frendes/[1] the stoute bruyn the bere/ and ysegrym the wulf/ whiche sore me [e5] repenteth/ and this goth ayenst my worship that I haue done amys ayenst my beste barons and that I trusted and beleuid so moche the fals horeson the foxe/ and my wyf is cause therof/ she prayde me so moche that I herde her prayer and that me repenteth/ thaugh it be to late/ what thawh sir kyng said the lupaerd/ yf ther be ony thyng mysdon/ it shal be amended we shal gyue to bruyn the bere to ysegrym the wulf/ and to erswyn hys wyf for the pece of his skynne and for their shoes for to haue good pees bellyn the ramme/ for he hath confessyd hym self that he gaf counseyl and consentyd to kywardes deth/ it is reson that he abye it/ And we alle shal goo fecche reynard and we shal areste hym and hange hym by the necke without lawe or Iugement/ and ther with alle shul be contente/

¶ How bellyn the ramme and alle his lignage were gyuen in the handes of ysegrym and bruyn and how he was slayn/

capitulo ¶ .xxij°.

THe kynge saide I wil do it gladly/ firapel the lupaerd wente tho to the pryson/ and vnbonde them firste/ and thenne he sayde ye sires I brynge to you a faste pardon and my lordes loue and frendship it repenteth hym and is sory that he euer hath don

[1] frendes/ that I C

spoken or trespaced ayenst you/ and therfore ye shal haue a good appoyntement/ And also amendes he shal/ gyue to you bellyn the ramme and alle his lignage fro now forthon to domesdaye/ in suche wyse that where someuer ye fynde them in felde or in wode that ye may frely/ byte and ete them [e5v] wythout ony forfayte/ And also the kynge graunteth to yow/ that ye maye hunte and do the werst that ye can to reynard and alle his lygnage wythoute mys-doyng This fayr grete pryuelage wylle the kynge graunte to you euer to holde of hym/ And the kynge wille that ye swere to hym neuer to mysdoo/ but doo hym homage and feawte I counseil yow to doo this/ For ye may doo it honorably/ Thus was the pees made by fyrapel the lupaerd frendly and wel/ And that coste bellyn the ramme his tabart and also his lyf/ and the wulfis lignage holde thise preuilegis of the kynge/ and in to thys daye they deuoure and ete bellyns lignage where that they may fynde them this debate was begonne in an euyl tyme/ For the pees coude neuer syth be made bytwene them/ The kynge dyde forth wyth his courte and feste lengthe xij· dayes lenger for loue of the bere and the wulf/ So glad was he of the makyng of this pees/

ℂ How the kynge helde his feeste/ and how lapreel the cony complayned vnto the kynge vpon reynart the foxe capitulo ℂ ·xxiij°.

TO this grete feste cam al maner of beestis/ For the kynge dyde do crye this feste ouer alle in that londe/ Ther was the moste Ioye and myrthe that euer was seen emonge beestis/ Ther was daunsed manerly the houedaunce with shalmouse trompettis and alle maner of menestralsye/ the kynge dyde do ordeyne so moche mete/ that euerych fonde ynough/ And ther was no beest [e6] in al his lande so grete ne so lytyl but he was there/ and ther were many fowles and byrdes also/ and alle they that desired the kynges frendship were there/ sauyng reynard the foxe/ the rede false pilgrym whiche laye in a wayte to doo harme/ and thoughte it was not good for hym to be there/ Mete and drynke flowed there/ Ther weere playes and esbatemens/ The feest was ful of melodye/ One myght haue luste to see suche a feeste/ and right as the feeste had dured viij dayes/ a boute mydday cam in the cony lapreel to fore the kynge where he satte on the table with the quene/ and sayde al heuyly that all they herde hym that were there/ My lorde haue pyte on my complaynt whiche is of grete force and murdre that reynard the foxe wold haue don to me/ yester morow as I cam rennyng by his borugh at maleperdhuys he stode byfore his dore without lyke a pylgryme/ I supposed to haue passed by hym peasibly toward this feste and whan he sawe me come/ he came ayenst me sayeng his bedes I salewed hym/ but/ he spack not one worde/ but he raught out his right foot and dubbed me in the necke bytwene myn Eeris/ that I had wende I sholde haue loste my heed/ but god be thanked I was so lyght that I sprange fro hym/ wyth moche payne cam I of his clawes/ he grymmed as he had ben angry by cause he helde me no faster/ tho I escaped from hym I loste myn one ere/ and I had foure grete holes in my heed of his sharpe nayles that the blood sprange out/ and that I was nyhe al a swoun/ but for the grete fere of my lyf I sprange and ran so faste fro hym that he coude not ouertake me/ See my lord thise [e6v] grete woundes that he hath made to me with his sharpe longe nayles/ I praye you to haue pite of me and that ye wil/ punysshe this false traytour and morderar/ or ellis shal ther noman goo and comen ouer the heth in saefte/ whyles he haunteth his false and shrewde rewle/

¶ How corbant the roke complayned on the foxe for the deth of his wyf capitulo ¶ .xxiiij°.

RYght as the cony had made an ende of his complaynt/ cam in corbant the roek flowen in the place to fore the kynge and sayde[1]/ dere lorde here me/ I brynge you hier a piteous[2] complaynt/ I wente to day by the morow wyth sharpebek my wyf for to playe vpon[3] the heth And there laye reynart the foxe doun on the grounde lyke a dede keytyf/ hys eyen stared and his tonge henge longe out of his mouth/ lyke an hounde had ben deed/ we tasted and felte his bely/ but we fonde theron no lyf/ tho wente my wyf and herkened and leyde her ere to fore his mouth for to wite yf he drewe his breeth/ whiche mysfylle her euyl/ For the false felle foxe awayted wel his tyme and whan he sawe her so nygh hym/ he caught her by the heed and boote it of/ tho was I in grete sorowe and cryde lowde/ Alas alas what is there happed/ thenne stode he hastely vp/ and raught so couetously after me that for feere of deth/ I trembled and

[1] andsayde C [2] pietous C [3] wpon C

flewh vpon a tree therby and sawe fro ferre how the false keytyf ete and slonked her in so hungerly that he lefte neyther flessh ne bone/ nomore but a fewe fethers/ the smal fethers he slange [e7] them in wyth the flessh/ he was so hungry/ he wolde wel haue eten tweyne/ Tho wente he his strete/ tho flewe I doun wyth grete sorow and gadred vp the fetheris for to shewe them to you here/ I wolde not be agayn in suche peryl and fere as I was there for a thousand marke/ of the fynest gold that euer cam out of arabye/ My lord the kyng see hier this pyteous werke/ Thise ben the fethers of sharpbecke my wyf/ my lord yf ye wil haue worship ye muste do herfore Iustyce and auenge you in suche wise as men may fere and holde of yow/ For yf ye suffre thus youre saufconduyt to be broken/ ye your self shal not goo peasibly in the hye way/ for tho lordes that do not Iustyce and suffre that the lawe be not executed vpon the theeuis/ morderars and them that mysdoo/ they be parteners to fore god of alle theyr mysdedes and trespaces/ and eueryche thenne/ wylle be a lord hym self/ dere lorde see wel to for to kepe your self·

ℂ How the kynge was sore angry of thise complayntes capitulo ℂ .xxv°.

NOble the kyng was sore meuyd and angry whan he had herde thise complayntes of the cony and of the roek/ he was so ferdful to loke on that his eyen glymmerd as fyre/ he brayed as lowde as a bulle in suche wise that alle the court quoke for feere/ at the laste he sayde cryeng/ by my crowne and by the trouthe that I owe to my wyf I shal so awreke and auenge this trespaces/ that it shal be longe spoken of after/ that my saufconduyt [e7v] and my commandement is thus broken I was ouer nyce that I beleuid so lyghtly the false shrewe/ his false flateryng speche deceyued me/ He tolde me he wolde go to rome/ and fro[1] thens ouer see to the holy londe/ I gaf hym male and palster and made of hym a pylgrym and mente al trouth/ O what false touches can he/ how can he stuffe the sleue wyth flockes/ but this caused my wyf/ it was al by her counseyl/ I am not the fyrst that haue ben deceyued by wymmens counseyl by whiche many a grete hurte hath byfallen/ I pray and comande alle them that holde of me and desire my frendship/ be

[1] for C

they here or wher someuer they be/ that they wyth theyr counseyl and dedes helpe me tauenge this ouer grete[1] trespaas/ that we and owris may abyde in honour and worship/ and this false theef in shame that he nomore trespace ayenst our saufgarde/ I wil my self[2] in my persone helpe therto al that I maye/

YSegrym the wulf and bruyn the bere herde wel the kynges wordes/ and hoped wel to be auengid on reynard the foxe but they durste not speke one word The kynge was so sore meuyd that none durste wel speke/ Atte laste the quene spak/ Sire pour dieu ne croyes mye toutes choses que on vous dye/ et ne Iures pas legierment/ A man of worship shold not lyghtly bileue/ ne swere gretly vnto the tyme he knewe the mater clerly. and also me ought by right here that other partye speke/ Ther ben many that complayne on other and ben in the defaute them self. **Audi alteram partem.** here that [e8] other partye/ I haue truly holden the foxe for good/ and vpon that/ that he mente no falshede/ I helped hym that I myghte but how someuer it cometh or gooth/ is he euyl or good/ me thynketh for your worship that ye shold not procede ayenst hym ouer hastely that were not good ne honeste/ For he may not escape fro you/ Ye maye prysone hym or flee hym/ he muste obeye your Iugement/ thenne saide fyrapel the lupaerd/ My lord me thynketh/ my lady here hath saide to you trouthe and gyuen yow good counseyl do ye wel and folowe her and take aduyse of your wyse counseyl/ And yf he be founden gylty in the trespaces that now to yow be shewd/ late hym be sore punysshid acordyng to[3] hys trespaces/ And yf he come not hyther/ er this feste be ended and excuse hym/ as he ought of right to doo/ thenne doo as the counseyl shal aduyse yow/ But and yf he were twyes as moche false and ylle as he/ is/ I wolde not counseylle that he sholde be done to more than right/ Isegrym the wulf saide sir fyrapal. all we agree to the same· as ferre as it pleseth my lord the kynge/ it can not be better. But though reynart were now here. and he cleryd hym of double so many playntes yet shold I brynge forth ayenst hym that he had forfayted his/ lyf. But I wyl now be stylle and saye not. by cause he is not presente and yet aboue alle this he hath tolde the kynge of certayn tresour lyeng in krekenpyt in hulsterlo. Ther was neuer lyed a greter lesyng. ther wyth he

[1] geete C [2] sell C [3] do C

hath vs alle begyled. and hath sore hyndred me and the bere. I dar leye my lyf theron that he sayd not therof a trewe worde. Now robbeth he and steleth vpon [e8v] the heth/ alle that gooth forth by his hows/ Neuertheles sir firapel what that pleseth the kynge and yow/ that muste wel be don/ But and yf he wolde haue comen hyther/ he myght haue ben here for he had knowleche by the kynges[1] messager/ The kynge sayde we wyl none otherwyse sende for hym/ but I commande alle them that owe me seruyse and wylle my honour and worshippe that they make them redy to the warre at the ende of vj dayes/ all them that ben archers and haue bowes/ gonnes bombardes horsemen/ and footemen that alle thise be redy to besiege maleperduys/ I shal destroye reynart the foxe/ yf I be a kynge[2]/ ye lordes and sires what saye ye hereto/ wille ye doo this wyth a good wyl/ And they sayd and cryed alle/ ye we lorde/ whan that ye wylle/ we shal alle goo with yow.

¶ How grymbert the dasse warned/ the foxe/ that the kynge was wroth with hym and wold slee hym capitulo ¶ .xxvj°.

Alle thise wordes herde grymbert the dasse whiche was his brother sone/ he was sory and angry yf it myght haue prouffyted he ranne thenne the hye way to maleperduys ward/ he spared nether busshe ne hawe/ but he hasted so sore that he swette/ he sorowed in hym self for reynart his rede eme/ and as he wente he saide to hym self Alas in what daunger be/ ye comen in/ where shal ye become shal I see you brought fro lyf to deth/ or elles exyled out of the lande/ truly I may be wel sorouful/ for ye be [f1] the heed of alle our lygnage/ ye be wyse of counseyl/ ye be redy to helpe your frendes whan they haue nede/ ye can so wel shewe your resons/ that where ye speke/ ye wynne all/ with suche maner wayllyng/ and pytous wordes cam grymbert to maleperduys/ And fonde reynart his eme there standyng/ whiche had goten two pygeons/ as they cam first[3] out of her neste to assaye yf they coude flee and bicause the fethers on her wyngis were to shorte/ they fylle doun to the ground/ And as reynart was gon out to seche his mete/ he espyed them and caught hem and was comen home with hem/ And whan he sawe grymbert comyng/ he taryed and said/ welcome my best beloued neuew that I knowe in al my kynrede/ ye haue ronne faste ye ben al

[1] kyn/| ges [2] akynge C [3] frrst C

be swette/ haue ye ony newe tydynges/ alas said he/ lyef eme it standeth euyl wyth yow/ ye haue loste both lyf and good/ the kynge hath sworn that he shal gyue you a shameful deth/ he hath commanded alle his folke withyn vj dayes for to be here/ Archers fotemen/ horsemen/ And peple in waynes· And he hath gunnes/ bombardes tentes and pauyllyons/ And also he hath do laaden torches/ See to fore yow/ For ye haue nede/ Ysegrym and bruyn ben better now wyth the kynge than I am wyth yow/ Alle that they wille/ Is doon/ Isegrym hath don hym to vnderstande that ye be a theef and a morderar· he hath grete enuye to yow. Lapreel the cony and Corbant the roek haue made a grete complaynt also. I sorow moche for your lyf. That for drede I am alle seke. Puf said the foxe/ dere neuew is ther nothyng ellis/ be ye so sore aferd [f1v] herof Make good chere hardely/ thaugh the kynge hym self and alle that ben in the court had sworn my deth/ yet shal I be exalted aboue them alle/ They maye alle faste Iangle clatre and yeue counseyl/ but the courte may not prospere wythoute[1] me and my wyles and subtylte

❡ How reynart the foxe cam another tyme to the courte capitulo ❡ .xxvij°.·

DEre neuew late alle thise thynges passe and come here in/ and see what I shal gyue you/ a good payre of fatte pygeons/ I loue no mete better/ They ben good to dygeste/ they may almost be swolowen in al hool the bones ben half blode/ I ete them wyth that other/ I fele my self other whyle encombred in my stomak therfore ete I gladly lyght mete. My wyf ermelyn shal receyue vs frendly/ but telle her nothyng of this thynge/ For she sholde take it ouer heuyly/ she is tendre of herte. she myght for fere falle in somme sekenes/ a lytyl thynge gooth sore to her herte/ And to morow erly I wil goo with yow to the courte/ And yf I may come to speche and may be herd/ I shal so ansuere/ that I shal touche somme nygh ynowh/ neuew wyl not ye stande by me/ as a frende ought to doo to another/ yes truly dere eme said grymbert my lyf[2] and alle my good is at your commandement/ god thanke you neuew said the foxe/ That is wel said. yf I may lyue I shal quyte it yow/ Eme said grymbert ye may wel come tofore alle the lordes and

[1] weythoute C [2] my lyf *omitted in* C

excuse yow ther shal none areste yow ne holde as longe as ye [f2] be in your wordes/ The quene and the lupaerd haue goten that/ then said the foxe/ therfor I am glad/ thenne I care[1] not for the beste of them an heer/ I shal wel saue my self/ they spake nomore herof/ but wente forth in to the burgh/ And fonde ermelyn there sittyng by her yonglyngs whiche aroose vp anon and receyuid them frendly/ Grymbert salewed his aunte and the chyldren wyth frendly wordes/ the ij pygeons were made redy for theyr soper/ Whiche reynard had taken/ eche of them toke his part as ferre as it wolde stratche/ yf eche of hem had had one more/ ther sholde but lytyl haue be[2] lefte ouer/ the foxe saide/ lief neuewe[3]/ how lyke/ ye my chyldren rosel and reynerdyn they shal do worship to alle our lygnage/ They begynne al redy to do wel/ that one catcheth wel a chyken and that other a pullet/ They· conne wel also duke in the water after lapwynches and dokys/ I wolde ofte sende them for prouande/ but I wil fyrste teche them how they shal kepe them fro the grynnes/ fro the hunters and fro the houndes/ yf they were so ferre comen that they were wyse/ I durste wel truste to them that they shold wel vytaylle vs in many good diuerses metes/ That we now lacke/ And they lyke and folowe me wel/ For they playe alle grymmyng and where they hate they loke frendly and meryly· For ther by they brynge them vnder their feet/ And byte the throte asondre/ This is the nature of the foxe/ They be swyfte in their takynge whiche pleseth me wel. [f2v]

EMe said grymbert ye may be glad that ye haue suche wyse chyldren/ And I am glad of them also by cause they be of my kynne/ Grymbert said the foxe ye haue swette and be wery it were hye tyde that ye were at your reste/ Eme yf it plese you it thynketh me good Tho laye they doun on a lytier made of strawe/ the foxe/ hys wyf and hys chyldren wente alle to slepe/ But the foxe was al heuy/ and laye. sighed and sorowed how he myght beste excuse hym self/ On the morow erly he ruymed his castel and wente with grymbart/ but he toke leue first of dame ermelyn his wyf and of his chyldren/ and sayde thynke not longe I muste goo to the court wyth grymbert my cosyn/ yf I tarye somwhat be not aferde/ and yf ye here ony ylle tydyngis/ take it alway for the beste. And see wel to your self and kepe our castel wel I shal doo yonder the beste

[1] car| re C [2] be *omitted in* C [3] nouewe C

I can after that I see how it gooth Alas reyner said she how haue ye now thus taken vpon yow for to go to the court agayn/ the last tyme that ye were there ye were in grete ieopardye of your lyf. And ye sayde ye wold neuer come there more. dame said the foxe. thauenture of the world is wonderly it goth otherwhyle by wenyng/ Many one weneth to haue a thing whiche he muste forgoo. I muste nedes now go thyder/ be content it is al wythoute drede/ I hope to come at alther lengest with in fyue dayes agayn/ Here wyth he departed and wente wyth grymbert to the court ward/ And whan they were vpon the heeth thenne sayde reyner/ Neuew syth I was laste shryuen I haue don many shrewde tornes/ I wolde ye wold here me now of alle that I haue [f3] trespaced in/ I made the bere to haue a grete wounde for the male whiche was cutte out of his skynne/ And also I made the wulf and his wyf to lese her shoon/ I peased the[1] kynge with grete lesyngis and bare hym on honde that the wulf and the bere wold haue betrayed hym and wolde haue slayn hym/ so I made the kynge right wroth with them· where they deseruyd it not/ also I tolde to the kynge that ther was grete tresour in hulsterlo of whiche he was neuer the better ne richer/ for I lyed al that I sayde/ I ledde bellyn the ramme and kywart the hare with me/ and slewe kyward and sente to the kynge by bellyn kywarts heed in skorn/ And I dowed the cony bytwene his eeris that almost I benamme his lyf from hym For he escaped ayenst my wyl/ he was to me ouerswyft/ The roeke may wel complayne/ for I swolowed in dame sharpbeck his wyf/ and also I haue forgoten on thyng the laste tyme that I was shreuen to you/ Which I haue syth bethought me/ And it was of grete deceyte that I dyde whiche I now wyll telle yow/ I cam wyth the wulf walkynge bytwene houthulst and eluerdynge/ There sawe we goo a rede mare/ And she had a black colte or a fool of iiij monethis olde/ which was good and fatte Isegrym was almost storuen for hunger/ And prayd me goo to the mare/ and wyte of her yf she wold selle her fool/ I ran faste to the mare/ And axed that of her/ she sayd she wold selle it for money/ I demaunded of her how she wold selle it/ she sayde it is wreton in my hyndre foot/ Yf ye conne rede and be a clerk ye may come see and rede it. Tho wyste I wel where she wold [f3v] be. and I saide nay for sothe I can not rede/ And also I desyre not to bye your chylde· Isegrym hath sente me hether. and wold fayn knowe the prys therof/ the mare

[1] the| the C

saide late hym come thenne hym self/ And I shal late hym haue knowleche/ I sayde/ I shal/ and hastely wente to ysegrym and saide/ eme wil ye ete your bely ful of this colte/ so goo faste to the mare for she taryeth after yow/ She hath do wryte the pris of her colte vnder her fote she wolde that I shold haue redde it/ but I can not one lettre/ whiche me sore repenteth/ For I wente neuer to scole/ eme wylle ye bye that colte/ conne ye rede so maye ye bye it/ oy neuew that can I wel what shold me lette/ I can wel frenshe latyn englissh and duche. I haue goon to scole at oxenford I haue also wyth olde and auncyent doctours ben in the audyence and herde plees/ and also haue gyuen sentence/ I am lycensyd in bothe lawes/ what maner wrytyng that ony man can deuyse/ I can rede it as perfyghtly as my name· I wyl goo to her and shal anon vnderstonde the prys/ and bad me to tarye for hym/ and he ranne to the mare/ and axed of her how she wold selle her fool or kepe it/ she sayde the somme of the money standeth wreton after on my fote he saide late me rede it/ she saide doo and lyfte vp her foot whiche was newe shood wyth yron and vj stronge nayles/ and she smote hym wythout myssyng on his heed that he fyl doun as he had ben deed/ a man shold wel haue ryden a myle er he aroos/ The mare trotted a way wyth her colte/ And she leet Isegrym lyeng shrewdly hurt and wounded He laye and bledde/ And howled as an hound/ I wente tho to hym and sayde/ [f4] Sir ysegrym dere eme how is it now wyth yow. haue ye eten ynowh of the colte. is your bely ful. why gyue ye me no part I dyde your erande. haue ye slepte your dyner I pray yow telle me what was wreton vnder the mares fote what was it. prose or ryme. metre or verse. I wold fayn knowe it. I trowe it was cantum. for I herde you synge me thoughte fro ferre. for ye were so wyse that noman coude rede it better than ye/ Alas reynart alas said the wulf I pray you to leue youre mockyng. I am so foule arayed and sore hurte. that an herte of stone myght haue pyte of me. The hore wyth her longe legge had an yron foot I wende the nayles therof had ben lettres/ and she hytte me at the fyrst stroke vj. grete woundes in my heed that almost it is clouen. suche maner lettres shal I neuer more desire to rede/

DEre eme is that trouthe that ye telle me/ I haue herof grete meruaylle/ I heelde you for one of the wysest clerkes that now lyue/ Now I here wel/ it is true that I long syth haue redde and herde/ that the beste clerkes/ ben not the wysest men/ the laye peple otherwhyle wexe wyse/ the cause that thise clerkes ben not the wysest/ is that they studye so moche in the connyng and science/ that they therin doole/ Thus brought I Isegrym in this grete laste and harme. That he vnneth byhelde his lyf/ Lyef neuew now haue I tolde you alle my synnes that I remembre. What so euer falle at the courte. I wote neuer how it shal stonde with me there. I am not now so sore aferd· For I am clere from synne [f4v] I wyl gladly come to mercy/ and receyue penance by your counseyl· grymbert sayde the trespaces ben grete/ neuertheles who that is deed muste abide deed. and therfore I wyl forgyue it you al togydre[1]/ With the fere that ye shal suffre therfore. er ye shal conne excuse you of the deth/ and hier vpon I wyl assoylle you. but the moste hyndre that ye shal haue shal be. that ye sente kywarts heed to the court And that ye blynded the kynge wyth suche[2] lyes/ Eme that was right euyl doon[3]/ The foxe sayde. what lyef neuew. Who that wyl goo thurgh the world this to here. and that to see/ and that other to telle. truly it may not clerly be done. how shold ony man handle hony. but yf he lycked his fyngres· I am oftymes rored and prycked in my conscience as to loue god aboue all thynge· and myn euen crysten as my self. as is to god wel acceptable. and acordyng to his lawe/ But how wene ye that reson wythin forth fyghteth ayenst the outeward wylle than stonde I alle stylle in my self that me thynketh I haue loste alle my wittes/ And wote not what me eyleth I am thenne in suche a thought/ I haue now alle lefte my synnes[4]/ And hate alle thynge that is not good/ and clymme in hye contemplacion[5] aboue his commandements but this specyal grace haue I whan I am alone/ But in a short whyle after whan the world cometh in me thenne fynde I in my waye so many stones/ and the fote spores that thyse loos prelates/ and riche preestys goo in/ that I am anone taken agayn/ thenne cometh the world and wyl haue this/ And the flesshe[6] wyl lyue plesantly/ whiche leye to fore me so many thinges that I thenne lose [f5] alle my good thoughtis and purpoos/ I here there synge pype/ lawhe/ playe/ and alle myrthe/ And I here that these prelates and riche curates preche and saye al other wyse/ than they thynke and doo/ There lerne I to lye/ the lesynges ben moste vsed in the lordes courtes certaynly lordes/ ladyes/ prestis and clerkes maken most lesyngis/ Men dar not telle to the lordes now the trouthe/ Ther is defaute/ I must flatre

[1] alto gydre C
[2] sutthe C
[3] euyldoon C
[4] symnes C
[5] comtemplacion C
[6] fhesshe C

and lye also/ or ellis I shold be shette wythout the dore/ I haue ofte herde men saye trouthe and rightfully/ and haue theyr reson made wyth a lesynge lyke to theyr purpose and brought it in and wente thurgh by cause their mater shold seme the fayrer/ The lesyng oftymes cometh vnauysed/ And falleth in the mater vnwetyngly/ And so whan she is wel cladde/ it goth forth thurgh with that other/

DEre neuew thus muste men now lye here/ and there saye soth flatre/ and menace/ praye· and curse/ And seke euery man vpon his feblest and wekest/ who otherwyse wylle now haunte and vse the world/ than deuyse a lesyng[1] in the fayrest wyse/ and that bywymple with kerchieuis aboute in suche wise that men take it for a trouthe/ he is not ronne away fro his maister/ Can he that subtylte in suche wise that he stamer not in his wordes/ and may thenne be herde/ neuew/ this man may doo wonder he may were skarlet and gryse/ he wynneth in the spyrituel lawe and temporal also and where sommeuer he hath to doo/ Now ben ther many false shrewis that haue grete enuye that they haue so grete fordele/ And [f5v] wene that they conne also wel lye/ And take on them to lye and to telle it forth/ he wolde fayn ete of the fatte morsellis. but he is not bileued ne herd/ And many ben ther that be so plompe and folisshe· that whan they wene beste to prononce and shewe their matere and conclude. They falle besyde and oute therof. And can not thenne helpe hem self/ and leue theyr mater wythout tayl or heed and he is a compted for a fool/ And many mocke them ther with/ but who can gyue to his lesynge a conclusion/ and prononce it without tatelyng lyke as it were wreton to fore hym/ and that he can so blynde the peple/ That his lesynge shal better be bileuid than the trouthe/ That is the man. What connyng is it to saye the trouth that is good to doo. How lawhe thise false subtyl shrewis that gyue counseyl to make thise lesynges. and sette them forth/ And maken vnright goo aboue right/ and make billes/ and/ sette in thynges that neuer were thought ne sayd/ and teche men see thurgh their fyngres And alle for to wynne money/ and late their tonges to hyre for to mayntene and strengthe their lesyngis alas neuewe this is an euyl connyng/ of whiche. lyf. scathe and hurte may come ther of/

[1] alesyng C

I Saye not but that otherwhyle men muste Iape/ bourde and lye in smale thyngis/ for who so sayth alway trouthe. he[1] may not now goo nowher thurgh the world. ther ben many that playe placebo. who so alleway sayth trouth. shal fynde many lettyngis in his way. Men may wel lye whan it is nede/ and after amende it [f6] by counseyl/ For alle trespaces/ ther is mercy. Ther is no man so wyse/ but he dooleth otherwhyle/ Grymbert sayde wel dere eme what thynge shal you lette. ye knowe al thyng at the narewest/ ye shulde brynge me hastely in dotyng your resons passen my vnderstandyng/ what nede haue ye to shryue you/ ye shulde your self by right be the preest/ And lete me and other sheep come to you for to be shryuen/ ye knowe the state of the world in suche wyse as noman may halte tofore you/ Wyth suche maner talkynge they cam walkyng in to the court/ The foxe sorowed somwhat in his herte/ Neuertheles he bare it out and stryked forth thurgh alle the folke til he cam in to the place where the kynge hym self was/ And grymbert was alway by the foxe and sayd eme be not a ferde. and make good chere/ who that is hardy/ thauenture helpeth hym/ Oftymes one day is better than somtyme an hole yere/ the foxe saide/ Neuew ye saye trouthe/ god thanke you ye comforte me wel/ And forth he wente and lokyd grymly here and there as who saith/ what wylle ye here come I/ he sawe there many of his kynne standyng whiche yonned hym but lytyl good/ as the otter beuer and other to the nombre of ·x. whome I shal. name afterward/ And somme were there that loued hym· The Foxe cam in and fyl doun on his knees to fore the kyng and began his wordes and sayde·

ℭ How reynart the foxe excused hym bifore the kynge capitulo ℭ .xxviij°. [f6v]

GOd fro whom nothyng may be hyd/ and aboue alle thyng is myghty saue my lord the kynge and my lady the quene and gyue hym grace to knowe who hath right and who hath wronge/ For ther lyue many in the world that seme otherwise outward than they be withinne/ I wolde[2] that god shewde openly euery mans mysdedes/ and alle theyr trespaces stoden wreton in theyr forehedes/ and it coste me more than I now saye/ And that ye my lord the kynge knewe as moche as/ I doo/ how I dispose me bothe erly

[1] be C [2] Iwolde C

and late in your seruyse/ And therfore am I complayned on of the euyl shrewys and wyth lesynges am put out of your grace and consayte/ and wold charge me with[1] grete offencis wythout deseruyng ayenst al right/ Wherfore I crye out harowe on them that so falsely haue belyed me/ and brought me in suche trouble/ how be it I hope and knowe you bothe my lord and my lady for so wyse and discrete/ that ye be not ledde nor bileue suche lesyngis ne false talis out of the right waye for ye haue not be woned so to doo/ Therfore dere lorde I biseche you to considre by your wysedom alle thynge by right and lawe/ is it in deede or in· speche/ do euery man right/ I desire no better he that is gylty and founde fawty late hym be punysshyd/ men shal wel knowe er I departe out of this courte/ who that I am/ I can[2] not flatre I wil allewey shewe openly my heed.

ℭ How the kynge answerd vpon reynarts excuse.

Alle they that were in the palays weren alle stylle and wondred that the foxe spack so stoutly/ the [f7] kynge sayde/ ha reynart how wel can ye your falacye and salutacion doon but your fayr wordes may not helpe you I thynke wel that ye shal this daye for your werkis be hanged by your necke/ I wil not moche chyde wyth you But I shal shorte your payne/ that ye loue vs wel/ that haue ye wel shewde on the cony and on corbant the roeck your falsenes/ and your false Inuencions shal without longe taryeng make you to deye/ A pot may goo so longe to water/ that at the laste it cometh to broken hoom/ I thynke your potte that so ofte hath deceyued vs/ shal now hastly be broken/ reynart was in grete fere of thise wordes· he wold wel. he had ben at coleyn/ whan he cam thedyr/ Thenne thought he I muste her thurgh/ how that I doo my lorde the kynge seyd he/ it were wel reson that ye herde my wordes alle out/ thaugh I were dampned to the deth/ yet ought ye to here my wordes out. I haue yet here to fore tyme gyuen to you many a good counseyl and prouffytable/ And in nede alwey haue byden by yow where other beestis haue wyked and goon theyr way/ yf now the euyl beestis with false maters haue to fore you wyth wronge belyed me/ and I myght not come to myn excuse/ ought I not thenne to playne/ I haue to fore this seen that I shold be herde by fore

[1] thith C [2] I an/ I cam C

another/ yet myght thise thyngis wel chaunge and come in theyr olde state/ Olde good dedes ought to be remembrid/ I see here many of my lygnage and frendes standyng that seme they sette now lytyl by me/ Whiche neuertheles sholde sore dere in theyr hertes. that ye my lord the kynge sholde destroye me wrongfully yf ye so dyde ye sholde destroye the [f7v] trewest seruaunt that ye haue in alle your landes/ what wene ye syr kynge/ hadde I knowen my self gylty in ony feat or broke. that I wold haue comen hether to the lawe emonge alle myne enemyes/ Nay sire nay/ not for alle the world of rede gold/ For I was fre and at large/ What nede had I to do that/ but god be thanked I knowe my self clere of alle mysdedes that I dar wel come openly in the lyghte and to answere to alle the complayntes that ony man can saye on me/ but whan grymbert brought me first thise tydyngis/ tho was I not wel plesed but half fro my self that I lepe here and there as an vnwyse man/ And had I not ben in the censures of the chyrche/ I had wythout taryeng haue comen/ but I wente dolynge on the heeth/ and wist not what to doo for sorowe/ And thenne it happed that mertyne myn eme the ape mette wyth me. Whiche is wyser in clergie than somme preest. he hath ben aduocate for the bysshop of cameryk ix yere duryng. he sawe me in this grete sorow and heuynes. and saide to me/ dere cosyn me thynketh ye ar not wel wyth your self/ what eyleth yow. who hath dysplesyd[1] yow. Thynge that toucheth[2] charge ought to be gyuen in knowleche to frendis. A triew frende is a grete helpe. he fyndeth ofte better counseyl than he that the charge resteth on. For who someuer is charged wyth maters is so heuy and acombred with them that ofte he can not begynne to fynde the remedye· For suche be so woo lyke as they had loste theyr Inwytte. I saide dere eme ye saye trouthe. For in lyke wyse is fallen to me. I am brought in to a grete heuynes vndeseruid and not [f8] gylty/ by one to whom I haue alway ben an herty and grete frende/ that is the cony whiche cam to me yesterday in the morenyng where as I satte to fore my hows and sayd matyns/ He tolde me he wolde goo to the court and salewed me frendly and I hym agayn/ Tho sayd he to me/ good reynard I am an hongred and am wery/ haue ye ony mete. I saide ye ynowh come nere· Tho gaf I hym a copel[3] of maynchettis with swete butter/ It was vpon a wednesday on whiche day I am not wonte to ete ony flessh/ And also I fasted by cause of this feste of whitsontyd

[1] dysplesyth C [2] thoucheth C [3] acopel C

whiche approuched/ For who that wylle taste of the ouerest wysehede/ and lyue goostly in kepyng the commandements[1] of our lord/ he muste faste and make hym redy ayenst the hye festes/ Et vos estote parati/ dere eme I gaf hym fayr whyte breed with swete butter/ wherwyth a man myght wel be easid that were moche hongry.·.

ANd whan he had eten his bely fulle/ tho cam russel my yongest sone/ and wold haue taken away that was lefte/ For yonge chyldren wold alway fayne eten/ And with that he tasted for to haue taken somwhat/ the cony smote russel to fore his mouthe that his teeth bledde/ and fyl doun half a swoun/ whan reynardyn myn eldest sone sawe that. he sprange to the cony and caught hym by the heed. and shold haue slayn hym. had I not reskowed hym I helpe hym that he wente from hym/ and bete my chylde sore therfore. lapreel the cony ran to my lord the kyng and saide I wold haue murdred hym/ [f8v] See eme thus come I in the wordes/ and I am leyde in the blame/ And yet he complayneth and I playne not/ After this cam corbant the roek fleyng wyth a sorouful noyse/ I asked what hym eyled. and he said alas my wyf is deed/ yonder lyeth a dede hare full of mathes and wormes/ and there she ete so moche therof. that the wormes haue byten a two her throte/ I axed hym how cometh that by/ he wold not speke a worde more but flewe his waye/ And lete me stande· Now saith he that I haue byten and slayn her/ how shold I come so nygh her/ for she fleeth/ and I goo a fote. beholde dere eme thus am I born an honde. I may saye wel that I am vnhappy/ But parauenture it is for myn olde synnes/ hit were good for me yf I coude paciently suffre it. The ape saide to me/ Neuew ye shal goo to the courte to fore the lordes and excuse yow/ alas eme that may not be. For the archedeken hath put me in the popes curse/ by cause I counseylled ysegrym the wulf for to leue his religyon at elmare and forsake his habyte/ he complayned to me that he lyuyd so straytly as in longe fastyng and many thyngis redyng and syngyng that he coude not endure it· Yf he shold longe abyde there he shold deye. I had pyte of his complaynyng/ And I helpe hym as a trewe frende that he cam oute. Whiche now me sore repenteth. for he laboureth al that he can ayenst me to the kynge for to do me be hanged.[2] thus doth he euyl for good. See eme thus am I at the ende of al my wyttes and of

[1] commandemts C [2] behanged C

counseyl. For I muste goo to rome for an absolucion. And thenne shal my wyf and chyldren suffre moche harme and blame. For thise euyl [g1] bestis that hate me/ shulle do to hem alle the hurte they maye and fordryue them wher they can/ And I wold wel defende hem yf I were fre of the curse/ for thenne wold I goo to the court and excuse me/ where now I dar not/ I shold do grete synne yf I cam emonge the good peple/ I am aferde god sholde plaghe me. Nay cosyn be not aferd· er I shold suffre you in this sorow I knowe the way to rome wel. I vnderstande me on this werke. I am called ther mertyne the bisshops clerke. and am wel byknowen there. I shal do syte the archedeken and take a plee ayenst hym. and shal brynge with me for you an absolucion ayenst his wil/ for I knowe there alle that is for to be doon or lefte there dwelleth symon myn eme whiche is grete and myghty ther. who that may gyue ought/ he helpeth hym anon/ ther is prentout· wayte scathe/ and other/ of my frendis and alyes Also I shal take somme money with me/ yf I nede ony. the preyer is wyth yeftes hardy. wyth money alleway the right goth forth. A trewe frende shal for his frende auenture both lyf and good/ and so shal I for you in your right

COsyn make good chere I shal not reste after to morow til I come to rome/ and I shal solycyte your maters/ And goo ye to the court as sone as ye may/ all your mysdedes/ and tho synnes that haue brought you in the grete sentence and curse/ I make you quyte of them and take them in my self/ whan ye come to the court ye shal fynde there rukenawe my wyf/ her two susters and my thre chyldren and many mo of our lignage/ dere cosyn speke to [g1v] them hardely/ my wyf his sondrely wyse/ and wil gladly do somme what for her frendis/ who that hath nede of helpe shal fynde on her grete frendship/ one shal alway seke on his frendis/ thaugh he haue angred them/ for blood muste krepe/ where it can not goo/ And yf so be that ye be so ouer chargyd that ye may haue no right/ thenne sende to me by nyght and day to the court of rome/ and late me haue knowleche therof/ and alle tho that ben in the lande is it kynge or quene/ wyf or man I shall brynge them alle in the popes curse/ and sende there an Interdicte[1] that noman shal rede ne syngen ne crystene chyldren/ ne burye the deede ne receyue sacramente/ tyl that ye shal haue good ryght/ Cosyn this shal I wel gete/ for the pope is so sore old that he is but lytil sette by/ And

[1] Inderdicte C

the cardynal of pure gold hath alle the myght of the court/ he is yonge and grete of frendis he hath a concubyne/ whom he moche loueth/ And what she desyreth that geteth she anone/ see cosyn/ she is myn nece/ and I am grete and may doo moche with her in suche wyse/ what I desyre/ I faylle not of it/ but am alway furtherd therin/ wherfore cosyn byd my lord the kyng that he doo you right/ I wote wel he wil not warne you/ for the right is heuy ynough to euery man/ my lord the kyng whan I herde this I lawhed/ and wyth grete gladnes cam hether and haue told you alle[1] trouthe/ yf ther be ony in this court that can leye on me ony other mater wyth good witnesse and preue it as ought to be to a noble man/ late me thenne make amendes acordyng to the lawe/ and yf he wil not leue of herbi/ thenne sette me day and feld and I shal make good on hym also ferre as he be of as good birthe as i am and to [g2] me lyke/ and who that can wyth fyghtyng gete the worship of the felde/ late hym haue it/ this right hath standen yet hetherto. And I wil not it sholde be broken by me. the lawe and right doth noman wrong/ alle the beestis both poure and riche were alle stylle whan[2] the foxe spak so stoutly/ the cony laprel and the roek were so sore aferde that they durste not speke· but pyked and stryked them out of the court bothe two. and whan they were a room fer in the playne they saide. god graunte that this felle murderare may fare euyl. he can bywrappe and couere his falshede. that his wordes seme as trewe as the gospel herof knoweth noman than we. how shold we brynge wytnesse. it is better that we wyke and departe· than we sholde holde a felde and fyghte with hym· he is so shrewde. ye thaugh ther of vs were fyue we coude not defende vs. but that he shold sle vs alle.

Isegrym the wulf and bruyn the bere/ were woo in hem self whan they sawe thise tweyne rume the court/ The kinge sayde/ yf ony man wil complayne late hym come forth/ and we shal here hym· yesterday camen here so many where ben they now Reynart is here/ The foxe saide. my lord ther ben many that complayne/ that and yf they sawe their aduersarye they wold be stylle and make no playnte/ witnes now of laprel the cony and Corbant the roek/ whiche haue complayned on me to yow in my absence/ but now that I am comen in your presence they flee away/ And dar not abyde by theyr wordes/ yf men shold byleue false shrewes/ it shold

[1] all e C [2] wban C

do moche harme and hurte to the good men/ as for me it skylleth not [g2ᵛ] Neuertheles my lord yf they had by your commandement[1] axed of me forgyfnes/ how be it they haue gretly trespaced/ yet I had for your sake pardoned and forgyue them/ for I wil not be out of charyte/ ne hate ne complayne on myne enemyes/ but I sette alle thyng in goddes hand he shal wreke[2] and auenge it as it plesyth hym.

THe kynge sayde reynart/ me thynketh ye be greuyd as ye saye/ ar ye withinforth as ye seme outward/ Nay it is not so cleer ne so open nowher nyghe/ as ye here haue shewed/ I muste saye what my gryef is/ whiche towcheth your worship and lyf/ that is to wete/ that ye haue don a foule and shameful trespaas/ whan I had pardonned you alle your offencis and trespacis/ and ye promysed to goo ouer the see on pylgremage/ And gaf to you male and staf/ And after this ye sente me by bellyn the ramme the male agayn and theryn Kywarts heed/ how myght[3] ye do a more[4] reprouable trespaas/ how were ye so hardy to dore to me doo suche a shame/ is it not euyl don to sende to a lorde/ his seruaunts heed/ ye can not saye nay here agaynst for bellyn the ram whiche was our chapelayn tolde vs al the mater how it happed/ suche reward as he had whan he brought vs the message/ the same shal ye haue or right shal faylle/ tho was reynart so[5] sore aferd that he wist not what to saye/ he was at his wittes ende/ and loked aboute hym pytously and sawe many of his kyn and alyes that herde alle this but nought they saide/ he was al pale in his visage but noman proferd hym hand ne fote to helpe hym/ the kinge said thou subtyl felaw and fals shrewe why spekest thou not [g3] art thow[6] now dombe/ The foxe stode in grete drede and syghed sore that alle herde hym/ But the wulf and the bere were glad herof.

ℭ How dame rukenawe answerd for the foxe to the kynge. capitulo ℭ xxix°.

DAme rukenawe the she ape reynarts aunte was not wel plesyd/ She was grete wyth the quene and wel belouyd/ hit happed wel for the foxe that she was there. For she vnderstood alle wysedom/ And she durste wel speke/ where as it to doo was/ where euer she cam euerich was glad of her/ she sayde my lord the kyng ye

[1] commandeent C [2] werke C [3] iuyght C
[4] amore C [5] fo C [6] art thow *omitted in* C

ought not to be angry whan ye sytte in Iugement/ For that becometh not your noblesse· A man that sytteth in Iugement ought to put fro hym alle wrath and angre/ A lorde ought to haue dyscrescion that shold sytte in Iustyse/ I knowe better the poyntes of the lawe/ than somme that were furryd gownes/ For I haue lerned many of them/ and was made connyng in the lawe/ I had in the popes palays of woerden a good bedde of heye/ where other beestes laye on the harde grounde and also whan I had there to doo/ I was suffred to speke/ and was herd to fore another/ by cause I knewe so wel the lawe/ Seneca wryteth that a lorde shal oueral doo right and lawe/ he shal charge none to whom he hath gyuen his saufgarde to aboue the right and lawe/ the lawe ought not to halte for noman/ And euery man that stondeth here wolde wel bethynke hym what he hath doon and bydryuen in his dayes he shold the better haue pacience and pyte on Reynart/ late euery man knowe hym self/ that is my counseyl/ ther is none that stondeth so [g3v] surely/ but otherwhyle he falleth or slydeth/ who that neuer mysdede ne synned/ is holy and good and hath no nede to amende hym/ whan a man doth amys/ and thenne by counseyl amendeth it/ that is humaynly/ and so ought he to doo/ but alway to mysdo and trespace/ and not to amende hym/ that ys euyl and a deuely lyf/ Merke thenne what is wreton in the gospel Estote misericordes/ be ye mercyful yet standeth ther more/ Nolite iudicare/ et non iudicabimini/ deme ye noman/ and ye shal not be demed/ Ther standeth also how the pharisees brought a woman[1] taken in aduoultrye and wold haue stoned her to deth/ they axed our lord what he said therto/ he said who of yow alle is withoute synne/ late hym caste the fyrst stone/ tho abode noman but lefte her there stondyng

ME thynketh it is so hyere/ ther be many that see a strawe in an others ye/ that can not see a balke in his owne/ ther be many that deme other/ and hym self is worst of alle/ thaugh one falle ofte/ and at laste aryseth vp and cometh to mercy/ he is not therof dampned God receyueth alle them that desyre hys mercy late noman condampne another/ though they wyste that he had don amys/ yet late them see theyr owne defawtes/ and thenne may they them self correcte fyrst/ and thenne reynert my cosyn shold not fare the werse for his fadre and his graunfadre/ haue alway

[1] awoman C

ben in more loue and reputacion in this court than Isegrym the wulf or bruyn the bere with al theyr frendis and lignage/ hit hath ben here to fore an vnlyke comparison/ the wysedom of Reynart my cosyn/ and [g4] the honour and worsship of hym that he hath doon and the counseyl of them/ For they knowe not how the world gooth/ me thynketh this court is al torned vp so doon/ Thise false shrewes flaterers and deceyuours arise and wexe grete by the lordes and ben enhaunsed vp/ And the good triewe and wyse ben put doun/ For they haue ben woned to counseylle truly and for thonour of the kyng I can not see how this may stonde longe/ Thenne said the kynge/ dame yf he had don to yow suche trespaas as he hath don to other it shold repente yow· Is it wonder that I hate hym/ he breketh alway my saufgarde/ haue ye not herde the complayntes that here haue ben shewde of hym of murdre/ of theefte/ And of treson/ haue ye suche trust in hym/ Thynke ye that he is thus good and cleer/ thenne sette hym vp on the awter and worshipe and praye to hym as to a saynte[1]/ But ther is none in alle the world that can saye ony good of hym/ ye maye saye moche for hym/ but in thende ye shal fynde hym al nought/ he hath nether kyn ne wyn ne frende that wylle entreprise to helpe hym he hath so deseruyd/ I haue grete meruaylle of yow/ I herde neuer of none that hath felawsshippid with hym that euer thanked hym or saide ony good of hym/ sauf you now/ but alway he hath stryked hem with his tayl/ the she ape ansuerd and said/ my lord I loue hym and haue hym in grete chierte/ And also I knowe a good dede that he ones in your presence dyde/ wherof ye coude hym grete thanke/ though now it be thus torned/ yet shal the heuyest/ weye moste/ a man shal loue his frende by mesure/ and not his enemye hate ouermoche/ stedfastnes and constaunce is syttyng and behoueth [g4ᵛ] to the lordes. how someuer[2] the world torneth. Me ought not preyse to moche the daye. tyl euen be come. good counseyl is good for hym that wil doo ther after.

ℂ A parable of a man[3] that delyuerd a serpent fro peryl of deth. capitulo ℂ xxx°.

NOw two yere passid cam a man and a serpent[4] here in to this court for to haue Iugement. whiche was to yow and youres right doubteful. The serpent stode in an hedche where as he

[1] asaynte C [2] someūer C [3] aman C [4] serpent-| C

supposed to haue gon thorugh/ but he was caught in a snare by the necke. that he myght not escape without helpe but shuld haue lost his lyf there. the man cam forth by. and the serpente called to hym and cryde. and prayd the man that he wolde helpe hym out of the snare. or ellis he muste there dye:

THe man had pyte of hym and saide/ yf thou promyse to me that thou wilt not enuenyme me ne do me none harme ne hurte I shal helpe the out of this peryl/ The serpente was redy and swore a grete othe that he now ne neuer sholde doo hym harme ne hurte· Thenne he vnlosed hym and delyuerd hym out of the snare/ And wente forth to gydre a good whyle/ that the serpente had grete hongre for he had not eten a grete while to fore. and sterte to the man and wold haue slayn hym. the man sterte awaye and was a ferde and said/ wilte thou now sle me/ hast thou forgoten the oth that thou madest to me that thou sholdest not mysdoo ne hurte me [g5] The serpent answerd I maye doo it good/ to fore al the world that I doo/ the nede of hongre may cause a man to breke his oth/ The man saide yf it may be not bettre/ gyue me so longe respyte tyl we mete and fynde that may Iuge the mater by right/ The serpente graunted therto/ thus they wente to gydre so longe that they fonde tyselyn the rauen/ And slyndpere his sone/ there rehersed they theyr resons/ Tiselyn the rauen Iuged anon that he shold ete the man/ he wolde fayn haue eten his parte and his sone also/ The serpent said to the man/ how is it now/ what thynke ye haue I not wonne/ The man saide/ how sholde a robber Iuge this he shold haue auayle therby/ and also he is allone/ ther muste be two or thre atte leste to gydre and that they vnderstande the right and lawe and that don/ late the sentence gon/ I am neuertheles yl on ynough/ They a greed and wente forth bothe to gydre so longe that they fonde the beer and the wulf to whom they tolde theyr mater/ And they anon Iuged that the serpent shold sle the man/ For the nede of hongre breketh oth alway/ the man thenne was in grete doubte and fere/ and the serpent cam and cast his venym at hym/ but the man lepe a way from hym with grete payne/ And said ye doo grete wronge that ye thus lye in a wayte to slee me/ ye haue no right therto/ The serpent sayde/ Is it not ynough yet/ hit hath ben twyes Iuged/ ye sayd the man that is of them that ben wonte to murdre and robbe/ Alle that euer they swere and promyse they holde not/ but I appele this mater in to the court to fore our lord the kyng/ And that thou mayst not forsake/ [g5v] And what Iugement that shal be gyuen there/ I shal obeye and suffre/ and neuer doo the contrarye.

THe bere and the wulf sayden that it shold be so/ And that the serpent desired no better/ They supposed yf it shold come to fore yow/ It shold goo there as they wolde. I trowe ye be wel remembrid herof· Tho cam they alle to the court to fore yow/ And the wulues two chyldren cam with theyr fader. Whiche were callyd empty bely and neuer full/ by cause they wold ete of the man. For they howlyd for grete hongre wherfore ye commaunded them to auoyde your court/ The man stode in grete drede/ and called vpon your good grace and tolde how the serpente wolde haue taken his lyf from hym to whom he had sauyd his lyf and that aboue his oth and promyse he wold haue deuoured hym/ The serpente answerd I haue not trespaced/ And that I reporte me hoolly vnto[1] the kyng/ For I dyde it to saue my lyf/ For nede of lyf/ one may breke his oth and promyse/ My lord that tyme were ye and alle your counseyl here wyth acombryd For your noble grace sawe the grete sorow of the man/ And ye wold not that the man shold for his gentilnes and kyndenes be Iuged to deth/ And on that other side[2] hongre and nede to saue the lyf seketh narowly to be holpen/ hier was none in al the court that coude ne knewe the right hierof/ Ther were somme that wolde fayn the man had be holpen/ I see them hier stondyng/ I wote wel they sayde that they coude not ende this mater/ Thenne commanded ye that reynard my neuew [g6] shold come and saye his aduys in this mater/ that tyme was he aboue alle other byleuyd and herd in the court/ And ye bad hym gyue sentence acordyng to the best right/ and we alle shal folowe hym/ For he knewe the grounde of the lawe/ reynard said my lord/ it is not possyble to[3] yeue a trewe sentence after theyr wordes/ for in here sayeng ben ofte lesynges/ But and yf I myght see the serpent in the same paryl and nede that he was in whan the man loosed hym and vnbounde/ Thenne wyste I wel what I shold saye/ And who that wolde doo otherwise he shold mysdoo agayn right/ Thenne sayd ye my lord reynard that is wel said we alle· acorde herto/ For noman can saye better/ Thenne wente the man and the serpent in to the place wher as he fonde the serpente/ Reynart bad that the serpent shold be sette in the snare in lyke wyse as he was/ And

[1] vn C [2] sith C [3] te C

it was don/ Thenne sayd ye my lord/ reynart how thynketh yow now/ what Iugement shal we gyue. Thenne said reynart the foxe. My lord now ben they bothe lyke as they were to fore. they haue neyther wonne ne loste See my lord how I Iuge for a right also ferre as it shal plese your noble grace. yf the man wil now lose and vnbynde the serpent vpon the promyse and oth. that he to fore made to hym. he may wel doo it. But yf he thynke that he for ony thyng shold be emcombryd or hyndred by the serpent. or for nede of hongre wold breke his oth and promyse. Thenne Iuge I that the man may goo frely where he wyl. and late the serpente abyde stylle bounden. lyke as he myght haue don at the begynnyng. For he[1] wold haue broken his oth and [g6v] promyse/ where as he helpe hym out of suche fereful peryl/ Thus thynketh me a ryghtful Iugement that the man shal haue his fre choys/ lyke as he to fore hadde.

LO my lord this Iugement thought[2] yow good/ and alle your counseyl whiche at that tyme were by you/ and folewed the same/ And preysed reynardis wysedom that he had made the man quyte and free/ Thus the foxe wysely kepte your noble honour and worship/ as a triewe seruaunt is bounde to doo to his lord/ wher hath the beer or the wulf don euer to yow so moche worship They conne wel huylen and blasen stele and robbe/ and ete fatte morsellis and fylle theyr belyes/ And thenne Iuge they for right and lawe that smale theuis that stele hennys and chekyns shold be hanged/ But they hem self that stelen kyen oxen and horses/ they shal goo quyte and be lordes/ And seme as though they were wyser than salamon/ Auycene or aristotiles/ And eche wil be holden hye proud/ and preised of grete dedes and hardy But and they come where as it is to doo/ they ben the firste that flee/ Thenne muste the symple goo forth to fore/ And they kepe the rereward behynde/ Och my lorde these and other lyke to them be not wyse/ but they destroye towne. castel. lande and peple. They retche not whos hows brenneth. so that they may warme them by the coles They seke alle theyr owne auayll and synguler proffyte/ But Reynart the foxe and alle his frendis and lygnage sorowen and thynke to preferre the honour worship. fordeel and proffyte of theyr lord. and for wise counseyl [g7] whiche ofte more prouffyteth here than pryde and boost/ This doth reynard/ thaugh he haue no thanke/ Atte

[1] fforhe C [2] thougt C

longe it shal be wel knowen/ who is beste and doth moste prouffyt/ My lord ye saye/ that his kynne and lignage drawe al afterward from hym/ and stonde not by hym/ for his falshede and deceyuable and subtyl touchis/ I wolde an other had sayde that/ ther sholde thenne suche wrake be taken therof/ that hym myght growle that euer he sawe hym/ But my lorde we wyl forbere you/ ye maye saye your playsir/ and also I saye it not by yow/ Were ther ony that wolde bedryue ony thyng ayenst yow with wordes or with werkes/ hym wold we soo doo to/ that men shold saye we had ben there/ Ther as fyghtyng is/ we ben not woned to be aferd· My lorde by your leue I may wel gyue you knoweleche of reynardis frendis and kynne. ther ben many of them that for his sake and loue wille auenture lyf and good. I know my self for one. I am a wyf. I shold yf he had nede sette my lyf and good for hym also I haue thre ful waxen children which ben hardy and stronge/ whom I wold alle to gydre auenture for his loue. rather than I shold see hym destroyed/ yet had I leuer dye than I sawe them myscarye to fore myn eyen. so wel loue I hym.

¶ Whiche ben frendes and kynne vnto Reynard the foxe. capitulo ¶ xxxj°.

THe fyrste chylde is named byteluys. whiche is moche cherysshyd and can make moche sporte and [g7v] game/ wherfore is gyuen to hym the fatte trenchours and moche other good mete whiche cometh wel to prouffyt of fulrompe hys brother/ and also my thyrde chylde is a doughter and is named hatenette/ she can wel pyke out lyse and netis out of mens heedis/ thise thre ben to eche other tryewe/ wherfor I loue them wel/ dame rukenawe called hem forth and sayde/ welcome my dere chyldren come forth and stande by reynard your dere neuew/ Thenne sayd she/ Come forth alle ye that ben of my kynne and reynarts/ and late us praye the kynge that he wille doo to reynart ryght of the lande/ Tho cam forth many a beest anon/ as the squyrel/ the musehont/ the fychews/ the martron/ the beuer wyth his wyf ordegale/ the genete/ the ostrole/ the bonssyng/ and the fyret/ thyse tweyne ete as fayne polayl as doth reynart/ The oter and pantecroet his wyf whom I had almoste forgoten/ yet were they to fore wyth the beuer enemyes to the foxe/ but they durst not gaynsaye dame rukenawe/ for they were aferd of her She was also the wysest of al his kynne of counseyl and was moste doubted/ Ther cam also mo than xx other by cause of her for to stande by Reynard[1]/ Ther cam also dame atrote with her ij sustres/ the wesel/ and hermell the asse. the backe/ The watreratte and many moo to the nombre of xl/ whiche alle camen and stoden by reynard the foxe/

MY lord the kyng saide rukenauwe come and see hier yf reynart haue ony frendis/ here may ye see/ we ben your trewe subgettis whiche For yow wold [g8] auenture both lyf and good yf ye had nede/ Though ye be hardy myghty and stronge/ Oure welwyllyd frendship can not hurte you/ late reynard the foxe wel bethynke hym vpon thise maters that ye haue leyd ayenst hym/ And yf he can not excuse hym/ thenne doo hym right we desire no better/ And this by right ought to noman be warned/ The quene thenne spack. this saide I to hym yesterday/ But he was so fyers and angry that he wold not here it. the lupaerd saide also. Syre ye may Iuge no ferther than your men gyue theyr verdyte. For yf ye wold goo forth by wyl and myghte that were not worshipful For your estate here allewaye bothe partyes and thenne by the beste and wysest counseyl gyue Iugement discretly acordyng to the beste right. the kynge saide. this is al trewe· but I was so sore meuyd whan I was enformed of kywarts deth and sawe his heed. that I was hoot and hasty. I shal here the foxe. can he answere and excuse hym of that is leyd ayenst hym. I shal gladly late hym goo quyte. And also atte requeste of his good frendis and kynne. Reynart was glad of thise wordis. and thoughte god thanke myn aunte· She hath the rys doo blosme agayn[2]· She hath wel holpen me forth now. I haue now a good foot to daunse on. I shal now loke out of myne eyen. And brynge forth the fayrest lesyngis that euer man herde. and brynge my self out of this daunger.

¶ How the foxe wyth subtylte excused hym for the deth of kywart the hare and of alle other maters that were leyde ayenst hym and how wyth Flateryng [g8v] gate agayn his pees of the kynge. capitulo ¶ xxxij°.

Thenne spak reynart the foxe and saide/ Alas what saye ye is kywart deed/ and where is bellyn the ramme/ what brought he to yow/ whan he cam agayn/ For I delyuerd to hym thre

[1] Rynard C [2] a-| agayn C

iewellis/ I wold fayn knowe where they ben be comen/ That one of hem shold he haue gyuen to yow my lord the kyng/ And the other ij to my lady the quene/ The kynge saide/ bellyn brought vs nought ellis but kywarts heed/ lyke as I saide you to fore/ wherof I toke on hym wrake/ I made hym to lose his lyf/ For the foule kaytyf said to me/ that he hym self was of the counseyl of the lettres makyng that were in the male/ Alas my lord is this very trouthe/ woo to me kaytyf that euer I was born sith that thise good Iewellis be thus lost myn herte wil breke for sorowe/ I am sory that I now lyue/ what shal my wyf saie whan she hereth herof/ she shal goo out of her wytte for sorow/ I shal neuer also longe as I lyue haue her frendship she shal make moche sorowe whan she hereth therof/ The she ape saide Reynard dere neuew/ what prouffyteth that ye make al this sorowe late it passe/ And telle vs what thise Iewellis were/ parauenture we shalle fynde counseyl to haue them agayn yf they be aboue erthe Mayster akeryn shal laboure for them in his bookis/ and also we shal curse for them in alle chirchys vnto the tyme that we haue knowleche wher they been/ They maye not be loste/ Nay aunte thynke not that/ For they that [hi] haue them wyl not lightly departe fro them. ther was neuer kynge that euer gaf so riche Iewellis as thise be/ Neuertheles ye haue somwhat wyth your wordes easyd myn herte and made it lighter than it was/ Alas loo here ye may see how he or they to whome[1] a man trusteth moost is ofte by hym or them deceyuyd/ thaugh I shold goo al the world thorugh and my lyf in auenture sette therfore/ I shal wyte wher thise Iewellis ben becomen.

WYth a dissymylyd and sorouful speche saide the foxe herken ye alle my kynne and frendys/ I shal name to yow/ thise Iewellis what they were/ And thenne may ye saye that I haue a grete losse/ that one of them was a rynge of fyn gold/ and within the rynge next the fyngre were wreton lettres enameld with sable and asure and ther were thre hebrews names therin/ I coude not my self rede ne spelle them/ for I vnderstonde not that langage/ but maister abrion of tryer he is a wyse man/ he vnderstandeth wel al maner of langages and the vertue of al maner herbes/ and ther is no beest so fiers ne stronge but he can dompte hym/ for yf he see hym ones he shal doo as hee wyl/ And yet he bileueth not

[1] whōme C

on god/ He is a Iewe/ The wysest in connyng and specially he knoweth the vertue of stones. I shewde hym ones this rynge/ he saide that they were tho thre names that seth brought out of paradys whan he brought to his fadre Adam the oyle of mercy/ And who someuer bereth on hym thise thre names/ he shal neuer be hurte by thondre ne lyghtnyng· ne no witchecraft shal haue power ouer hym [h1v] ne be tempted to doo synne/ And also he shal neuer take harm by colde/ thaugh he laye thre wynters longe nyghtis in the feelde/ thaugh it snowed stormed or frore neuer so sore/ so grete myght haue thise wordes/ wytnes of maister abrion/ withought forth on the rynge stode a stone of thre maner colours/ the one part was lyke rede cristalle/ and shoon lyke as fyre had ben therin/ in suche wyse that yf one wold goo by nyght/ hym behoued non other lighte for the shynyng of the stone made and gaf as grete[1] a light as it had ben mydday/ That other parte of the stone was whyte and clere as it had ben burnysshid/ Who so had in his eyen ony smarte or sorenes/ or in his body ony swellyng/ or heed ache/ or ony sykenes withoutforth yf he stryked this stone on the place wher the gryef is/ he shal anon be hole/ or yf ony man be seke in his body of venym/ or ylle mete in his stomack/ of colyk/ stranguyllyon/ stone/ fystel or kanker or ony other sekenes/ sauf only the very deth late hym leye this stone in a litle watre/ And late hym drynke it/ and he shal forthwyth be hole and al quyte of his seknessis/ Alas said the foxe we haue good cause to be sory to lese suche a Iewel/ Forthermore the thirde colour was grene lyke glas/ But ther were somme sprynklis therin lyke purpure/ the maister told for trouthe/ that who that bare this stone vpon hym shold neuer be hurte of his enemye/ and that noman were he neuer so stronge and hardy that myght mysdoo hym/ and where euer that he fought he shold haue vyctorye were it by nyght or by daye also ferre as he behelde it fastyng/ and also therto where someuer he wente and in what felawship/ he shold be bylouyd/ though they hadde [h2] hated hym to fore/ yf he had the ring vpon hym/ they shold forgete theyr angre as sone as they sawe hym/ Also though he were al naked in a felde agayn an hondred armed men/ he shold be wel herted and escape fro them with worship/ but he muste be a noble gentle man/ and haue no chorles condicions/ For thenne the stone had no/ myght and by cause this stone was so precious and good/ I thought in my self that I was not able ne

[1] gretr C

worthy to bere it/ and there fore i sente it to my dere lord the kyng/ for i knowe hym for the most noble that now lyueth/ and also alle our welfare and worship lyeth on hym/ and for he shold be kepte fro alle drede nede and vngheluck.

I Fonde this rynge in my fadres tresour/ and in the same place I toke a glasse or a mirrour and a combe[1] whiche my wyf wold algates haue/ a man myght wondre that sawe thise Iewellis/ I sente thyse to my lady the quene/ for I haue founden her good and gracious to me/ this Combe myght not be to moche preysed/ Hit was made of the bone of a clene noble beest named Panthera/ whiche fedeth hym bytwene the grete Inde and erthly paradyse/ he is so lusty fayr and of colour/ that ther is no colour vnder the heuen/ but somme lyknes is in hym/ therto he smelleth so swete/ that the sauour of hym boteth alle syknessis and for his beaute and swete smellyng all other beestis folowe hym/ for by his swete sauour they ben heled of alle syknessis/ this panthera hath a fair boon brode and thynne/ whan so is that this beeste is slayn al the swete odour restith[2] in the bone whiche can not be broken ne shal neuer [h2v] rote ne be destroyed by fyre/ by water/ ne by smytyng/ hit is so hard tyht and faste/ and yet it is lyght of weyght/ The swete odour of it hath grete myght/ that who that smelleth it sette nought by none other luste in the world and is easyd and quyte of alle maner diseases and Infirmytes/ And also he is ioconde and glad in his herte/ this combe is polysshid as it were fyne syluer/ and the teeth of it ben smal and straite/ And bytwen the gretter teeth and the smaller is a large felde and space where is coruen many an ymage subtilly[3] made and enameld aboute with fyn gold/ the felde is checked with sable and siluer/ enameld with cybore and asure/ And ther in is thistorye how venus Iuno and pallas strof for thapple of gold/ whiche eche of them wold haue had/ whiche contrauersye was sette vpon parys/ that he shold gyue it to the fayrest of them thre.

PArys was that tyme an herde man and kepte his faders beestis and sheep without troye/ whan he had resceyuid thapple/ Iuno promysyd to hym yf he wolde Iuge that she myght haue thapple/ he shold haue the moste richesse of the world/ pallas said yf she

[1] acombe C [2] restid C [3] subtlly C

myght haue thapple she wold gyue hym wysedom and strengthe and make hym so grete a lorde that he shold ouercome alle his enemyes/ and whom he wold/ venus saide what nedest thou richesse or strengthe/ art not thou pryamus sone/ and hector is thy brother whiche haue al asye vnder their power/ art not thou one of the possessours of grete troye/ yf thou wylt gyue to me thapple i shal gyue the the richest tresour of the world and that shal be the fayrest woman that euer had lyf on erthe/ ne neuer shal none be born fairer than she/ thenne shal thou be richer [h3] than riche/ And shal clymme aboue al other/ For that is the tresour that noman can preyse ynough/ for honest/ fair and good women can put a way many a sorow fro the herte/ they be shamefast and wyse/ and brynge a man in very Ioye and blysse/ Parys herde this venus whiche presented hym this grete Ioye and fayr lady and prayd her to name this fayr lady/ that was so fair and where she was/ venus saide it is helene kynge menelaus wyf of grece/ ther lyueth not a nobler[1]. richer. gentiller. ne wyser wyf in al the world/ Thenne parys gaf to her thapple and said that she was fayrest/ how that he gate afterward helene by the helpe of venus and how he brought her in to troye and wedded her/ the grete loue and ioly lyf that they had to gydre/ was al coruen in the felde euery thyng by hym self/ and the storye wreton.

NOw ye shal here of the mirrour/ the glas that stode theron was of suche vertu that men myght see therin/ all that was don within a myle/ of men of beestis and of al thynge that me wold desire to wyte and knowe/ and what man loked in the glasse had he ony dissease/ of prickyng or motes/ smarte or perles in his eyen he shold be anon heled of it/ Suche grete vertue had the glas/ is it thenne wondre yf I be meuyd and angry for to lose suche maner Iewellis. The tree in whiche this glas stode was lyght and faste and was named cetyne/ hit sholde endure euer er it wold rote or wormes shold hurte it/ and therfore kynge salamon seelyd his temple wyth the same wode withynforth/ Men preysed it derrer than fyn gold hit is like to tre of hebenus[2]/ of whiche wode kynge [h3v] Crompart made his hors of tree for loue of kynge morcadigas doughter that was so fayr/ whom he had wende for to haue wonne/ That hors was so made within/ that wo someuer rode

1 anobler C

2 helenus JR, BM[2], EC, PM; hebenus BM[1]

on hit yf he wolde/ he shold be within lesse than on hour/ an hondred myle thens/ And that was wel preuyd For cleomedes the kynges sone wolde not byleue that/ That hors of tree had suche myght and vertue/ He was yonge/ lusty and hardy/ And desyred to doo grete dedes of prys for to be renomed in this world/ And leep on this hors of tree/ Crompart torned a pynne that stode on his brest/ And anon the horse lyfte hym vp and wente out of the halle by the wyndowe and er one myght saye his pater noster/ He was goon more ten myle waye cleomedes was sore aferd and supposed neuer to haue torned agayn/ as thistorye therof telleth more playnly/ but how grete drede he had/ and how ferre that he rood vpon that horse made of the tree of hebenus er he coude knowe the arte and crafte how he shold torne hym/ and how Ioyeful he was whan he knewe it/ and how men sorowed for hym/ and how he knewe alle this and the ioye therof whan he cam agayn al this I passe ouer for losyng of tyme/ but the moste parte of alle cam to by the vertue of the wode/ of whiche wode the tree that the glas stode in was made/ and that was without forth of the glas half a foot brood/ wherin stode somme strange hystoryes whiche were of gold/ of sable of siluer/ of yelow/ asure and cynope/ thyse sixe colowrs were therin wrought in suche wise as it behoued/ and vnder euery hystorye the wordes were grauen and enameld that euery man myght vnderstande what eche historye was/ After my [h4] Iugement ther was neuer myrour so costly so lustly ne so playsaunt/ in the begynnyng stode there an horse made fatte stronge and sore enuyous vpon an herte whiche ran in the feeld so ferre and swyftly that the hors was angry that he ran so ferre to fore hym· and coude not ouertake hym· he thought he shold cacche hym and subdue hym. though he shold suffre moche payne therfore. the horse spack tho to a herdeman in this wyse. yf thou cowdest taken an herte that I wel can shewe the/ thou sholdest haue grete prouffyt therof. thou sholdest selle dere his hornes his skyn and his flesshe. the herdeman sayd how may I come by hym. the hors saide sytte vpon me. and I shall bere the and we shal hunte hym til he be take· The herdeman sprange and satte vpon the hors and sawe the herte and he rode after but the herte was lyght of foot and swyft. and out ran the hors ferre they honted so ferre after hym that the horse was wery and said to the herdeman that satte on hym. now sytte of I wil reste me/ I am al wery. and gyue me leue to goo fro the. The herdeman saide I haue arested the thow mayst not escape fro me· I haue a brydle on thy hede and sporis on my heles thou shalt neuer haue thanke herof/ I shal bydwynge and subdue the haddest thou sworn the contrarye. see how the horse brought hym self in thraldom and was taken in his owne nette. how may one better be taken than by his owne propre enuye suffre hym self to be taken[1] and riden· ther ben many that laboure to hurte other· and they them seluen ben hurt and rewarded with the same

THer was also made an asse and an hound/ whiche dwelled bothe with a riche man/ The man louyd his hound [h4v] wel/ For he pleyde ofte with hym as folke doo with houndis/ the hound leep vp and pleyd with his tayl/ And lyckyd his maister aboute the mouth/ this sawe bowdwyn the asse/ and had grete spyte therof in his herte/ and said to hym self/ how may this be and what may my lorde see on this fowle hound/ whom I neuer see doth good ne proffyt/ sauf spryngeth on hym and kysseth hym/ But me whom men putten to laboure/ to bere and drawe/ and doo more in a weke than he wyth his xv shold doo in a hole yere and yet sytteth he neuertheles by hym at the table/ and there eteth bones flessh and fatte trenchours/ And I haue nothyng but thystles and nettles/ And lye on nyghtes on the harde erthe and suffre many a scorn[2]/ I wyl no lenger suffre this/ I wylle thynke how I may gete my lordes loue and frendship lyke as the hounde doth/ Therwyth cam the lorde/ And the asse lyft vp his tayl and sprang with his fore feet on the lordes sholdres/ And blered grennyd and songe and with his feet made two grete bules aboute his eres/ And put forth his mouth and wolde haue kyssed the lordes mouth as he had seen the hound doon/ Tho cryde the lorde sore aferde help/ help/ this asse wil slee me/ Thenne cam his seruauntis with good stauis and smyten and bete the asse so sore that he had wende he shold haue loste his lyf/ Tho retorned he to his stable and ete thistles and nettles and was an asse as he to fore was. In lyke wyse who so haue enuye and spyte of an others welfare/ and were seruyd in lyke wyse/ it shold be wel behoefful/ Therfor it is concluded that the asse shal ete thistelis and netteles and bere the sacke/ though [h5] men wold doo hym worship he can not vnderstonde it/ but must vse olde lewde maners/ Where as asses geten lordshippis/

[1] betaken C   [2] ascorn C

there men see selde good rewle/ For they take hede of nothyng but on theyr synguler prouffyt/ yet ben they take up and rysen grete/ the more pyte is/

HErken ferther how my fadre and tybert the catte wende to gydre/ and had sworn by theyr trouthe that for loue ne hate they shold not departe. And what they gate/ they shold departe to eche the half/ Thenne on a tyme[1] they sawe hunters comyng ouer the felde with many houndes/ They leep and ronne faste fro them ward al that they myghte as they that were aferd of theyr lyf/ Tybert said the foxe whyther shal we now best flee/ the hunters haue espyed vs/ knowe ye ony helpe my fadre trusted on the promyse that eche made to other/ And that he wolde for no nede departe fro hym/ Tybert said he/ I haue a sack ful of wyles yf we haue nede/ as ferre as we abyde to gydre we nede not to doubte hunters ne houndes/ Tybert bigan to syghe and was sore aferd/ And saide/ Reynart what auayllen many wordes/ I knowe but one wyle. and theder must I too. And tho clamme he vpon on hye tree in to the toppe vnder the leuys/ Where as hunter ne hounde myght doo hym non harme· And lefte my fadre allone in Ieoparde of his lyf. For the hunters sette on hym the houndes alle that they coude/ Men blewe the hornes and cryed and halowed the foxe/ Slee and take. Whan tybert the catte sawe that. he mocked and [h5v] scorned my fadre and said what reynart cosyn vnbynde now your sakke wher al the wylis ben in/ it is now tyme ye be so wyse called/ helpe your self/ For ye haue nede/ this mocke muste my fadre here of hym to whom he had most his trust on/ And was almoste taken and nygh his deth and he ranne and fledde wyth grete fere of his lyf and lete his male slyde of by cause he wold be the lighter/ yet al that coude not helpe hym for the houndes were to swyft and shold haue byten hym/ But he had one auenture that ther by he fond an old hole/ wherin he crepte/ and escaped thus the honters and houndes/ Thus helde this false deceyuer tibaert his sykernes that he had promysed/ Alas how many ben there now a dayes that kepe not theyr promyse/ and sette not therby though they breke it/ And though I hate tybaert herfore/ is it wonder but I doo not sikerly/ I loue my sowle to wel therto/ Neuertheles yf

[1] atyme C

I sawe hym in auenture and mysfalle in his body or in his goodes/ I trowe hit shold not moche goo to my herte so that another dyde it/ Neuertheles I shal neyther hate hym ne haue/ enuye at hym/ I shal For goddes loue forgyue hym yet is it not so clere out of myn herte/ but a lytyl ylle wylle to hymward abideth therin as this cometh to my remembraunce/ And the cause is that the sensualyte of my flessh fyghteth ayenst reson.

THer stode also in that myrrour of the wulf/ how he fonde ones vpon an heth a dede hors flayn· but al the flessh was eten thenne wente he and bote grete [h6] morsellis of the bones that for hungre he toke thre or iiij attones and swolowed them in/ For he was so gredy that one of the bones stack thwart in his mouth/ Wherof he had grete payne/ And was in grete fere of his lyf/ He soughte al aboute for wyse maisters and surgyens and promysed grete yeftis for to be heled of his disease/ Atte laste whan he coude nowher fynde remedye he cam to the crane wyth his longe necke and bille/ and prayde hym to helpe hym and he wolde loue and rewarde hym so wel that he sholde euer be the better/ The crane herked after this grete rewarde and put his heed in to his throte and brought out the boon wyth his bylle/ The wulf sterte a syde wyth the pluckyng/ and cryde out alas thou doost me harme/ but I forgyue it the/ doo no more soo/ I wolde not suffre it of an other/ The crane saide/ Sir Isegrym goo and be mery for ye be al hool now gyue to me that ye promysed The wulf saide/ wyl ye here what he sayth/ I am he that hath suffred and haue cause to playne/ and he wille haue good of me/ he thanketh not me of the kyndnes that I dyde to hym he put his heed in my mouth/ and I suffred hym to drawe it out hole without hurtyng/ And he dyde to me also harme/ And yf ony hier shold haue a reward it shold be I by ryght/ Thus the vnkynde men now adayes rewarde them that doo them good/ whan the false and subtyl aryse and become grete/ thenne goth worship and prouffyt al to nought/ Ther ben many of right that ought reward and doo good to suche as haue holpen hem in her nede/ that now fynde causes and saye they be hurte and wolde haue amendis/ where they ought to rewarde [h6v] and make amendes them self/ Therfore it is said and trowthe it is/ whoo that wyl chyde or chastyse/ see that he be clere hym self.

Alle this and moche more than I now can wel remembre was made and wrought in this glasse/ The maister that ordeyned it/ was a connyng[1] man and a profounde clerk in many sciencis/ And by cause thise Iewells were ouer good and precious for me to kepe and haue/ Therfore I sente them to my dere lord the kynge and to the quene in presente/ Where ben they now that gyue to theyr lordes suche presentes/ The sorowe that my ij chyldren made whan I sente away the glasse was grete for they were woned to loke therin and see them self how theyr clothyng and araye bycam them on their bodyes/ O alas I knewe not that kywart the hare was so nyghe his deth whan I delyueryd hym the male with thise iewellis/ I wiste not to whom I myght better haue taken them. though It shold haue coste me my lyf. than hym and bellart the ramme/ They were two of my best frendis/ Oute alas I crye vpon the murderar/ I shal knowe who it was. though I shold renne thurgh al the world to seke hym. For murdre abydeth not hyd. it shal come out perauenture he is in this companye that knoweth where kywart is bicomen. though he telleth it not. For many false shrewys walke wyth good men. fro whom noman can kepe hym· they knowen theyr craft so wel and can wel couere their falsenes. but the most wondre that I haue is that my lord the kyng hier saith so felly. that my fadre [h7] nor I dyde hym neuer good/ that thynketh me meruayl of a kynge/ but ther come so many thyngis to fore hym that he forgeteth that one wyth that other/ and so faryth by me/ Dere lorde remembre not ye whan my lord your fadre lyuyd/ and ye an yonglyng of two yere were that my fadre cam fro skole fro Monpellier/ where as he had fyue yere studyed in receptes of medycynes/ he knewe al the tokenes of the vryne as wel as his honde/ And also alle the herbes and nature of them whiche were viscose or laxatyf/ he was a synguler maister in that science/ he myght wel were cloth of sylke and a gylt gyrdle/ whan he cam to court he fonde the kynge in a grete sekenes/ wherof he was sory in his hert/ For he louyd hym aboue alle other lordes/ The kynge wold not forgoo hym/ For whan he cam alle other had leue to walke where they wold he trusted none so moche as hym/ he said reynard I am seke and fele me the lenger the werse/ My fadre said/ my dere lord here is an vrynal/ make youre water therin and as sone[2] as I may see it I shal telle what sekenes it is and also how ye shal be holpen/ the kynge dyde as he conseilled hym for he

[1] aconnyng C [2] assone C

trusted noman better that lyuyd/ Though so were that my fader dyde not as he shold haue don to you/ But that was by counseyl of euyl and foule beestis/ I had wonder therof/ but it was a rasyng ayenst his deth/ he sayd my lord yf ye wyl be[1] hole/ Ye muste ete the lyuer of a wulf of vij yere old/ that may ye not leue/ or ellis ye shal deye/ for your vryne sheweth it playnly/ the wulf stode ther by and said nought/ But the kynge said to hym sir ysegrym now ye here wel that I muste haue your [h7v] lyuer/ yf I wil be hool/ Tho answerd the wulf and saide/ Nay my lord not soo/ I wote wel I am not yet fyue yere olde/ I haue herde my moder saie soo/ My fadre sayd/ what skylleth his wordes/ late hym be opened and I shal knowe by the lyuer yf it be good for yow or not/ And therwyth the wulf was had to kychen/ and his lyuer taken out/ whiche the kynge ete and was anon al hole of alle his sekenes/ thenne thanked[2] he my fadre moche/ and commanded alle his houshold upon their lyuys that after that tyme they shold calle hym mayster reynard

HE abode stylle by the kynge and was byleuid of alle thyngis/ and muste allewey go by his syde/ And the kynge gaf to/[3] hym a garlond of rooses. whiche he muste alway were on his heed. but now this is al torned· Alle the old good thinges that he dyde. ben forgeten· And thise couetouse and rauenous shrewys ben taken vp and sette on the hye benche and ben herde and made grete. And the wyse folke ben put a back. by whiche thise lordes ofte lacke. And cause them to be in moche trouble and sorowe For whan a couetous man of lowe byrthe is made a lord· and is moche greet and aboue his neyghbours hath power and myght/ Thenne he knoweth not hym self/ ne whens he is comen And hath no pyte on nomans/ hurte. ne hereth nomans requeste. but yf he may haue grete yeftis. al his entent and desyre is to gadre good and to be gretter. O how many couetous men ben now in lordes courtes. they flatre [h8] and smeke/ and plese the prynce for theyr synguler auayl/ But and the prynce had nede of them or their good they sholde rather suffre hym to deye or fare right hard er they wold gyue or lene hym/ They be lyke the wulf/ that had leuer the kynge had deyed than he wolde gyue hym his lyuer/ Yet had I leuer er that the kynge or the quene shold fare amys/ that xx suche

[1] he C [2] thanketh C [3] to- C

wulues shold lose theyr lyues/ hit were also the leest losse/ My lorde al this bifelle in your yongthe that my fader dyde thus/ I trowe ye haue forgoten it/ And also I haue my self don yow reuerence worship and courtosye/ Vnroused be it/ thaugh ye now thanke me but lytyl/ but parauenture ye remembred not that I shal now saye/ not to ony forwyttyng of yow/ for ye be worthy alle worship and reuerence that ony man can doo/ that haue ye of almyghty god by enheritaunce of your noble progenytours/ wherfor I your humble subgette and seruaunt am bounden to doo to yow alle the seruyse that I can or maye/ I cam on a tyme walkyng with the wulfe Isegrym/ And we hadde goten vnder vs bothe a swyne/ And for his lowde cryyng we bote hym to deth/ and syre ye cam fro ferre out of a groue ayenst vs ye salewed vs frendly and saide we were welcome. and that ye and my lady the quene whiche cam after yow hadde grete hongre. and had nothyng for to ete/ and prayd vs for to gyue yow parte of our wynnyng/ Isegrym spack so softe that a man vnnethe myght here hym. but I spack out and saide. ye my lord with a good will. though it were more we wil wel that ye haue parte And thenne the wulf departed as he was wont to doo/ [h8v] he departed and toke that on half for hym self/ And he gaf yow a quarter/ For yow and for the quene/ That other quarter he ete and bote as hastely as he myghte/ bicause he wolde ete it allone/ And he gaf to me but half the longes that I pray god that euyl mote he fare.

THus shewde he his condicions and nature/ er men shold haue songen a Credo ye my lord had eten your part/ And yet wold ye fayn haue had more/ For ye were not ful/ And bicause he gaf yow no more ne profred yow/ Ye lyft vp your right fote and smote hym bytwene the eris that ye tare his skynne ouer his eyen/ and tho he myght no lengre abyde but he bledde/ howled and ran away and lefte his part there lye/ Tho said ye to hym haste yow agayn hether and brynge to vs more/ And here after see better to how ye dele and parte/ Thenne saide I my lord yf it plese yow I wyll goo wyth hym/ I wote wel what ye saide/ I wente wyth hym/ he bledde/ and groned as sore as he was al softly/ he durst not crye lowde/ we wente so ferre. that we brought a calf/ And whan ye saw vs come therwyth. ye lawhyd for ye were wel plesyd/ ye said to me that I was swyft in hontyng· I see wel that ye can fynde wel whan ye take it vpon yow/ ye be good to sende forth in a nede/ The calf is good and fatte. herof shal ye be the delar I saide my lord wyth a good wyl/ The one half my lord shal be for yow. And that other half for my lady the quene. the moghettis. Lyuer longes and the Inward shal be for [π^{r}] your chyldren/ the heed shal Isegrym the wulf haue/ and I wil haue the feet· Tho said ye Reynart who hath taught you to departe so courtoisly/ my lord said I. that hath don this preest that sytteth her with the blody crowne/ he lost his skynne[1] wyth the vncourtoys departyng of the swyn/ And for his couetyse and rauyne he hath bothe hurte and shame/ Alas[2] ther ben many wulues now a dayes/ that without right and reson destroye and ete them that they may haue the ouerhand of/ they spare neyther flesh ne blood frende ne enemye/ wha they can gete· that take they/ O woo be to that lande and to townes· where as the wulues haue the ouerhand/ My lord this and many other good thing haue I don for you/ that I cowde wel telle yf it were not to long/ of whiche now ye remembre litil by the wordes that I her of you. yf ye wold al thyng ouersee wel/ ye [π^{v}] wold not saye as ye doo· I haue seen the day/ that ther shold no grete mater be concluded in this court without myn aduyse/ al be yt that this auenture is now fallen[3]/ It myght happen yet that my wordes shal be herd and also bileuyd as wel as an others as ferre as right wyl for I desyre none other/ For yf ther be ony can saye and make good by suffycient witnessis that I haue trespaced I wil abyd al the right and lawe that may come therof. and yf ony saie on me ony thyng of whiche he can brynge no wytnesses. Late me thenne[4] be rewlyd after the lawe and custome of thys court the kynge said Reynart ye saye resonably I knowe not of Kywarts deth more than that bellyn the Ramme brought his heed hether In the male/ therof I lete yow goo quyte·[5] For I [i1] haue no wytnes therof/ My dere lord said Reynart[6] god thanke yow/ sykerly ye doo wel for his deth maketh me so sorowful/ that me thynketh my herte wyl breke in two/ o whan they departed fro me myn herte was so heuy/ that me thought I shold haue swowned/ I wote wel it was a token of the losse that tho was so nyghe comyng to me/ alle the moost parte of them that were there and herde the foxes wordes of the Iewellis and how he

[1] skynne BM[1], BM[2], EC, PM; skynn JR
[2] *sic* BM[1], BM[2], EC, PM; shame And as JR
[3] now fallen BM[1], BM[2], EC, PM; nowfall en JR
[4] thenme C
[5] qnyte BM[1], BM[2], JR; quyte EC, PM
[6] Reynart *omitted in* C

made his contenance and stratchid hym/ had veryly supposed that it had not be fayned but that it had be tryewe. they were sory of his losse and mysauenture. and also of his sorowe· The kynge and the quene had bothe pyte of hym. And bad hym to make not to moche sorowe/ But that he sholde endeuore hym to seche hem. For he had so moche preysed hem. that they had grete wyl and desyre to haue them/ And by cause he had made them to vnderstonde that he had sente these Iewellis to them. though they neuer had them· yet they thankyd hym. And prayd hym to helpe that they myght haue them.

THe foxe vnderstode theyr menyng wel. he thought toward them but lytyl good for al that· he said god thanke yow my lord and my lady that ye so frendly comforte me in my sorow. I shal not reste nyght ne day ne alle they that wyl doo ony thyng for me but Renne and praye/ Thretene and aske alle the four corners of the world[1]/ Thaugh I shold euer seche tyl that I knowe where they ben bicomen/ and I pray you my lord the kynge/ That yf they were in suche place as I cowde not gete them by prayer/ by myght ne by request [11v] that ye wold assiste me and abide by me/ For it towcheth your self/ and the good is youris/ And also it is your part to doo Iustyse on thefte and murdre whiche bothe ben in this caas/ Reynart said the kynge that shal I not leue whan ye knowe wher they ben/ Myn helpe shal be alway redy for you/ O dere lorde this is to moche presented to me/ yf I had power and myght I sholde deserue ayenst yow/ Now hath the foxe his mater fast and fayr/ For he hath the kynge in his hand as he wold/ hym thought that he was in better caas than it was lyke to haue be/ he hath made so many lesynges/ that he may goo frely wher he wyl without complaynyng of ony of them alle/ Sauf of Isegrym which was to hymward angry and dysplesyd and saide/ O noble kynge ar ye so moche chyldyssh that ye byleue this false and subtyl shrewe/ and suffre your self wyth false lyes thus to be deceyuyd/ Of fayth it shold be longe or I sholde byleue hym/ he is in murdre and treson al be wrapped/ And he mocketh you to fore your visage/ I shal telle hym a nother tale I am glad that I see now hym here/ al his lesynges shal not a vaylle hym er he departe fro me.

[1] wolrd C

¶ How ysegrym the wulf complayned agayn on the foxe. capitulo ¶ xxxiij°

MY lord I pray you to take hede/ this false theef betraied my wyf ones fowle and dishonestly/ hit was so that in a wynters day that they wente to gyder thurgh a grete water/ and he[1] bare/ my wyf an honde that he wold teche her take fysshe wyth her tayl/ and that she [i2] shold late it hange in the water a good while and ther shold so moche fysshe cleue on it that foure of them shold not conne ete it. The fool my wyf supposed he had said trouthe/ And she wente in the myre to the bely to er she cam in to the water/ And whan she was in the deppest of the water. he bad her holde her tayl stylle. til that the fysshe were comen. she helde her tayl so longe that it was frorn harde in the yse and coude not plucke it out. And whan he sawe that. he sprange vp after on her body. Alas there rauysshyd he and forcyd my wyf so knauisshly that I am ashamed to telle it. she coude not defende her self the sely beest· she stode so depe in the myre. herof he can not saye naye· For I fonde hym with the dede. for as I wente aboue vpon the banke I sawe hym bynethe vpon my wyf shouyng and stekyng as men doo whan they doo suche werke and playe. Alas what payne suffred I tho at my herte I had almost for sorow loste my fyue wyttes and cryde as lowde as I myght reynart what do ye there/ and whan he sawe me so nyghe tho leep he of. and wente his waye. I wente to her in a grete heuinesse. And wente depe in that myre and that water er I coude breke the yse and moche payne suffred she er she coude haue out her taylle/ and yet lefte a gobet of her tayle behynd her/ And we were lyke bothe therby to haue lost our lyues/ for she galped and cryde so lowde for the smarte that she had er she cam out/ that the men of the village cam out with stauys and byllis/ wyth flaylis and pykforkes/ And the wyuis wyth theyr distauis/ and cryed dyspytously sle/ sle/ and smyte doun right/ I was neuer in my lyf so a [i2v] ferde/ For vnnethe we escaped[2]/ we ran so fast that we swette ther was a vylayne that stake on vs wyth a pyke/ whiche hurted vs sore he was stronge and swyfte a fote/ hadde it not be nyght/ Certaynly we had ben slayn/ The fowle olde quenes wold fayn haue beten vs/ they saide that we had byten theyr sheep/ They cursed vs with many a curse/ Tho cam we in to a felde ful of brome and brembles there hydde we vs fro the

[1] be C [2] escape C

vylaynes/ And they durst not folowe vs ferther by nyght/ but retorned home agayn See my lorde thys fowle mater/ this is murdre/ rape/ and treson/ whiche ye ought to doo Iustyce theron sharply.

REynard answerd and said/ yf this were trewe/ it shold go to nyghe myn honour and worship/ god forbede that it shold be founde trewe/ hit is wel trewe that I taught her how she sholde[1] in a place catche fysshe/ and shewde her a good way for to goo ouer in to the water without goyng in to the myre/ But she ranne so desyrously whan she herde me name the fyssh/ That she nether way no path helde/ But wente in to the yse wherein she was forfrorn/ And that was by cause she abode to longe she had fissh ynough yf she coude haue be plesyd wyth mesure it falleth ofte[2]/ who that wold haue all/ leseth alle/ Ouer couetous was neuer good/ For the beest can not be satisfyed/ And whan I sawe her in the yse so faste/ I wende to haue holpen her/ and heef and shoef and stack here and there to haue brought her out/ But it was al payne loste/ For she was to heuy for me/ Tho [i3] cam ysegrym and sawe how I shoef and stack and dyde al my beste and he as a fowle chorle· fowle and rybadously sklaundryth me wyth her. as thyse fowle vnthriftes ben wonte to doo· But my dere lord it was none otherwyse. he belyeth me falsely parauenture his eyen daselyd as he loked from aboue doun. he cryde and cursed me and swore many an oth I shold dere abye it/ whan I herde hym so curse and thretene/ I wente my waye/ and lete hym curse and menace til he was wery/ And tho wente he and heef and shoef and halpe his wyf out/ and thenne he leep and ran and she also for to gete them an hete and to warme them/ or ellis they shold haue deyed for colde/ And what someuer I haue said a fore or after/ that is clerely al trouthe/ I wolde not for a thousand marke of fyn gold lye to[3] yow one lesyng it were not syttyng for me/ what someuer falle of me I shal saye the trouthe/ lyke as myn elders haue alway don/ syth the tyme that we fyrst vnderstode reson/ and yf ye be in doubte of ony thyng that I haue said otherwyse than trouth/ gyue me respyte of viij dayes that I may haue counseyl/ and I shal brynge suche Informacion wyth good tryew and suffycient recorde/ that ye shal alle your lyf duryng truste and byleue me/ and so shal all your counseyl also/ what haue I to doo wyth the wulf/ hit is to fore

[1] holde C [2] falle thofte C [3] lyeto C

clerly ynowh shewde that he is a foule vylaynous kaytyf/ and an vnclene beest/ Whan he deled and departed the swyn/ So is it now knowen to yow alle by hys owen wordes that is a deffamer of wymmen as moche as in hym is ye may wel marke euerychone/ Who shold luste to do that game to [i3v] one so stedfast a wyf beyng in so[1] grete peryll of deth now aske ye hys wyf/ yf it be so as he sayth/ yf she wyl saye the trouth I wote wel/ she shal saye as I doo/ Tho spack erswynde the wulfis wyf/ Ach felle reynart/ noman can kepe hym self fro the/ thou canst so wel vttre thy wordes and thy falsenes and treson sette forth/ but it shall be euyl rewarded in the ende/ How broughtest thou me ones in to the welle where the two bokettys henge by one corde rennyng thurgh one polley whiche wente one vp and another doun/ thou sattest in that one boket bynethe in the pytte in grete drede/ I cam theder and herde the syghe and make sorowe/ And axed the how thou camest there/ thou saidest that thou haddest there so many good fysshes eten out of the water that thy bely wolde breste/ I said telle me how I shal come to the/ Thenne saidest thou aunte sprynge in to that boket that hangeth there/ and ye shal come anon to me/ I dyde so/ and I wente dounward/ and ye cam vpward tho was I alle angry/ thou saidest thus fareth the world that one goth vp/ and another goth doun/ tho sprang ye forth and wente your waye and I abode there allone syttyng an hole day sore an hongryd and a colde/ And therto had I many a stroke er I coude gete thens/ Aunte sayd the foxe/ thaugh the strokes dyde you harme I had leuer ye had them than I/ For ye may better bere them/ for one/ of vs must nedes haue had them/ I taught yow good/ wyl ye vnderstande it and thynke on it/ that ye another tyme take better hede and bileue noman ouer hastely/ is he frende or cosyn/ for euery man seketh his owne prouffyt/ They be now fooles that do not soo/ And [i4] specyally whan they be in Ieopardye of theyr lyues.

ℂ A fayr parable of the foxe and the wulf· Ca° xxxiiij°

MY lord said dame Erswyn I pray yow here how he can blowe with alle wyndes/ And how fayr bryngeth he his maters forth/ Thus hath he brought me many tyme in scathe and hurte said the wulf/ he hath ones bytrayed me to the she ape myn aunte/

[1] inso C

where I was in grete drede and fere/ for I lefte there almost myn one ere/ yf the foxe wil telle it how it byfel/ I wyl gyue hym the fordele therof/ for I can not telle it so wel/ but he shal/ beryspe me/ wel said the foxe I shal telle it wythout stameryng I shal saye the trouth/ I pray yow herken me/ he cam in to the wode and complayned to me/ that he had grete hongre For I sawe hym neuer so ful/ but he wold alway haue had fayn more/ I haue wonder where the mete becometh that he destroyeth/ I see now on his contenance that he begynneth to grymme for hongre/ Whan I herde hym so complayne I had pyte of hym/ And I saide I was also hongry/ thenne wente we half a day to gydre and fond nothyng/ tho whyned he and cryted/ and said he myght goo no ferther Thenne espyed I a grete hool standyng in the myddys vnder an hawe whiche was thyck of brembles/ and I herde a russhyng therin I wist not what it was/ thenne said I goo therin and loke yf ther be ony thyng ther for vs/ I wote wel ther is somwhat/ tho said he cosyn I wolde not crepe in to that hole for twenty pound but I wist fyrst what [14v] is therin/ me thynketh that ther is some perylous thyng but I shal abyde here vnder this tree/ yf ye wil goo therin to fore/ but come anon agayn/ And late me wete what thyng is therin/ Ye can many a subtylte and can wel helpe your self and moche better than I/ See my lord the kynge/ Thus he made me poure wight to goo to fore in to the daunger/ and he whiche is grete longe and stronge abode withoute and rested hym in pees/ awayte yf I dyde not for hym there.

I wold not suffre the drede and fere that I there suffred for al the good in erthe/ but yf I wyste how to escape/ I wente hardyly in/ I fonde the way derke/ longe and brood/ Er I right in the hool cam soo espyed I a grete light whiche cam in fro that one syde ther laye in a grete ape with tweyne grete wyde eyen/ and they glymmed as a fyre/ And she had a grete mouth with longe teeth and sharp naylles on hir feet and on hir handes/ I wende hit had be a mermoyse/ a baubyn or a mercatte/ for I sawe neuer fowler beest/ and by her laye thre of her children whiche were right fowle For they were ryght lyke the moder/ whan they sawe me come/ they gapeden wyde on me and were al stylle/ I was aferd/ And wold wel I had ben thens/ but I thoughte I am therin/ I muste ther thurgh and come out as wel as I maye/ as I sawe her me thought she semed more than ysegrym the wulf/ And her chyldren were more than I/ I sawe neuer a fowler meyne/ they laye on fowle heye whiche was al be pyssed/ [i5] They were byslabbed and byclagged to their eres to in her owen donge/ hit stanke that I was almost smoldred therof I durst not saye but good/ and thenne I saide/ Aunte god[1] gyue yow good[2] daye and alle my cosyns your fayr chyldren/ they be of theyr age the fayrest that euer I sawe O lord god how wel plese they me/ how louely/ how fayr ben they eche of them for their beaute myght be a grete kyngis sone/ Of right we ought to thanke yow/ that ye thus encrece oure lygnage/ Dere aunte whan I herde saye that ye were delyuerd and leyd doun I coude no lenger abyde but muste come and frendly vysite yow/ I am sory that I had not erst knowen it/ Reynard cosyn said she ye be welcome/ For that ye haue founde me and thus come see me I thanke yow/ Dere cosyn ye be right trewe and named right wyse in alle londes/ and also that ye gladly furthre and brynge your lignage in grete worship/ Ye muste teche my chyldren with the youris som wysedom that they may knowe what they shal doo and leue/ I haue thought on yow/ for gladly ye goo and felawship with the good/ O how wel was I plesyd whan I herde thise wordes/ this deseruyd I at the begynnyng whan I callyd her aunte/ how be it that she was nothyng sybbe to me/ For my right aunte is dame rukenawe that yonder standeth/ Whiche is woned to brynge forth wyse chyldren/ I saide aunte my lyf and my good is at your commandement/ and what I may doo for yow by nyght and by daye/ I wylle gladly teche them alle that I can. I wolde fayn haue be thens for the stenche of them. and also I had pyte of the grete [i5v] hongre that Isegrym had/ I saide aunte I shal commytte yow and your fayr chyldren to god and take my leue/ My wyf shal thynke longe after me/ Dere cosyn said she ye shal not departe til ye haue eten/ for yf ye dyde I wold saie ye were not kynde/ Tho stode she vp and brought me in an other hool where as was moche mete of hertes and hyndes/ roes/ fesaunts/ partrychs and moche other venyson that I wondred fro[3] whens al this mete myght come/ And whan I had eten my bely ful she gaf me a grete pece of an hynde for[4] to ete wyth my wyf and[5] wyth my houshold/ whan I come home/ I was a shamed to take it/ But I myght none other wyse doo/ I thankyd her and toke my leue/ she bad me I shold come sone agayn/ I sayd I wolde/ And so departed thens meryly/ that I so wel had spedde/

[1] good C [2] god C [3] for C [4] fro C [5] amd C

I hasted me out/ and whan I cam and sawe ysegrym whiche laye gronyng. And I axed hym how he ferde/ he said neuew al euyll· For it is wonder that I lyue/ brynge ye ony mete to ete I deye for honger. tho had I compassion of hym and gaf hym that I had. And saued hym there his lyf· wherof thenne he thanked me gretly. how be it that he now oweth me euyl wyl.

HE had eten this vp anon. tho said he Reynard dere cosyn what fonde ye in that hool. I am more hongry now than I was to fore. my teeth ben now sharped to ete. I said thenne. Eme haste yow thenne lyghtly in to that hool. Ye shal fynde there ynough. there lieth myn aunte wyth her chyldren· yf ye wyl spare the trouth [i6] and lye grete lesynges/ ye shal haue there al your desire/ But and ye saye trouth/ ye shal take harme/ My lord was not this ynough sayd and warned/ who so wold vnderstonde it/ that al that he fonde he shold saye the contrarye But rude and plompe beestis can not vnderstonde wysedom/ therfore hate they alle subtyl Inuencions/ For they can not conceyue them. Yet neuertheles/ he saide he wolde goo Inne/ and lye so many lesyngis er he sholde myshappe that all man sholde haue wondre of it. and so wente forth in to that fowle stynkyng hool. and fonde the marmosette. She was lyke the deuyls doughter. and on her chyldren hynge moche fylth cloterd in gobettis. Tho cryde he alas me growleth of thyse fowle nyckers/ Come they out of helle. men may make deuylles a ferd of hem. goo and drowne them that euyl mote they fare· I sawe neuer fowler wormes. they make al myn heer to stande right vp/ sir ysegrym said she. what may I doo therto. they ben my chyldren. And I muste be their moder. what lyeth that in your weye· whether they be fowl or fayr. They haue yow nothyng coste. here hath ben one to day byfore yow whiche was to them nyhe of kyn· And was your better and wyser and he sayde that they ware fayr. who hath sente yow hyther with thyse tydynges. dame wyl ye wytte I wylle ete of your mete. hit is better bestowed on me than on thyse fowle wyghtes. She sayde hier is no mete/ he saide here is ynough. And ther wyth he sterte with his hede toward the mete. and wolde haue goon in to the hool[1] wher the mete was. But myn aunte sterte vp wyth her chyldren. and ronne to hym wyth their sharp longe nayles [i6v] so sore that the blode ran ouer his eyen/ I herde hym crye sore and

[1] hoool C

howle/ but I knowe of no defence that he made/ but that he ran faste out of the hool/ And he was there cratched and byten/ and many an hool had they made in his cote and skyn/ his visage was alle on a blood/ and almost he had loste his one ere/ he groned and complayned to me sore/ thenne asked I hym yf he had wel lyed he sayd I saide lyke as I sawe and fonde/ and that was a fowle bytche wyth many fowle wyghtis/ Nay eme said I/ ye shold haue said/ Fayr nece how fare ye and your fair chyldren whiche ben my welbelouid cosyns/ the wulf sayd/ I had leuer that they were hanged er I that saide/ ye eme therfore muste ye resseyue suche maner payment/ hit is better otherwhile to lye than to saye trouthe/ They that ben better/ wyser and strenger than we be haue doon so to fore vs/ See my lord the kyng thus gate he his rede coyf/ Now stondeth he al so symply as he knewe no harme/ I pray yow aske ye hym yf it was not thus/ he was not fer of yf I wote it wel·

¶ How ysegrym proferd his gloue to the foxe for to fyght wyth hym· capitulo ¶ xxxv°.

THe wulf sayd I may wel forbere your mockes and your scornes and also your felle venymous wordes strong theef that ye ar/ ye saide that I was almost dede for hungre/ when ye helpe me in my nede/ that is falsely lyed/ for it was but a boon[1] that ye gaf to me/ ye had eten away alle the flessh that was theron/ And ye [i7] mocke me and saye that I am hongry here where I stande/ that toucheth my worship to nygh/ what many a spyty worde haue ye brought forth wyth false lesyngis/ And that I haue conspyred the kynges deth for[2] the tresour that ye haue seid to hym/ is in hulsterlo/ And ye haue also my wyf shamed and sklandred/ that she shal neuer recoure it/ and I shold euer be disworshipped therby yf I auengyd it not/ I haue forborn yow longe/ but now ye shal not escape me/ I can not make her of greet preef/ But I saye here to fore my lord and to fore alle them that ben here that thow art a false traytour and a morderar/ And that shal I proue and make good on thy body wythin lystes in the felde. and that body ayenst body And thenne shal our stryf haue an ende/ And therto I caste to the my gloue/ and take thou it vp/ I shal haue right of the or deye therfore/ Reynard the foxe thought how come I on this Campyng/ we ben

[1] aboon C [2] fro C

not bothe lyke/ I shal not wel conne stonde ayenst this stronge theef/ all my proof is now come to an ende.

❡ How the foxe toke vp the gloue. And how the kynge sette to them daye and felde for to come and doo theyr bataylle capitulo ❡ xxxvj°

YEt thought the foxe I haue good auauntage. the clawes of his for feet ben of. and his feet ben yet sore therof. whan for my sake he was vnshoed. he shal be somwhat the weyker. Thenne sayde the foxe who that saith that I am a traytour or a morderar. I saie he lieth [i7v] falsely and that art thou specyally ysegrym/ thou bryngest me/ there as I wold be/ this haue I ofte desyred/ lo here is my plegge/ that alle thy wordes ben falls/ And that I shal defende me/ and make good that thou lyest/ The kynge receyuyd the plegges/ and amytted the bateyll And asked borowes of them bothe/ that on the morn they shold come and parforme theyr batayll/ and doo as they ought to doo/ Thenne the bere and the catte were borowes for the wulf/ And for the foxe were borowys grymbert the dasse/ and byteluys·

❡ How rukenawe the she ape counseylled the foxe how he sholde byhaue hym in the felde ayenst the wulf Capitulo ❡ xxxvij°

THe she ape saide to the foxe/ Reyner neuew/ See that ye take hede in your batayll/ be colde and wyse Your eme taught me ones a prayer that is of moche vertue to hym that shal fyghte/ And a grete maister and a wyse clerk. and was abbot of boudelo that taughted hym/ he saide who that sayde deuoutly this prayer fastyng shal not that day be ouercomen in batayl ne in fyghting therfore dere neuew be not aferd/ I shal rede it ouer yow to morow/ thenne may ye be sure ynough of the wulf hit is bettre to fyghte/ than to haue the necke asondre/ I thanke you dere aunte said the foxe/ The quarel that I haue is rightful therfore I hope I shal spede[1] wel/ and that shal gretely be myne helpe/ Alle his lygnage abode by hym al[2] the nyght/ and helpe hym to dryue a way the tyme/ [i8] Dame rukenawe the she ape his aunte thoughte alway on his prouffyt and fordele/ And she dyde alle his heer fro the heed to the

[1] shalspede C [2] hymal C

tayl be shorn of smothe/ and she anoynted alle his body wyth oyle of olyue/ And thenne was his body also glat and slyper/ that the wulf sholde haue none holde on hym/ And he was round and fatte also on his body/ And she said to hym dere cosyn ye muste now drynke moche/ that to morow ye may the better make your vryne/ but ye shal holde it in tyl ye come to the felde/ And whan nede is and tyme/ so shal ye pysse ful your rowhe tayll/ and smyte the wulf therwyth in his berde/ And yf ye myght hytte hym therwyth in his eyen· thenne shal ye byneme hym his syght/ that shold moche hyndre hym/ but ellis hold alway your tayl faste bytwene your legges that he catche you not therby/ and holde doun your eris lyeng plat after your heed/ that he holde you not therby/ And see wisely to your self/ and at begynnyng flee fro his strokes. And late hym sprynge and renne after yow/ and renne to fore where as moste dust is/ and styre it wyth your feet that it may flee in his eyen and that shal moche hyndre his syght/ And whyle he rubbeth his eyen take your auantage and smyte and byte hym there as ye may most hurte hym/ And alleway to hytte hym wyth your tayll ful of pysse in his visage and that shal make hym so woo/ that he shal not wyte where he is/ And late hym renne after yow for to make hym wery/ Yet his feet ben sore/ of that ye made hym to lose his shooes/ and though he be greet/ he hath no herte/ Neuew certaynly this is my counseyll. [i8v]

THe connyng goth to fore strenghte/ therfore see for your self/ And sette your self wysely atte defence/ that ye and we alle may haue worship therof/ I wold be sory yf ye myshapped/ I shal teche you the wordes that your eme mertyn taught me/ that ye may ouercome your enemye/ as I hope ye shal doo wythout doubte/ therwyth she leyde her hand vpon his heed and saide these wordes/ Blaerde Shay Alphenio/ Kasbue Gorfons alsbuifrio/ Neuew now be ye sure fro alle myschief and drede/ and I counseyle yow that ye reste you a lytyl/ for it is by the daye/ ye shal be the better dysposed/ we shal awake you al in tyme/ aunte said the foxe I am now glad/ god thanke you ye haue don to me suche good/ I can neuer deserue it fully agayn/ me thynketh ther may no thynge hurte me syth that ye haue said thyse holy wordes ouer me/ Tho wente he and leyd hym doun vnder a tre in the grasse and slepte tyl the sonne was rysen/ tho cam the otter and waked hym and bad hym aryse/ and gaf hym a good[1] yong doke/ and said/ dere cosyn I haue this nyght made many a leep in the water er I coude gete this yong fatte doke/ I haue taken if fro a fowler/ take and ete it/ Reynart sayde this is good hansele/ yf I refused this I were a fool/ I thanke yow cosyn that ye remembre me/ yf I lyue I shal rewarde yow/ The foxe ete the doke with oute sawce or breed it sauourd hym wel and wente wel in/ And he dranke therto iiij grete draughtis of water/ Thenne wente he to the bataylle ward and alle they that louyd hym wente wyth hym. [k1]

¶ How the Foxe cam in to the felde and how they foughten/ capitulo ¶ xxxviij°.

WHan the kynge sawe reynart thus shorn and oyled he said to hym/ Ey foxe how wel can ye see for your self/ he wondred therof he was fowle to loke on/ but the foxe said not one worde but kneled doun lowe to therthe vnto the kynge and to the quene and stryked hym forth in to the felde/ The wulf was ther redy and spack many a proud word/ the rulers and kepars of the felde was the lupaert and the losse/ they brought forth the booke/ on whiche sware the wulf that the foxe was a traytour and a morderar/ and none myght be falser than he was/ and that he wolde preue on his body and make it good/ Reynart the foxe sware that he lyed as a false knaue and a cursyd theef and that he wold doo good on his body/ Whan this was don the gouernours of the felde/ bad them doo theyr deuoyr/ Thenne romed they alle the felde sauf dame ruken-awe the she ape/ she abode by the foxe and bad hym remembre wel the wordes that she had sayd to hym/ she said see wel too/ whan ye were vij yer olde ye were wyse ynowh to goo by nyght wythout lanterne/ or mone shyne/ Where ye wyste to wynne ony goode/ ye ben named emong the peple wyse and subtyl/ payne your self to werke soo that ye wynne the prys/ thenne may ye haue euer honour. and worship/ and al we that ben your frendys/ he answerd my derest aunte I knowe it wel/ I shal doo my beste and thynke on your counseyl/ I hope so to doo that alle my lignage shal haue worship therby/ and myn enemyes shame and confusion/ she sayde god graunte it yow. [k1v]

[1] agood C

ℭ How the foxe and the wulf foughten to gydre ca° xxxix°

THerwyth she wente out of the felde/ and lete them tweyne goo to gydre/ the wulf trade forth to the foxe in grete wrath and opened his fore[1] feet/ and supposed to haue taken the foxe in hem/ But the foxe sprang fro hym lyghtly/ For he was lyghter to fote than he/ The wulf sprange after and hunted the foxe sore/ theyr frendes stode/ without the lystes and loked vpon hem/ The wulf strode wyder than reynard dyde and ofte ouertoke hym/ And lyfte vp his foot and wende to haue smyten hym/ but the foxe sawe to/ and smote hym wyth his rowhe tayle/ Whiche he had al be pyssed in his visage/ tho wende the wulf to haue ben plat blynde/ the pysse sterte in his eyen/ thenne muste he reste for to make clene[2] his eyen/ Reyner thougthe on his fordele and stode aboue the wynde skrabbing and casting wyth his feet the duste that it flewe the wulfis eyen ful/ the wulf was sore blynded therwyth/ in suche wyse that he muste leue the rennyng after hym/ For the sonde and pysse cleuyd vnder his eyen that it smerted so sore/ that he must rubbe and wasshe it a way/ Tho cam reyner in a grete angre and bote hym thre grete woundes on his heed wyth his teeth/ and said/ what is that syr wulf/ hath one there byten yow/ how is it wyth yow/ I wyl al otherwyse on yow yet/ abyde I shal brynge yow somm newe thyng/ ye haue stole many a lambe and destroyed many a symple beest/ and now falsely haue appeled me and brought me in this trouble/ al this shal I now auenge on the/ I am chosen to reward the for thyn[3] old synnes [k2] For god[4] wyl no lenger suffre the in thy grete rauayn and shrewdnes I shal now assoylle the and that shal be good for thy sowle take paciently this penaunce/ for thou shalt lyue no lenger/ the helle shal be thy purgatorye/ Thy lyf is now in my mercy/ but and yf thou wilt knele doun and aske me forgyfnes/ and knowleche the to be ouercomen/ yet though thou be euyl/ yet I wyl spare the/ for my conscience counseylleth me/ I shold not gladly slee no man/ Isegrym wende wyth thyse mockyng and spytous wordes to haue goon out of his wytte/ And that dered hym so moche that he wyste not what to saye buff ne baff/ he was so angry in his herte/ The woundes that reynart had gyuen hym bledde and smerted sore/ And he thought how he myghte best auenge it

[1] sore C [2] elene C [3] forthyn C [4] good C

WYth grete angre he lyft vp his foot and smote the foxe on the heed so grete a stroke/ that he fyl to the ground/ tho sterte the wulf to and wende to haue take hym/ but the foxe was lyght and wyly and roose lyghtly vp and mette wyth hym fiersly/ and there began a felle bataylle whiche dured longe/ the wulf had grete spyte on the foxe as it wel semed/ he sprange after hym x tymes eche after other/ and wold fayn haue had hym faste/ but his skyn was so slyper and fatte of the oyle that alway he escaped fro hym O so subtyl and snelle was the foxe/ that many tymes whan the wulf wende wel to be sure of hym/ he sterte thenne bytwene his legges and vnder his bely and thenne torned he agayn and gaf the wulf a stroke wyth his tail ful of pysse in his eyen that Isegrym wende he sholde haue loste his [k2^{v}] sight[1]/ and this dyde he often tymes/ And alwey whan he had so smyten hym thenne wold he goo aboue the wynde and reyse the duste/ that it made his eyen ful of stufs/ Isegrym was woo begon/ and thought he was at an afterdele/ yet was his strengthe and myght moche more than the foxes/ Reynard had many a sore stroke of hym whan he raught hym/ They gaf eche other many a stroke and many a byte whan they saw theyr auauntage/ And eche of hem dyde his best to destroye that other/ I wold I myght see suche a bataylle[2]/ that one was wyly/ and that other was stronge/ that one faught wyth strengthe/ and that other with subtylte.

THe wulf was angry that the foxe endured so longe ayenst hym yf his formest feet had ben hole/ the foxe had not endured so longe/ but the sores were so open that he myght not wel renne/ And the foxe myght better of and on than he/ And also he swange his tayl wyth pysse ofte vnder his eyen/ and made hym that hym thougthe that his eyen shold goo out/ Atte laste he sayd to hym self/ I wyl make an ende of this bataylle/ How longe shal this caytyf dure thus ayenst me/ I am so grete/ I shold yf I laye vpon hym presse hym to deth/ hit is to me a grete[3] shame that I spare hym so longe/ Men shal mocke and poynte me wyth fyngres to my shame and rebuke for I am yet on the werst syde/ I am sore wounded/ I blede sore/ and he drowneth me/ wyth his pysse/ and caste so moche dust and sande in myne eyen/ that hastely I shal not conne see/ yf I suffre hym ony lenger/ I wyl sette it in auenture/

[1] ght BM[1]; sight BM[2], JR, PM, EC   [2] abataylle C   [3] agrete C

and seen what shal come therof/ wyth that he smote wyth his [k3] foot reynard on the heed that he fyll doun to the ground And er he cowde aryse he caught hym in his feet· and laye vpon hym as he wold haue pressed hym to deth. Tho began the foxe to be a ferd. and so were alle his frendis whan they sawe hym lye vnder· And on that other syde alle ysegryms frendes were ioyeful and glad. The foxe defended hym faste wyth his clawes as he laye vpward wyth his feet· And gaf hym many a clope· The wulf durste not wyth his feet doo hym moche harme but wyth his teeth snatched at hym as he wold haue byten hym. whan the foxe sawe that he shold be byten and was in grete drede. he smote the wulf in the heed wyth his formest clawes and tare the skynne of bytwene his browes and hys eeris. and that one of his eyen henge out. Whiche dyde hym moche payne· he howlyd. he wepte· he cryde lowde. and made a pyteuous noyse/ for the blode rann doun as it had ben a streme

¶ How the foxe beyng vnder the wulf· wyth flateryng wordes glosed[1] hym. that the foxe cam to his aboue agayn.

capitulo ¶ xl°

THe wulf wyped his eyen. the foxe was glad whan he sawe that/ he wrastled so sore/ that he sprang on his feet whyles he rubbed his eyen/ the wulf was not wel plesyd ther wythalle[2]/ And smote after hym er he escaped and caught hym in his armes and helde hym faste/ notwythstandyng that he bledde/ Reynard was woo thenne/ There wrastled they longe and sore/ The wulf wexe so angry that he forgat al his smarte and payne and threw the foxe al plat vnder hym/ whiche cam hym [k3v] euyl to passe/ For his one hand by whiche he deffended hym sterte in the fallyng in to ysegryms throte/ and thenne was he aferd to lese his hand/ The wulf sayd tho to the foxe/ Now chese whether ye wyl yelde yow as ouercome/ or ellis I shal certaynly slee yow/ the skateryng of the dust thy pysse/ thy mockyng ne thy deffence/ ne alle thy false wylys/ may not now helpe the/ thou mayste not escape me/ Thou hast here to fore don me so moche harme and shame/ and now I haue lost myne one eye/ and therto sore wounded[3]/ Whan reynard herde that it stode so rowme/ that he shold chese to knowleche hym

[1] wordesg losed C [2] therwyth alle C [3] woundeed C

ouercomen and yelde hym/ Or ellis to take the deth/ he thought the choys was worth ten marke/ And that he muste saye that one or that other/ he had anon concluded what he wold saie/ and began to saye to hym wyth fayr wordes in this wyse/ Dere eme I wyl gladly become your man wyth alle my good/ And I wyl goo for you to the holy graue/ and shal gete pardon and wynnyng for your cloistre/ of alle the chyrches that ben in the holy lande/ Whiche shal moche prouffyte to your sowle and your elders sowles also/ I trowe ther was neuer suche a prouffre/ prouffred to ony kynge/ And I shal serue you/ lyke as I shold serue our holy fader the pope/ I shal holde of you al that I haue and euer ben your seruaunt and forth I shal make that al my lignage shal do in lyke wyse/ Thenne shal ye be a lord a boue alle lordes/ who shold thenne dare doo ony thyng ayenst you/ And furthermore whatsomeuer I take of polaylle/ ghees/ partrych or plouyer/ fysshe or flesshe or what someuer it be/ therof [k4] shal ye fyrst haue the choys/ and your wyf and your chyldren/ er ony come in my body/ Therto I wyl alway abyde by you/ that where ye be ther shal no hurte ne scathe come to yow/ ye be strong and I am wyly/ late vs abyde to gydre/ that one wyth the counseyl and that other wyth the dede/ then may ther nothyng mysfalle to vs ward/ and we ben so nygh of kynne eche to other/ that of right shold be no angre bytwene vs/ I wold not haue foughten ayenst you yf I myght haue escaped/ But ye appeled me fyrst vnto fyghte/ Tho muste I doo/ that I not doo wold gladly/ And in this bataylle I haue ben curtoys to yow/ I haue not yet shewde the vtterist of my myght on yow/ lyke as I wold haue doon yf ye had ben a straunger to me/ For the neuew ought to spare the eme/ it is good reson and it ought so to bee/ Dere eme so haue I now doo/ And that maye ye marke wel whan I ran to fore yow. myn herte wold not consente therto. For I myght haue hurte yow moche more than I dyde. but I thought it neuer For I haue not hurte yow ne don yow so moche harm that may hyndre yow· sauf only that myshappe that is fallen on your eye/ ach therfore[1] I am sory and suffre moche sorow in my herte. I wold wel dere Eme that it had not happed yow. But that it had fallen on me. so that ye therwyth had ben plesyd. how be it. that ye shal haue therby a grete auauntage. For whan ye here after shal slepe ye nede not to shette but one wyndowe. where another muste shette two. My wyf and my children. and my lignage shal falle dounn to your

[1] thersore C

feet/ to fore the kynge and to fore alle them that ye wyl desyre and praye [k4v] yow humbly/ that ye wyl suffre reynart your neuew lyue and also I shal knoweleche ofte to haue trespaced ayenst yow/ and what lesynges I haue lyed vpon yow/ How myght ony lord haue more honour than I proffre yow/ I wold for no good do this to another/ therfore I pray yow to be plesyd here wyth al

I Wote wel yf ye wolde ye myght now slee me/ but and ye so don had/ what had ye wonne/ so muste ye euer after this tyme kepe yow fro my frendes and lignage/ Therfore he is wyse that can in his angre/ mesure hym self and not be ouer hasty/ and to see wel what may falle or happe afterward to hym/ what man that in his angre can wel aduyse hym certaynly he is wyse/ Men fynde many fooles that in hete hasten hem so moche/ that after they repente hem/ and thenne it is[1] to late/ but dere Eme I trowe that ye be to wyse so to doo/ hit is better to haue prys honour/ reste/ and pees/ And many frendes that be redy to helpe hym/ than to haue shame/ hurte/ vnreste/ and also many enemyes lyeng in a wayte to doo/ hym harme/ Also it is lityl worship to hym that hath ouercomen a man[2]/ thenne to slee hym/ it is grete shame/ not for my lyf/ Thaugh I were deed/ that were a lytyll hurte.

ISegrym the wulf said/ Ay/ theef how fayn woldest thow be losed and dyscharged fro me/ that here I wel by thy wordes/ were thou now fro me on thy free feet/ Thou woldest not sette by me an egge shelle/ [k5] Though thou promysedest to me alle the world of fyn rede/ gold/ I wold not late the escape/ I sette lytyl by the and alle thy frendes and lignage/ Alle that thou hast here said is but lesyngis and fayned falsenes/ Wenest thou thus to deceyue me/ it is longe syth that I knewe the/ I am no byrde to be locked ne take by chaf/ I know wel ynowh good corn/ O how woldest thou mocke me/ yf I lete the thus escape/ thou myghtest wel haue said this to one that knewe the not/ but to me thou losest thy flateryng and swete floytyng/ For I vnderstande to wel thy subtyl lyeng talys/ Thow hast so ofte deceyued me/ that me behoueth now to take good hede of the. Thow false stynkyng knaue thow saist that thou hast spared me in this batayl. loke hetherward to me. is not myn one

[1] this C [2] aman C

eye out. and therto hast thou wounded me in xx places in my heed. thou woldest not suffre me so longe to reste. as to take ones my breeth. I were ouer moche a fool yf I shold now spare the. or be mercyful to the. so many a confusion and shame as thou hast don to me. and that also that toucheth me most of alle. that thou hast disworshiped and sklaundred erswyn my wyf· Whom I loue as wel as my self. and falsely forsedest[1] and deceyuedest her. whiche shal neuer out of my herte. For as ofte as it cometh to myn mynde/ alle myn angre and hate that I haue to the reneweth. In the mene wylle that ysegrym was thus spekyng. The foxe bithought hym how he myght helpe hym self. And stack his other hond after bytwene his legges. And grepe the wulf fast by the colyons. And he wronge hem so sore that for woo and [k5v] payne/ he muste crye lowde and howle/ Thenne the foxe drewe his other hond out of his mouth/ The wulf had so moche payne and anguyssh of the sore wryngyng that the foxe dowed and wronge his genytours/ that he spytte blood/ And for grete payne he byshote hym self

¶ How ysegrym the wulf was ouercomen and how the batayl was taken vp and fynysshid/ And how the foxe had the worship

capitulo ¶ xlj°

THis payne dyde hym more sorow and woo/ than his eye dyde that so sore bledde/ and also it made hym to ouerthrowe alle in a swowne For he had so moche bledde/ and also the threstyng that he suffred in his colyons made hym so faynt that he had lost his myght/ Thenne reynard the foxe lepe vpon hym wyth al his myght/ And caught hym by the legges and drewe hym forth thurgh the felde/ that they alle myght see it/ and he stack and smote hym sore/ Thenne were ysegryms frendes al ful of sorowe/ and wente al wepyng vnto theyr lord the kynge/ And prayde hym that he wold doo sece the batayll and take it vp in to his handes/ The kynge graunted it/ and thenne wente the kepars of the felde the lupaerd and the lossem and saide to the foxe and to the wulf/ Our lord the kynge wil speke wyth yow/ and wyl that this batayl be ended/ he wil take it in to his hand/ he desyreth that ye wyl gyue your stryf vnto hym For yf ony of yow here were slayn/ it shold be grete shame on bothe sydes/ For ye haue as moche worship of this felde

1 forsest C

[k6] as ye may haue/ and they sayde to the foxe/ Alle the beestis gyue to yow the prys/ that haue seen this bataylle/ The foxe said therof I thanke hem/ and what that shal plese my lord to commande that shal not I gaynsaye/ I desire no better/ but to haue wonne the felde/ late my frendes come hether to me/ I wil take aduyse of them what I shal doo/ They saide/ that they thought it good/ And also it was reson in weyghty maters a man shold take aduys of his frendes/ thenne cam dame slopecade/ and grymbert the dasse her husbond/ dame rukenawe wyth her ij susters/ Byteluys and fulrompe her ij sones and hatenet her doughter/ the flyndermows and the wezel/ And ther cam moo than xx/ whiche wold not haue comen yf the foxe had lost the feeld· So who that wynneth and cometh to hys aboue. he geteth grete loos and worship/ And who that is ouer throwen· And hath the werse. to hym wyl noman gladly come. Ther cam also to the foxe. the beuer. the otter and bothe theyr wyues panthecrote and ordegale. And the ostrole· the Martre the fychews. the fyret. the mowse. and the squyrel and many moo than I can name. And alle bycause he had wonne the feeld. ye some cam that to fore had complayned on hym and were now of his next kynne. and they shewde hym right frendly chier and contenance. Thus fareth the world now. who that is riche and hye on the wheel. he hath many kynnesmen and frendes· that shal helpe to bere out his welthe. But who that is nedy and in payne or in pouerte. fyndeth but fewe frendes and kynnesmen· For euery man almost escheweth[1] his companye and waye. There was thenne grete [k6v] feste they blewe vp trompettis and pyped wyth shalmoyses/ They sayden alle dere neuew blessyd be god that ye haue sped wel/ we were in grete drede and fere whan we saw yow lye vnder/ reynart[2] the foxe thanked alle them frendly/ and resceyued them with grete Ioye and gladnes/ Thenne he asked of them what they counseylled hym/ yf he sholde[3] gyue the felde vnto the kynge or noo/ Dame slopecade sayde/ ye hardely cosyn/ Ye may wyth worship wel sette it in to his handes/ And truste hym wel ynough/ Thoo wente they alle wyth the kepars of the feelde vnto the kynge/ And Reynard the foxe wente to fore them alle/ wyth trompes and pypes and moche other mynstralcye/ The foxe kneled doun to fore the kynge/ The kynge bad hym stande vp/ and said to hym/ reynard ye be now Ioyeful/ ye haue kepte your day worshipfully/

1 esheweth C

2 reynart EC, PM, BM[1], BM[2]; reynart. JR

3 hesholde C

I discharge yow. and late yow goo frely quyte where it plesyth yow/ And the debate bytwene yow I holde it on me. And shal discusse it by reson and by counseyl of noble men and wil ordeyne therof that ought be doon by reson. at suche tyme as ysegrym shal be hool. And thenne I shal. sende for yow to come to me· And thenne by goddes grace I shal yeue out the sentence and Iugement·

¶ An ensample that the foxe told to the kynge whan he had wonne the felde. capitulo ¶ xlij°

MY worthy and dere lord the kynge. saide the foxe I am wel a greed and payd therwyth. But whan I cam fyrst in to your court. ther were many that were felle [li] and enuyous to me. Whiche neuer had hurte ne cause of scathe by me/ but they thought that they myght beste ouer me/ And alle they cryden wyth myn enemyes ayenst me/ and wold fayn haue destroyed me/ by cause they thought that the wulf was better withholden and gretter wyth you than I was whiche am your humble subget/ They knewe none other thyng why ne wherfore/ They thoughte not as the wyse be woned to doo/ that is what the ende may happen/ My lorde thyse ben lyke a grete heep of houndes[1] whiche I ones sawe stonde at a lordes place vpon a donghil/ where as they awayted that men sholde brynge them mete/ Thenne sawe they an hound come out of the kychen/ and had taken there a fayr rybbe of beef er it was gyuen hym/ And he ran fast away wyth all/ but the cook had espyed or he wente away/ and toke a grete bolle full of scaldyng water/ and caste it on his hyppes behynde/ Wherof he thankyd nothyng the cook/ For the heer behynde was skalded of/ And his skyn semed as it had be thurgh soden/ Neuertheles he escaped away/ and kepte that he had wonne/ And whan his felaws the other houndes saw hym come wyth this fayr rybbe/ They called hym alle and saide to hym/ O how good a frende is the cook to the/ Whiche hath gyuen to the so good a boone/ Wheron his so moche flessh/ The hound saide ye knowe nothyng therof/ Ye preyse me lyke as ye see me to fore wyth the bone/ But ye haue not seen me behynde/ take hede and beholde me afterward on myn buttokkis/ And thenne ye shal knowe how I haue deseruyd it. [li^v]

[1] ofhoūndes C

ANd whan they had seen hym behynde on his hyppes how that his skynne and his flessh was al rawe and thurgh soden/ tho growled them alle and were aferd of that syedyng water/ and wold not of his felawship/ but fledde and ran away from hym/ and lete hym there allone/ See my lord this right haue thyse false beestis/ whan they be made lordes and may gete their desire/ and whan they be myghty and doubted/ thenne ben they extorcionners and scatte and pylle the peple/ and eten them lyke as they were forhongred houndes/ These ben they that bere the bone in her mouth/ Noman dar haue to doo wyth hem/ but preyse alle that they bedryue/ Noman dar saye other wyse/ but suche as shal plese hem by cause they wold not be shorn/ and somme helpe them forth in theyr vnryghtwys dedes by cause they wold haue parte and lykke theyr fyngres/ and strengthe them in theyr euyl lyf and werkis/ O dere lorde how lytyl seen they that do thus after behynde them what the ende shal be atte laste they fal fro hye to lowe in grete shame and sorowe/ and thenne theyr werkis[1] come to knowleche and be opene in suche wyse that noman hath pyte ne compascion on them/ in theyr meschief and trouble/ and euery man curse them and saye euyl by them to their shame and vylanye/ many of suche haue ben blamed and shorn ful nyghe that they had no worshipe ne prouffyt/ but lose theyr heer as the hound dyde. that is theyr frendes. whiche haue holpe them to couere their mysdedes and extorcions. lyke as the heer coueryth the skynn/ And whan[2] they haue sorow and shame for theyr olde trespaces. thenne eche body pluckyth his hand fro hym. And flee. lyke as the houndes dyde [l2] fro hym that was scalded wyth[3] the syedyng water/ and lete men[4] thyse extorcioners[5] in her sorow and nede/

MY dere lorde kynge I beseche you to remembre this example of me/ it shal not be ayenst your worship ne wysedom/ What wene ye how many ben ther suche false extorcionners now in thise dayes/ ye moche werse than an hound/ that bereth suche a bone in his mouth/ in townes/ in grete lordes courtes/ whiche wyth grete facing and bracyng oppresse the poure peple wyth grete wronge/ and selle theyr fredom and pryuelages/ and bere them on hond of thyngis that they neuer knewe ne thoughte/ And all for

[1] weerkis C [2] wehan C [3] thyth C
[4] hym C [5] extorcions C

to gete good for theyr synguler proffyt/ God gyue them all shame and soone destroye them who somme euer they be that so doo/ but god be thanked said the foxe/ ther may noman endwyte me ne my lygnage ne kynne of suche werkys/ but that we shal acquyte vs/ And comen in the lyghte/ I am not a ferd of ony/ that can saye on me ony thyng that I haue don otherwyse than a trewe man ought to doo/ Alleway the foxe/ shal a byde the foxe though alle his enemyes hadde sworn the contrarye/ My dere lord the kynge I loue you wyth my herte aboue alle other lordes/ And neuer for noman wold I torne fro yow/ But abyde by yow to the vtterist[1] how wel it hath ben otherwyse enformed your hyenes/ I haue neuertheles[2] alway do the best/ and forth so wylle doo alle my lyf that I can or may/ [l2v]

¶ How the kyng forgaf the foxe alle thyngis/ and made hym souerayn and grettest ouer al his landes. ca° xliij°

THe kynge sayde Reynard ye be one of them that oweth me homage· whiche I wyl that ye allway so doo. And also I wylle that erly and late ye be of my counseyl. and one of my Iustyses/ See wel to that ye not mysdoo/ ne trespace nomore. I sette yow agayn in alle your myght and power. lyke as ye were to fore and see that ye further alle maters to the beste righte· For whan ye sette your wytte and counseyl to vertue and goodnesse· thenne may not our court be wythout your aduyse and counseyl. For here is non that is lyke to yow in sharp and hye counseyll ne subtyller in fyndyng a remedye for a meschief. And thynke ye on thexample that ye your self haue tolde. And that ye haunte rightwysnes/ and be to me trewe. I will fro hensforth[3] werke and doo by your aduyse and counseyll. he lyueth not that yf he mysdede yow. But I shold sharply aduenge and wreke it on hym ye shalle oueralle speke and saye my wordes. And in alle my lande shall ye be aboue alle other souerayne and my bayle. That Offyce I gyue yow. ye may wel occupye it wyth worship/ Alle reynardis frendis and lignage thanketh the kyng hyely[4]/ The kynge sayde/ I wolde doo more For your sake/ than ye wene/ I pray yow alle that ye remembre hym that he be trewe/ Dame rukenawe thenne sayd yes sykerly my lord/ that shal he euer be/ And thynke ye not the contrary/ for yf

[1] wtterist C [2] neuerthe-| theles C [3] frohens forth C [4] heyly C

he were otherwyse/ He were not of our kynne ne lignage [l3] And I wold euer myssake hym/ and wold euer hyndre hym to my power/ Reynart the foxe thanked the kynge with fayr curtoys wordes/ And sayd/ dere lorde I am not worthy to haue the worship[1] that ye doo to me/ I shal thynke theron and be trewe to you also longe as I lyue/ and shal gyue you as holsom counseyl as shal be expedient to your good grace/ here wyth he departed wyth his frendes fro the kynge/ Now herke how Isegrym the wulf dyde/ bruyn the bere/ tybert[2] the catte/ and erswynde and her chyldren wyth their lignage drewen the wulf out of the felde/ and leyde hym vpon a lyter of heye/ and couerd hym warm/ and loked to his woundes whiche were wel .xxv· and ther cam wyse maistres and surgyens/ Whiche bonde them and weeshe hem he was so seke and feble/ that he had lost his felynge/ But they rubbed and wryued hym vnder his temples and eyen/ that he sprange out of his swoun[3]/ and cryde so lowde that alle they were aferde/ they had wende that he had ben wood

Bvt the maistres gaf hym a drynke/ that comforted his herte and made hym to slepe/ They comforted his wyf/ And tolde to her that ther was no deth wounde ne paryl of his lyf/ Thenne the court brake vp/ and the beestis departed and wente to theyr places and homes that they cam froo.

¶ How the foxe wyth his frendis and lignage departed nobly fro the kynge/ and wente to his castel malleperduys/
capitulo ¶ xliij° [l3v]

REynart the foxe toke his leue honestly of the kynge and of the quene. And they bad hym he shold not tarye longe. But shortly retorne to them agayn· he answerd and said dere kynge and quene alway at your commandement I shal be redy/ yf ye nede ony thyng whiche god forbede I wold alway be redy wyth my body and my good to helpe yow/ and also al my frendes and lignage in lyke wyse shal obeye your commandement and desire/ ye haue hyely deseruyd it/ god quyte it yow and yeue you grace longe to lyue/ And I desyre your licence and leue to goo home to

[1] wership C [2] thybert C [3] swoun̄ C

my wyf and chyldren/ And yf your good grace wil ony thyng/ late me haue knowleche of it/ And ye shal fynde me alway redy/ Thus departed the foxe wyth fayr wordes fro the kynge. ¶ Now who that coude sette hym in reynardis crafte/ and coude behaue hym in flateryng and lyeng as he dyde/ he shold I trowe be herde/ bothe wyth the lordes spyrytuel and temporel/ They[1] ben many and also the moste parte that crepe after his waye and his hole/ The name that was gyuen to hym/ abydeth alway stylle wyth hym/ he hath lefte many of his crafte in this world/ Whiche allewaye wexe and become myghty/ for who that wyl not vse reynardis crafte now is nought worth in the world now in ony estate that is of myght/ But yf he can crepe in reynardis nette/ and hath ben his scoler/ thenne may he dwelle with vs/ For thenne knoweth he wel the way how he may aryse/ And is sette vp aboue of euery man/ Ther is in the world moche seed left of the foxe/ whiche now oueral groweth and cometh sore vp/ though they haue no rede berdes/ Yet [14] ther ben founden mo foxes now/ than euer were here to fore/ The rightwys peple ben al loste/ trouthe and rightwysnes ben exyled and fordriuen/ And for them ben abyden wyth vs couetyse/ falshede/ hate and enuye/ Thyse regne now moche in euery contre/ For is it in the popes court/ the emperours/ the kynges dukes or ony other lordes where someuer it be eche man laboureth to put other out fro his worship/ offyce and power/ for to make hym sylf to clymme hye with lyes/ wyth flateryng/ wyth symonye/ wyth money/ or wyth strengthe and force/ ther is none thyng byloued ne knowen in the court now adays but money/ the money is better byloued than god/ For men doo moche more therfore/ For who someuer bryngeth money/ shal be wel receyuyd and shal haue alle his desyre/ is it of lordes or of ladyes or ony other/ that money doth moche harme/ Money bryngeth many in shame and drede of his lyf/ and bryngeth false wytnes ayenst true peple for to gete money. Hit causeth vnclennes of lyuyng. lyeng. and lecherye. Now clerkes goon to rome/ to parys and to many another place. for to lerne reynardis crafte· is he clerke/ is he laye man· eueriche of them tredeth in the foxes path. and seketh his hole. The world is of suche condycion now. that euery[2] man seketh hym self in alle maters. I wote not what ende shal come to vs herof Alle wyse men may sorowe wel herfore. I fere that for the grete falsenes thefte robberye and murdre that is now vsed so

[1] The| C [1] eueey C

moche and comonly. and also the vnshamefast lecherye and auoultry bosted and blowen a brood with the auauntyng of the same. that wythout grete repentaunce [l4v] and penaunce therfore/ that god will take vengeaunce and punysshe vs sore therfore/ whom I humbly beseche and to whom nothyng is hyd that he wylle gyue vs grace to make amendes to hym therfore/ and that we maye rewle vs to his playsyr/ And her wyth wil I leue For what haue I to wryte of thise mysdedis/ I haue ynowh to doo with myn owne self/ And so it were better that I helde my pees and suffre/ And the beste that I can doo for to amende my self now in this tyme/ And so I counseyle euery man to doo here in this present lyf/ and that shal be most our prouffyt/ For after this lyf/ cometh no tyme that we may occupye to our auantage for to amende vs For thenne shal euery man answere for hym self and bere his owen burthen/ Reynardis frendes and lignage to the nombre of xl haue taken also theyr leue of the kynge/ And wente alle to gydre wyth the foxe/ whiche was right glad that he had so wel sped/ And that he stode so wel in the kynges grace. he thought. that he had no shame. but that he was so grete with the kyng that he myght helpe and further his frendes/ and hyndre his enemyes/ and also to doo what he wolde. wythout he shold be blamed yf he wold be wyse/

The Foxe and his frendis wente so longe to gydre that they camen to his burgh to Maleperduys. ther they alle toke leue eche of other wyth fayr and courtoys wordes/ Reynard dyde to them grete reuerence and thanked them alle frendly. of theyr good fayth and also worship that they had don and shewd to hym. And profred to [l5] eche of them his seruyse yf they had nede wyth body and goodes/ And herwyth they departed/ and eche of them wente to theyr owne howses/ The foxe wente to dame ermelyn his wyf whiche welcomed hym frendly he tolde to her and to his chyldren/ alle the wonder/ that to hym was befallen in the court/ And forgate not a worde/ but tolde to them euery dele/ how he had escaped/ Thenne were they glad that theyr fader was so enhaunsed and grete wyth the kynge/ And the foxe lyued forthon wyth his wyf and his chyldren in grete Ioye and gladnes/ Now who that said to yow of the Foxe more or lesse than ye haue herd or red/ I holde it for lesynge/ but this that ye haue herd or red/ that may ye byleue wel/ and who that byleueth it not/ is not therfore out of the right byleue/ how be it/ ther be many yf that they had seen it/

they shold haue the lasse doubte of it/ for ther ben many thynges in the world whiche ben byleuyd though they were neuer seen/ Also ther ben many fygures/ playes founden/ that neuer were don ne happed/ But for an example to the peple/ that they may ther by the better/ vse and folowe vertue/ and teschewe synne and vyces/ in lyke wyse may it be by this booke/ that who that wyl rede this mater/ though it be of iapes and bourdes/ yet he may fynde therin many a good wysedom and lernynges/ By whiche he may come to vertue and worship. Ther is no good man blamed herin/ hit is spoken generally/ Late euery man take his owne part as it belongeth and behoueth/ and he that fyndeth hym gylty in ony dele or part therof/ late hym bettre and amende hym And he that is veryly good/ I pray god kepe hym therin [l5v] And yf ony thyng be said or wreton herin/ that may greue or dysplease ony man/ blame not me/ but the foxe/ for they be his wordes and not myne/ Prayeng alle them that shal see this lytyl treatis/ to correcte and amende/ Where they shal fynde faute/ For I haue not added ne mynusshed but haue folowed as nyghe as I can my copye whiche was in dutche/ and by me william Caxton translated in to this rude and symple englyssh in thabbey of westmestre. fynysshed the vj daye of Iuyn the yere of our lord ·M.CCCC.Lxxxj. and the xxj yere of the regne of kynge Edward the iiijth/

¶ Here endeth the historye of Reynard the foxe etc.

NOTES

3/6–7 Caxton added *and of the catte Tybert*, in which the *of* means 'concerning, about' (cf. *Of them that were frendis . . .* 4/29), for the cat makes no complaint against Reynard in this chapter.

5/12 *to his aboue*: *te bouen* (P p. 3); the phrase occurs frequently in Caxton's writings. The *his* refers to the fox, and the whole phrase means 'how the fox came out on top'. This idiom occurs in English from the thirteenth to the fifteenth century, the last quotation being from Caxton. See OED. *Above*, C. 2, and MED. *above(n, adv.* as *n.* 2 (a).

5/19 ff. Caxton omits the penultimate chapter heading found in P, but he includes it in the body of the text (108/14–15) with the result that he has two chapters numbered 43.

6/2 There is no need to emend *lerynge* to *lernynge*, the reading in PL, for *lerynge* is found occasionally in ME. (see OED. *Lering*, where the last quotation is dated *c.* 1460) and Caxton was probably influenced by the Dutch text which has *leren* (3).

6/7 In C *good* and *god* are both spelt indiscriminately with a single or a double *o*, though in PL they are spelt in conformity with modern orthographic practice. This confusion is rare in other ME. texts, and the confusion in C perhaps originated with the compositor rather than with Caxton. In general, however, I have emended the forms only when *good* and *god* occur in proximity to each other, where corruption could have crept in more easily.

6/8 *mowe* translates P's *mogen* (12). Although Kellner found in *Blanchardyn and Eglantine* (1489) that *mowe* was used more frequently by Caxton than *may* (Introduction, pp. liii–liv), this is the only time it is used in C; see Blake, p. 314.

6/16 *wyth ones ouer redyng*: 'by glancing through it only once'.

6/22 For a discussion of the feudal and legal background of the Reynard story and how this may have influenced the characterization in it see J. Graven, *Le Procès criminel du Roman de Renart*, 1950. Royal courts were normally held at the great church festivals. The *that* has the sense of 'when', see OED. *That, relative pron.* 7. The sense is: It was at Whitsun, when the trees become green . . ., that Noble decided to hold an assembly. Cf. 10/36.

6/27 *on open Court at stade*: cf. *te stade een eerlic hof* (P 33). *Open* must here have the sense 'not confined or limited to a few, generally accessible or available', see OED. *Open, a.* 14, though MD. *eerlic* means 'noble, honourable'. The interpretation of C's *at stade* is disputed. Dutch scholars, however, are agreed that P's *te stade* means 'in great state', cf. RII's *myt groten loue* (B 57), and that it is not a place-name; see Teirlinck, pp. 225–6, and Muller–Logeman, p. 159. Stallybrass, p. 2, and Morley–Thoms, p. 44, translate C's *at stade* as 'at state'; but it is more likely that Caxton thought the MD. *stade* was a place-name, and there is a village named Staden in W. Flanders. For similar mistakes cf. *in the popes palays of woerden* (69/7 and note) and *dame pogge of chafporte* (17/12 and note). The later printers understood *stade* to be a place-name: *Staden* PL a1; *stade* RP a1; *Staden* TG a4v; *great palace of Sanden* 1629 a3.

6/31 The names of the animals are taken over direct from the Dutch, though most of them are found already in RR. Some of the animals were known under these names in England before 1481. The fox, for example, is called *Reynarde* in *Sir Gawain and the Green Knight*, l. 1920, but in NPT. VII. 3334 the fox is called Russell, a name derived from his red colour. For earlier accounts of the fox and the wolf in England see Introduction, § 1 and F. Mossé, *Les Langues modernes*, xlv (1951), 70–84.

7/6 ff. The account of Reynard's visit to Isegrim's house is told in detail in RR. branch II and it forms the basis of Isegrim's complaint before Noble in RR. branch Va.

7/16 *the book wyth the sayntes* translates *die heiligen* (58) which may well mean only 'the holy relics', although at P 5437 a book is clearly implied. It was common legal practice to attest one's innocence by taking an oath on the Bible or some other holy book. Thus we find an early sixteenth-century merchant swearing 'uppon the holy evangelistes' (J. Webb, *Great Tooley*, 1962, p. 69). This incident in C is ultimately based on an episode in RR. branch Va in which Reynard was to have sworn upon the relics of St. Roonel the dog in order to clear himself of the charge of defiling Isegrim's wife and children. But because Roonel, who had allied himself with Isegrim, was only feigning death and was waiting for Reynard to approach close enough so that he could seize him, Reynard refused to swear the oath. The previous clause, *and haue sworen on the holy sayntes that he was not gylty therof*, was added by Caxton; see Introduction, § 3.

7/19–24 Stallybrass, p. 3, puts these lines after '. . . woxen blynde' (7/13), claiming that they are misplaced in C. But Caxton follows the Dutch text closely here and emendation is unnecessary.

7/21 *he is not lyuyng*: 'there is no person alive, i.e. nobody'.

7/26 ff. In RR. branch XXVI Reynard steals a sausage from Tibert; the part of Curtois is apparently the work of the Flemish adaptor of RI.

7/33 It is only here that Tibert is on Reynard's side; otherwise he is his implacable foe. Muller II, p. 23, suggested that Tibert supports Reynard here because of the perpetual enmity between cat and dog.

8/2–3 Sands, p. 48, punctuates *How be it that I complain not?* But this clause goes with what follows and *how be it* means 'even though', cf. *Al* (P 82). See OED. *Howbeit*, B. *conj*.

8/5 *that cam by me to*: Stallybrass, p. 4, and Sands, p. 48, modernize *to* as *too*. There is no equivalent in P, which has a different construction (86). But there is a MD. expression *toe comen*, 'to come about, arise', which Caxton may have imitated unconsciously here, cf. *the moste parte of alle cam to by the vertue of the wode* (80/16, P 4329–30 *quam . . . toe*; and see Introduction, § 2). The use of adverbial prepositions closely linked with a verb is a feature of C which is taken over from the Dutch, see de Reul, pp. 193–6.

8/5 In C *panther* is used as a personal name, not as a generic one. In this Caxton follows the Dutch. Stallybrass, p. 4, takes Panther to be the beaver, for this is the name of the beaver in RI (A 126); but at 30/14 he is described as *the boore* (cf. P 1361 *everzwijn*). See note to 30/14.

8/8 *that*: 'but that'.

8/14 P has it that Reynard held the hare fast between his feet when the hare sat there.

8/31 For this proverb see Jente, no. 766, and ODEP., p. 172.

8/31–32 Sands modernizes *leye* as *lie* (p. 49) and Stallybrass translates it as *lie* (p. 5). But *what leye ye* is not found in the Dutch text, and was no doubt added by Caxton as a doublet of *wyte* 'to lay blame or guilt upon someone'. So *leye* must mean 'to bring forward as a charge or accusation' and is part of the verb 'to lay', OE. *lecgan*; see OED. *Lay, v.*[1] 27. The sense is 'What do you accuse my uncle Reynard of?' Cf. 24/6.

8/35–36 *it shold not be thought in hym/ that it were ynowh*: 'it would not be reckoned a sufficient (requital) in the king's eyes that . . .'. Caxton may, however, have meant the *in hym* to refer to Reynard, though in the Dutch the king is referred to (P 133–4).

8/36–9/1 Caxton misunderstood the Dutch which reads *en sout hem dat niet te vergheues ghedaen hebben* (P 135–6, 'and you would not have done that to him with impunity'). Caxton probably understood *te vergheues* 'for nothing, unpunished' (see Muller–Logeman, p. 160) as 'forgiveness' (cf. MD. *vergeven*, 'to forgive').

9/3 ff. The story of the merchants and the fish is told in RR. branch III. But there Reynard lies down in the road feigning death, is thrown on to the cart and then eats some fish before jumping down with others. Isegrim does not appear in that account. In branch XIV, however, the wolf Primaut tries the same trick, but is discovered and soundly beaten.

9/7 ff. In RR. branch V Reynard and Isegrim fall upon a villain who was carrying a large ham. The man let the ham fall and chased Reynard. In the meantime Isegrim took the ham and kept it to himself so that when Reynard returned all that he found was the rope which had been used to hang the ham up with. The story is found earlier in *Ysengrimus*.

9/8 *that*: 'which', cf. *die* (P 148).

9/22 Stallybrass, p. 6, mistranslates *he shold haue lefte that* as 'he should have believed that . . .'. But the clause means 'he should not have mentioned that . . .'. See OED. *Leave, v.*[1] 4.

9/25–27 The chastisement of children was generally encouraged by medieval writers, who took the proverb 'Who spares the rod spoils the child' as their text. Cf. *Piers Plowman* C vi 139–41 and OED. *Spare*, *v.*[1] 6.

9/31–32 For this proverbial expression see Jente, no. 598.

9/34 There is no counterpart in P to the *that he*. It must be accepted with de Reul, pp. 65–66, as an example of the supplementary pronoun in Caxton. The *that he* supplements the *who that* (9/33) and merely repeats its meaning. For another example cf. *who can gyue to his lesynge a conclusion . . . and that he can so blynde the peple* (61/26–28). In a modern rendering *that he* may be omitted. Stallybrass, p. 6, and Morley–Thoms, p. 47, change the sense by omitting *whiche* (9/35). Thoms, p. 7, and Sands, p. 50, begin a new sentence with *who that* (9/33), but this makes less sense. The clause beginning *who that* is closely linked to what has gone before as P 186–7 shows. The sense must be: If he took stolen goods from a thief, it is quite in order as anyone [knows] who is [as] acquainted with the law, etc., as my uncle Reynard is. The corresponding sentence in P is also difficult, cf. Muller–Logeman, p. 161.

9/37 *Menowr* from AN. *meinoure*, *mainoure*, etc., is a legal term meaning 'a stolen object found in a thief's possession when he is arrested'; see OED. *Mainour*, *manner*. P has *mit dieften* (191).

10/3 Cf. P 196 *scadet*. For the confusion of final *-d* and *-th* see *English Versions*, pp. 70–71.

10/9–10 It makes better sense to take the *as I yesterday herd saye of them that cam fro hym* with what follows (cf. Stallybrass, p. 7) rather than with what precedes (cf. Sands, p. 51), though either is possible.

10/11 On *Maleperduys*, ultimately from OF. *Malpertuis*, *Maupertius*, 'a robber hole', see Teirlinck, pp. 166–81.

10/16 Caxton has mistranslated the Dutch, which has that Grimberd was speaking about his uncle (P 219–21). Caxton has made it seem as though the badger is Reynard's uncle, but the relationship is the opposite (cf. 12/7).

10/25 *two the fayrest hennes*: i.e. 'the two most beautiful hens', see OED. *Two*, B. I. 1b and cf. *one the best chylde* (33/20). See de Reul, pp. 20–21, and T. Mustanoja, *A Middle English Syntax*, 1960, pp. 299–300.

10/28 *susters*: P 236 has *broeders*.

10/36 It is better to emend the passage to bring it into line with P 249–50 *Alsoe dat ick koene ende hoemoedich was*, for otherwise the *I* remains isolated with no predicate, cf. Morley–Thoms, p. 49. See de Reul, p. 211. Caxton's *as that* (translating *Alsoe dat*) means merely 'that'.

11/12 P has *dat hem sinen pels stoef* (267, 'so that the hair flew out from his skin like dust'), so the sense of *smoked* is probably 'to give off dust'; see OED. *Smoke*, *v.* 2.

11/15 There are many late medieval carvings and pictures extant in which the fox is dressed in some form of ecclesiastical garb. Usually, however, the audience consists of geese, not hens. See K. Varty, *Reynard the Fox*, 1967.

11/21 The slavin is a pilgrim's mantle, but the pilch is an outer garment usually made of skin dressed with hair. The pilch has no particular connexion with clerical dress.

11/27 Caxton has changed the Dutch *haghe* (290) into a *hawthorn*, though at 11/30 it is merely a *busshe*. In NPT. the fox lies in a *bed of wortes* (VII. 3221).

11/29 One of the few occasions when Caxton uses a more expressive word than the Dutch, for he translates *namse te gadere* (293) as *clucked hem to gydre*. For a general discussion of Caxton's language, see N. F. Blake, *Neuphilologische Mitteilungen*, lxvii (1966), 122–32.

11/32 In some versions Reynard puts the captured fowl in his bag, otherwise he merely puts it *on his bak*, as in NPT. VII. 3336.

11/34 The sense would be better if the *hym* and the *vs* were transposed, for *kepe* here has the sense of 'guard, keep in safety' and is parallel to *saue*, cf. P 301 *ons beschermen of bewaren*. But the confusion may have arisen in translation with some misunderstanding over the meaning of *kepe* rather than in the printing, and so no emendation has been made.

12/8 Arber, p. 11 and elsewhere, emends *abye* to *abyde*. But P has *becopen* (315) for which *abye* is a suitable translation. See OED. *Aby, abye, v. arch.* 2, and de Reul, p. 88.

12/14–15 *Placebo Domino* are the words which open the first antiphon of the Vespers of the Dead. Thus they come to mean the Vespers themselves. Cf. *Piers Plowman* C iv 467.

12/16 The vigil is the Office for the Dead. Similarly the commendation is an office for the dead which gets its name from the closing prayer *Tibi, Domine, commendamus* in which the soul of the dead person was 'commended' to God.

12/20 *Byte* here has the sense of 'to bite to death'; P has *verbeten* (338). See Introduction, § 2.

12/20 Previous commentators have been misled by the stroke in C and have understood *for* as a preposition, e.g. Sands, p. 54: 'Complain You for Her! She Is Shamefully . . .'. But *complayne* is a transitive verb, see OED. *Complain, v.* 1, and *for* is a conjunction, cf. *want* (P 339). The sense is: Mourn for her because she suffered a shameful death.

12/29 The idiomatic expression *see wel to* has often been misunderstood by previous commentators. It means 'take care, take heed' and does not need to be altered; see OED. *See, v.* B. 25 and Introduction, § 2. But Stallybrass, p. 10 and elsewhere, emends to *see well to* [*it*], and Sands occasionally alters the idiom: on p. 70 he incorrectly modernizes to *see well tofore you*, where the phrase means 'take care of yourself'.

12/33 *casus*: 'an elementary lesson, an ABC', cf. *casus* (P 359). The word is not found in OED. In the Dutch versions it is found only in P, where it is a loan from medieval Latin. From the meaning 'case (of a substantive etc.)', *casus* developed the meaning 'grammar, an elementary lesson'. See further Muller–Logeman, p. 163. In TG the word is replaced by *lesson.*

13/5 The first *as* perhaps has the sense of 'thus, so' here from the Dutch *Also* (P 367). *Forest* means 'a waste region'; cf. P's *in eenre woestenien* (368) and see OED. *Forest, sb.* 3. *Ther bysyde* (13/6) means 'at the edge of the wilderness'; cf. *Besiden der woestinen* (P 369–70).

13/7 *and lande* translates *ende lant* (P 370–1). Possibly *lant* could mean 'a piece of land', but it is more probably a misprint for MD. *lanc* 'long'; cf. RII *Een wech hooch ende lanck* (B 532) and *this longe hylle* (C 13/35).

13/24 Caxton has translated *noot* 'prey' (P 376) as 'need'; see Muller–Logeman, p. xlvii.

13/25 *that*: here 'when', cf. *als* (P 396).

14/3–4 Sands, p. 56, following Morley–Thoms, p. 52, and Stallybrass, p. 12, modernizes 'the most gentle and richest of levies and of land'. It is doubtful whether either the spelling or the sense supports an interpretation of *leeuys* as 'levies'. P has *die meeste van loue van alden lande* (423–4) where *loue* means 'praise'. Perhaps because of *lande* Caxton confused this word with MD. *loueren* 'leaves' (cf. P 30 *loueren*: *leuys* 6/24); and note that Caxton later translated *tymmerman van groten loue* (P 497) as *carpenter of grete tymbre* (15/12–13). See Blake, p. 307. Thoms, p. 172, and Stallybrass, p. 264, suggest that the phrase might be an alliterative formula, but it does not occur elsewhere. Though it makes little sense, the text is not emended as this is a translation error on Caxton's part.

14/9–10 To make sense of *that I ete what myght it helpe yow that yf I tolde yow* understand the second *that* in the sense 'as to that'. It probably arose through hasty translation of *dat ick at wat helpet v dat ick v dat veel seide* (P 431–2). Caxton may have intended to replace P's *dat* by *yf*, but perhaps included the *that* by mistake as well.

14/23 Red is the usual colour of the fox, though the additional sense of 'cunning, false' may be implied; see R. Sprenger, *Germania*, xxi (1876), 350–1. In NPT. the fox is described as a *col-fox* (VII. 3215).

14/27 i.e. 'all the honey that is to be found from here to Portugal'. But P 457 reads *poertegale* and it is possible that a south Dutch village called Poortugaal was referred to. See Teirlinck, pp. 197–201.

14/35 *vij hamber barelis*: OED. *Hamber* and *Amber, sb.*[2] derives *hamber* from *amber* 'a liquid measure'. No forms are found in English between 1100 and 1481. But the word *ambra* is found in medieval Latin during this time, see R. E. Latham, *Revised Medieval Latin Word-List*, 1965, s.v. [1]*ambra* and *manbra*. A *hamber barel* is therefore a barrel designed to hold an 'amber' of any fluid. It may be that Caxton had come across this measure in his business life; P has *seuen aemen* (470–1). Cf. MED. *ambre, n.*

15/14 ff. For the story of the bear caught in the oak compare the originally oriental story of the ape who watched the carpenter splitting a log by the use of wedges. After the carpenter goes away, the ape sits on the log, pulls out the wedges and is caught in the tree by the testicles. On the carpenter's return he gets a good thrashing. See L. Hervieux, *Les Fabulistes latins*, 1899, v. 114, 345–7, 450.

15/24 It makes the irony more pointed if we accept with Sands, p. 58, that *mesure is good in alle mete* is spoken by Bruin. Stallybrass, p. 15, and Morley–Thoms, p. 54, make it part of Reynard's speech. Note the play on the word *mesure* which occurs throughout this interchange.

15/35 Previous editors have not emended *crutched*, though OED. *Crutch, v.*[2] suggested it was a misprint or error for *cratch*. This seems the most probable explanation, for P 531 has *crassede*; and *cratch* is used elsewhere in C: 37/27, 95/2. In all instances *cratched* means 'scratched'.

16/19 Only those who had proceeded to the higher orders of the priestly calling were obliged to remain celibate; those in the lower orders, such as clerks, could marry if they wished. See Muller II, pp. 54–57. Nevertheless in view of the general tone of the work, it is likely that Julok was the priest's concubine and that she was introduced as part of the general satire against the church.

16/20 *she sat tho and spanne*: i.e. 'she had been sitting and spinning at that time'.

16/21–2 Cf. P 567 *Nv naket brunen veel scanden*; see de Reul, p. 13, on the transformation of the dative into the nominative.

16/22–3 *that he allone muste stande ayenst them alle*. In his haste Caxton may have misread *dat een op al setten*, 'he must do his utmost' (P 568), as *dat al op een setten*; see Muller–Logeman, p. xlvii.

17/3 As Bertolt is called 'Sir', it is possible that he was some kind of cleric, though he is not the priest of the village. Otherwise the title may be used ironically to imply someone who gives himself airs; cf. *my dame baue* (17/6). The description of him as *with the longe fyngers* implies someone who knows how to steal.

17/5–6 For games in medieval England see A. L. Poole, *Medieval England*, 2nd ed., 1958, pp. 605–32 and references there.

17/6 *Aue* is the name of the woman Abelquak. She is not another woman as Stallybrass, p. 17, and Morley–Thoms, p. 56, suppose.

17/12 *dame pogge of chafporte*: *vrou pogge van cafpoerten* (P 612), which corresponds to RII *Vrou Julocke vander after poorten* (B 844). MD. *cafpoerte* (literally 'chaff-gate', i.e. exit for waste) is a scornful and impolite nickname which Caxton misunderstood as a place-name; cf. 6/27 and 69/7.

17/13–14 Thoms, p. 18, Stallybrass, p. 17, Morley–Thoms, p. 56, and Sands, p. 60, all put a full-stop after *stowte man*. This ruins the humour of the passage, for Macob was a brave man only so long as he had no one to fight against. We may assume that Lantfert his son was tarred with the same brush.

17/20–1 Sands, p. 61, and other commentators punctuate 'wherefore he was full of sorrow when he saw his wife lie in the water. Him lusted no longer to smite the bear, . . .'. It would perhaps be better to punctuate with a full-stop after 'sorrow' and a comma after 'water'; cf. P 623–6.

17/24 The way in which pardons were distributed by the church was one of the major complaints of the protestant preachers. On pardons and pardoners see particularly J. Jusserand, *English Wayfaring Life in the Middle Ages*, 2nd ed., 1889, p. 309 ff.

17/31 Caxton has changed the parishioners of the Dutch text to the priest (17/28), but he forgot to change *them* to the singular.

18/12 *hym*: *v* (P 673). The Dutch has direct speech here.

18/19 The bear is called a priest because he has lost all the hair on top of his head and thus Reynard implies he has taken the tonsure. The joke is repeated about the wolf later, 87/7–8.

18/27 It seems better to emend the text here to bring it in line with P, which reads *Weer sidi een moninck of een abt* (694–5), 'Where are you a monk or an abbot?' (i.e. In what monastery do you live?). Attempts to explain the text as given in C are not particularly happy. Thoms, p. 20, reads *Were ye a monke or an abbot*?, though we should have expected *Are ye*. . . . Sands, p. 62, modernizes to 'Were you a monk or an abbot, he that shaved your crown . . .', presumably implying 'If you were a monk . . .'.

18/29 *don of your gloues* continues the joke and refers to the gloves which an abbot would wear. He would take them off to officiate at divine services, and so Reynard thinks Bruin is going to sing compline.

19/24 *another tyme*: 'on the second occasion'; cf. *this seconde tyme* (19/27). Both instances translate MD. *anderweruen*.

20/2 *ther lyeth not on*: 'that has no bearing on this matter', see Introduction, § 2. For the proverb which follows cf. *The Owl and the Nightingale*, 761 ff. and see the references in E. G. Stanley, *The Owl and the Nightingale*, 1960, pp. 160–3.

20/6 *Tybert made hym sone redy* translates *makede hem haesteliken heen* (P 770, 'made his way speedily from there'), and thus it is that the next action occurs when Tibert is on his way, although this is not so clear in C.

20/7 *one of seynt martyns byrdes*: *enen sinte martijns voegelen* (P 772). The significance of St. Martin is uncertain here, as is the kind of bird implied; see du Cange, *Glossarium Mediæ et Infimæ Latinitatis*, 1884–7, s.v. *Avis S. Martini*; commentators have suggested the hen-harrier, the crow, raven, or goose. Clearly it is a bird of ill-omen. Birds were frequently used in divination and augury in almost all European countries. See further Muller I, pp. 109–10.

20/21 *whad*: a variant spelling found occasionally in the fifteenth century, so there is no need to emend.

21/5 Without reference to the Dutch text it is not always possible to tell whether *ye* is a pronoun or an interjection. But in *ye tybert saye ye me trouthe* the first *ye* means 'yea', and the second 'you'; cf. P 827–8 *Iae tybert. segdi mi oec waer*. See de Reul, p. 33.

21/8 *flawnes*: 'tarts', or even like the modern 'flans'; commonly in ME. associated with pasties, *Havelok*, l. 644. See T. Austin, *Two Fifteenth-Century Cookery-Books*, EETS., o.s. 91, 1888 repr. 1964, pp. 51, 73 (where the by-form *flathon* is used).

21/15 The sense must be 'Full? That would be many (mice)'. Cf. P 841 *zat dat waer al vele*, though RII reads *wat* for *zat* (B 1168).

21/18 *quod the foxe* is added in C, but *foxe* is here a mistake for *catte*, for Tibert speaks these lines. It was later realized that a mistake had been made, and in PL *reyner quod the foxe* is changed (incorrectly) to *Tybert quod the foxe*. *Reyner* is the correct reading here, for this is found in P 846. The attempt by Thoms, p. 25, to make sense out of the passage as it stands in C is not convincing.

21/19 Montpelier was the site of a famous medical school which was already in existence at the beginning of the twelfth century and received its first statutes in 1220. See Teirlinck, pp. 184–7.

22/17 People in the Middle Ages went to bed naked. Muller–Logeman, p. lii, include *moder naked* among their list of Dutch loan-words in C, but OED. *Mother naked*, *a*. records examples earlier than C.

22/18 *Locken* is probably a clipped form of the name *Iulock*; and although P has *locken* (907), RII has *Julocken* (B 1267). They are the same priest and his wife who appeared in the story of Bruin and the honey.

22/24–5 Originally there may have been a satirical meaning behind the priest's castration. The implication would be that he was now in a better position to fulfil his priestly functions without being diverted by the sins of the flesh. See Muller II, pp. 73–4.

23/11 The snare consisted of a string with a running noose, which got tauter the more one struggled. By gnawing through the string Tibert could run away with the noose still round his neck. This piece of string is said to be in his possession later (31/22).

23/21 Caxton has altered P 973 *sijn broeder soen* to *the foxes suster sone*, for that is the relationship given earlier in chapter 4 (8/29).

23/24–5 Sands, p. 69, punctuates '. . . the third time. For all and . . .'; but it is better to put the full-stop after *all*. For the phrase *third time for all* cf. the more modern *once for all*; see OED. *All*, A. *adj*. 9a.

24/21 Stallybrass, p. 28, translates *for ther lacketh my counseyl* as 'for there my counsel was at fault'. But the sense is 'the court is in need of my advice' and this thought is developed by Reynard at 24/25–30. P 1022–3 reads *want daer is mijns raets ghebrec*.

24/25–6 i.e. their enmity is only skin-deep, cf. P 1029 *ten gaet hem niet ter herten*.

24/33 Caxton's *that shal hurte me* is a literal translation of P 1039 *dat sal mi deeren*. In RII the clause read *Dit heb ic anxt sel my dair deren* (B 1435, 'I am afraid that I shall suffer harm there'). The *heb ic anxt* was omitted in P, but Caxton did not realize that this left his *that shal hurte me* rather isolated.

25/4 For the name *rosel* cf. *daun Russell the fox* (NPT. VII. 3334). No satisfactory origin for the name has yet been found; see C. Dahlberg, 'Chaucer's Cock and Fox', *JEGP*. liii (1954), 277 ff.

25/25 *whom . . . his*: i.e. 'whose'; cf. P 1080 *dien ic sijn crune*.

25/26 *her . . . she*: Tibert is otherwise portrayed as a male, but Caxton has confused the sex here.

26/1 C omits *at*, but at 65/31 we find *at elmare*, though in PL the omission at 26/1 is corrected by the addition of an *of*. Elmare was a Benedictine priory between Aardenburg and Biervliet which was founded in 1144 as a daughter house of St. Peter's in Ghent. It was destroyed by a flood in 1424. See Teirlinck, pp. 43–53. The story of how Reynard made Isegrim a monk is told in RR. branch III.

26/2 ff. The bell-ringing episode originates from RR. branch XIV, although there the principal actors are the wolf Primaut and Reynard. A similar account is found in RR. branch XII, though in this branch it is Tibert whom Reynard deceives.

26/7 The meaning of *to axe the religyon* is obscure. P 1103–4 reads *eer hi te woerde conde comen ende segghen ick wil mi begheuen*, 'before he could speak and say "I will become a monk",' for MD. *begeven* has the meaning 'to leave the world and enter a monastery'. Since Caxton uses *religyon* elsewhere (41/24) to mean 'a monastery', probably *to axe the religyon* means 'to ask [if he could join] the monastery', though it is not clear whether the phrase by itself means that or whether the text should be emended to include some words such as *to join*.

26/8–9 At 89/3 ff. it is said that it is Isegrim's wife who was taught to catch fish by Reynard. The original story is found in RR. branch III.

26/10 *Vermedos* is the ancient French province of Vermandois in East Picardy, linked by the marriage of its rulers to Flanders in 1156–86; see Teirlinck, pp. 241–3 and also pp. 7–15, and Muller I, p. 126. For this story cf. RR. branch XIV where the episode is told of the wolf.

26/20 In RI this chicken was a tame one belonging to the pastor. It may have been intended to satirize the dogs and birds which religious kept as pets; see Muller II, pp. 92–3.

28/12 The black nuns were probably members of the Benedictine order. Augustinian nuns also wore black, but they were not established in the Low Countries when RI was written; see Muller II, p. 103.

29/16 C reads *syttyng* here and at 70/29 and 90/30, though Thoms, Stallybrass, Morley–Thoms, and Sands all read *fitting* on these three occasions. But see OED. *Sitting, ppl. a.* 2. The word is not changed in the sixteenth- and seventeenth-century versions.

29/21 *ones*: i.e. 'one day'. There is no parallel in P; the reference is presumably to Doomsday.

29/25 Cf. P 1320–1 *als ghi te hant wel aen mi vernemen selt.*

30/14 Sands, p. 79, Morley–Thoms, p. 72, and Stallybrass, p. 36, punctuate 'panther, the boar', as if Panther and the boar were two different animals. Although in RI Panther was the name of the beaver and not of the boar (A 1855–7), in P we find *dat everzwijn panther* (1361–2) corresponding to *panther the boore*, and so we must accept that Caxton understood Panther to be the boar's name.

30/15 The name Brunel was usually applied to an ass, cf. Chaucer's *Daun Burnel the Asse* (NPT. VII. 3312) and Nigellus's poem about the ass entitled *Burnellus seu Speculum Stultorum.*

30/16 *hamel the oxe*: in P 1365 the animal is merely described as *harmel* (a weasel), but Caxton may have confused it with MD. *hamel* (a wether) or merely taken it as a name and added 'the ox'. Cf. 75/3 n.

30/17 Caxton added the name Pertelot, which is not found in any of the Dutch versions, from NPT.; see Blake, p. 309, and Muller–Logeman, p. xlvi (note).

30/33 Caxton mistranslated the Dutch; cf. P 1388 and see Introduction, § 3.

31/1 *yonglyng*: *iongelinc* (P 1397). The MD. word was part of the epic style of the romances, and it may have been used by the author of RI to parody that style; see Muller II, p. 112.

31/6 ff. The sense of the passage is: Because it is almost dark and because there are so many hedges and bushes in which Reynard could hide himself, he would never be found again if he escaped. The punctuation in Stallybrass, p. 37, Morley–Thoms, pp. 72–73, and Sands, p. 80, hardly makes this clear.

31/9 *thus*: i.e. inactive.

31/14 In RI the two brothers are said to have been called *Rumen* and *Wijde lancken* (A 1924), but the story behind this allusion is not known. See Muller II, pp. 113–14.

31/18 *balked*: OED. *Balk, v.*[1] 3 glosses this word as 'To stop short as at an obstacle, to pull up'. But Sands, p. 207, writes 'Probably "bellowed", which is the sense of the Gouda edition's *ballech*, preterite of *belken*/*belleken*'. Stallybrass, p. 37, translates it as 'growled'; Morley–Thoms, p. 73, n. 1, as 'brayed'. Thoms, p. 177, glosses as 'Was angry, from the Flemish *belgen*, in past tense *balch*, to be angry'. This is the sense accepted by Muller–Logeman, p. l, who reject OED.'s translation. It is best to accept this sense here; see further Introduction, § 2.

31/20 ff. Reynard urges his enemies to expedite his execution in order that they should go on ahead to prepare the gallows. This will allow him to flatter the king and queen in their absence. After Reynard is forgiven, the raven has to fly off to tell his enemies what has happened (42/25 ff.). However, the actual progression of events is not entirely clear in C.

31/36 Arber misread C's *pray* as *pay* (p. 32), a reading adopted by other editors, e.g. Sands, p. 81. P, however, reads *dorst ic. ick woude v ghenade doen* (1445–6, 'If I dared, I would show you mercy'), which is not very fitting in the context. But Caxton does make minor improvements in the text; see Blake, pp. 307–8.

32/5 *I wote wherto I shal*: cf. P 1452–3 *Ic ben des op deser vren al ghetroest*, a corruption of RII's *Jc bins getroost te dese werue* (B 2003). Caxton made nothing of the Dutch and introduced his own interpretation. But the relevance of his *I wote wherto I shal* is not obvious. Possibly the fox is suggesting that after death he will go to heaven and this is a source of comfort to him.

32/30 The meaning of this passage is not clear. P 1493–4 has *nv quamen si daer die galghe stont*, 'now they came to where the gallows stood'. Stallybrass, p. 39 n., suggests 'I shall rise in esteem as high as they would raise me on the gallows' as a translation, and all previous commentators make this sentence part of Reynard's monologue, though the sense is somewhat harsh. Yet this is the most satisfactory solution unless one accepts that Caxton related this sentence to (*he*) *thought* (32/24); *as fer as* could then mean 'all the time until'. He was thinking of these things all the way to the gallows.

33/3 C's reading *helpe* makes little sense, although it is kept by all previous commentators. P 1507 reads *bewaren*, 'guard', which is the sense required here. So I suggest emending to *kepe*, although *holde* would also be a possible emendation. *Helpe* may have been introduced because of its occurrence two lines above.

34/16 The omission of the subject pronoun is common in Caxton, see de Reul, pp. 30–2. The sense is: You would have been murdered . . . and it would have. . . .

34/25 *packe*: i.e. a bag of lies, cf. 82/13 *sack ful of wyles*. The idea of the fox or another animal keeping all his tricks in a bag or purse is a common one. See E. G. Stanley, *The Owl and the Nightingale*, 1960, l. 694 and note.

34/27–30 The sense is: Because I must die, even if you had not exhorted me [to confess] so strongly, I will not encumber my soul [with unconfessed sins]. If I did so [i.e. if I did encumber my soul with unconfessed sins], my soul would go to hell. Stallybrass, p. 42, Morley–Thoms, p. 77, and Sands, p. 84, misunderstand the passage by taking *dyde* (34/29) as 'died' instead of 'did'. The passage is somewhat harsh because of the *and hadde ye me not so sore coniured*. Reynard is saying that because he is going to die he will confess, but because the queen has urged him to confess he does it the more readily. Not to confess would mean that his soul would go to hell. If this were not so, he would not want to confess because he must implicate his kinsmen in his confession.

35/21 Ermanaric was a ruler of the Goths in the fourth century. He quickly became for Germanic authors the typical tyrant and rich king, and he is constantly referred to in earlier Germanic literature. 'A remarkable piece of evidence to prove the significance of heroes in Church circles is provided not by legends of the saints but by a document of the tenth century, the *Miracula S. Bavonis,* which contains the information that a King Hermenrik was supposed to have founded his imperial castle in Ghent. This also explains how the Dutch poem *Reinaert* still knows about the treasures of this Gothic king.' (J. de Vries, *Heroic Song and Heroic Legend*, trans. B. J. Timmer, 1963, p. 237.)

35/26 Many of the adventures described in *Reynard the Fox* take place in Flanders which was the homeland of the poet of RI and possibly also of the poet of RII; see Teirlinck, pp. 245–7.

35/31 *gaunt*: *ghent* (P 1664). *Yfte* appears in the Dutch texts as Hijfte (or Yfte) and Yste. In the Middle Ages Hijfte was a small village which was situated just outside Ghent on the north-east side. See Teirlinck, pp. 79–84.

35/36 Akon, that is Aachen or Aix-la-Chapelle, is the city in which the German kings were traditionally crowned from 832 to 1531.

36/10 *the holy thre kynges of coleyne*: Caxton added *of coleyne*, see Introduction, § 3. The relics of the three holy kings were brought to Cologne from Milan by Frederick I (Barbarossa) in 1162.

36/17 ff. The story of the frogs and the stork is based ultimately on one of Aesop's fables, though there the frogs are given a water-snake as their ruler; see Lenaghan, pp. 90–91, for Caxton's version.

36/27 *to strengthe theyr kynge*: *den oudeuaer horen coninck* (P 1715). P's reading has led most previous commentators to take *strengthe* as an abstract noun personified. But de Reul, p. 2, suggests that as Caxton did not translate *oudeuaer* a few lines earlier, he probably did not know its meaning. So it is better to take *strengthe* as the verb 'to support' here; cf. 61/35.

37/21 In the bestiaries it is the lion who erases his footprints by sweeping his tail over them; see McCulloch, p. 137.

38/2 As OED. distinguishes between *sold* and *souldie*, the latter is included in the list of Dutch loans in C, see Introduction, § 2. But the phrase *sould and wages* was common in the fifteenth century in proclamations concerning the French war, and even the verbal phrase *to be soulded or waged* is found; see R. W. Chambers and M. Daunt, *A Book of London English 1384–1425*, 1931, pp. 70, 77. Caxton may well have based his *souldye or wagis* on this common phrase, though he took the actual form *souldye* from MD.

38/16 *dassen*: i.e. 'of the dasse (badger)'. Caxton has taken over the Dutch genitive in *-en*; see Introduction, § 2.

38/24–25 'In this way Bruin's treacherous plan remained unfulfilled on account of my subtlety.' For *abide after* see Introduction, § 2.

39/3–4 Caxton translates *In dien dat . . . Ende dat* (P 1859–60) as *yf . . . and that*.

39/20 *stoundmele*: cf. P 1885 *belopen*; see Muller–Logeman, p. xlviii.

39/22 Cf. 39/31. The straw was used as a legal symbol, particularly in Frankish law, to represent the conveyance or quit-claim of land or other possessions, and also to confirm the handing over of gifts. The symbol was normally a straw, Latin *festuca* hence *festucatio*, but it could also be a stick covered with runes or some other token. See du Cange, *Glossarium* s.v. *Festuca*, and F. Pollock and F. W. Maitland, *The History of English Law before the Time of Edward I*, 2nd ed., 1898, ii. 184 ff.

39/27–28 Caxton translates P 1897–8 closely, which has in its turn somewhat abbreviated the passage in RII: *Jc sel dair om dencken bin ic vroet / Ende v des dancken hogelijck* (B 2577–8).

40/2 Hulsterlo was probably a district between Hulst and Kieldrecht. The name Hulsterlo occurs first in Dutch records in 1136. It appears to have been a district with woodland and moor, etc., which was not entirely barren. It is now called Kauter; see further Teirlinck, pp. 88–110.

40/2 Krekenpit, like Hulsterlo, lies in the neighbourhood of Kieldrecht in Waas; see further Teirlinck, pp. 123–40.

40/29 *fro rome to maye*: *van romen tot meye* (P 1954), but in the other Dutch texts the phrase is slightly different. The expression exhibits a humorous mixture of a spatial and a temporal measure of reckoning. Instead of saying 'from Rome to London' or 'from January to May', the Dutch author combined the two. The sense is: Your statement is as far from the mark as Rome is distant from May. For similar expressions see Teirlinck, pp. 120–3.

40/30 The River Jordan is often referred to as a *flomme* in ME., see OED. *Flume, sb.* 1. As a biblical river it was probably well known, though its relevance in this phrase is not clear. The expression appears to be equivalent to the modern 'lead up the garden path'. See Teirlinck, pp. 112–13.

41/6 The original reading of RI was probably *reynout de ries* (A 2668, 'Reynout the dog'). This was transformed in the Dutch texts to *Pater simonet die vriese* (P 1977). Simonet is a punning name on simony, but the relevance of 'Frisian' (*vriese*) is not apparent. See Teirlinck, pp. 247–54.

41/29–32 On pilgrims, their dress and their reasons for embarking on a pilgrimage see particularly J. Jusserand, *English Wayfaring Life*, 2nd ed., 1889, p. 338 ff.

43/20 Caxton mistranslated the Dutch *wildi* (P 2109 'would you arrange for Erswind to give me two of her shoes') as a conditional through inversion, and so he rendered as *yf ye myght*. He failed to provide an apodosis for the protasis he had created. By the *she may wel doo it* we are to understand 'she may easily give me them', though P adds 'with honour' (2111).

44/16–17 *grece his shoes*: cf. *Sayme of hereng; Men enoynte therwyth shoes*. (H. Bradley, *Dialogues in French and English by William Caxton*, EETS., E.S. 79, 1900, p. 20.)

44/26 In RI the authority quoted is Meester Jufroet (A 2952), on whom see Tinbergen–Dis, pp. 36–37. There is no agreement as to which theologian is meant, but Geoffroy d'Angers, a twelfth-century theologian, and his teacher, a certain Guillelmus, have been suggested.

44/29 MD. *hem* is dative singular and plural of the third person of the personal pronoun. Caxton has here confused singular and plural, a not uncommon feature of his translation, cf. 17/31, 61/25. The sense is: . . . if he would abandon those sins, confess, receive penance and act in accordance with his priest's advice, God will forgive them (*for* him?) and be merciful unto him.

44/33–34 These names, which refer to the grasping and deceitful nature of the clergy, were introduced by the poet of RII. They show that poet's more outspoken and satirical attitude towards the church.

45/19 Although P has only *hebt goods oerlof* (2220–1), it seems better to assume the omission of *yow* here; particularly as the compositor may have omitted the word when he began the next line. For a similar omission, see 68/27.

45/29 *deux aas*: *doys aes* (P 2238). The lowest cast in the game of dice is two aces, i.e. two ones. Hence Reynard was a pilgrim of the lowest possible worth. OED. *Ace*, 2 quotes examples of *ace* in the sense 'worthless' before this, but this is the first occurrence of *deux aas* listed. But cf. OED. *Ambs-ace*, 1 which is recorded from 1297.

47/1–2 This ironic remark by Reynard, which does not fit the context too well, goes back to RII (B 3138–9). In RI Reynard says that the king will give them gifts which he himself would not wish to receive (A 3139–43).

47/11 *wodekokkis*: Thoms, Arber, and Sands retain C's *wododekkis*, which is surely a misprint. There is no corresponding word in P. It is emended in both PL and RP.

48/1 Cf. the proverbial expression 'A forced oath has no worth'; Jente, no. 112, and ODEP., p. 467.

48/6 Cf. ODEP., p. 280.

48/31 *two lettres*: *twee brieuen* (P 2418–19). But RI (A 3252) reads *een paer lettren*, which is based on the Latin *par litterarum*, 'one letter'; see Tinbergen–Dis, p. 201, and Muller II, p. 175. Cf. 49/9.

50/17 The *that I* may have been included by the compositor because of the *that I* in the line above. P 2514 reads *Als*. Thoms, p. 70, Stallybrass, p. 64, and Morley–Thoms, p. 95, omit *that I*; Sands, p. 106, includes it, though he accepts that it may be a typographical error.

51/2 *appoyntement*: P 2541 has *soene*, a technical term used to express the agreement reached between two feuding parties after a murder. A money payment was usually involved. The meaning is here 'pact, agreement', cf. OED. *Appointment*, 2.

51/17–18 This sentence has been consistently misunderstood by earlier commentators: Sands, p. 107, modernizes 'The king did forth with his court and feasted length twelve days longer'; and Stallybrass, p. 66, renders 'The King continued with his Court and feast length twelve days longer'. But *dyde . . . lengthe* means 'prolonged, caused to be prolonged,'; cf. *lengthe* 32/7. The meaning is 'Forthwith the king prolonged his court and feast twelve days longer . . .', cf. P 2566–7 *Die coninc dede ter stont sijn hof xij. dage verlangen. Feste* is a substantive, not a verb, the phrase *courte and feste* translating *hof*; cf. *feest and court* 6/21. See de Reul, p. 14 n.

51/20 This marks the beginning of the continuation by the poet of RII.

52/26 ff. The story of how the fox captured birds by feigning death is found in the medieval bestiaries, see McCulloch, p. 119.

53/32–3 OED. glosses *Flock, sb.*[2] 2 as 'coarse tufts and refuse of wool or cotton . . . used for quilting garments'. This proverb is not recorded in ODEP., but *sleeve* appears in many proverbial expressions and idioms. Muller–Logeman, p. li, record *flockes* among their list of loan-words, but OED. records examples earlier than C. For a discussion of the meaning of the Dutch idiom see Muller–Logeman, p. 176.

54/20 *flee* has here to be understood as 'cause him to be exiled'. It translates *ontvlien* (P 2739) which is probably a misprint for *ontliuen* 'to put to death', the reading in RII (B 3692); see Muller–Logeman, p. 176. For *flee* cf. *or elles exyled out of the lande* (55/24–5). Thoms, p. 76, reads *slee*; Stallybrass, p. 70, and Morley–Thoms, p. 100, read *flay*. See MED. *flen, v.* (1) 1c.

54/30 *more than right*: *bouen recht* (P 2752), see Muller–Logeman, p. xlviii.

54/34 *ayenst hym*: 'evidence enough against him to show' (Sands, p. 210).

55/7 *otherwyse*: 'another time', cf. *anders* (P 2775).

55/18–19 *his brother sone* is added in C, but Grimberd is elsewhere said to be Reynard's sister's son, cf. 8/29, 23/21 n.

55/19–20 *yf it myght haue prouffyted*: Stallybrass, p. 71, Morley–Thoms, p. 101, and Sands, p. 112, take this clause with what follows; but it is perhaps better to understand it with what goes before. 'He was angry and grieved—as if that could be of any help.' This is how the sentence was understood by Thoms, p. 78.

55/20–1 *hye way* translates *rechten wech* (P 2790–1, 'direct way'). The 'most direct road' is the meaning that *hye way* has in Caxton generally, cf. OED. *Highway*, 2. But in pursuing the shortest way Grimberd had to go over or through all the hedges and bushes, so that *hye way* here probably means not the most direct road, but the shortest possible way. For *he spared nether busshe ne hawe* cf. *Sir Orfeo*, l. 346: *He no spard noiþer stub no ston.*

56/4 *for to be here*: *heeruaert* (P 2824), see Introduction, § 3.

56/33 One line of C ends with *grymbert* and probably when the compositor began setting up the next line he omitted *my lyf*; cf. *mijn lijf ende mijn goet* (P 2865) and *both lyf and good* (56/2).

57/12 Reynerdyn, the son of Reynard, is the same as Reynkyn (25/2). For some reason RII's *reynaerdijn* (B 1453) is changed to *reynken* at P 1049, but not elsewhere. Caxton did not bother to compare and correct the names.

57/34 *thynke not longe*: cf. *laet v niet verlanghen* (P 2926–7, 'Don't yearn too much for me'). See OED. *Think, v.*[2] B. 10c, and de Reul, p. 163.

58/5 *by wenyng*: *si gaet bi wylen wtghissen* (P 2940–1; cf. RII *buten gissen*, B 3947). Stallybrass, p. 75, translates 'it goeth otherwise [than] by expectation', and Sands, p. 210, 'Things sometimes go unpredictably'. The sense is certainly 'Things do not always go as expected', as the Dutch shows. *Wenyng* is 'expectation', but the interpretation of *goth by* is difficult. Caxton may have been confused by the Dutch *bi* to include *by*, though *otherwhyle* represents *bi wylen* accurately. Perhaps one could take *go by* in the sense 'go past, pass', cf. OED. *Go, v.* B. 77.

58/29 Houthulst and Elverdinghe are situated in Flanders about ten kilometres apart, Elverdinghe being about seven kilometres from Ieperen. The two place-names are found only in P, for RII has Honthorst and Everdingen (B 3997) and these may be two place-names in Holland. See Teirlinck, pp. 54–57.

58/29 ff. For the story of the fox, the wolf, and the mare, see P. F. Baum, 'The Mare and the Wolf', *Modern Language Notes*, xxxvii (1922), 350–3.

59/9 Caxton changed the Erfurt of P to Oxford, just as in *The Mirrour of the World* whenever Paris is mentioned in the French original he adds Cambridge and Oxford; see N. S. Aurner, *Caxton*, 1926, p. 133.

59/11–12 *bothe lawes*: i.e. canon and civil law; cf. 61/16. The phrase is first recorded in OED. *Law, sb.*[1] 4b from 1577–87.

59/28 *cantum*: 'song, devotional song', cf. *cantum* (P 3041); see Muller–Logeman, p. 178. In OED. Suppl. *Cantus* 'A song or melody, especially ecclesiastical melody' is recorded only from 1590; cf. also *Cant, sb.*[3] I. Caxton took the word straight from P, which in its turn borrowed it direct from medieval Latin; it is not part of normal MD. vocabulary. *Cantum* may be a subtle reminder of the wolf's experience as a monk. From 1629 onward it appears in English versions as *pricksong*.

59/39 *the beste clerkes / ben not the wysest men*: cf. Chaucer's *Reeve's Tale* l. 134 (I. 4054), Henryson's *Morall Fabillis*, l. 1064. See also Jente, no. 288, and ODEP., p. 97.

60/11–12 *er ye shal conne excuse you of the deth*: this passage has been mistranslated from the Dutch by Caxton, who took *doet* (2nd plur. pres. indic. of the verb *doen* 'to do') as the noun *doot/doet* 'death'. P 3075 reads *eer ghi noch v onscult daer of doet*, 'before you can make your excuses in this matter'. The sense of the Dutch passage is: Uncle, I shall forgive you for that as well as for all the anxiety you ought to suffer for it, before you can even excuse yourself for it.

60/14 C reads *sutthe*, which Thoms, p. 86, Stallybrass, p. 78, and Sands, p. 119, emend to *subtle*. But in view of the reading in P 3078–9, *Ende den coninck mit loghentaelen alsoe verblinde*, an emendation to *suche* (or *sutche*) is better, with *suche* corresponding to *alsoe*. Morley–Thoms, p. 107, retain C's *sutthe* which they gloss as 'flattering'; but I can find no justification for this interpretation.

60/15 ff. The sense is: Anyone who lives in this world and uses his ears, eyes, and tongue can expect to become tainted with some of the world's faults, just as anyone who handles honey can expect to get sticky fingers. *Clerly* means 'without taint, without becoming infected'.

60/24 *thought*: *verdriet* (P 3095).

61/3–4 '. . . and [they] introduced it [i.e. the lie] and [the lie] was adopted to make their argument more attractive'.

61/10–16 The syntax of this passage is not clear, for the interpretation of *he is not ronne away fro his maister* is uncertain. Stallybrass, p. 80, and Morley–Thoms, p. 108, would attach it to the previous clause, meaning 'If anyone does not act in this way, he has not run away from his master (i.e. he has not completed his training)'. This is the most probable interpretation and the construction is one found elsewhere in C, cf. 61/26–9. The second part of the passage will then mean 'If anyone knows how to lie without stammering, he can do great things'. Sands, p. 120, interprets the first sentence as a question and takes the *he is not ronne away fro his maister* with what follows meaning 'he is well taught, i.e. he has not left his master before he has learnt all the tricks'. This interpretation is somewhat less convincing. For a discussion of the meaning of the corresponding Dutch phrase see Muller–Logeman, p. 179.

61/16 *skarlet and gryse*: *bont ende scarlaken* (P 3140). Scarlet refers to the colour and quality of the cloak and *gryse* to its fur trimming. The man who can lie is fit to be a high officer of the realm, someone who would wear clothes of this sort. It is doubtful whether there is reference to the dress of a particular profession.

61/25 Another example of Caxton changing number in the middle of a sentence, cf. 17/31. The Dutch has *hi*, 'he', throughout, which Caxton has changed to the plural except here. Cf. de Reul, p. 80.

61/28 *that he*: see note to 9/34.

61/34 *see thurgh their fyngres*: *doer den vingher sien* (P 3170). The phrase appears to mean 'to connive at some wrong by failing to look at it firmly, to overlook something'. OED. *Finger, sb.* 3a gives its first quotation for the idiom from 1549; in C it was taken over direct from P.

61/36 *lyf. scathe* is a compound meaning 'damage to life'. Sands, p. 121, wrongly modernizes 'life, scathe, and hurt'. See Introduction, § 2.

62/4 See note to 12/14–15. To *play placebo* means 'to flatter, be a time-server', cf. OED. *Placebo*, 2. The man who wants to get on in this world has to flatter his superiors.

62/6–7 With this proverb compare the OF. *N'est si sages qui ne foloit*, M. Roques, *Le Roman de Renart*, 1951 ff., vol. ii, l. 4419 (Martin's branch II, l. 429).

62/18 Cf. ODEP., p. 221.

62/19 See Jente, no. 347, and ODEP., p. 130.

63/24–5 See Jente, no. 42, and ODEP., p. 502.

64/21 *Cameryk* (Cambrai) is situated on the Schelde. It was originally a bishopric, but became an archbishopric in 1559. The bishopric extended fairly far north and it included parts of Flanders. Some scholars have tried to identify Martin with one of the officers of the bishopric; but no convincing identification has yet been made. Otherwise it is possible that Martin is a reference to the abbey of St. Martin which was noted for its lax discipline. It should be noted that many of the names given to the apes are names of scorn and mockery: Symon (simony), Prentout (French *prends tout*), Biteluys (someone who eats lice), Fulrompe (foul rump), Hatenette (someone who picks out ticks), and Rukenawe (someone who stinks). Nevertheless, Martin is a name which was often applied to apes, see OED. *Martin*[2], and H. Janson, *Apes and Ape Lore*, 1952, p. 352, n. 63. See also Teirlinck, pp. 116–20.

65/16 *thus come I in the wordes*: i.e. 'a charge is presented against me'. The idiom seems not to be attested elsewhere in English; it is translated literally from the Dutch *soe come ic inden woerden* (P 3372).

65/25 *am I born an honde*: cf. *ben ic bedraghen ende belast* (P 3387). *To bear on hand* is 'to accuse someone wrongly, to abuse with false pretences', see OED. *Bear*, *v.*[1] 3e.

66/8–9 The sentence as it stands is difficult because P misunderstood RII, which reads *Jc ken te romen wel den staet* (B 4538, 'I know how things are arranged in Rome'). Leeu appears to have misread *staet* as *straet* and printed *ick kenne den wech te romen wel* (3417–18). So one has to understand Caxton's prose as elliptical for: 'rather than let you be humiliated in this way, [I shall go to Rome for] I know the way to Rome perfectly'.

66/15 Cf. *Freir Wolff Waitskaith* in Henryson's *Morall Fabillis*, l. 667.

66/21 It was normal for an excommunicated person to appeal to Rome through an advocate against the excommunication. Although it was often considered that while an appeal was pending the excommunication was not binding, there is no evidence to suggest it was possible for the advocate to assume the sins and excommunication of his client. But the ape's actions represent the perversion of the normal processes. See *Dictionnaire de Théologie catholique*, s.v. *Excommunication*.

66/30 See Jente, no. 621, and cf. ODEP., p. 336.

67/1 The cardinal of pure gold is a satirical thrust suggesting that you can get what you want in Rome only by bribing the officials there. See particularly J. A. Yunck, *The Lineage of Lady Meed*, 1963, pp. 93–117, and P. Lehmann, *Die Parodie im Mittelalter*, 1922, pp. 58–70.

67/21–2 *they were a room fer in the playne*: Sands, p. 128, glosses *room* as 'area', and Stallybrass, p. 88, translates 'they were in the open far in the plain'. P 3504 reads *si op dat ruyme waren*. Although C's *room* has probably been suggested by P's *ruyme* ('the open'), it is best to take it as an adverb here. OED. *Room*, *adv.* 1 quotes from Pecock (*c.* 1449) *Whilis thei stonden or sitten or knelen rombe fer ech from othir*. The meaning therefore is 'very (far)'.

68/8 *greuyd*: P 3539 reads *vermuyt*, 'changed, altered'. It is difficult to account for Caxton's translation; see Muller–Logeman, p. 182. Cf. 42/4.

69/7 *popes palays of woerden*: cf. P 3594 *in des paeus hof van weerden* (i.e. honourable); and cf. RII *Jnt spaeus hoff door mijn weerde* (B 4752). Caxton has misunderstood *weerden* as a place-name; cf. *at stade* (6/27 and note) and *of chafporte* (17/12 and note). See Muller–Logeman, p. 183.

69/8–9 *whan I had there to doo*: *als ic daer een saeke te doen hadde* (P 3596–7 'When I had a suit to plead there').

69/10 Seneca, the Roman rhetorician, often plays the part of a wise man or philosopher in the Middle Ages. Many of his stories were well known because they had been incorporated in the *Gesta Romanorum*.

69/12 *halte*: i.e. 'to proceed imperfectly or faultily', OED. *Halt*, *v.*[1] 4. Sands, p. 130, modernizes it wrongly as *hold*. Cf. P 3602–3 *Men en sal dat recht doer nyement mencken*.

69/13 *And* means 'if' here, for the inverted word order in Dutch implies condition: *Wil een yghelijc* . . . (P 3603); see OED. *And*, C. Sands, p. 130, punctuates the passage to give two sentences: 'And every man . . . in his days. He should the better. . . '. But this makes little sense. Stallybrass, p. 91, rearranges the word order, 'And would every man that standeth here well bethink him . . .', to give the required conditional sense.

69/23 *Nolite iudicare*: Matthew vii. 1–2. The biblical passage about those that cannot see their own faults introduced a few lines later (69/30–1) follows immediately after this text (Matthew vii. 3–5). The expression became proverbial in ME. literature, cf. Chaucer's *Reeve's Tale*, ll. 65–6 (I. 3919–20).

69/24 ff. John viii. 3–11.

70/23–4 *he hath stryked hem with his tayl*: *hi en strijct altoos sinen stert* (P 3671–2). The expression, which is not found elsewhere in English, means 'he has deceived them in the end'.

70/27 'In the end those that offer the best counsel shall be appreciated.' The metaphor is from a pair of scales: the weightiest and best advice will always make the beam finally fall on that side. See Jente, no. 704.

70/35 ff. The story of the man and the ungrateful serpent goes back to Aesop's fables, though it has undergone considerable modification. See Lenaghan, pp. 139–40.

71/16 *I maye doo it good*: i.e. 'I may answer for my actions before the whole world'; cf. P 3712–13 *voer allen luden mach ic dat verantwoerden dat ic di doe*. Cf. 98/23.

71/17–18 Cf. *for neid may haif na Law* (Henryson's *Morall Fabillis*, l. 731).

71/27 See note to 9/34.

72/15 *that*: i.e. 'as to that'; see de Reul, p. 15.

72/20 *on that other side*: Sands, p. 135, keeps C's reading and translates *sith* as 'hand'. The common typographical confusion of *-th* and *-d* (see *English Versions*, pp. 70–1) suggests that it is better to emend to *side*; cf. 30/26. Thoms, p. 105, Morley–Thoms, p. 121, and Stallybrass, p. 96, interpret *sith* as 'because, since'; but the syntax hardly supports this interpretation.

72/29 The passage in direct speech follows uncomfortably upon that in indirect speech. In P both sentences are in direct speech (3796–8).

73/21 ff. With the general meaning of this sentence compare the medieval proverb 'Little thieves are hanged, the big ones escape'; see Jente, no. 274, and ODEP., p. 375.

73/27 Solomon and Aristotle are often referred to in medieval literature as wise men as, for example, in *Piers Plowman* C xii 211–20. Avicenna (980–1037) is less often mentioned, though cf. Chaucer's *Pardoner's Tale*, VI. 889 f. He was a famous Arabian writer on medicine and philosophy, who was especially noted for his commentaries on Aristotle.

73/37 *here*: Caxton mistranslated *datten here* ('to the lord', P 3870), taking *here* 'lord' as *hier* 'here'.

74/21 ff. The corresponding passage in P (3903–54) was drastically shortened by Caxton. Biteluys attends to men's clothes and consequently is given food for his services. As he gets more than he can eat, Fulrompe also benefits. Hatenette receives food for her services which she likewise divides with Fulrompe. For his part Fulrompe would give up his life for his kinsfolk. That is why Rukenawe says her three children are *to eche other tryewe* (74/26–7).

74/32 *musehont*: cf. P 3965 *muushont*, RII *mvshont* (B 5183). The animal referred to is almost certainly a weasel, see OED. *Mouse-hunt*[1], though Stallybrass, p. 99, translates 'Musk-rat'. See Introduction, § 2.

74/34 *bonssyng*: earlier editors, except Stallybrass, keep C's form *boussyng*, but in P and RII the word is spelt with an *n* (*bonssinc* P 3968, *bunsing* B 5187). It is better to assume that there is a turned *n* in C; see Stallybrass, p. 274, and Introduction, § 2.

75/3 *hermell the asse*: cf. P 3980–1 *dat hermel ende den egel*. Caxton must have misread *egel* as *ezel*, 'ass', see Muller–Logeman, p. 186. It is difficult to decide whether Caxton meant *hermell* to be a common noun, 'weasel', or a proper noun, the name of the ass. The omission of *ende*, 'and', and the fact that Caxton took *harmel* (P 1365) as the name of the ox at 30/16 incline me to accept the latter alternative. Previous commentators have taken *hermell* as a common noun and assumed that the weasel and the hermell were Dame Atrote's sisters. In that case C's *hermell* would be a MD. loan-word, for OED., s.v. *Ermelin*, records no form earlier than 1555.

75/27 *a good foot to daunse on*: cf. the proverb *hij danst op eenen voet*, Jente, no. 414. The idiomatic expression *I shal now loke out of myne eyen* is translated literally from the Dutch, cf. P 4025 *Ick wille nv wt minen oeghen sien*. Sands, p. 214, suggests that it means 'Keep my eyes open'.

76/16 No explanation for this name has yet been found.

76/17 *we shal curse for them in alle chirchys*: the sense in P is slightly different: *Ende oeck soe salmen se veruloecken ende in alle kercken te banne doen die daer of weten soe langhe dat si dair bescheyt of doen* (4061–4, 'those who know anything about them will be cursed and excommunicated in all churches until they give information about them').

76/32 *hebrews* is the plural of the adjective agreeing with *names*; cf. *diuerses metes* 57/19, and see de Reul, p. 25. Sands, p. 141, mistranslates as 'three Hebrews' names'; cf. P 4085 *drie hebreesche namen*.

76/34 *maister abrion of tryer*: cf. P 4087 *abrioen*, RII *abrioen* (B 5330). Teirlinck, pp. 226–38, suggests that *Abrioen* in RII is a Dutch form of *Auberon* who appears in the OF. *Huon of Bordeaux*. Auberon is a magician, which would account for his title of 'maister'. In *Huon of Bordeaux* Auberon is also a very wise man who can control the beasts and who knows the power of stones. But Abrioen is a Jew and did not believe in God, which is not true of Auberon. This may have been an invention by the poet of RII. Nevertheless, there was also an archbishop of Trier who died in 1152 whose name was Alberon. Teirlinck thinks that the two figures might have been amalgamated to give us *maister abrion of tryer*. It is, however, possible that the name is fictitious.

76/36–7 Caxton's *for yf he see hym ones he shal doo as hee wyl* does not quite correspond to P 4094–6 *Niet dan als hijt aen siet soe moet dan doen alle sinen wille* (If Abrioen merely looks upon the animal it has to do what he wants). In the bestiaries a wolf is said to lose its fierceness if a man sees it before it sees the man, see McCulloch, p. 189.

77/1 On the position of the Jews in the Middle Ages see I. Abrahams, *Jewish Life in the Middle Ages*, 2nd ed., 1932.

77/2 *the vertue of stones*: the attributes that this ring possesses are closely linked with precious stones in the Middle Ages. See particularly P. J. Heather, 'Precious Stones in the Middle-English Verse of the Fourteenth Century', *Folk-Lore*, xlii (1931), 217–64 and 345–404. Most of the information is taken from the medieval lapidaries, for which see P. Studer and J. Evans, *Anglo-Norman Lapidaries*, 1924, and L. Pannier, *Les Lapidaires français du Moyen Age*, 1882.

77/3–4 The apocryphal story of how Seth went to Paradise to get the oil is related, for example, in *The Golden Legend* which Caxton was to translate and print. See G. Ryan and H. Ripperger, *The Golden Legend of Jacobus de Voragine*, part I, 1941, pp. 269 f. See also E. C. Quinn, *The Quest of Seth for the Oil of Life*, 1962.

77/8 *wynters longe*: *winter lancshe* (P 4112); cf. OED. *Winter, sb.*[1] 5, and Muller–Logeman, p. 187.

77/28–9 *and that noman were he neuer so stronge and hardy that myght mysdoo hym* translates P 4147–8 *Gheen van sinen vianden soe machtich soe starc of soe koen die hem misdoen mocht*. The second *that* in C would seem to mean 'who'. The sense is best understood as 'and that [there was] no one no matter how strong or brave he might be who could do him an injury'.

78/11 In the Middle Ages the Earthly Paradise was normally considered to lie at the easternmost edge of the world. This is its location on the Hereford Mappa Mundi, see W. L. Bevan and H. W. Phillott, *Medieval Geography*, 1873, pp. xx–xxi. India was situated just to the west of Paradise.

78/13 The sweet smell associated with the panther is a feature of the bestiaries, see McCulloch, pp. 148–50.

78/18 The sense demands the present tense *restith*; cf. P 4205 *blijft*. As the typographical interchange of final *-d* and *-th* is common, the emendation is justified; see *English Versions*, pp. 70–1.

78/29 ff. The tales of the judgement of Paris, the rape of Helen, and the Trojan War were well known in the Middle Ages and frequently cited. Caxton himself had translated the *Recuyell of the Historyes of Troye*, although the account there differs in detail from the summary here. Certain features of the story, which are not found in P, have been added in C; see Introduction, § 3.

79/22 *and the storye wreton*: cf. P 4280–1 *Ende van elcken dat onderscheyt daer neder gescreuen* (And the distinguishing features of each one were also written down underneath); cf. 80/21–3.

79/23 For a mirror with similar properties compare the story of Virgil's mirror in Gower's *Confessio Amantis*, v. 2031 ff. and the account of the mirror in Chaucer's *Squire's Tale* (v. 132–6).

79/34 *tre of hebenus*: not as Stallybrass, p. 106, translates 'tree of ebony', but 'the wood of the ebony tree' for Caxton's *tre* translates Dutch *hout*. The phrase *of whiche wode* means 'from this wood'; *wode* is the noun, not the adjective.

79/35 ff. This story is based ultimately on a thirteenth-century French poem called *Cléomadès*, by Adenet le Roi, for an English paraphrase of which see H. S. V. Jones, 'The Cléomadès, the Méliacin, and the Arabian tale of the "Enchanted Horse",' *JEGP*, vi (1906–7), 221–43.

80/24 ff. The story of the deer and the jealous horse is told originally in Aesop's fables of a boar and a horse. For Caxton's version see Lenaghan, p. 129.

81/6 The subject of *suffre* is the unexpressed pronoun 'he' referring back to 'one'. The pronoun is often omitted in Caxton; cf. P 4375 *die*, and see de Reul, pp. 30–2.

81/9 ff. The story of the hound and the jealous ass is found in Aesop's fables. For Caxton's version see Lenaghan, pp. 85–6. The sense of *made* (81/9) is 'carved (the story of)'.

81/17 In P *Mer mi* (4392; *But me*) anticipates syntactically *Ende mi* (4399; *And I* 81/20). Caxton forgot this connexion when he came to translate the *Ende mi* and he used a different construction, thus leaving the *But me* in the air. This change of construction occurs commonly in Caxton, see R. R. Aurner, 'Caxton and the English Sentence', *University of Wisconsin Studies in Language and Literature*, xviii (1923), 56–57.

82/4 ff. For other versions of this tale, see E. G. Stanley, *The Owl and the Nightingale*, 1960, pp. 160–3. For Caxton's version of the fable see Lenaghan, pp. 140–1.

82/22 The cry that the hunters uttered is 'Slee and take'; cf. 26/22.

83/1 Sands, p. 149, interprets *mysfalle* as a noun, 'misfortune', here; but it is better to understand it as a verb, cf. P 4487 *misuille.*

83/8 ff. The story of the wolf and the crane is based ultimately on Aesop's fables. For the fable as printed by Caxton see Lenaghan, pp. 78–9.

84/13 *bellart*: otherwise spelt *Bellin,* but Caxton here follows P which reads *bellaert* (4565), although RII has *bellijn* (B 5905); cf. 57/12.

84/16 *murdre abydeth not hyd*: see ODEP., p. 439, and Jente, no. 516.

84/25 ff. The story of the curing of the sick lion is one of the recurrent features of the stories about Reynard the fox. See Introduction, § 1, and also H. Janson, *Apes and Ape Lore*, 1952, p. 82. For Caxton's version of the fable of the sick lion see Lenaghan, pp. 146–9.

84/36 i.e. 'the longer I live, the worse I feel'.

85/16 *mayster*: a title of honour to imply the recipient's distinction in learning and surgery.

85/24 The subject of *cause* must be the *couetouse and rauenous shrewys*; the *them* refers to the lords.

85/36 *fare amys*: *storue* (P 4670).

86/5 ff. The dividing of the spoils is a common fable which is found in many ancient collections, see Introduction, § 1.

86/36 *brought*: *vingen* (P 4731).

87/21 *It myght happen*: P 4779–81 refers to the wheel of fortune which might restore Reynard to his fortune sometime in the future.

87/35 *alle the moost parte*: *Als die meesten hoep* ('When most of them' P 4806).

88/1 *stratchid hym*: the exact sense of *stratch* is not clear, though it might have been suggested by the Dutch which reads *ende hoe hi voert sijn ghelaet daer op stercte* (P 4808–9). Since this clause is translated by Caxton as *how he made his contenance and stratchid hym*, we should perhaps take the two English phrases as parallel to each other and understand *stratchid hym* as 'made (appropriate) facial expressions'. Though *stratchid* echoes *op stercte*, it can hardly be taken as a loan-word.

89/3 ff. In most versions Reynard instructs Isegrim in the art of fishing (cf. 26/8–9). This episode was invented by the poet of RII on the basis of the older account.

89/15 The rape of the wolf's wife forms the major complaint also in the *branche du Plaid*.

90/13 See Jente, no. 270, and ODEP., p. 7.

91/11 ff. The original story in RR. branch IV is told of the fox and the wolf. These are likewise the two personages in the story as found in *The Fox and the Wolf*, see J. A. W. Bennett and G. V. Smithers, *Early Middle English Verse and Prose*, 2nd ed., 1968, pp. 65–76. In C the wolf's part is played by his wife.

91/21–2 Cf. ODEP., p. 731.

92/3 *fordele*: cf. P 5033 *vorwaerde*. On the meaning of the Dutch expression which appears to mean 'I shall let Reynard speak first', see Muller–Logeman, pp. 193–4. OED. *Fordeal*, 2 records the meaning 'precedence', which is the sense required here, from 1513 onwards. Although the meaning of C's *fordele* might have been influenced by P's *vorwaerde*, it cannot be classified among C's MD. loan-words because there is no corresponding MD. word with both this form and sense.

92/4 Cf. 61/14.

92/24–5 *awayte yf I dyde not for hym there* translates *Besiet of ic hem daer gheen trouwe an en dede mijns onghelucks* (P 5071–2, 'Note if I kept my word to him there and if I did him an evil turn').

92/32–3 See H. Logeman, ' "Mermoyse," "Baubyn," "Mercatte",' *The Academy*, xli, part i (1892), 567, who points out that these words already have a pejorative sense.

93/25 i.e. 'do what I can for you', cf. P 5141.

93/29–30 *My wyf shal thynke longe after me* translates *mijn wiue sal nae mij verlanghen* (P 5148–9, 'My wife will be anxious about my long absence'). Cf. 57/34.

95/4 *on a blood*: *met enen bloede* (P 5240–1).

95/13 *rede coyf*: another joking reference to the fact that Isegrim looked like a monk with a red tonsure; cf. 87/8.

95/33 *and that body ayenst body*: *Ende dat sal wesen lijf teghen lijf* (P 5286–7); cf. *Sir Gawain and the Green Knight* l. 98.

96/10 *and that art thou specyally ysegrym* is syntactically clumsy. One has to understand it in the sense 'and you are the one in particular, Isegrim, [who is a liar]'. P 5302 reads *ende ghi ysegrym sonderlinghe*, which is to be read with what follows, 'You in particular, Isegrim, you lead me where I would be'.

96/24 There was an abbey at Baudeloo, which was founded *c.* 1195 by Boudewijn van Boekle; see Teirlinck, pp. 28–31. The sentence as a whole has to be understood as 'and [it was] a great master . . ., and [he] was abbot of Baudeloo, that taught him'.

96/28–9 A common proverbial expression in Dutch, see Jente, no. 141.

96/31 The *that* refers to the prayer.

97/30 These are nonsense words in P, which have become corrupted in the transmission of the Dutch texts. RII reads *Blaerde scaeye sal penis / Carsbij gor sous abe firnis* (B 6857–8). The prayer is perhaps a sarcastic thrust at church Latin. For a similar jibe at the commoners' use of Latin, see *Ysengrimus* ii. 97–100.

98/13 Although originally the work of the poet of RII, the battle exemplifies all that is best in the Reynard story. The narrative which is lively and humorous can be read for its own sake. Yet there is an undercurrent of parody: the contest is a distortion of the descriptions of single combat common in the romances. This distortion is emphasized by the partly animal and partly human character of the protagonists. Here neither opponent behaves in a courtly manner, and the final victory is won by most underhand means.

99/16 Caxton misread the Dutch, cf. P 5492–3 and Introduction, § 3.

99/34 *buff ne baff*: *boe noch bau* (P 5531). Arber, Morley–Thoms, and Stallybrass misread C's text as *buff ne haff*, though all the copies have *baff*. It is an alliterative expression also found elsewhere, see OED. *Buff*, *sb.*[5] and *int.*, and Introduction, § 2.

100/15–16 *ful of stufs*: Caxton took over the Dutch form as well as including an *of*, cf. P 5564 *vol stofs*. See also Introduction, § 2.

102/6–7 The sepulchre in Jerusalem is meant. P's *cloester winninghe* (5678–9) means gaining a share in the good deeds of the monks in order to mitigate one's own sins, *opera supererogatoria*; see MNW. *Cloosterwinninge*. Caxton appears not to have understood this.

102/31 *but I thought it neuer*: 'such a thought never entered my head'; cf. *mer neen so arghen ghedacht en creghe ic nye* ('But I never have such a wicked thought', P 5724–5).

104/26 *legges*: cf. P 5840 *kuwen*, which is a misprint for *kullen*, 'testicles'. Caxton clearly made nothing of the ghostword *kuwen* and put in 'legs' which he thought would make good sense. See Muller–Logeman, pp. 200–1.

104/30, 33 Caxton gradually changes his translation of *op nemen* 'to bring (a fight) to an end'. At 104/19 *taken vp and fynysshid* translates *opghenomen* (P p. 325). P 5846 *den camp op nemen wilde* is translated *doo sece the batayll and take it vp in to his handes* (104/30); and P 5852–3 *hij wil desen camp op nemen* is translated *wyl that this batayl be ended/ he wil take it in to his hand* (104/33–4). The phrase *take it into his hand* would appear to mean 'have jurisdiction in the matter, decide the issue', cf. 105/33.

104/32 The *lossem* is the same animal as the *losse* (98/19). P 5849 reads *loessem*, though RII has *oss* or *los* (B 7366, C 7360). See Introduction, § 2.

105/10 *flyndermows*: *vledermuys* (P 5875); see N. F. Blake, *Neuphilologische Mitteilungen*, lxvii (1966), 130.

105/17 *Martre* (P 5884 *maerter*) is the same animal as the *martron* 74/33 (P 3966 *marter*). Caxton has merely failed to anglicize the spelling here.

105/22 The reference is to the wheel of fortune, see H. R. Patch, *The Goddess Fortuna in Mediaeval Literature*, 1927, pp. 147–77.

106/12 *hurte ne cause of scathe*: *scade of verdriet* (P 5932).

106/13 *they myght beste ouer me*: understand *myght* in the sense 'to be strong, to prevail'; see OED. *May*, *v.*[1] B. 1. Cf. 33/30, and see E. G. Stanley, *The Owl and the Nightingale*, 1960, p. 106.

106/16–17 *They knewe none other thyng why ne wherfore*: cf. *Anders en wisten si gheen sake waer om* (P 5938–9, 'They knew of no other charge that they could justly raise against me').

107/13–14 *lykke theyr fyngres*: see OED. *Lick*, *v.* 1b, and cf. 60/18.

107/15 *after behynde them*: cf. P 5997 *achter ten sterte*, 'backwards behind themselves (i.e. glance back at their tails)'.

107/27–8 Caxton has not followed the syntax of the Dutch and so it is not clear how one should understand *and lete hym thyse extorcions in her sorow and nede*. P 6017–20 has *Recht als die honde gingen lopen. vanden hont dien si soe mitten siedenden water versoden sagen Aldus so laetmen dese ende deser gelike alle wege in horen noden* (i.e. just as the dogs fled from the scalded dog, so these [extortioners] and their like are abandoned in their necessity). Although the confusion in C may have arisen from Caxton's failure to understand P, it seems better to emend. Two emendations are possible. Firstly, one can substitute PL's reading *and lete thyse extorcioners*. Then the subject of *lete* will be *eche body* and the clause introduced by *lyke as* will stand in parenthesis. Secondly, one can emend to *and lete men thyse extorcioners*, with *men* (i.e. one) as the subject of *lete*. The second emendation is preferable for it is closer to the Dutch and it provides a better reason for the corruption to *hym* in the text. In general the application of the moral to the example is somewhat clumsy, though Caxton is not alone to blame for that. The dog with the bone in his mouth represents bad rulers who destroy the people through excessive taxation. People pander to him when he is in the ascendant, just as the dogs welcomed their fellow when they saw the bone. But when the bad ruler falls from power, he loses all his accomplices just as the dog lost his hair which was scalded off. Then everyone who before had pandered to him leaves him, just as the dogs abandoned the dog with the bone.

108/14–15 Caxton left out this chapter heading in the table of contents, and so both this and the next chapter are numbered 43; see note to 5/19 ff.

108/28–9 The sense is: If any man at all wronged you, I should take severe vengeance upon him for it. *He lyueth not* i.e. 'there is no man alive'.

110/6 The phrase *the lordes spyrytuel and temporel* provides a good illustration of how Caxton gradually improved as a translator and how he freed himself more and more from the Dutch text. At 6/5–6 he had used *lordes and prelates gostly and worldly* as a translation of *heren ende prelaten gheestelic ende waerlic* (P 7–8) right at the beginning of his work. Yet the similar phrase at the end of P *heren. sijn si gheestelic of waerlic* (6137) is translated as *the lordes spyrytuel and temporel*.

110/33 It was a common complaint of the moralists that many monks and priests abandoned their monastery or living to go abroad. This forms the basis of Nigellus's poem *Burnellus seu Speculum Stultorum*.

111/7–9 Caxton alters the sense of the Dutch which reads *wat wil ick vele die werelt berechten van zaken die my mede selue ane vechten daer ick toe ondanck of crighe* (P 6184–6). Caxton's *I haue ynowh to doo with myn owne self* means 'I am fully occupied attending to my own sins'.

111/10 *And the beste that I can doo for to amende my self*: cf. P 6188–9 *dat beste is dat elck dat beste doet in sijnre tijt tot synen profyte* ('and the best thing that each one of us can do is to do the best for his own profit in his lifetime'). Caxton has rewritten the sentence, but his syntax is difficult to follow. Stallybrass, p. 149, Morley–Thoms, p. 164, and Sands, p. 186, punctuate 'and the best that I can, do, for to amend myself', i.e. do the best I can to reform my ways. This is a possible interpretation, though the syntax seems somewhat clumsy. It is also possible, from the preceding *were*, to understand a part of the verb 'to be', cf. 77/28–9 and note. The sentence would then mean: 'It would be better for me to hold my peace and suffer, and the best thing I can do [would be] to reform my ways'.

111/35 Editors of Caxton's prologues and epilogues include from *Now who that said* . . . in their editions and thus imply that all that follows is Caxton's own composition. This is not so, for Caxton is still translating here. Only the colophon is Caxton's own.

112/3 ff. It was common in the Middle Ages to use humorous stories to inculcate a moral lesson. For a similar injunction not to forget the real meaning, cf. NPT. (VII. 3438–40):

> But ye that holden this tale a folye,
> As of a fox, or of a cok and hen,
> Taketh the moralite, goode men.

GLOSSARY

THE glossary is designed for a reader who has at least an elementary knowledge of Middle English and it is not a complete concordance. Special attention has been given to words which have retained their form but changed their meaning, to words which have not survived into Modern English, and to words whose meaning might not be immediately apparent to a modern reader on account of their Middle English spellings. Words which occur commonly in Middle English, such as the pronouns, have not normally been glossed and no attempt has been made to record orthographical variants or complete inflexions. But words which occur in the text only in the plural or the preterite have sometimes been glossed under that form; and cross-references have been provided where necessary for words which have more than one form. When a word occurs with two meanings in the text, one of which would be familiar and the other strange to a modern reader, only the latter meaning is given. Thus *by cause* is glossed as 'so that, in order that'; its modern meaning 'since, for the reason that' which also occurs, e.g. at 41/27, is not listed. It should, therefore, never be assumed that the meaning given is the only meaning a word has in the text. No etymological information is given, but the Dutch loan-words which occur in the text are marked with an asterisk and they are discussed more fully in the Introduction, § 2. Select line references are given to all words, but the references do not necessarily indicate the first occurrence of the word. The form of the headword given is that of the first line reference.

ARRANGEMENT

The following initial letters are listed together: vocalic **i** and vocalic **y**; and **u** and **v**. Consonantal **i** follows vocalic **i**/**y**; consonantal **y** follows **w**. The use of capitals in the text has been disregarded in the glossary. Many phrases are recorded in the glossary; they are recorded under the following headwords. If there is a noun in the phrase, it is recorded under that noun; if there is no noun but an adjective, see under the adjective; other phrases are listed under the verb. Thus the following phrases, *come I in the wordes*, *make it good*, and *come agayn*, are to be found under *wordes*, *good*, and *come* respectively.

ABBREVIATIONS

adj. (adjective), *adv.* (adverb), *comp.* (comparative), *conj.* (conjunction), *gen.* (genitive), *impers.* (impersonal), *interj.* (interjection), *intrans.* (intransitive), *n.* (noun), *phr.* (phrase), *pl.* (plural), *prep.* (preposition), *pp.* (past participle), *pr. p.* (present participle), *pt.* (preterite), *refl.* (reflexive), *s.* (singular), *superl.* (superlative), *trans.* (transitive), *v.* (verb). It should be noted that whereas *n.* means 'noun', the abbreviation 'n.' after a page and line reference means 'see note'. Page and line references to emended forms are italicized.

a *interj.* oh 44/10

aas *n.* ace: *deux* ~ little worth 45/29 n.

abhorren *v.* regard with horror 10/34

abyde *v.* accept, submit to 13/16; stay the same, remain unaltered 108/7; *intrans.* restrain oneself 86/30; *~ *after* remained unaccomplished 38/24–5 n.; ~ *by* support, remain true to 14/18; stay with 96/31; ~ *togydre* remain in an alliance 102/19

abye *v.* pay for, atone 12/8 n.

aboue *prep.* beyond 69/12; despite 72/13; *to his* ~ gain a commanding position, come out on top 5/12 n.; succeed, obtain the mastery 32/29

accompanye *v. refl.* travel in the company of 41/35

***ach** *interj.* alas 102/33

a colde *adj.* cold 40/34

a combred *pp. adj.* oppressed 33/8; cf. **encombred**

a compted *pp.* accounted, reckoned 61/25

acorde *v.* assent to, consent to 72/35; **acordyng** *pr. p.*, ~ *to* in agreement with 60/21

a cursyd *pp. adj.* under sentence of excommunication 41/37

a doo *n.*, *make moche* ~ make a great fuss 31/18

aduenge *v.* revenge 108/29

aduys *n.* deliberation, consultation 12/22; opinion, judgement 72/26

aduyse *v. refl.* reflect, consider 103/12

aduocate *n.* one whose profession it is to plead the cause of someone in a court of justice 64/20

aduoultrye *n.* adultery 69/26

a ferde *pp. adj.* frightened, afraid 22/1

a fore *adv.*, *prep.* before 90/28

a fote *adv.* on foot 65/25

after *adv.* behind 59/16; afterwards 90/28; *prep.* in accordance with 8/22; with 17/30; for 21/30; towards, at 28/29; ~ *that* (*conj.*, *phr.*) in accordance as, as 13/24

***afterdele** *n.* disadvantage 100/17

***afterfeet** *n. pl.* hindlegs 45/34

***afterward** *adv.* back, away from 74/2

agayn *adv.* in return, in reply 44/25; *prep.* against 72/34

age *n.*, *for* ~ because of their (old) age 16/21

a goon *pp. adj.* ago 41/3

agrauate *pp. adj.* excommunicated 41/36

a greed *pp. adj.*, *wel* ~ pleased, satisfied 106/9–10

al *adv.* intensive strengthening the action of the participle, e.g. ~ *lawhyng* 27/10–11; very, completely, entirely 68/25; *quasi-conj.* (with inversion) although 10/2; ~ *that* as much as, as fast as 17/28, 65/36; ~ *be yt* although 87/20

algates *adv.* always 78/7

allyance *n.* kinship 33/33

almesse *n.* alms 10/13

also *adv.* so 13/35; ~ *that* furthermore 93/16; ~ *therto* furthermore 77/31

alther [used with intensifying force, OED. *All*, D. 3] s.v. **lengest, next**

al togydre *adv. phr.* entirely 60/10–11

amende *v.* correct, reform 11/13

amendes *n. pl.* compensation 51/2; reward 83/35

amys *adv.* wrongly 69/19

amytte *v.* allow, permit 96/14

and *conj.* if 69/13 n.; when 73/28; ~ *yf* if 47/11; unless 99/29; ~ *that* while 13/30; so that 61/28; ~ *to* in order to 64/12

an hete *adv. phr.* warm 90/26–27

an hongryd *pp. adj.* hungry 91/23

anoynt *v.* smear (with oil) 97/1

anon *adv.* immediately, forthwith 21/37

another *adj.* a second 19/24 n., 56/19

answere *v. intrans.* rebut a charge 75/23

a payd *pp. adj.* pleased, satisfied 28/34

appech *v.* bring a charge against 39/12

appele *v.* accuse (of a crime) 35/16; refer to a tribunal 71/39

apoynt *v. intrans.* agree, arrange definitely 12/24

appoyntement *n.* pact, agreement 51/2 n.

araye *v.* handle badly, discomfit, rout 23/17

arette *v.* impute 41/38

a right *adv.* correctly, properly 9/25

arise *v. intrans.* gain influence 70/7; rise to a prominent position 83/31, 110/14
armonye *n.* melodious sound 6/26
arte *n.* skill, method of doing something 80/12
as *adv.* thus, so 13/5 n.; *conj.* when 22/1; as if 35/4; as soon as 41/30; ~ *that* (*conj., phr.*) that 10/36 n.; ~ *to* in order to 60/19; *right* ~ just as if 40/25; as soon as 52/23; *prep.* like 59/22; ~ *in* for instance, from 65/32
asaye *v.* make trial, try 15/19
a sondre *adv.* asunder, apart 23/11
aspye *v.* see 38/19
assoylle *v.* pardon, grant absolution to 27/35
asure *n.* bright blue 78/28
a swoune, al a swoun *adj.* or *adv. phr.* in a swoon or faint 23/6, 52/14; *half* ~ in a faint 65/11
at *prep.* through 26/15; in 89/21; *with gen.* at the house of 18/22
atte *prep.* at 11/14; at the 22/19; s.v. **longe**
attones *adv.* at once, together 83/11
a two *adv. phr.* in or into two parts 46/33
auayle *n.* benefit, advantage 71/26
auaylle *v.* help, assist 24/16; **a vaylle** 88/36
auauntage *n.* advantage 96/6; opportunity 100/20
auauntyng *n.* boasting 111/2
audyence *n.* judicial hearing 59/10
auenge *v.* revenge, take revenge for 99/37
auenture *n.* happening, event 24/16; piece of good luck 82/30; jeopardy, 83/1; misfortune, chance 87/20; **thauenture** fortune 62/18; *sette* (*it*) *in* ~ endanger 76/25; put it to the test 100/37
auenture *v.* risk 6/33; **a venture** 8/32; *intrans.* take a risk 27/14–15
auyse *v.* advise, counsel 23/19
auncyent *adj.* venerable 59/10
auoyde *v.* vacate, quit 72/11
auoultry *n.* adultery 111/2
a wayte *v. intrans.* lie in hiding, lie in ambush 37/10
awreke *v.* avenge 53/26
awter *n.* altar 45/1
axe *v.* ask 26/7 n.
ayenst *prep.* towards, to meet 86/13; in preparation for, towards the time 65/3; contrary to 107/30

backe *n.* bat 75/4
***baff** *n.*, *buff ne* ~ not a single word 99/34 n.
bayle *n.* bailiff, an officer of justice 108/31
***balk** *v. intrans.* be angry 31/18 n.
balke *n.* beam of timber 69/31
balock stone *n.* testicle 22/25
bann *v.* curse, swear at 17/32
***banne** *n.* excommunication 41/29
batayll *n.* single combat 96/16
baubyn *n.* baboon, ape 92/33
be *v.*, *how is it now wyth yow* how are you? 59/23–4; *as moche as in hym* ~ to the limit of his capability 91/4; ~ *it of* whether it be from 110/29; *what* ~ *that to me* how am I responsible? 29/36; *ye ar not wel wyth your self* you are so distraught as not to know what you are doing 64/22–3; *it was so* it happened 10/35; *what* ~ *that* what does that matter? 9/20; *though so were* though it came to pass 85/1; *yf it* ~ *so wyth me* if I were in a position 41/19; *yf he* ~ *as wel* if he stood as high 8/34
bebled *pp. adj.* covered with blood 18/17
become *v.* end up 92/8; *where shal ye* ~ what will happen to you? 55/23–24; *becometh wel* (*impers.*) is fitting, appropriate 31/25; **bycam** *pt.* (*pl.*) were suitable, sat well 84/9; ~ *yl* turned out unfavourably 22/25; **be comen** *pp.*, *where they ben* ~ what has happened to them 76/1
bedes *n. pl.* prayers 52/7
beest *n.* animal 6/29
behoefful *adj.* advantageous, necessary 81/34
behoue *v. impers.* be fitting, necessary 43/23
belye *v.* calumniate by false statements 63/5
***belyke** *v.* resemble 25/3
belong *v. impers.* be fitting, pertain to 44/21

benche *n.*, *hye* ~ seat of the judiciary, judicial bench *38/27*; *sette on the hye* ~ promoted to a position of authority 85/22

benyngne *adj.* benign 36/33

be pyss *v.* defile by urinating 7/12

bere *v.* carry 15/9; wear 77/5; endure 91/26; ~ *out* spend 105/23; **bare out** *pt. s.* supported, sustained 41/7–8; acted bravely 62/15; **borne vp** *pp.* advanced in status 29/20

***beryspe** *v.* censure, reprove 92/3

besyly *adv.* fervently 43/18

bestow *v.* dispose of 94/32

be swette *pp. adj.* covered with sweat 56/1

***betel** *n.* wedge 15/15

bethynke *v. refl.* consider, recollect 69/13; **bethought** *pt. s.* reflected 32/1; thought of 58/27; ~ *hym other wyse* changed his mind 7/17; (*pp.*) *I was sore* ~ I racked my mind 37/9

bettre *v.* improve, amend *24/37*, 42/22

bewaylle *v.* lament, mourn 38/23

beware *v. intrans.* take a warning 16/34; take care 24/5

bewraye *v.* reveal, expose 34/33

be wrapped *pp. adj.* implicated, involved 88/34; cf. **bywrappe**

by *adj.* situated to one side, less important 47/29; *adv.* nearby, round about 27/8; *prep.* in accordance with 19/29; with 20/35; beside, next to 21/2; near 37/13; via, through the agency of 48/27; with respect to, with reference to 74/7; concerning 107/20

by cause *conj.* so that, in order that 38/28, 61/4

byclagged *pp. adj.* covered with any sticky substance 93/3

byde by *v. phr.* give support to 63/32

***bydryue** *v.* have sexual intercourse with 27/26; perpetrate, accomplish 74/8

***bydwynge** *v.* subdue, render submissive 81/2; ***bydwongen** *pp. adj.* subjugated 36/19; forced 48/1

byfylle *pt. s.* befell 36/17; **bifelle** 86/2

byhaue *v. refl.* act, conduct oneself 96/20

byhelde *pt. s.* kept 60/4

byknowen *pp. adj.* familiar, acquainted 66/10

byleue *n.*, *out of the right* ~ unbelieving 111/38–9

bill *n.* written document 61/33

bille *n.* beak 83/17

byllis *n. pl.* halberds 89/30

bylouyd *pp. adj.* respected, loved 77/32

byneme *v.* deprive of 97/9; **benamme** *pt. s.* took away 58/23

by path *n.* secondary path 18/3

birchen *adj.* of or pertaining to birch 40/9

byshote *pt. s. refl.* excreted, deposited ordure 104/17

***byslabbed** *pp. adj.* beplastered 93/3

bytake *v.* commit, entrust 11/26

byte *v.* *bite to death 12/20; **bote** (*pt.*) ~ *of* bit off 31/23; **boote** *pt. s.* bit 52/34

bytymes *adv.* early in the morning 41/30

bywymple *v.* cover, disguise 61/12

bywrappe *v.* conceal, disguise 67/23

blasen *v.* blow, puff 73/22

blasme *v.* reproach 15/22

bleef *pt. s.* remained 16/15

blere *v.* protrude the tongue 81/25

blewe vp *phr.* (*pt. pl.*) blew, sounded 105/26

blocke *n.* piece of rock or stone 27/2

blood *n.*, *on a* ~ bleeding 95/4

blosme *v.* blossom, bloom 75/26

blowen *pp.*, ~ *a brood* made public far and wide 111/2

bolle *n.* bowl, cauldron 106/24

bombardes *n. pl.* cannons 55/11

bonde *adj.* enslaved 36/26

bone *n.* request, petition 33/6

***bonssyng** *n.* polecat 74/34 n.

boost *n.* vain-glory 73/38

borde *v.* mock, jest 27/12

borowe *n.* pledge 96/14

borugh, burgh *n.* city 38/10; castle 52/4

bosted *pp. adj.* vaunted, bragged of 111/2

bote *v.* cure 78/14

bote s.v. **byte**

bounde *pp. adj.* obliged, under obligation of duty 73/20

bourd *n.* idle tale, raillery 112/7

bowyng *pr. p.* bending 28/1
bracyng *n.* the action of assuming a bold attitude 107/34
braye *v. intrans.* shout, cry aloud (in pain) 15/35
brede *n.* roast meat 46/8
breke *v.* destroy, bring to nought 37/3; **brak** *pt. s.* knocked out 15/29; ~ *vp* (*intrans.*) was dissolved 109/21
brenne *v. intrans.* burn, be aflame 34/12; **brennyng** *pr. p.* burning *10/26*
breste *v. intrans.* break, burst 91/17
brynge *v.*, ~ *forth* present 34/26; **brought** *pt. pl.* captured 86/36 n.
***broke** *n.* crime 42/30
brokes *n. pl.* brooks 47/13
brouke *v.* use, employ 32/28
browes *n. pl.* eyebrows 101/13
***buff** s.v. ***baff**
***bule** *n.* swelling 81/26
burgh *n.* s.v. **borugh**
burnysshid *pp.* polished 77/16
but *conj.* unless 32/4; ~ *yf* unless 60/18; *none . . . but that he* no-one who had not 7/2; before 21/27; ~ *that* but rather, on the contrary 7/22; except 23/9; yet the fact that 47/2; ~ *tyl* until 36/12

caas *n.* suit, lawsuit 13/15; condition, plight 34/28; *in better* ~ in a more advantageous position 88/27
caytyf *n.* wretch, fool 15/9
***campyng** *n.* battle, single combat 95/36
can, conne *v.* know, have learned 59/8, 61/13; know how to 61/19; **coude** *pt. s.* 110/4; s.v. **thanke** *n.*
cantum *n.* song, liturgical song 59/28 n.
carre *n.* cart, waggon 9/4
caste *n.* volley 17/15
caste *pt. s.* threw down 5/1; **casted** *pt. s.* threw 26/25
casus *n.* ABC, elementary lesson 12/33 n.
catch *v.* take hold of, capture 26/21; acquire, gain 32/32
cause *n.* suit, matter for litigation 83/34; *is* ~ *therof* brought it about 50/20–21; ~ *of scathe* injury 106/12
censures *n. pl.* condemnation, excommunication 41/37
certaynly *adv.* indeed 42/32
cetyne *n.* shittim, acacia 79/31
chambre *n.* room 13/27
chapelayn *n.* chaplain, clerk 8/13
charge *n.* trouble 13/30; moral weight, importance 64/24
charge *v.* command, order 41/1; accuse 63/3
charyte *n.* Christian love of our fellow men 68/5
chastyse *v. intrans.* make criticisms 83/37
check *v.* mark out in squares 78/28
chere *n.*, *wyth an heuy* ~ miserably 44/2; *with a glad* ~ joyfully 44/19; *make good* ~ be cheerful 50/12
cherysshyd *pp. adj.* beloved, held dear 74/21–22
chese *v.* choose 101/30
chyde *v. intrans.* express dissatisfaction 29/33; ~ *wyth* complain against 63/20
chydyng *n.* vehement expression of displeasure 15/30
chierte *n.* affection 70/25
chorle *n.* peasant 37/4
***cybore** *n.* vermilion colour of cinnabar 78/28
cynope *n.* vermilion colour of cinnabar 80/20
clatre *v. intrans.* talk noisily 56/16
clene *adj.* pure 78/10
clere *adj.* transparent 12/18; pure, free from guilt or sin 25/17; free from the taint 25/31; evident 30/7; brilliant 77/16
clere *adv.* completely, entirely 83/4
clere *v. refl.* prove oneself innocent 8/1
clergie *n.* learning 64/20
clerke *n.* scholar 59/39 n.; secretary 66/10
clerly *adv.* honestly, frankly 33/8; thoroughly, entirely 54/12; *without entanglement, without becoming infected 60/17 n.
cleue *v.* break 14/7; **clouen** *pp.* 59/34; split 15/14
cleue *v.* stick, adhere 99/17
clyft *n.* cleft 15/28
clymme *v. intrans.* climb 27/8; ~ *aboue* (*trans.*) excel 79/10
cloyster *n.* nunnery 28/12; monastery 102/7

cloysterer *n.* monk 11/19
***clope** *n.* blow, stroke 101/8
closyd *pp. adj.* enclosed 11/19
cloterd *pp. adj.* covered with clots 94/21
cluck *v.* call chickens together by clucking 11/29 n.
***cluse** *n.* eremitical cell 10/11
coyf *n.* close-fitting cap 95/13 n.
colde *adj.* unimpassioned 96/22
coles *n. pl.* charcoal 73/33
colyk *n.* colic, severe stomach pains 77/21
colyon *n.* testicle 22/25
colour *n.*, *of* ~ so adorned with colours 78/12
come *v.* used like *go* as a kind of auxiliary, e.g. *come see* 58/36; *come and see* 75/6 [OED. *Come, v.* B. 3d, e]; ~ *agayn* come back, return 42/24; ~ *by* come to pass, happen 65/22; capture 80/33; ~ *of* hurry up 21/31; ~ *out* be made known to all 84/17; ~ *to* happen to, befall 102/19; ~ *vp* flourish 110/16; ~ *to late* be too slow 12/34; **cam** *pt.* (*subj.*) should come 12/25; ~ *by* fell in with *33/30*; ~ *forth by* was walking past 71/3; *~ *of* escaped from 52/11; *how come I on* how did I get involved in? 95/36; **cam* (*by*) *to* was brought about (by) 8/5 n., 80/16; ~ *out* escaped 9/14; ~ *hym euyl* (*to passe*) it turned out badly for him 101/27; **comen** *pp.*, *so ferre* ~ had learned so much 57/17–18; ~ *of* descended from 11/1
comfort *v.* relieve, strengthen 109/18
comynte *n.* state, commonwealth 36/19
command to *v. phr.* enjoin upon *42/7*
commandement *n.* command, bidding 56/34
commendacion *n.* office for the dead 12/16 n.
commyssyon *n.* order, command *6/29*
commytte *v.* commend to (someone's) keeping 93/28
complayne *v.* lament, bewail 12/20 n., 36/24; ~, ~ *on*, *~ *ouer* raise a charge (against someone) 3/4
complaynyng *n.* complaint 65/35
complaynt *n.* charge, accusation 3/6
complyn *n.* compline, last service of the day 18/30
comprise *v.* understand, comprehend 6/17
conceyue *v.* understand, comprehend 94/17
conclude *v. intrans.* agree, come to a decision 12/24; ~ *moche by me* frequently come to their decision through my advice 24/26
condampne *v.* condemn 69/35
condycion *n.* state, state of affairs 110/36; *pl.* rank, estate 46/5; personal qualities 86/25
confusion *n.* humiliation, discomfiture 98/35
cony *n.* rabbit 4/14
coniure *v.* constrain (a person to some action) by appealing to something sacred, implore 34/19
conne *v.* s.v. **can**
connyng *adj.* skilled, versed in a subject 69/6
connyng *n.* wisdom, intelligence 20/2; knowledge, learning 61/36
consayte *n.* estimation 63/3
considre *v.* weigh, give heed to 63/9
conspyre *v.* join a conspiracy (to accomplish something) 95/25
constaunce *n.* constancy, resolution 70/29
contenance *n.* facial expression 34/27; good cheer, favour 105/21; *made his* ~ assumed a certain demeanour 88/1
contrarye *adj.* opposed 36/2
contrauersye *n.* dispute, contention 78/30
conueyne *v.* conduct, escort 45/20
correccion *n.* authority, control 30/8
coruen *pp.* carved, engraved 78/26
cosyn *n.* kinsman, relative 20/29, 91/29
***coste** *n.* food, sustenance 9/29
coste *v.* involve an expenditure (of time, trouble, etc.) 94/28
costely *adj.* valuable 39/6; splendid, magnificent 80/24
coude s.v. **can, conne**
couere *v.* conceal, disguise 84/20
couetyse *n.* covetousness 34/12
couetouse *adj.* avaricious 85/21

couetously *adv.* greedily 52/36

counseyl *n.* assembly, council 6/5; advice, plan 19/23, 32/13; *fynde* ~ devise a plan 76/15; *in* ~ in secrecy 36/7; *was of the* ~ had been party to the plan 76/6; *wyth oute* ~ without taking advice 38/32

courtoys *adj.* having manners fit for the court of a prince 46/4; graciously polite 109/3

courtoisly *adv.* in a noble manner, nobly 87/7

crafte *n.* strength 15/32; intellectual power 20/2; skill 80/13; deceit 110/4; *of his* ~ who follow his practice 110/9

craftely *adv.* skilfully 49/35

cratch *v.* scratch *15/35* n., 37/27

credo *n.* Creed 8/13

crye *n.* shouting, noise 16/23

crye *v.* proclaim 51/24; shout 55/14

crystene *v.* baptize 66/36

***cryte** *v. intrans.* cry, howl 92/12

crope *pt. s. intrans.* crept 27/11; **cropen** *pp.* crept 17/33

croppe *n.* neck 32/12

crowne *n.* top of the head 25/25

curse *n.* excommunication 42/1

curse *v. intrans.* utter ecclesiastical imprecations 76/17 n.; **cursyd** *pp. adj.* wretched 28/19; excommunicated 41/36

curtosye *n.* courtly behaviour 9/20; *don* ~ pay respect as to a superior 86/4

day *n.* appointed day 7/14, 96/4; *by the* ~ almost dawn 97/32; *kepte your* ~ acquitted yourself 105/38

***day** *v.* summon to appear on a certain day 19/20

daluyst *pt. 2 s.* you dug, buried 40/20

damage *n.* loss 12/4

dame *n.* as a form of address, 'Madam' 47/4; as a title, Lady, Mistress 47/24

dampne *v.* damn, condemn 35/1

danger *n.* risk, peril 3/30; power 47/21

dasel *v. intrans.* be blinded by a bright light 90/21

***dasse** *n.* badger 8/27; **dassen** badger's 38/16 n.

dawnyng *n.* dawn, daybreak 20/24

debate *n.* contention 51/15

deceyte *n.* deceitful trick 31/8; wickedness 58/28

deceyuable *adj.* deceitful, deceptive 74/3

dede *adj.*, *sholde be* ~ should be put to death 30/32

dede *n.*, *with the* ~ in the act 89/18

dede *pt. s.* s.v. **do**

deel *n.* part, share 14/17; a number 17/18

defaute *n.* wrong 54/14

deffamer *n.* one who raises imputations (against another) 91/3

deye *v. intrans.* die 65/34

delar *n.* one who divides or distributes 87/2

dele *n.* s.v. **deel**

dele *v.* share, participate in 44/7; divide, distribute 86/33

deme *v.* judge 69/24

departe *v. intrans.* part company 82/6; *trans. and intrans.* divide 82/6, 86/20; ~ *fro* give up, relinquish 76/20; *be departed* escaped 47/4

departyng *n.* division, distribution 87/9

dere *adj.* noble, worthy 7/19

dere *adv.* at a high price 90/23

dere *v.* grieve 64/4

derrer *adj. comp.* more highly 79/34

deserue *v.* earn, merit 70/20; pay for 106/35; ~ *ayenst/agayn* repay, requite 97/34

deseruyng *n.* merit, desert: *wythout* ~ unjustifiably 63/3–4

desire *n.* will, pleasure 109/32

desyrously *adv.* eagerly, longingly 90/9

despyte *n.* contempt, scorn: *had in* ~ regarded with contempt 35/23

deth *n.*, *to the* ~ mortally 27/23; *take the* ~ be killed 102/1; *the very* ~ death itself 77/22

deth wounde *n.* mortal wound 109/20

deuely *adj.* evil, wicked 69/21

deuyse *v.* contrive, fashion 59/12; invent 61/11

deuocion *n.* prayer 28/31

deuoyr *n.* duty 98/25

diere *n.* animal 18/20

dyscharge *v.* set free 103/22
dyscrescion *n.* discernment, discrimination 69/3–4
discrete *adj.* prudent, judicious 63/7
discretly *adv.* prudently 75/19
disease *n.* illness, sickness 83/15
dishonestly *adv.* disgracefully, shamefully 89/4
dyspytously *adv.* mercilessly 89/31
dysplesyd *pp.* wronged, offended *64/23*
dispose *v. refl.* make oneself ready 62/36; *pp. adj.* inclined, able 97/32
dissymyl *v. intrans.* dissemble 40/28; *pp. adj.* feigned 76/27
dyssymylyng *n.* dissimulation *35/4*
dystaf *n.* distaff, staff for spinning wool 16/20; **distauis** *pl.* 89/31
disworshippe *v.* dishonour 95/28
diuerses *adj. pl.* varied, of various kinds 57/19
do *v.* cause (to do something): (*with infin.*) 6/28, (*with pp.*) 10/6; perform 44/23; repay 65/37; behave, act 85/2; ~ *moche with* be on good terms with 67/4; ~ *to* treat, handle 74/9; ~ *wyth you* behave towards you 23/3; do or say anything against 107/10; *it is to* ~ there is any concern, business 73/29; *it to* ~ *was* it was necessary 68/35; *what haue I to* ~ *wyth* why should I concern myself with? 90/37; *we may not* ~ *amys* we shall not be acting unwisely 47/30–31; *how that I* ~ whatever happen to me 63/28; ~ *ye wel* be wise 54/23; **dyde** *pt. s.*, ~ *on* put on 4/4; **doon** *pp.* concluded 34/21; ~ *to* treated 23/23; *euyl* ~ a wicked action 68/18; ~ *amys ayenst* acted unjustly towards 50/19
***dolynge** s.v. ***doole**
doluen *pp. adj.* buried 35/21
dompte *v.* subdue 76/36
***doole** *v. intrans.* go astray 60/3; **dolynge** *pr. p.* behaving like a madman 64/17
dore *v.* dare 68/17
dotyng *n.* stupidity: *brynge me in* ~ show me to be an idiot 62/9
doubte *n.* fear 71/33; *wythout* ~ indeed, truly 97/28
doubte *v.* fear 82/14
doubteful *adj.* involved in uncertainty 70/37
***dow** *v.* hit, nip 58/22; wring 104/16
drede *n.* fear 9/13; *it is al wythoute* ~ there is nothing to worry about 58/7
drede *v.* fear: *to* ~ to be feared 12/35
drewe *pt. s.* dragged 104/26
dryue *v.*, ~ *a way* pass 96/32; **droof** *pt. s.* journeyed 17/35
drough *pt. s.* drew 17/38
***dubbe** *v.* hit, nip 52/8
duke *v. intrans.* dive 57/14
dure *v. intrans.* last, continue 51/36
duryng *pr. p.*, *ix yere* ~ for the space of nine years 64/21; *alle your lyf* ~ throughout your life 90/36

easid *pp.* relieved, refreshed 65/5; cured 78/22
eche *adj., pron.*, ~ *after other* one after another 100/7
eche body *n.* everybody 107/25
eyen *n. pl.* eyes 28/34; *vnder his* ~ face to face 24/23; in his eyes 100/28; *leyde his* ~ turned his eyes, looked 37/12; *loke out of myne* ~ see with my own eyes, look after myself 75/28 n.
eyer *n.* air 47/13
eyle *v.* worry, cause anxiety 21/36
elder *n.* forefather 90/31
elenge *adj.* remote, lonely 47/25
ellis *adv.* else 20/38
eme *n.* uncle 24/4
encombred *pp. adj.* burdened, inconvenienced 56/25; **emcombryd** hindered, embarrassed 73/8
***ende** *conj.* and 17/6
ende *n.*, *what the* ~ *may happen* what might turn up in the end 106/18
ende *v.* find a conclusion to 72/24
endeuore *v. refl.* exert oneself 88/5
endite *v.* compose 49/9
endyttyng *n.* composition 48/33
endure *v. intrans.* survive 14/14
***endwyte** *v.* reproach 108/3
enhaunse, enhaunse vp *v., v. phr.* exalt in dignity or rank 70/8, 111/33
enheritaunce *n.*, *by* ~ *of* as a birthright from 86/8
ensample *n.* parable, illustrative example 106/7

entente *n.*, *to thentente* with the object 6/10; *brought hym to his owne* ~ made him follow his own desire 45/28
entreprise *v.* take upon oneself 70/20
enuenyme *v.* poison 71/7
enuye *n.* malice, enmity 56/10
er *conj.* before 47/31; ~ *that* rather than 85/36
erly and late *adv. phr.* always, at all times 108/18
erm *v.* grieve 46/1
ernest *adj.* in earnest, true 14/23
erst *adv.*, *not* ~ not till then 93/13
erthe *n.*, *brynge on* ~ bury 12/11–12
esbatemens *n. pl.* amusements, diversions 51/34
escape *v. intrans.* be free of doing something 102/23
eschewe *v.* avoid, shun 112/5
eschewyng *n.* avoidance: *in* ~ in order to avoid 35/6
especyal *adj.*, *in* ~ especially, particularly 25/24
espye *v.* see, catch sight of 92/29
estate *n.* rank, position 42/9
ete *v.* devour, destroy 107/8
euen *adj.* level 37/19
euen crysten *n.* fellow Christian 60/20
euerich *pron.* everybody 68/36
euerychone *pron.* everyone 91/4
euesong *n.* evensong 13/32
euyl *adj.* difficult 9/29; wicked, malicious 63/2
euyl *adv.* maliciously 8/30; wrongfully 9/32; *al* ~ very badly 94/2
euil willed *adj.* unwilling 20/5–6
example *n.* parable, illustrative story 5/17
excuse *n.* defence 30/26; *come to myn* ~ present my defence 63/35
excuse *v.* deny a charge 3/23
execute *v.* enforce 53/14
expedient *adj.* conducive to advantage, fit 109/6
extorcionner *n.* one who practises extortion 107/7

facing *n.* the action of putting on a bold front 107/34
faylle *v. intrans.* be wanting 68/21
fayn *adv.* gladly 8/26
fayn *v.* feign, pretend 45/9; *pp. adj.* fictitious 40/26
fayr *adj.* beautiful 79/14; polite, courteous, of or pertaining to a court 109/3
fayth *n.* obligation 46/27; *of* ~ truly 88/32
***falacye** *n.* guile, trickery 63/18
***faldore** *n.* trapdoor 27/8
falle *v. intrans.* happen, befall 60/6; sin, fall into sin 69/33; ~ *better* turn out more favourably 33/18; ~ *in* become part of 61/5; ~ *besyde and oute* be unable to complete (something) 61/23
fallyng *n.*, *in the* ~ as he fell 101/28
fals *adj.* evil, wicked 37/4
falsely *adv.* wickedly, dishonestly 104/7
falsenes *n.* fabrication 103/27
falshede *n.* deceitfulness, faithlessness 110/20
fare *v. intrans.* experience (good or bad) fortune 32/8; ~ *amys* die 85/36; ~ *by* befall, turn out 84/25; ~ *euyl* come to a bad end 86/24; ~ *right hard* endure great distress 85/33; ~ *the werse* undergo greater hardship 69/38
fast *adj.* secure 13/10; firm 50/36; hard 78/20
fast *adv.* securely 13/12; diligently, zealously 37/17; readily 56/16
faste *v. intrans.* keep fast-days 28/7
fatte *adj.* greasy 100/8
fawty *adj.* guilty 6/32
feawte *n.* obligation of fidelity by a feudal tenant to his lord, fealty 51/10
feblest *adj. superl.*, *vpon his* ~ on his weakest spot 61/10
fecche *v.* go in quest of, convey back 44/8
***fede** *v. refl.* live, exist 78/11
feest *n.* courtly assembly 6/21; church festival 64/39
feet *n.* deed 28/38
felaws *n. pl.* companions, partners 33/33
felawship *n.* partnership 33/35; companionship 41/8; *wold not of his* ~ did not wish for his company 107/3–4
felawsshippe *v.* hold company (with someone) 70/22

feld *n.* battlefield, lists *5/6*; *holde a ~* fight in single combat 67/26; *gyue the ~ vnto* submit the battle to someone's arbitration 105/31

felde *n.* surface on which a picture is drawn 78/26

fele *v.* perceive, understand 6/9; (*refl.*) *~ me the lenger the werse* I feel more ill every minute 84/36

felynge *n.* physical sensibility 109/14

felle *adj.* vicious, sharp 9/1; enraged 33/29; wicked, evil 52/32

felly *adv.* cruelly 84/22

ferde *pt. s.* s.v. **fare**

ferdful *adj.* awe-inspiring 53/23

ferners *n. pl.* past years 32/1

ferre *adv.* afar 10/31; *fro ~* from or at a great distance 9/5; *so ~* for so long 80/37; *as ~ as* in so far as 6/8; as long as 28/27; as high as 32/30 n.; *was not ~ of* was near the mark 95/15; *as/also ~ as* (*conj. phr.*) provided that 77/31; s.v. **room**

fesaunt *n.* pheasant 93/33

feste s.v. **feest**

fette *pp.* fetched 23/20

fychew *n.* pole-cat, foumart 74/32–3

fiers *adj.* high-spirited, brave 76/36

fyghte *n.*, *appel vnto ~* challenge to single combat by way of settling a dispute 102/24

fygure *n.* representation 112/3

fyl *pt. s.* fell 23/6; **fyll** 101/2; cf. **falle**

fyn *adj.* pure, refined 78/27

fyngres *n. pl.*, *see thurgh their ~* overlook something 61/34 n.; *poynte me wyth ~* point at me in scorn 100/33; *lykke theyr ~* meddle in a matter and take their part 107/13–14

fyret *n.* ferret 105/17

first *adv.* for the first time *55/31*; **forst** first 17/15

fystel *n.* internal disease, ulcer 77/21

flayel *n.* flail, instrument for threshing corn by hand 16/18

flayn *pp. adj.* flayed, with the skin removed 83/9

flateryng *n.* flattery 103/31

flawn *n.* tart, flan 21/8 n.

flee *v.* exile, cause to flee 54/20 n.; *intrans.* fly 55/31; **flowen** *pp.* flying 52/24

flesshe *n.* meat 11/23

flycche s.v. **vlycche**

flyndermows *n.* bat 105/10 n.

flockes *n. pl.* coarse tufts of wool (used for quilting garments): *how can he stuffe the sleue wyth ~* how easily he can deceive others with plausible stories 53/32–3 n.

floytyng *n.* singing in flute-like tones 103/32

flomme *n.* river 40/30 n.

flowen s.v. **flee**

folke *n.* followers, liegemen 56/4

foot *n.*, *~ brode* (*longe*) a foot in breadth (length) 43/12; *to ~* on foot 99/5; *on thy free feet* able to go freely where you want 103/23; *brynge them vnder their ~* get the better of them 57/22

***footspore** *n.* track, foot-print 37/21

for *conj.* because 12/20 n.; because of 69/38; so that 78/3; to prevent 80/15; *~ to* to 28/37; in order to 38/30; *prep.* in exchange for 21/16; *~ alle that* (*phr.*) in return for anything that 21/5; in spite of that 88/12

forbede *v.* forbid 34/16

forbere *v.* spare, show mercy to 74/6; bear with, have patience with 95/18

force *n.* violence 52/2

force *v.* s.v. **forse**

fordele *n.* advantage, profit 61/18; precedence 92/3 n.

fordoo *v.* destroy, bring to nought 37/3

fordryue *v.* expel, drive out 36/3

forest *n.* waste region 13/5 n.

forfayte *n.* offence, transgression 51/5

forfayte *v.* forfeit, lose the right to 54/34

forfrorn *pp.* frozen, stuck fast 90/10–11

forgate *pt. s.* forgot 111/32

forgoo *v.* part with, go without 84/34

forhongred *pp. adj.* starving 107/8

forlorn *pp. adj.* lost, depraved 47/35

formably *adv.* in accordance with set forms 30/26–7

formest *adj. superl.* front, fore 100/25

forsake *v.* abandon, relinquish 44/28; decline, refuse 72/1

forse *v.* rape *104/7*

***for slynger** *v.* beat, belabour 17/2

***forslongen** *pp.* swallowed down, gobbled up 12/1
for sothe *adv. phr.* indeed, truly 8/20
forst s.v. **first**
for sworn *pp. adj.* perjured 47/34–5
forth *adv.* moreover, also 16/31; forward 18/37; then 43/10; ~ *wyth* at once 51/17
forthon *adv.* moreover 11/24; henceforth 28/6; thenceforth 35/19; ~ *to* (*prep.*, *phr.*) until 51/3
***forwynterd** *pp. adj.* reduced to straits by the winter 7/29
***forwyttyng** *n.* reproach 86/6
***forwrought** *pp.* destroyed, sinned against 50/16
foryeuenes *n.* absolution 42/23
foule *adv.* shamefully, disgracefully 59/31
founden *pp.* written, composed 112/3
fowl *n.* bird 6/25
fowle *adj.* wicked 28/28; ugly 94/27
fowler *n.* one who hunts birds 98/4
franke *adj.* free 39/25
free *adj.* noble, honourable 23/23; not subject to a lord 36/18
frendis *n. pl.*, *grete of* ~ having many friends 67/2
frese *v. intrans.* freeze: **frore** *pt. s.* 77/9; **frorn** *pp.* 89/13
fresshe *adj.* not healed *8/20*
***friese** *adj.* Frisian 41/6
fro *prep.* from 32/20
fro . . . ward *prep.* away from 82/8–9
frore, frorn s.v. **frese**
frossh *n.* frog 36/18
ful waxen *pp. adj.* grown-up 74/14–15
furryd *pp. adj.* adorned, trimmed with fur 69/5

gaynsaye *v.* deny, oppose 74/37
***galp** *v. intrans.* yell 22/11
game *n.* sport 91/5
gape *v.* stare, gaze at 92/35
generally *adv.* without reference to individuals 112/ 10
genete *n.* cat, civet-cat 74/33
genytoirs *n. pl.* testicles 31/23
gentil *adj.* noble, of noble birth 10/4
gentilnes *n.* nobility, courtesy 72/20
gete *v.* bring about 66/38; ~ *thens* escape from there 91/24; *to* ~ obtainable 25/16; **gate** *pt. s.* acquired, won 79/19; **goten** *pp.* captured 55/30; accomplished 57/2; ~ *vnder* captured 86/11
ghest *n.* guest 21/38
ghoos *n.* goose 30/15; **ghees** *pl.* 28/13
ghoot *n.* goat 30/15; **gheet** *pl.* 33/26
gybet *n.* gallows 31/11
gyue *v.* exchange 21/16; **geuen ouer** *pp.* relinquished 10/11
gladly *adv.* willingly, rather 14/22
gladsom *adj.* productive of gladness, cheering 6/23
glasse *n.* mirror 78/6
***glat** *adj.* smooth, slippery 97/2
***glymme** *v. intrans.* shine, gleam 92/30
glymmer *v. intrans.* shine 53/23
glose *v.* flatter 101/18; **glosyng** *pr. p.* flattering 5/11
go *v. intrans.* used as an intensive to strengthen the meaning of the verb, e.g. *goo sytte* 8/13–14, *go synge* 18/29; walk 18/36; pass over 50/12; go forward 71/28; befall 72/6; ~ *aboue* precede 61/32; ~ *after* follow 28/29; ~ *ayenst* be detrimental to 50/18; ~ *away* escape 31/28; ~ *by* go past, pass 58/5 n.; ~ *forth* proceed 75/17; ~ *out* be blinded 100/29; ~ *to fore* surpass 24/30; ~ *to nyghe* touch too closely 90/4–5; *but how it euer* ~ no matter what happens 47/20; *it goth forth thurgh* it is accepted 61/6; *how* ~ *it now* how are things with you? 42/27; *how someuer it cometh or* ~ however it turns out 54/17; **wente** *pt.*, ~ *from* escaped from 65/14; ~ *wel in* was readily digestible 98/8; ~ *in to* joined, became a member of 41/23; * ~ *to* shut 22/2; ~ *with* accompanied on a journey 47/35; **gon** *pp.*, ~ *forth* had been accomplished 40/15
gobet *n.* part, portion 89/26; a solidified mass (of a substance) 94/22
good *adj.*, *adv.*, *n.* pleasing, welcome 40/27; reliable *40/31*; easy 56/23; *doo* ~ make it good, show it to be the truth 98/23; *maye doo it* ~ answer for my actions 71/16 n.; *make* (*it*) ~ prove (it) to be the truth 95/32, 98/22; **better** *comp.* something better 16/9; *ben* ~ are on better

good (*cont.*):
terms 56/8; *hym had be* ~ it would have been better for him 9/30; *dyde al my* **beste** (*superl.*) did as much as I could 90/18; *take it alway for the* ~ make the most of it 57/36
good *adv.* well 91/27
good *n.* property, possessions 8/9
good willes *n. pl.* favour 34/23
goon *pp. adj.* ago, past 8/2
gostly *adj.* spiritual 6/5; devout 46/6
grace *n.* favour 3/32; *your good* ~ complimentary periphrasis for 'you' 29/13
***grate** *n.* bone, backbone (of a fish) 9/6
graue *n.* sepulchre 102/6 n.
grauen *pp.* engraved 80/22
graunt *v.* agree, concur 71/20
grece *v.* prepare by applying grease 44/16 n.
greet s.v. **grete**
gren(ne) s.v. **gryn**
grenne *v. intrans.* draw back one's lips and display one's teeth 81/25
***grepe** *pt. s.* gripped 104/12
grete *adj.* big 6/30; extensive 7/8; powerful 85/25; *be* ~ *wyth* be in high favour with (someone) 68/32; *become* ~ become important 83/31; *make* ~ advance to power 85/22; *rysen* ~ have risen to power 82/2–3; *wexe* ~ (*by*) grow in favour (with) 70/7; **grettest** *superl.* all-powerful 108/15
gretely *adv.* to a great extent, in a great degree 96/31
greuyd *pp.* incensed, made angry 68/8 n.
gryef *n.* injury, suffering 68/11; disease, malady 77/19
grymly *adj.* fiercely 62/21
grimme *v. intrans.* be angry, look fierce 34/2; **grymmyng** *pr. p.*, *alle* ~ with a very fierce expression 57/20–1
gryn *n.* trap, snare 21/37
gryse *n.* grey fur 61/16 n.
grounde *n.* basis, fundamental principles 72/29
***growle** *v. impers.* feel terror for 74/5
guyse *n.* manner, habit 22/8

habyte *n.* habit, monastic dress 65/31
hale *v.* pull, draw 43/34
half *adj.*, ~ *fro my self* almost out of my mind 64/15
halyday *n.* church festival 28/8
halow *v.* chase with shouts 82/21
halte *v. intrans.* play false, use shifts 62/13; proceed imperfectly or faultily 69/12 n.
hamber *n.* a measure 14/35 n.
***hamme** *n.* buttock, back of thigh 18/38
handle *v.* treat, behave towards 19/11; touch 60/18
hansele *n.* present (as a token of good fortune) 98/5
happe *n.* luck, fortune 40/21
happe *v. intrans.* come about 32/13; *hit happed wel* it was fortunate 68/33–4
happy *adj.* fortunate 30/5
harde *adv.* vigorously 16/24; with difficulty 47/19
hardely *adv.* bravely 66/27; indeed, assuredly 105/32
hardy *adj.* proud 10/36; bold 66/17; **hardyer** *comp.* more presumptuous 26/24
harme *n.*, *cacche no* ~ suffer no injury 15/22; *do* ~ cause pain 83/28; *take* ~ come to grief 94/13
harmles *adj.* unharmed 44/32
harneys *n.* genitals 22/32
harowe *interj.* harrow (as a cry of distress or alarm) 63/4
hastely *adv.* quickly 42/2; soon 100/36
hasty *adj.* quick-tempered 75/22
haue *v.* employ, use 6/5; possess, own 39/33; get possession of 88/10; ~ *them agayn* get them back 76/15; ~ *a waye* take (something) away 27/15–16; ~ *out* extricate 89/26; *what* ~ *I* why should I? 111/7–8
haunt *v.* use, employ 52/20
hawe *n.* hedge, bush 37/34
hebenus *n.* ebony 79/34 n.
hebrews *adj. pl.* Jewish, Aramaic 76/32 n.
hedche *n.* hedge 70/37
hede *n.*, *take better* ~ be more careful 91/28; *take no* ~ have no anxiety 11/23
heed *n.* chief, leader 55/25; *shewe*

openly my ~ make it clear where I stand 63/13–14
***heed offycer** *n.* principal officer 42/12
heef *pt. s.* pushed 90/15
heelde *pt. s.* considered, regarded 59/37
heep *n.* gathering, group 17/18
heer *n.* hair: *sherte of* ~ hair shirt 10/8–9
heeryng *pr. p.* listening (to) 6/8
hele *v.* cure 83/15
helpe *n.* support 30/9; aid, assistance 82/11; *toke to* ~ obtained (someone's) services 37/31
helpe *v. refl.* extricate oneself from a difficulty 92/21, 104/11; *pt.* helped 95/20; **holpen** *pp.* alleviated, cured 84/39
henge s.v. **hynge**
herdeman *n.* herdsman 80/30
here *v.* listen to (in confession) 58/12; understand 59/38; *ben* **herde** (*pp.*) their advice is followed 85/22
heren *adj.* made or consisting of hairs 11/21
hereto *adv.* to this, about this 55/13
here wyth al *adv. phr.* at that 103/6
herked after *phr.* gave ear to 83/19
hert *n.* hart 93/32
herte *n.* courage 97/22; *it goth not to the* ~ (the enmity) is only skin-deep 24/25–6; *gooth to her* ~ affects her 56/29; *shal neuer out of my* ~ I shall never forget 104/7–8
herty *adj.* heartfelt, warm 64/32
hete *n.* anger, passion 103/13
heuy *adj.* oppressed, despondent 17/37
heuyly *adv.* sorrowfully 10/30
heuinesse *n.* sorrow, anguish 89/24
hye *adj.* noble, glorious 7/7; chief, principal 65/3; profound 108/24
hyely *adv.* with honour 109/33
hier by *adv.* in the neighbourhood 14/28; from this example 16/34
hyer fore *adv.* on account of which 36/27
hierof *adv.* in respect of this 9/21
hieron *adv.* of that 8/5
hye way *n.* direct route 55/20 n.
hynder *adj.* back 44/3
hyndre *n.* hindrance 60/13
hyndre *v.* injure, impair 55/1
hynge, henge *pt. s.* hanged 38/24; hung 45/6
his *pr. s.* is 106/31
hystorye *n.* story, account, tale 6/1
holde *n.* possession 14/30; *haue none* ~ be unable to get a grip 97/3
holde *v.* keep, retain 37/7; hold (land or privileges) in feudal sense 51/9; constrain, restrain 57/1; keep to 90/10; ~ *faste* keep good watch 33/1; * ~ *of* fear 53/11–12; ~ *wyth* side with, support 32/22–3; *I* ~ *it on me* I take the responsibility for it 106/2; **holden** *pp.* regarded, considered 54/15
hole *n.*, *seketh his* ~ follow his precepts 110/35–6
holsom *adj.* beneficial 109/6
homage *n.*, *do to hym* ~ swear allegiance to him 35/25; *oweth me* ~ is under obligation to render allegiance 108/16–17
hond *n.*, *bare an* ~ deluded, tricked 89/5–6; *born an* ~ calumniated 65/25; *gyuen in the* ~ *of* given into the power of 50/32; *hath in his* ~ has influence over someone 88/26; *sette it in to his* ~ let him decide the outcome 105/33; *take on* ~ undertake 19/37; *take it vp in to his* ~ decide the matter himself 104/30 n.; *taken to his* ~ captured 18/14
honeste *adj.* honourable, seemly 18/24
honestly *adv.* in a seemly manner 109/26
hood *n.* skin on top of the head 17/34; monastic headdress 18/27
hool *adj.* unhurt 43/25; *al* ~ all in one piece 56/24; cured 77/19
hoot *adj.* angry 75/22
hope *v.* expect 18/5
hore *n.* whore (as term of abuse) 59/32
horeson *n.* whoreson (as term of abuse) 50/20
houedaunce *n.* court dance 51/26
hour *n.*, *in an euyl* ~ unhappily, at a bad time 46/17–18
how *adv.* why 31/5; no matter how 32/28; to what an extent 40/34; for how much, at what price 58/35; what 80/11; ~ *more . . .* ~ *more* the more . . . the more 47/34–5; ~ *that*

that 16/6; in what manner 18/34; however, whatever 63/28; ~ *wel oftymes* how many times 11/8; ~ *wel* (*that*) (*conj.*) although, albeit 37/26; ~ *be it* (*that*) however, although 8/2 n.
how someuer *adv.* in whatever way *70/30*
huylen *v.* howl 73/22
***humaynly** *adj.* in the manner of human beings 69/20
hungerly *adv.* hungrily 53/2
hurt *v.* be detrimental to 20/21
hurte *n.* wrong, damage 36/25; loss, harm 103/20
hurtyng *n.* harm, injury 83/28
husbondman *n.* peasant, village labourer 14/28

ye *n.* eye 69/31
yf *conj.* lest 32/18; provided that 38/18; as if 55/19 n.; ~ *that* if *49/30*
ylle *adj.* evil, wicked 43/4; bad 77/20
ylle *adv.* badly, insufficiently 12/33; *I am ~ on ynough* I am in a bad enough position 71/28–9
ylle wylle *n.* hatred, dislike 83/5
ymage *n.* picture 78/26
in *prep.* upon 66/24; to 77/39; on 101/11; into, within 102/17
informacion *n.* material for a charge or indictment 90/35
infortune *n.* misfortune 38/25
inne *adv.* within, inside 13/10
ynowh *adj.* enough 8/1
interdicte *n.* ban of general excommunication *66/35*
in to *prep.* until, up to 51/14
inuencion *n.* lie, fictitious story 30/25
inward *n.* entrails 87/4
inwytte *n.* intelligence, reason 64/29
irous *adj.* angry, irate 7/33

iangle *v. intrans.* chatter, talk noisily 56/16
iape *n.* idle talk, joke 112/7
iape *v. intrans.* jest, joke 14/21
ieopardye *n.* uncertainty, chance 23/8; danger 27/24
ioconde *adj.* happy, glad 78/23
ioyous *adj.* inspiring joy, cheerful 6/19
ioly *adj.* amorous, wanton 79/20
iuge *v.* assign or award judgement, adjudge 3/25; decree 7/14; **iugged** *pp.* adjudged 4/11
iugement *n.* sentence 30/34
iustyse *n.* court of justice 69/4; *don ~* inflict punishment 10/1

kaytyf s.v. **caytyf**
kakle *v. intrans.* cackle 10/30
kanker *n.* ulcer, spreading sore 77/21
kepars of the feelde *phr.* marshals of the lists 105/34
kepe *v.* protect, guard 11/34 n.; observe 28/7; ~ *from* avoid, shun 6/11
kyen *n. pl.* cows 73/25
kyndenes *n.* natural affection, love 72/20
kynne *n.* family: *of my next ~* my immediate relatives 34/33; *nyghe of his ~* closely related to him 31/2–3
kynrede *n.* family, kin 55/36
knaue *n.* wretch, rogue 103/34
knauisshly *adv.* dishonestly, villainously 89/15
knowe *v.* recognize, acknowledge 14/11; experience, find out 29/25; *knoweth not hym self* forgets who he is 85/27; **knewe** *pt. s.*, ~ *nothyng* was ignorant 16/1; *it is longe syth that I ~ the* I have been well acquainted with your character for a long time 103/28; **knowen** *pp. adj.* recognized, familiar 110/26
knoweleche *v.* acknowledge 103/3
knowleche *n.* cognizance, notice 10/20; *had ~* was informed 55/6; *gyuen in ~* made known 64/24; *come to ~* are made known 107/17

***laaden** *v.* load, load up 56/6
labour *n.* exerting influence 43/1; *pl.* endeavours 49/16
labour *v.* exert oneself to obtain (something) 43/11; ~ *fore* strive on someone's behalf 15/6; strive for (something) 34/24
lacke *v. intrans.* be wanting 24/21 n.; be at a loss 85/23
lande *n.* 13/7 n.
lapen *v.* drink greedily 33/23
lapwynches *n. pl.* lapwings 57/15
laste *quasi-n.*, *atte ~*, *at the ~* in the end 19/2, 33/23

***laste** *n.* distress, sorrow 60/4
late allone *v. phr.* do not worry (about something) 12/32–3
lawe *n.* justice, retribution 12/14; trial according to legal procedure 50/29; court of law 61/16
lawhe *v.* laugh 14/37
ledde *pp.* deceived (by lies) 63/7
leep *pt. s.* leapt, hastened 42/25; ~ *of* leapt off 89/23
leet *pt. s.* s.v. **lete**
leeuys *n. pl.* leaves 14/4 n.
leye *v.* prefer a charge against someone 8/31 n., 23/26; lie in wait 11/9; wager 55/2; ~ *to fore* offer (as temptation) 60/31; **leyd** *pp.*, ~ *doun* delivered of a child 93/11
lene *v.* support, assist 85/34
lengest *adj. superl.*, *at alther* ~ at the very latest 58/8
lengthe *v.* lengthen, prolong 51/18 n.
lepe *pt. s.* s.v. **leep**
lerynge *n.* teaching 6/2 n.
lernynge *n.* lesson 112/8
lese *v.* lose 58/15
lesyng *n.* lie, falsehood 32/22
leste *adj. superl.*, *of the* ~ but the least thing 34/5
lete *v.* leave 16/27; **leet** *pt. s.* 59/21
lette *v.* hinder, impede 62/8
lettyng *n.* delay 21/21; *pl.* hindrances 62/4
lettres *n. pl.* writs 38/3
leue *n.* permission 33/17; *toke* ~ (*of*) bade farewell (to) 57/33
leue *v.* abandon 8/16; omit, neglect to do (something) 12/25; ~ *of* give up, stop 67/12–13; *he shold haue lefte that* he should not have mentioned that 9/22 n.
leuer *adj. comp.* rather 44/36
lewde *adj.* ignorant 18/12; rude, vulgar 81/37
licence *n.* permission 109/34
lycensyd *pp. adj.* allowed to practise 59/11
lycourous *adj.* greedy, desirous 33/25
lye *v.*, * ~ *on* come in question 20/2 n.; be dependent on 78/3; **laye** *pt. s.*, ~ *better* was more conveniently situated 37/33–4; **leyn** *pp.*, ~ *by* had intercourse with 9/18
lyef *adj.* dear 14/8
lyeng *pr. p.* false 103/32
lyf *n.*, *touche their* ~ cost them their lives 43/28; *for nede of* ~ when it's a question of life and death 72/16; *upon their lyuys* on penalty of death 85/15–16; s.v. **duryng**
***lyf scathe** *n.* mortal injury 61/36 n.
lyfte vp *v. phr.* raised his arms 22/22
lyght *adj.* easily digestible 56/26; nimble 52/10, *superl.* 32/35; *comp.* more cheerful 76/22
lyghte *n.*, *comen in the* ~ be exonerated 108/5
lyghtly *adv.* nimbly 15/28; readily 29/17
lygnage, lynage *n.* family, relations, kin 4/10
lyke *adj.* similar 96/1; ~ *to* similar to 37/19–20; fitting for 61/3; *ryght* ~ similar to 92/35; *to me* ~ my equal 67/14–15; *it was* ~ *to haue be* (than) was to have been expected 88/27; *we were* ~ *to haue lost* we were within an ace of losing 89/27; ~ *as* (*conj.*) even as 6/15, 45/13
lyke *v.* imitate 57/20
lyknes *n.* guise, shape 11/15; parable 36/17; reflection, semblance 78/13
lynage s.v. **lygnage**
lynde *n.* tree, bough of a tree 32/34
lyne *n.* string, cord 31/24
lyste *pt. s.* desired 30/33
lytier *n.* bed 57/29
lytyl *adj.*, *but* ~ very little 88/12; *I wil not doo* ~ *ne moche herin* I will not stir a finger in the business 44/32
lyue *v.*, *he lyueth not* there is no man alive 108/28 n.
***lock** *v.* entice 103/28
loke *v.*, ~ *aboute* take care 23/35; ~ *to* attend to 109/11
londe *n.*, *alle the* ~ *a boute* up and down the whole country 37/37
longe *adv.* far, a long way 52/28; for a long time 53/27; *atte* ~ in the end 74/1
longen *pr. pl.* are appropriate to, are part of 12/15
longes *n. pl.* lungs 87/4
***loos** *adj.* free from moral restraint 60/29
loos *n.* praise 105/13

lordshippis *n. pl.* dominion, rule 81/37
lose *v.* set free 103/21; waste 103/31
losyng *n.* loss: *for ~ of tyme* in order to save time 80/15–16
***losse, lossem** *n.* lynx 98/19
loste *pp. adj.* useless 22/33; *al ~* destroyed 110/18
lothlyer *adj. comp.* more repulsive 16/26
loue *n.* esteem 70/1
luck *v. intrans.* befall, come to pass 34/5
lupaerd *n.* leopard 50/10
lust *v. impers.* be pleased, want to 17/21
luste *n.* pleasure, delight 78/22
lusty *adj.* beautiful, pleasing 6/23; vigorous, confident 80/4
lustly *adj.* beautiful 80/24

maynchettis *n. pl.* small loaves made of fine wheat bread 64/37
mayntene *v.* uphold, support 61/35
maister *n.* teacher 9/26; doctor 83/14; used as a title to signify a man's learning 44/26
make *v.* bring it about 21/14; have (something) done (to a person or thing) 26/2; compose, write 49/9; depict, make a picture of 81/9; **made** *pp.* put forward, supported 61/2
makyng *n.* composition 49/34; arrangement 51/19
male *n.* bag 48/37
malle *n.* club 17/1
mandementis *n. pl.* command, summons 6/20
maner *n.* species, kind, sort 9/14; bearing, behaviour 28/28
manerly *adv.* properly, courteously 51/26
mark *v.* s.v. **merk**
marke *n.* mark, unit of money 20/28
market *n.* bargain, transaction 16/28
marmosette *n.* small monkey 94/20
martre, martron *n.* marten 74/33, 105/17 n.
masse *n.*, *do ~* say mass 44/23
mater *n.* theme, topic 61/4; affair, business 87/19; *hath his ~ fast and fayr* achieved a satisfactory conclusion to his business 88/25
mathes *n. pl.* maggots, worms 65/20
matyns *n. pl.* canonical hour recited at daybreak 64/34
***maw** *v. intrans.* mew (like a cat) 22/11
me *pron.* one 14/15
meyne *n.* family, household 93/2
membre *n.* limb 42/17
menace *v.* threaten 20/18
mene *n.* agency, action 32/32
menestralsye *n.* music 51/27
menowr *n.* stolen object found in thief's possession 9/37 n.
***mercatte** *n.* monkey 92/33
mercy *n.*, *come to ~* receive pardon 60/8
merk, mark *v.* give heed to 6/3; understand 15/9
***mermoyse** *n.* monkey 92/32–3
meruaylle *n.* wonder, surprise 59/36–7
meruaylle *v.* wonder, be amazed 26/6
meschief *n.* misfortune 107/19
messager *n.* messenger 18/24
mesure *n.* moderation 26/15; *by ~* in moderation 15/2; *without ~* unlimited 15/19
mesure *v.* moderate, restrain 103/10
mete *adj.* suitable, fitting 31/19
mete *n.* food 7/29
mette wyth *phr.* (*pt. s.*) came across, met 64/19
meuyd *pp. adj.* angry, upset 75/21
myddys *n. pl.*, *in the ~* in the middle 92/13
myghte *n.* force, power 75/17
myghte *v.*, *that I ~* as much as I could 54/17; *al that they ~* as quickly as they could 82/9; *~ ouer* (*v. phr.*) prevail against 33/30, 106/13 n.
mynstralcye s.v. **menestralsye**
mynussh *v.* reduce, cut down 112/18
mysauenture *n.* misfortune 45/33–4
myscarye *v. intrans.* come to grief, be destroyed 74/17
***mysdele** *v. intrans.* distribute unfairly 9/3
mysdo *v. intrans.* do wrong, act incorrectly 9/37; **mysdede** *pt. s.* 69/18
mysdoyng *n.* transgression of the law 51/7–8

mysfalle *v. intrans.* come to grief 83/1 n.; **mysfylle euyl** *pt. s.* turned out badly 52/32
myshappe *n.* accident 102/33
myshappe *v. intrans.* meet with misfortune 94/18
myspreyse *v.* blame 8/24
***myssake** *v.* deny, renounce 109/2
mo, moo *adj.* more 9/2
moche *adj.* much, great 11/30; *adv.* greatly 9/17; very 10/15; *in so ~ that* (*conj., phr.*) with the result that 42/16
mocke *n.* taunt, derision 82/25
moder naked *adj. phr.* stark naked 22/17 n.
moed, mood *n.* frame of mind, temper 7/33
moghettis *n. pl.* intestines 87/4
moke *v. intrans.* mock, jest 21/12
more *adj. comp.* bigger, greater 24/19; *~ than* beyond what (is) 54/30; *adv.* further, in addition 11/19
morow *n., good ~* good morning 44/20; *by the ~* in the morning 52/26
morowtyde *n.* morning 36/5
morsellis *n. pl.* tit-bits 61/20; bite, mouthful 83/10
moste *adj. superl.* greatest, biggest 37/29, 60/13
mote *v.* must, may 29/17; may 86/24
motes *n. pl.* particles of dust causing irritation in the eyes or throat 79/27
mouth *n., holde your ~* be quiet 29/28
mowe *v.* be able 6/8 n.
***musehont** *n.* weasel 74/32 n.
muste *v., I ~ her thurgh* I must go through with it 63/28; *theder ~ I too* I must follow it 82/17

nay *interj.* no 14/22
naked *adj.* unarmed 77/35
name *n., in the deueles ~* accursedly 22/31
name *v.* refer to by name 40/24; relate, tell 76/28; *pp.* reputed 98/30
narewest *adj. superl., at the ~* fully, completely 62/8
narowly *adv.* urgently 72/21
nature *n.* properties 84/29; character, temperament 86/25
nede *n.* benefit 6/7; trouble 13/30; necessity 13/36
nedes *adv.* of necessity 14/13
ner, nerrer *adv. comp.* nearer 8/16
netis *n. pl.* nits 74/26
nette *n., crepe in reynardis ~* follow in R.'s footsteps 110/12; *taken in his owne ~* caused his own downfall 81/4–5
neue, neuew *n.* nephew 14/8
neuer *adv.* not 48/33, 60/6
new *adj.* fresh 14/6
newe shood *phr.* (*adv.+pp.*) recently shod 59/18
next *n., alther ~* right beside 40/10
***nycker** *n.* demon, devil 94/22
nygh *adv.* almost 23/9; closely 31/34; *also ~* as near 40/29; **nyhe** 52/14
nyght *n., an hole derke ~ longe* for the total length of a dark night 35/32; *on nyghtes* by night 81/21
nyp *v.* catch between two surfaces 16/3; **nypte** *pt. s.* vexed 9/1; **nyped** *pp.* cut off 18/28
noble *n.* gold coin 21/17
noblesse *n.* nobility 69/2
nobly *adv.* in a lofty or exalted manner 5/19
noman *n.* nobody 8/7
nombred *pp.* counted 39/6
nomoo *adj.* no more 42/20
nomore *n., ~ but* nothing else except 53/3
none *adj.* no 11/28; *~ other* nothing else *23/9*
none *n.* canonical office said at ninth hour 11/25
none *pron.* nobody 15/5
noo *adv.* not 105/32
not *n.* nothing 54/35
nothyng *adv.* not 16/1; not at all 38/21
notwythstandyng *conj., ~ that* although 101/24
nought *n.* nothing 9/11; *goth al to ~* is destroyed 83/31–32
nowher *adv.* in no way 14/14

***och** *interj.* oh 31/35
of *prep.* concerning, about 4/29; from 10/10; through, on account of 10/15; off 27/37; by 34/32; out of 53/31; *~ that* (*conj., phr.*) because 97/21

of and on *adv. phr.* to and fro 100/27

***offryng candel** *n.* candle used in act of worship 22/18

ofter *adv. comp.* more often 25/32

oy *interj.* yes 59/8

on *art.* an, a 82/17

on *prep.* about, upon 43/5; at 51/37; in 66/28

one *pron.* anyone at all 66/29; ~ *the best* the very best 33/20

ones *adv.* (*quasi-adj.*) a single 6/16; *adv.* one day 29/21 n.

ony *pron.* one, a man 25/5

open *adj.* public 3/27; generally accessible 6/27 n.; evident 68/10; not healed 100/26; revealed, made public 107/18

open *v.* cut open, make an incision in 85/11

openly *adv.* publicly, aloud 35/8

or *conj.* before 16/27

ordeyne *v.* appoint 36/21; provide 51/27; make 84/2

ordre *n.* monastic order 18/26

orguillous *adj.* proud 35/22

***ostrole** *n.* [of uncertain meaning] 74/34

other *pron.* the remainder 45/11, 61/7; another 54/14

other whyle *adv.* sometimes 56/25

other wyse *adv.* differently: *bythought hym* ~ changed his mind 7/17; *none* ~ not for a second time 55/7 n.; ~ *than* in a different way from 39/11

ouer *adv.* too 54/19, 84/4

ouer *prep.* beyond, past 15/27; on 18/38; about, concerning 45/2

oueral *adv., prep.* everywhere, throughout 11/17; **ouer alle** 6/28

ouer chargyd *pp.* oppressed 66/31

ouercome *v.* defeat 79/2; *pp.* 104/18

***ouerest** *adj. superl.* highest in quality 65/1

ouerhand *n., haue the* ~ *of* get the better of 87/12; *haue the* ~ be all-powerful, rule 87/15

ouermoche *adv.* excessively, exceedingly 70/28, 104/3

***ouer redyng** *n.* (superficial) reading (of a document) 6/16 n.

ouer see *adv.* abroad 48/20

ouersee *v.* consider, examine mentally 87/18

ouerswyft *adj.* too fast 58/24

ouerthrowe *v. intrans.* fall down, tumble 104/22

ought *n.* anything 18/21

ought *v.*, ~ *to doo* were in duty bound to do 96/16

out *adv.* to the end 63/31; *alle* ~ 63/29

oute alas *phr.* indeed (as exclamation implying indignation) 84/14

outeward *adv.* externally, in appearance 45/24

ouwher *adv.* anywhere 33/21

paas *n.* pace, step: *a good* ~ quickly 15/7–8

packe *n.* bag (of lies) 34/25 n.

payd *pp. adj.* pleased, satisfied 19/5

payment *n.* reward, retribution 95/11

payne *n.* sorrow, suffering 31/21; difficulty, trouble 71/34; ~ *loste* wasted effort 90/16

payne *v. refl.* take pains, exert oneself 15/4

***palster** *n.* pilgrim's staff 45/7

parable *n.* allegory, illustrative example 6/2

parauenture *adv.* perhaps 20/33

pardon *n.* remission 17/24

paryl *n.* danger 109/20

parlament *n.* discussion, debate 30/21

parte *n.* share 9/9; duty, concern 88/20; *a* ~ somewhat 24/31–2; *alle the moost* ~ almost everyone 87/35 n.

parte *v.* distribute, divide 86/33

partener *n.* partaker 44/7; accomplice 53/15

partrych *n.* partridge 93/33

passe *v.* traverse 43/25; *intrans.* depart 76/14; **passyd** *pp.* taken place 8/2; *adj.* ago 70/35

passyng *adv.* very, exceedingly 19/6

pasteyes *n. pl.* pies, meat-pies 21/8

pater *n.* used as title 'Father' for priest or monk 41/6

pater noster *n.* Our Father 28/31

path *n., tredeth in the foxes* ~ follow the fox's behaviour 110/35

pauyllyons *n. pl.* tents 56/6

pease *v.* pacify, appease 58/15
pees *n.* friendship, pardon 4/33; safety, protection 8/11; tranquillity 92/24; *made ~ wyth* effected a reconciliation with 42/16; *to haue holde his ~* to have kept quiet 9/30
perfyghtly *adv.* correctly 59/13
perylous *adj.* greatly to be dreaded, terrible 92/18
perles *n. pl.* eye disease, kind of cataract 79/27
person *n.* parson, priest 17/19
***personably** *adv.* with such an appearance as to create a favourable impression 45/22
pyk *v.* depart 67/20
pykforkes *n. pl.* pitchforks 89/30
pylche *n.* coarse woollen outer garment 11/21
pilgremage *n., a ~* on a pilgrimage 46/23
pylle *v.* despoil 107/8
pype *v. intrans.* squeak 21/28
pitously *adv.* lamentably, so as to inspire pity 10/28
pytte *n.* grave 12/17; hole 41/18
place *n.* house, habitation 106/20
placebo *n.* vespers 12/14 n.; *playe ~* flatter 62/3–4 n.
***plaghe** *v.* afflict, torment 66/7
playn *adj.* flat 37/19
playn *v. intrans.* make a complaint or a charge 9/23; complain 41/26
playnly *adv.* fully 80/10; distinctly, clearly 85/6
plays *n.* plaice 9/4
playsaunt *adj.* agreeable, beautiful 80/24
playsyr *n., to his ~* in accordance with his will 111/7; *saye your ~* tell what is your desire 74/6–7
plat *adv., al ~* level with the ground 37/15
***plat blynde** *adj. phr.* completely blind 99/11
plee *n.* suit at law 19/28; *take a ~ ayenst* file a suit against 66/11
plegge *n.* pledge 46/24
pley with *v. phr.* wag 81/12
plente *n.* abundance 37/29
plesantly *adv.* with gratification, voluptuously 60/31
plesyd *pp. adj.* satisfied 46/7; *wel ~* 68/32
plete *v.* plead 13/15
***plompe** *adj.* foolish, ignorant 61/22
plouyer *n.* plover 102/15
pluck *v. intrans.* deprive of hair or skin 11/5; pull 16/24
pluckyng *n., wyth the ~* when it was pulled out 83/21
poyntes *n. pl.* matters 6/3; particulars 9/3
polaylle *n.* poultry 28/24
polete *n.* pullet 28/20
possessour *n.* owner, ruler 79/6
poure *adj.* wretched 29/32
pouruey *v.* furnish with provisions 25/10
power *n., haue vnder their ~* have authority, control over 79/5; *to my ~* as much as I could 109/2
pray for *v. phr.* intercede on someone's behalf 42/15–16; beg (you) to do 44/37
prech *v.* proclaim, speak 10/16
preef *n.* proof 95/30
preferre *v.* promote 73/36
present *v.* offer 79/14
presente *n.* gift: *in ~* as a gift 84/6
preue *v.* prove 98/21
preuy *adj.* intimate, familiar 38/26
prickyng *n.* smarting, tingling 79/27
pryncypal *adj., most ~* the leaders 34/32
prys *n.* value, worth 18/25
prysone *v.* imprison 54/20
pryuelage *n.* right 51/8
profounde *adj.* learned 84/3
profre *v.* make an offer (of something) 86/28
progenytours *n. pl.* ancestors 86/8
proye *n.* prey 13/25
prononce *v.* relate, utter 61/22
proof *n.* attempt to prove oneself 96/2
propre *adj.* own 81/5
prouende *n.* provisions, food 41/24
prouffyt *v.* be of avail, avail 15/33
prouffyte *n.* gain, advantage 26/2; benefit, well-being 83/32; *cometh wel to ~* benefits 74/24
prouffytable *adj.* advantageous 63/32
puddyng *n.* a kind of sausage 7/30
puf *interj.* pooh (as an expression of contempt) 56/12

purpoos *n.* intention, resolution 60/33
putte *v.* cause 81/17; ~ *a back* repulse, reject 85/23; ~ *away* dispel 32/24; ~ *doun* deprive of their influence 70/8; ~ *out* expel 110/23; ~ *out of* (*refl.*) free oneself from 42/1

quene *n.* trollop 89/36
quyte *adj.* free, unpunished 8/21; free from, rid of 11/14; *make* ~ deprive 25/28; *al* ~ unscathed 25/30
quyte *v.* repay, requite 32/14
quoke *pt. s. intrans.* quaked 45/1

racke *n.* rack, an instrument of torture 24/12
***rasyng** *n.* fit of madness 85/3
***ratte** *n.* wheel 13/18
rauener *n.* despoiler 36/31
rauenous *adj.* rapacious, given to plundering 85/21
raught *pt. s.* stretched, extended 52/8; caught 100/18; ~ *out* pulled out 22/25
rauyne, rauayn *n.* robbery, rapine 87/10, 99/26
rauyssh *v.* rape 89/15
rebuke *n.* shame, disgrace 100/34
receptes *n. pl.* prescriptions, formulae 84/28
recluse *n.* monk, hermit 11/19
recorde *n.* evidence, proof 90/35
recoure *v.* remedy, make good again 95/28
rede *adj.* red, cunning 14/23 n.
rede *v. intrans.* read (divine service) 66/35; **radde** *pt. s. trans.* read 45/2
refrayne *v. refl.* stop oneself, restrain oneself 28/25
refuse *v.* reject 36/35
regne *v. intrans.* be dominant, prevail 110/20
reherse *v.* relate, enumerate 71/22
reyse *v. intrans.* travel 41/35
***reken** *v.* reckon out, allege 33/32
relece *v.* grant remission or discharge (of sins) 17/24
religion *n.* monastery 41/24
remembraunce *n.* memory 83/6
remembre *v.* think of 11/24; remind 108/34
renne *v. intrans.* run 13/36; **ronne** *pt. pl.* 94/36
rennyng *n.* running 99/16
renomed *pp. adj.* renowned 80/5
repent *v.* cause grief, be a cause of sorrow to 44/5
reporte *v. refl.* appeal 72/15
repref *n.* shame, disgrace 41/34
reprise *v.* reprove, reprehend 9/27
reprouable *adj.* reprehensible 68/16
rereward *n.*, *kepe the* ~ *behynde* stay in the rear 73/30–1
reskow *v.* rescue 65/13
reson *n.* action or matter agreeable to reason 9/33; advice 106/3; *pl.* arguments 71/22; *it is* ~ it is just 102/28
resonably *adv.* in accordance with reason 87/28
resseyue *v.* take delivery of 9/35
rest *v. intrans.* remain, be located *78/18*
reste *n.* peace, repose 22/9
retche *v.* care for 46/7
retorne agayn *v. phr.* turn back home 45/30
reuerence *n.* respect, deference 86/7; *sauf your* ~ with no discourtesy meant to you 39/7–8; *dyde grete* ~ paid obeisance to 111/24–5
rewarde *v.* repay 32/33; *euyl rewarded* repaid with misfortune 91/10
rewle *n.* conduct, behaviour 52/20; government, control 82/1
rewle *v. refl.* behave, conduct oneself 111/7; **rewlyd** (*pp.*) ~ *after* be treated in accordance with 87/26
rybadously *adv.* wickedly 90/19
rybaud *n.* one who jests and uses scurrilous language 18/20
riche *adj.* choice 18/15; *almighty 20/17; happy, blessed 79/17; *richer than* ~ the most fortunate among men 79/9
ridge *n.* back 43/12
rydynge knotte *phr.* (*quasi-n.*) slipknot 32/34
ryght *adj.* true, just 6/17; direct, straight 28/15
right *adv.* very 18/17
ryght *n.* justice 7/8; *by/of* ~ rightfully, properly 18/8, 54/27; *as ferre as* ~ *wyl* in so far as justice allows 87/22; *the dethes* ~ funeral ceremonies 12/9–10
rightful *adj.* just 96/30

rightwys *adj.* good, virtuous 110/18
rightwysnes *n.* virtue, good justice 108/26
rys *n.* twig, small branch 75/26
roches *n. pl.* rocks 43/26
rodde *n.* twig, branch 27/37
royame *n.* kingdom 11/17
rome, ruym *v.* leave, vacate 30/37
room *adv.* widely, very (far) 67/21 n.
***rore** *v.* move 43/9; affect with some feeling 60/18
rouer *n.* robber 8/7
roughe *adj.* hairy 16/27
***rouynge** *n.* robbery, theft 25/18
***rowme** *adj.* far, advanced 101/36
rude *adj.* inelegant, lacking in literary merit 112/20
ruym *s.v.* **rome**
rumour *n.* noise, uproar 15/36
russhyng *n.* noise made by rapid or violent movement 92/14
***rutsele** *v. intrans.* slide 18/38

sable *n.* black 78/28
sack *n.* bag (of lies) 48/5
saye *v.* speak 87/27; ~ *euyl by* speak to someone's detriment, denigrate 107/19–20; ~ *moche for* speak strongly for someone 70/18; ~ *naye* deny 89/17; ~ *on* raise against 64/13; *I ~ not but that* I do not deny 62/1; *so ferre sayd* implicated himself so much 50/1
sayeng *n.*, *in here ~* in their testimony 72/30–1
salewe *v.* salute, greet 24/4
salutacion *n.* greeting 63/18
saue *v.* keep, protect 44/32
sauf *prep.* except 6/31; ~ *that* (*conj., phr.*) except that 45/3
saufconduyt *n.* safe-conduct 21/19
saufgarde *n.* protection, safe-conduct 54/4
sauyng *prep.* except 51/31
sauour *n.* smell 78/14
sauour *v. intrans.* smell, give off an aroma 9/8; taste 21/8; *impers.* 98/7
scathe *n.* harm, injury 10/34
***scatte** *n.* treasure 34/10
***scatte** *v.* oppress by exactions 107/7
science *n.* knowledge, learning 60/3; *pl.* various kinds of knowledge 84/3
scole *n.* university 59/9, 84/27
scoler *n.* pupil, disciple 110/13
scorn *n.* taunt, sign of contempt 81/22
scryppe *n.* pilgrim's bag or wallet 43/13
sece *v.* stop, put an end to 104/30
seche *v.* seek 48/6
see *v.*, * ~ *to* take care 12/29 n.; ~ *for your self* be on your guard 97/24
seel *v.* wainscot, cover with woodwork 79/32
seeld *adv.* seldom 8/31
seke *adj.* ill 41/27
seke *v.* demand 72/21; *seketh hym self* seeks his own advantage 110/37; ~ *on* resort to for help 66/29
sekenes *n.* illness 56/29
sely *adj.* deserving of pity 89/17
semed *pt. s.*, *as it wel ~* as was readily apparent 100/6
senewis *n. pl.* sinews 43/34
sensualyte *n.* lust, fondness for pleasures of the body 83/6
sentence *n.* judgement, excommunication 41/29
serue *v.* treat in a specified manner 81/33
seruyse *n.* feudal obligation to serve lord in warfare 55/8
sette *v.* stake (life and goods) upon 74/14; appoint 96/3; ~ *by* take account of 7/18–19; value 14/15; ~ *them forth* propagate them 61/32; ~ *hym in* learn 110/4; *pp.* composed 6/15; ~ *a syde* deposed 37/9; ~ *therto* determined on that course of action 31/26; ~ *vp* promoted 110/14; ~ *vpon* laid on 78/31
sexte *n.* third of the lesser canonical hours 11/25
shadde *n.* shed 11/4
shalmouse, shalmoyses *n. pl.* reed instruments, shawms 51/26, 105/26–27
shame *n.* disgrace 22/32; *brynge to ~* discredit 32/21; (*quasi-adj.*) *a shames deth* a shameful death 18/12–13
shame *v.* bring disgrace upon 95/27
shamefast *adj.* modest 79/12
shameful *adj.* dishonourable 56/3
sharp *v.* sharpen 94/9
sharpe *adj.* rugged, provided with sharp rocks 43/25; acute, cunning 108/24

sharply *adv.* attentively 15/18; vigorously 90/3; severely, sternly 108/29
she ape *n.* female ape 4/25
shette *v.* shut 102/38
shew *v. refl.* present oneself 45/24; **shewde** *pp.* given witness to 70/14
shoef *pt. s.* shaved 18/28
shoys *n. pl.* shoes 4/3; **shoon** 43/16
shooue *v.* shove, push 27/16; **shoof** *pt. s.* pushed 26/26
shorn *pp. adj.* with a tonsure 41/24; *deprived of privileges, possessions 107/12
shorte *v.* shorten, abbreviate 31/21
shrew *n.* villain 6/11
shrewd *adj.* unfavourable, ill-omened 20/11; loud 22/4; severe, grievous 26/36; wicked 52/20
shrewdly *adv.* wickedly, maliciously 20/27; severely 59/21
shrewdnes *n.* wickedness 99/26
shrifte *n.* confession 4/22
shryue *v.* take shrift, be confessed 3/22; *refl.* confess, make one's confession 25/22; **shroef** *pt. s.* 25/11; **shreuen** *pp.* 58/26
sybbe *n., adj.* kin, related by blood 50/10
syde *n., on the werst* ~ on the losing side 100/34
***side hole** *n.* smaller hole leading off a larger one 47/29
***siede** *v.* boil 30/7; **syedyng** *pr. p.* 107/3
sykerly *adv.* assuredly, certainly 8/24
***sykernes** *n.* promise, faith 82/33
symple *adj.* plain 14/10; of low rank 73/30; innocent 99/22; inelegant 112/20
syngen *v. intrans.* sing chants (at divine service) 66/36
synguler *adj.* exclusive, own particular 73/34; distinguished 84/30
***syte** *v.* summon to court 66/11
syth *adv.* afterwards 27/3
syth *conj.* since 20/3; ~ *that* 10/5–6
sytte *v.,* * ~ *of* dismount 80/39; ~ *vpon* mount 80/34
syttyng *adj.* befitting 29/16 n.
skarlet *n.* rich cloth (often red in colour) 61/16 n.
skathe *v.* hurt, harm *10/3* n.
skateryng *n.* stirring up 101/31
***skylle (quyte)** *v.* make free or quit of 42/29
skylle *v. impers.* make a difference, be of importance 68/1
sklandre *v.* slander 25/30
***skrabbe** *v.* scrape 99/14
***slange** *pt. s.* devoured 53/3
slauyne *n.* pilgrim's mantle 11/21
slee *v.* slay, kill 26/22
slepe *pt. s.* slept 8/4
***slepe** *v.* drag 27/1
***slepte** *pp.* digested by means of sleep 59/25
slyde *v.* slip, fall 69/17
slyper *adj.* slippery 100/8
***slonk** *v.* devour, swallow greedily 53/2
slowe *adj.* sluggish 41/27
smal *adj.* slender 26/17; petty 73/24
smarte *n.* pain 79/27
smeke *v.* flatter 85/31
smellyng *n.* odour, smell 78/15
smerte *v. impers.* smart, cause pain 99/17
smyte *v.* strike 17/21; ~ *doun right* destroy, kill 89/31; **smeton** *pt. pl.* 27/23; **smyten, smeten** *pp.* punished, chastised 9/26; hammered 15/15
smoke *v. intrans.* give off dust 11/12 n.
***smoldre** *v. intrans.* smother, suffocate 93/4
smothe *adj.* free from hair or bristles 97/1
snatch *v. intrans.* make a sudden bite 101/9
snelle *adj.* cunning, keen-witted 100/9
so *adv.* to such an extent 16/29; ~ *as* (*conj., phr.*) so that 19/10; as 29/25; ~ *that* provided that 83/2
softly *adv.* quietly 48/11
solycyte *v.* prosecute 66/21
somme *adj.* any 64/20; *pron.* one 16/16; some men 49/15
somwhat *adv.* to some extent, to a slight degree 50/10
sonde *n.* dust 99/16
***sondrely** *adv.* especially, particularly 66/27
sore *adj.* grievous 16/33; painful 104/16

sore *adv.* strongly 7/2; very, greatly 7/28
sorenes *n.* pain 77/17
sorouful *adj.* lamentable, doleful 65/18
sorowe *v.* lament 38/23; *intrans.* have anxiety 73/35; ~ *for* fear for 56/12; *provide for 25/9
soth *n.* truth 24/20
souerayn *adj.* supreme, holding superior rank 108/15
***souldye** *n.* salary, wages 38/2 n.
souldyour *n.* soldier 38/7
spare *v.* refrain from 45/17; abstain from destroying or injuring 55/20; avoid the use of, forbear 94/11; leave (someone) uninjured 100/32
speche *n.*, *may come to* ~ am allowed to speak 56/30–1
specyally *adv.* in particular 96/10 n.
spede *v. intrans.* fare 3/14; ~ *wel* succeed 96/30; **sped** (*pp.*) *was* ~ was treated 13/1
spekyng *n.* interchange, dialogue 42/6
spelle *v.* read 76/33
***spynde** *n.* larder, pantry 26/11
spyte *n.* grudge, malice 81/13
***spyty** *adj.* scornful 95/24
spytous *adj.* scornful 99/33
sprynge *v. intrans.* jump 97/14
***sprynklis** *n. pl.* spots, speckles 77/26
squyer *n.* officer in attendance on a sovereign 42/28
stack *pt. s.* stuck 83/12
stack(e) s.v. **steke**
stade *n.* 6/27 n.
stage *n.* elevated platform 42/7
standeth s.v. **stonde**
stappes *n. pl.* footsteps 25/4
***stare** *v. intrans.* gaze lifelessly, be glazed (as in death) 52/28
stately *adj.* royal, noble 36/35
steke, sticke *v.* push, thrust as in sexual intercourse 89/19; **stake, stack(e)** *pt.* hit, struck 17/9, 104/27; ~ *on* 89/33
stere *v.* move 43/9; **styre** cause to rise 97/15
sterte *pt. s.* jumped, moved suddenly 18/32; went 99/12; fell, entered 101/28
sticke s.v. **steke**
stylle *adj.* quiet 23/1
stynkynge *adj.* disgusting 36/35
styre s.v. **stere**
***stokke** *n.* stick, stave 26/35
stole *n.* throne 35/36
stonde *v.* remain, exist 24/24; ~ *by* support 74/3; ~ *euyl wyth* be unfavourably situated 56/2; *how it standeth with me* how I am placed 35/1
stone *n.* testicle 23/2; disease causing formation of gall-stones 77/21
stoppe *v.* fill up 37/19
***stoppelmaker** *n.* reaper of stubble 17/13
storuen *pp.* dead 58/32
stoundmele *adv.* at intervals 39/20 n.
stoutly *adv.* bravely, boldly 63/17
stowte *adj.* valiant 13/3
strayte *adj.* stringent 6/29
straytly *adv.* strictly 65/32
strange *adj.* helpless, at a disadvantage 47/25; unfamiliar 80/19
stranguyllyon *n.* quinsy 77/21
stratche *v. intrans.* extend 57/10; *refl.* make a facial expression 88/1 n.
streem *n.* river, current 18/33; *the beste of the* ~ where the current was strongest 17/30–1
strenger *adj. comp.* stronger 95/12
strengthe *v.* support 36/27 n., 61/35
strete *n.* road: *hyest* ~ principal avenue 29/8; *wente he his* ~ departed 53/5
stryk *v.* rub, stroke 37/21, 77/18; *intrans.* make one's way 62/15; *refl.* 98/17
***stryke** *n.* trap 32/12
***strode wyder** *phr.* (*pt. s.*) took longer steps 99/8
stroke *n.* blow 97/13
strong *adj.* flagrantly guilty 95/19
***strope** *n.* noose 32/34
study *v.* set oneself deliberately (to do something) 32/23
***stufs** *n.* dust 100/16 n.
subgettis *n. pl.* subjects 75/8
subtyl *adj.* cunning, crafty, wicked 61/31, 83/31
subtylitee *n.* stratagem, trick 37/23
subtilly *adv.* cleverly, cunningly 78/27
suche *pron.* such a one, someone of this type 20/32

suppose *v.* believe as a fact, be of the opinion 13/4; intend, think 52/5

sure *adj.* safe 97/31; *be ~ ynough of* be confident to get the better of 96/28

surely *adv.* securely 69/17

swange *pt. s.* swung 100/27

swere *v.* make an oath 54/11

swete *adj.* dear 15/22

sworn *pp.* ordered to be enforced 29/26

swoun *n.* swoon, faint 48/21; s.v. **a swoune**

swown *v. intrans.* faint 87/34

tabart *n.* coat, skin 51/13

tabyde s.v. **abyde**

table *n.* table of contents 3/1

tayl *n.*, *a cattes ~* something of no value 48/2–3; *he hath stryked hem with his ~* he has deceived them in the end 70/23–4 n.

take *v.* capture 26/22; catch 89/6; **toke** (*pt. pl.*) *~ to* joined to their following 38/32; **taken** *pp.* ensnared 60/30; committed 84/12; *~ vp* promoted, taken into one's protection 85/21; concluded 104/19; *~ vpon yow* decided, undertaken 58/2

takynge *n.* hunting, capture 57/24

tale *n.* conversation, discourse 42/25; *I shal telle hym a nother ~* I shall teach him a lesson 88/34–5; **talys** *pl.* stories, fabrications 103/32

tare *pt. s.* wounded, lacerated 86/29

tarye *v.* delay 15/3

taryeng *n.* delay: *without longe ~* immediately 63/23

taste *v.* feel, grope 27/11; try, attempt 65/9

***tatelyng** *n.* faltering, stammering 61/27

telle *v.*, *~ hit forth* relate 30/28; make (false) assertions 61/20

tendre *adj.* of fine and delicate feelings 56/28

thanke *n.* credit, honour 49/16; *can hym no ~* acknowledge no gratitude to him 13/34; *conne ~* express gratitude 19/16; *haue ~* have reward 81/2

thanke *v.* reward, repay 31/15; *that ~ I* thanks to 47/22; **thankyd** *pt. s.*, *~ nothyng* expressed absolutely no gratitude 106/25–6

that *adv.* as to that 14/9 n., 72/15; indeed, also 41/10; *conj.* when 6/22 n., 13/25 n.; but that 8/8; in that 16/22; if 27/9, 39/4 n.; because, in that 53/23; as much as 54/17

that *art.*, *~ one . . . ~ other* the one . . . the other 17/1

that *pron.* that which 38/21; someone who 71/19; who 71/27 n.

thaugh *conj.* even supposing that 50/11

thefte *n.* thieving 28/9

thentente s.v. **entente**

ther *adv.* used with adv. or prep. to form another adv. or conj. phrase: *~ after* accordingly 70/32; *~ as* where, wherever 74/10; *~ by* next to it, as well 45/7; near by 85/6–7; *~ that* where 47/9; *~ by there that* past the place where 8/15; *~ of* for which, on account of which 33/25; *~ to* in addition to that 78/13; *~ with* at that, then 50/29; *~ with all* with that, at that 34/8, *101/22*

thyder that *adv. phr.* where 15/1

thyng *n.*, *of suche ~ as* of whatever 40/37; *knewe none other ~ why ne wherfore* they were moved by no other reason 106/17; *pl.* matters, affairs 64/24; *doo his ~* attend to his business 37/24–5

thynke *v.* contrive, devise 73/35; *~ longe* yearn, be weary with waiting 57/34 n.; *~ on* meditate on 43/18, 91/28; *~ wel* expect 63/19; **thought** *pt.* meant 26/28; called to mind, remembered 36/17; *~ it neuer* did not intend it 102/31

thynne *adj.* lukewarm, strained 47/5

tho *adj.* those 40/10

tho *adv.* then 7/17; *conj.* when 52/12

thombe *n.*, *I haue now goten my ~ out of his mouth* I have escaped from his power 47/22

thorpe *n.* village 16/15

thought *n.* confusion, perplexity 60/24 n.

thought *pt. s.* seemed 26/4; *hym ~ good* it seemed fitting to him 45/2; *~ yow* seemed to you *73/16*

thraldom *n.* slavery, servitude 81/4
threstyng *n.* squeezing 104/23
thretene *v. intrans.* utter threats and curses 88/15
thryes *adv.* three times 27/37
throte *n.* mouth 101/29
thurgh *prep.* on account of, because of 9/15
***thurgh soden** *pp. adj.* very sodden 106/27
thwart *adv.* crosswise, transversely 83/12
tyde *n.* time 57/28
tyht *adj.* hard 78/20
tyl *conj.*, ~ *that* until 88/16
tyme *n.* opportunity, occasion 32/32; *in/on a* ~ on one occasion 37/15; *vnto the* ~ (*that*) until 54/12; *in an euyl* ~ unhappily 22/14; *al in* ~ in good time 97/33; *that* ~ then, at that time 78/33; *to fore/a fore* ~ earlier 36/17; *after that* ~ from then onwards 85/16; *at suche* ~ *as* when 106/4; *thirde* ~ *for al* for the third and final time 23/24–5 n.; *at al tymes* always 37/10–11; *often* ~ frequently 100/13–14
to *adv.* too, also 26/27; *prep.* against 9/18; at 30/4; towards 31/25; up to 89/10, 93/3
to beten *pp. adj.* excessively beaten 23/16
to broken *pp. adj.* broken in pieces 63/25
to fore *adv.* ago, earlier 9/19; *prep.* before, in front of 33/12
tokenys *n. pl.* signs, characteristic marks 36/14
tomble *v. intrans.* proceed by stumbling and rolling 19/1
toppe *n.* hair on top of the head 18/29
torne *v.*, ~ *agayn* return 80/10; ~ *fro* abandon 108/10; ~ *to* result in 20/13; **al torned** changed, altered 85/20
tornes *n. pl.* stratagems, tricks 58/11
to tore *pp.* torn to pieces 11/5
touch *n.* deceitful trick 53/32
touch *v.* grieve 47/34; accuse, involve 56/31; concern, appertain to *64/24*
touchyng *prep.* about, concerning 3/12
to . . . ward *prep.* towards 20/15
trade forth to *phr.* (*pt. s.*) advanced towards 99/3
traytour *n.* someone who betrays anyone who trusts him, betrayer 20/27
tree *n.* wood 79/30
trenchours *n. pl.* slices of bread used instead of plates 81/20
treson *n.* breach of faith, wicked behaviour 28/9
trespace *v.* wrong, commit wrong (against) 25/27; ~ *to* 7/20
trespas *n.* wrong, insult 7/9; misdeed 62/34
trewe *adj.* honest, virtuous 10/4; loyal 74/27
trompe *n.* trumpet 105/35
trouthe *n.* faith, loyalty 36/10; *mente al* ~ thought it was all genuine 53/32; *for* ~ as a fact 77/27
trowe *v.* think, believe 12/34
truantrye *n.* truancy 9/27
truly *adv.* sincerely 14/33; indeed 48/24
truste to *v. phr.* place reliance on 57/18
tubbe *n.* barrel 26/13
tweyne *num.* two 92/30
two *num.*, ~ *the fayrest* the two most beautiful 10/25 n.

valdore s.v. **faldore**
vane *n.* banner 16/19
venym *n.* poison 77/20
venymous *adj.* pernicious, slanderous 95/19
venyson *n.* meat (gained by hunting) 18/13
venture *n.* chance 24/35; jeopardy 38/10
verdyte *n.* decision, conclusion 75/17
very *adj.* real, true 6/12; absolute, complete 76/7
veryly *adv.* in truth, indeed 21/13
vertue *n.* power, efficacy 77/2 n.
vigilye *n.* prayers for the dead 12/16 n.
vylayne *n.* low rustic 89/33
vylaynous *adj.* depraved, churlish 91/1
vyllonye *n.* infamous conduct 7/22; ignominy, disgrace 41/22
visage *n.* face 16/33

viscose *adj.* viscous 84/30
***vyseuase** *n.* trifle 9/24
vitaylle *v.* provide with victuals 25/10
vytayller *n.* the bread-winner 25/8
vlycche *n.* flitch, side 9/7
vnauysed *pp. adj.* unintentionally 61/5
***vnberisped** *pp. adj.* without censure or blame 35/9
vnbynde *v.* open, untie 34/25
vnborn *pp.* not carried, not delivered 48/37
vnclene *adj.* morally impure, wicked 91/2
vnclennes *n.* moral impurity 110/32
vncourtoys *adj.* discourteous, not pertaining to noble character 87/9
vnder *adv.* underneath 101/5; *prep.* at the foot of 37/34; in 99/17
vnderstandyng *n.* meaning, sense 6/13
vnderstonde *v.* discover, learn 59/13–14
vndeseruid *pp. adj.* not merited 64/31
***vngheluck** *n.* misfortune 78/4
vnhappe *n.* misfortune 20/13
vnkynde *adj.* unnatural, ungrateful 83/30
vnlyke *adj.* unequal 70/3
vnlose *v.* free 71/10
vnnethe, vnnethis *adv.* hardly 22/36
vnresonable *adj.* going beyond reason excessive 7/10
vnreste *n.* turmoil, trouble 103/17
vnright *n.* wrong, injustice 61/32
vnryghtwys *adj.* wicked, evil 107/13
***vnroused** *pp. adj.* [of uncertain meaning] 86/4
vnshamefast *adj.* immodest 111/1
***vnshoed** *pp. adj.* with shoes removed 44/1
vnther doluen *pp.* buried 40/11
vnthriftes *n. pl.* dissolute persons 90/20
vnthrifty *adj.* wanton, foolish 37/1
vnwetyngly *adv.* unintentionally 61/5
vnwyse *adj.* foolish, mad 64/15
vouchesauf *v.* confer, bestow 39/30
vpon *prep.* under the condition of 73/6; ~ *that that* on the assumption that 54/16
vp so doon *adv. phr.* upside down 70/6
vrynal *n.* glass used for medical examination of urine 84/37
vsed *pp.* practised, employed 6/5
vtterist *n.* full extent 102/26; limit, extreme end *108/10*

waer *adj.* aware, conscious of 22/1
wages *n. pl.*, *take* ~ enlist, take service 38/1
waye *n.* road, path 28/35; means, method 41/17; whereabouts 105/25; *fynde the* ~ devise a plan 37/8; *take my* ~ go 41/30; *torned in to a good* ~ turned over a new leaf 42/4; *out of the right* ~ mistakenly 63/8; *lyeth in your* ~ what business is it of yours? 94/27; *crepe after his* ~ follow in his footsteps 110/7; **weyes** *pl.* gates, openings 13/23
waylle *v. intrans.* complain, lament 41/26
wayllyng *n.* complaint, sorrowing words 55/28
waynes *n. pl.* waggons 56/5
wayte *v. intrans.* lie in ambush 11/34; ~ *after* wait for 21/32
wayte *n.*, *laye in a* ~ lurked in an ambush 51/32
wakyng *n.* keeping vigils in devotion 10/15
walke wyth *v. phr.* be found in the company of 84/19
walled *pp.* provided with a wall 11/4
wandre *v. intrans.* travel, roam 33/35
***wapper** *n.* leaden ball attached to a strap 17/2
***wapper** *v.* strike with a wapper 17/2
***warande** *n.* hunting land, abode of animals 41/4
ward s.v. **to . . . ward, fro . . . ward**
ware *pt. s.* wore 40/14
warm *adv.* warmly 109/11
warne *v.* notify, inform of a command 23/24
warne *v.* refuse 67/7
warnyng *n.* intimation, notification 24/9
water *n.* lake 40/2
waxe, wexe *v.* grow 17/35, 33/27; **wexe** *pt. s.* 18/30; **waxen, woxen** *pp.* become, gone 7/13

weder *n.* castrated ram, wether 34/2
weeshe *pt. pl.* washed 109/13
weyker *adj. comp.* weaker 96/8
wel *adv.* used as an intensive to strengthen the action of the verb 16/35, 54/7; very 33/3; readily, easily 37/8
welbelouid *adj.* very dear 95/9
weleaway *interj.* alas, alack 34/18
welfare *n.* good fortune, prosperity 81/33
wel herted *adj.* stouthearted, courageous 77/36
welwyllyd *adj.* favourably disposed 75/10
wende *v. intrans.* go, make one's way 82/4
wene *v.* think 60/21
wenyng *n.* doubt, uncertainty: *brynge you out of* ~ remove all your doubts 40/30; expectation 58/5 n.
***wentle** *v. intrans.* roll, tumble about 19/1; **wentelyng** *pr. p.* 19/4
were as *adv. phr.* where 13/5
werk *n.* ornamentation 40/16; deed 53/9; business 66/9
werke *v.* bring it about 98/31
wete, wyte *v.* know 23/19; find out 37/10; *that is to* ~ namely 7/11; **wist** *pt. s.* 92/17
whad s.v. **what**
what *adj.* whatever 41/34; how 95/24; ~ *thawh* what matter, though (it be too late) 50/22; ~ *therof* what does that matter 44/26; *interj.* lo, now 35/32
what that *pron. phr.* whatever 35/11
whatsomeuer *pron.* whatever, whatsoever 102/14
wher *adv.* whenever 66/4; when, on what occasion 73/20; used with adv. or prep. to form another adv.: ~ *for* on account of which 36/31; ~ *of* as a result of which 11/30; of which 26/14; ~ *on* on which 106/31; ~ *someuer* wherever, wheresoever 42/19; ~ *that* wherever 51/15; ~ *upon* for which reason 7/13–14; ~ *wyth* with which 41/7
whiche *pron.* who 4/27; *by* ~ on account of which 13/28; through whom 53/35
whyle *n.* time 11/14; *in a short* ~ *after* not long afterwards 60/27; *a good* ~, *a grete* ~ a long time 71/12; *in the mene* ~ *that* while 37/34
whiles *conj.* while 30/10
who *pron.* he who 6/12; if anyone 16/34
who someuer *pron.* whosoever, whoever 77/5
wyde *adj.* big 92/30
***wyde** *adv.* with a wide open expression 92/36
***wyder** *adv. comp.* s.v. **strode**
wyf *n.* woman (of low rank) 16/15; woman 74/13; **wyuis** *pl.* 17/18
wyght *n.* being, person 23/14; ***wyghtis** *pl.* children 95/7
***wyke** *v. intrans.* withdraw, give way 63/33
wyl *n.* individual determination 75/17; desire 88/6; *by my* ~ willingly 47/21; *outeward* ~ carnal desire 60/22; *dyde with her his* ~ had his pleasure of her 9/20; *see your* ~ *of* see your desire carried out with respect to 32/35; *were at his* ~ were ready to do what he wanted 39/38; *al thus haue your* ~ everything turns out as you want 44/10; *oweth me euyl* ~ is hostilely inclined towards me 94/6; cf. **good willes**
wyle *n.* deceitful trick, ruse 12/30
wyly *adj.* crafty, sly 21/34
wylle *v.* want to, wish to 25/22; wish for 55/8; **wolde** *pt. s.* intended 35/25; *wel* ~ would be content 8/8; could easily 53/4; would have preferred 63/27; *where she* ~ *be* what was in her mind 58/37; **willyd** *pp.* wanted to 30/1
wyn *n.* friend 70/19
wynde *n.*, *aboue the* ~ in the wind 100/15; *blowe with alle wyndes* trim his sails to all winds, suit his actions to all conditions 91/33–4
wynne *v.* acquire 38/31
wynnynge *n.* gain, acquisition 10/12; spoils of hunting 86/16; gain, profit 102/6 n.
wynters day *n.* winter-day 89/4–5
wynters longe *adj. phr.* as (tediously) long as the winter 77/8 n.
wise *n.* manner: *in suche* ~ (*that*/*as*) so that 43/5; *in this* ~ thus 12/19; *in lyke*

wise (*cont.*):
~ similarly 81/32; *in lyke ~ as* just as 72/38; *al other ~ than* the opposite of what 60/35
wysehede *n.* wisdom 65/2
wysely *adj.* like a wise man 45/24
wist s.v. **wete**
wit, wyte s.v. **wete**
wyte *v.* accuse, blame 8/32
wyth *prep.* at the coming of 38/16; by 110/6; ~ *that* when 65/9
wyth al *adv.* with it, herewith 106/23
withholden *pp. adj., be ~ wyth* be in (someone's) favour 106/15–16
wythholdyng (you) *phr., n.* action of staying away 24/7
withinforth *adv.* within, on the inside 68/9
withought forth *adv.* on the outside 77/11
wythoute *adv., prep.* outside, on the outside 22/35; besides, in addition to 38/15
wytnes *n.* witness: ~ *of* according to 77/10
wytte *n.* mind, sense 38/37; *out of his ~* mad 99/33; *at his wittes* [*s.*] *ende* 68/23; *at the ende of al my wyttes and of counseyl* in despair at finding any plan or solution 65/38; *loste my fyue ~* gone mad 89/21–2
wonder *n.* an astonishing happening 26/23; miracle 61/15; *most ~ that I haue* I am amazed 84/21; *is it ~* is it surprising? 82/35
wonder *v.* be amazed 63/16
wonderly *adj.* marvellous 58/5
wonder thyng *phr.* marvel 41/18
wonte, woned *pp.* accustomed 13/20
woo *adj., n.* sorrow, misery, sorrowful 20/11; ~ *begon* oppressed with sorrow 100/16; *dyde hym ~ of* was still painful from 32/12
wood *adj.* mad, rabid 43/7
worden *pt. pl.* became 33/28
wordes *n. pl., began his ~* began to speak 62/26; *by the ~* judging from the words 87/17; *brouke my ~* get to speak 32/28–9; *come in the ~* be charged, accused 65/16 n.; *in your ~* able to speak 57/2
world *n., thus fareth the ~* such is the way of the world 91/21; *how the ~ gooth* the way of the world 70/5; *alle the ~ of* a vast quantity 103/24; *not goo nowher thurgh the ~* may not succeed anywhere 62/2–3
worldly *adj.* temporal 6/6
***worme** *n.* monster 94/25
worship *n.* honour, renown 5/16; *gete the ~ of the felde* win the battle-honours 67/15
worshipful *adj.* honourable 75/18
worshipfully *adv.* with dignity and honour 12/11
worthiest *adj. superl.* noblest 17/11
wrake *n.* vengeance 74/5
wrange *pt. s.* struggled, writhed 16/4
wrastle *v. intrans.* struggle 16/4; wrestle 101/21
***wrawen** *v. intrans.* cry aloud, screech 22/2
wreke *v.* avenge 44/11, *68/6*
wryngyng *n.* squeezing, action of squeezing 104/16
wrytyng *n.* what has been written, composition 48/33
***wryue** *v.* rub 109/14
wronge *pt. s.* squeezed 104/13
wrongfully *adv.* unjustly 64/5
wroth *adj.* fierce, savage 33/29
wrought *pp.* made, worked 84/2
wroughten to *phr.* (*pt. pl.*) inflicted upon 17/6–7

***yamer** *v. intrans.* grieve, have pity 45/10
yate *n.* gate 13/12
ye *interj.* indeed 9/36
yeft *n.* money gift 66/17
yelde *v. refl.* give oneself up 101/30
yere s.v. **duryng**
***yester morow** *phr.* yesterday morning 52/3
yeue out *v. phr.* publish, announce 106/6
yonglyng *n.* young man 31/1; young animal 57/6
yongthe *n.* youth 86/2
***yonne** *v.* wish 62/23
***yonste** *n.* favour, goodwill 15/4

INDEX OF NAMES

Abrion, 76, 77
Adam, 77
Akeryn, 76
Akon, 35, 40
Arabye, 53
Arderne, 10, 35
Aristotiles, 73
Asye, 79
Atrote, 75
Aue Abelquak, 17
Auycene, 73

Baetkyn, 17
Baue, 17
Bellyn, the ram, 4, 30, 44–6, 48–51, 58, 68, 75, 84, 87
Bellart s.v. Bellyn
Bertolt, 17
Byteluys, the ape's son, 74, 96, 105
Bokart, 49, 50
Borre, the bull, 30
Boudelo, 96
Boudewyn, the ass, 30, 81
Brownyng, s.v. Bruyn
Bruyn, the bear, 1, 12–20, 25, 29, 31–3, 35–8, 42, 45, 46, 50, 54, 56, 67, 70, 109
Brunel, the goose, 30

Cameryk, 64
Cantart, the cock's daughter, 10
Caxton, William, 112
Chafporte, 17/12 n.
Chantecler, the cock, 1, 10–12, 25, 29, 30
Cleomedes, 80
Coleyne, 36, 40, 63
Coppe(n), the cock's daughter, 10, 12
Corbant, the rook, 4, 52, 56, 63, 65, 67
Crayant, the cock's daughter, 10
Crompart, 79, 80
Curtoys, the dog, 3, 7–9
Cuwaert, s.v. Kywart

Edward IV, 112
Eelmare, 26, 65

Elue, 38
Eluerdynge, 58
Empty Bely, the wolf's child, 72
Ermelyn, the fox's wife, 24, 25, 37, 46–8, 56, 57, 111
Ermeryk, 35, 39, 40
Erswynde, the wolf's wife, 27, 43, 44, 50, 91, 104, 109

Firapeel, the leopard, 50, 51, 54, 55
Flaundres, 35, 40
Fulrompe, the ape's son, 74, 105

Gaunt, 35
Gelys, 44
Grece, 79
Grymbert, the badger, 3, 4, 8, 10, 23–5, 27–30, 35, 36, 55–8, 60, 62, 64, 96, 105

Hamel, the ox, 30
Hatenette, the ape's daughter, 74, 105
Hector, 79
Helene, 79
Hermell, the ass, 75
Holland, 10
Houthulst, 58
Hughelyn, 16
Hulsterlo, 40, 41, 54, 58, 95

Yfte, 35
Inde, 78
Iordayn, 40
Isegrym, the wolf, 3, 5, 7–9, 22, 25–7, 30–5, 38, 41–4, 46, 50, 54, 56, 58–60, 65, 67, 70, 83, 85–7, 89, 90, 93–6, 99–101, 103–4, 106, 109
Iulok, the priest's wife, 16, 17, 22, 23
Iuno, 78

Kywart, the hare, 4, 8, 9, 30, 40, 41, 46, 48–50, 58, 60, 68, 75, 76, 84, 87
Krekenpyt, 40, 41, 47, 54

Lantfert, a carpenter, 14–18, 29

Lapreel, the rabbit, 4, 51, 56, 65, 67
Locken, s.v. Iulok
London, 40
Loosuynde, 44
Ludolf, 16

Macob, 17
Maleperduys, 5, 10, 13, 20, 24, 25, 46, 52, 55, 109, 111
Menelaus, 79
Mertyne, the ape, 64, 66, 97
Mertynet, the priest's son, 22
Monpelier, 21, 84
Morcadigas, 79

Neuer Full, the wolf's child, 72
Noble, the lion, 29, 32, 42, 53

Olewey, the ewe, 30
Ordegale, the beaver's wife, 74, 105
Ottram, 17
Oxenford, 59

Pallas, 78
Pantecroet, the otter's wife, 74, 105
Panther, the boar, 8, 30
Panthera, 78
Parys, son of Pryamus, 78, 79
Parys, 40, 110
Pertelot, the cock's wife, 30
Pogge, 17
Portyngale, 14
Prendelor, 44
Prentout, 66
Pryamus, 79

Rapiamus, 44
Reynart, the fox, 3, 6–16, 18–25, 27–34, 38–52, 54–9, 62–4, 67–70, 72–6, 87–8, 90–1, 93–6, 98–101, 104, 105, 108–12
Reynart, the fox's father, 82, 85
Reynerdyn, the fox's son, 25, 57, 65
Reynkyn, s.v. Reynerdyn
Ryn, the dog, 41
Rome, 40–3, 53, 66, 110
Rosel, the fox's son, 25, 57, 65
Rukenawe, the ape's wife, 4, 5, 66, 68, 75, 93, 96, 98, 105, 108

St. Martyn, 20
Salamon, 73, 79
Saxone, 38
Seneca, 69
Seth, 77
Sharpebek, the rook's wife, 52, 53, 58
Symon, the ape's uncle, 66
Symonet, the Frisian, 41
Slyndpere, the raven's son, 71
Sloepcade, the badger's wife, 36, 105
Somme, 38
Stade, 6/27 n.

Tybert, the cat, 3, 7, 19–23, 25, 29–32, 35, 42, 44, 49, 82, 109
Tyselyn, the raven, 42, 71
Tryer, 76
Troye, 78, 79

Venus, 78, 79
Vermedos, 26

Wayte Scathe, 66
Westmestre, 112
Woerden, 69/7 n.

PRINTED IN GREAT BRITAIN
AT THE UNIVERSITY PRESS, OXFORD
BY VIVIAN RIDLER
PRINTER TO THE UNIVERSITY